EXPLAINING U.S. **IMPRISONMENT**

MARY BOSWORTH
Oxford University

Los Angeles | London | New Delhi
Singapore | Washington DC

For information:

SAGE Publications, Inc.
2455 Teller Road
Thousand Oaks, California 91320
E-mail: order@sagepub.com

SAGE Publications Ltd.
1 Oliver's Yard
55 City Road
London EC1Y 1SP
United Kingdom

SAGE Publications India Pvt. Ltd.
B 1/I 1 Mohan Cooperative
Industrial Area
Mathura Road, New Delhi 110 044
India

SAGE Publications Asia-Pacific Pte. Ltd.
33 Pekin Street #02-01
Far East Square
Singapore 048763

Printed in the United States of America.

Library of Congress Cataloging-in-Publication Data

Bosworth, Mary.
Explaining U.S. imprisonment / Mary Bosworth.
p. cm.
Includes bibliographical references and index.
ISBN 978-1-4129-2486-3 (cloth)
ISBN 978-1-4129-2487-0 (pbk.)
1. Imprisonment—United States. 2. Prisons—United States.
3. Prisoners–United States. I. Title. II. Title: Explaining US imprisonment.

HV9471.B675 2010
365′.973—dc22 2009019945

09 10 11 12 13 10 9 8 7 6 5 4 3 2 1

Acquisitions Editor: Jerry Westby
Editorial Assistant: Eve Oettinger
Production Editor: Karen Wiley
Copy Editor: Bill Bowers
Typesetter: C&M Digitals (P) Ltd.
Proofreader: Sally Jaskold
Indexer: Gloria Tierney
Cover Designer: Candice Harman
Marketing Manager: Jennifer Reed Banando

EXPLAINING U.S.
IMPRISONMENT

For Anthony, Ella, and Sophia

Contents

Preface

Despite growing evidence of the prison's significant social and economic costs, in addition to longer-term concerns over its effectiveness and criticism of conditions behind bars, the United States appears committed to mass incarceration. The government relies on the prison not only to manage its domestic offenders but also, increasingly, to safeguard its borders from undocumented immigrants. Under the Bush administration, prisons were also deployed to hold suspected terrorists and those labeled "enemy combatants." This book asks why? What explains the enduring appeal of the prison?

There are a number of reasons why a critical analysis of the purpose and nature of imprisonment is apposite. Well before the official acknowledgment of a financial meltdown, states were struggling to fund existing prison places, siphoning off money from other crucial responsibilities in education, health, and welfare. In the current economic climate, such problems will only worsen. So, too, as a result of sentencing and policing, many states and the federal system are struggling to deal with high levels of overcrowding. Even the most conscientious of wardens must find it difficult to offer meaningful time out of cell, counseling, treatment, adequate care, or job training. Indeed, evidence, including the number of states under various forms of judicial oversight, suggests that conditions in many facilities fail to meet legal thresholds of acceptability. Finally, the ever-expanding overrepresentation of Black and Hispanic men, women, and children behind bars raises troubling questions about the nation's commitment to race equality.

In order to understand how we have arrived at the prisons of today, this book takes a long view of incarceration. Starting with accounts from the first colonies, it considers changing examples and explanations of imprisonment around the country. It is a work of historiography as much as history, setting out the dominant ideas behind imprisonment, as well as aspects of the prison across a range of states and time frames.

Though focused on the prison, this book has been conceived within the context of the broader theoretical body of work referred to as the sociology of punishment. It also reflects my own interest in issues of race and gender, and my belief that these topics continue to be inadequately dealt with in many criminological studies. It has been written for a number of audiences, from undergraduates to those conducting research on and even living in prison. Drawing on a range of source material that includes unpublished archives, statutes, court cases, academic studies, firsthand accounts, and newspaper articles, it maps out the changing debates that have framed, underpinned, and, it should not be forgotten, challenged U.S. prison. Indeed, a key theme of this study is to identify how people have opposed and criticized incarceration almost as much as they have lauded it.

Now that the new administration of President Barack Obama has taken the reins of power, the United States may be ready to revisit the logic of imprisonment and reduce its reliance on it. Second only to the death penalty, imprisonment is the most severe sanction the state can impose on any individual. It must, therefore, be constantly evaluated and justified. Yet, when was there last a serious public discussion of imprisonment? All too often, in the face of considerable evidence against it, its legitimacy is simply taken for granted. The problem of the prison is not simply that most of these people—even those labeled enemy combatants—will one day be released, but simply that it is an institution suffused with suffering, failure, injustice, and inadequacy. This is not a book arguing for abolition. It is, however, one that calls for a reduction in prison numbers and curbing of punitive sentiment. As the chapters will show, the prison has never lived up to our expectations; it is time for a change.

Acknowledgments

In writing this book I have, as ever, benefited from the assistance from many colleagues, students, and family members. I have also been fortunate in my publisher and in my academic institution.

When I first began research for this book, in 2004, I was a visiting fellow at the Centre for Socio-Legal Studies at the University of Oxford, on sabbatical from a university post in the U.S., and anticipating an eventual return to America. In fact, I have, happily, remained in Oxford, taking up a University Lectureship at the Centre for Criminology and a Fellowship at St Cross College. This move has been extremely rewarding, and I am indebted to my colleagues and students here for providing such a friendly and rich intellectual environment. Oxford is a special place to live and work.

Moving jobs and countries, along with the arrival of my second daughter Sophia, have contributed to a significant delay in completing this manuscript. Either that, or I have finally joined the ranks of "real" academics, notorious as a group for always running late. Notwithstanding my delinquency in this area, Jerry Westby and the team at Sage have been understanding, and, above all, patient.

In compiling the historical material, I was helped by a number of librarians and archivists from around the country, particularly Katherine Wilkins from the Virginia Historical Society and Jeff Kintop, the State Archives Manager at Nevada State Library and Archives. Kathy Kirkpatrick from GenTracer aided me in my research on prisoner of war camps, while Melinda Gales and Teresa Roane from the Museum of the Confederacy and Lee Shepard from Virginia Historical Society helped with research on Civil War prisons. Alan Barnett from the Research Center of the Utah State Archives and Utah State Library and staff from the Texas State Library and Archives Commission helped me identify files on 19th- and early

20th-century inmates and institutions. In Oxford, Paul Honey from the Centre for Socio-Legal Studies provided some vital research assistance when I was on maternity leave, and in the U.S. Jeneve Brooks-Klinger, while still at Fordham University, thoughtfully visited the New York Public Library for me when I could not. Robert Perkinson and Ethan Blue, "proper" prison historians, assisted and inspired me as well.

In addition to those who helped me gather my research materials, I would like to thank those who have read all or part of the book manuscript at various stages of its rather lengthy gestation, including Lucia Zedner, University of Oxford, and Carolyn Hoyle, University of Oxford; Jeanne Flavin, Fordham University; Larry Sullivan, City University of New York, John Jay College of Criminal Justice; Vanessa Barker, Florida State University; Jim Thomas, Northern Illinois University; Ashley Blackburn, University of North Texas; Richard Tewksbury, University of Louisville; Cathy Lavery, Iona College; Mary Dodge, University of Colorado at Denver Health Sciences Center; Jim Houston, Grand Valley State University; Beth Huebner, University of Missouri Saint Louis; Ojmarrh Mitchell, University of Cincinnati; Connie Ireland, California State University Long Beach; Pam Schram, California State University San Bernardino; and Stacy L. Mallicoat, California State University Fullerton. To my parents, Richard and Michal Bosworth, who read all my work with a critical and supportive eye, I owe a particular debt of gratitude.

I would like to dedicate this book to my three favorite Americans: Anthony, Ella, and Sophia; may they never be imprisoned.

Introduction: Explaining U.S. Imprisonment

Those who look for philosophical consistency in prison policies are apt not to find it.

(Toch, 1997, p. 4).

The United States has a punishment system that no one would knowingly have built from the ground up. It is often unjust, it is unduly severe, it is wasteful, and it does enormous damage to the lives of black Americans.

(Tonry, 2004, p. vii).

Life in prison is frustration and loneliness and boredom and futility.

(Runyon, 1954, p. 9)

The United States has the dubious honor of incarcerating more people per capita than any other nation, whether industrialized, democratic, undemocratic, or developing. It comes first in all published listings of incarceration rates, and has done so for some time.[1] Presently more than one person per 100 of the adult population is behind bars (Pew Charitable Trusts, 2008). Not surprisingly, then, prisons in the U.S. are big business. They underpin national webs of commerce, particularly in the economically fragile hinterland, as well as global markets that spread far beyond the country's borders. Prisons also loom large in the popular imagination. Notwithstanding a range of sentencing options, all too often prison is viewed by the populace as the inevitable and appropriate response to crime. In short, despite criticism leveled at them by academics, prisoners, lobby groups, inmate families, criminal justice practitioners, church members, and even some politicians, prisons are ubiquitous in 21st-century America.

This book asks why. Why does the U.S. place so many people in custody? What is their confinement meant to achieve? How is it that, despite their manifest failings, prisons are seemingly so legitimate and uncontested? Has it always been so? In answering such questions, this book traces the historical development of the professional and popular justifications of imprisonment, at the same time as it describes the changing nature of the prison itself. It is, as a result, a history of ideas and arguments as well as one of institutions and individuals. While undoubtedly more of a "history of the present" than a straightforward narrative of the past, it engages in some detail with texts and documents from earlier periods in a bid to uncover some missing and marginalized elements of the evolution of America's prisons.

Statistical Overview

At year-end 2008, the U.S. was incarcerating more than 2.4 million men, women, and children in 5,000 or so custodial institutions scattered around the country. Over one and a half million (1,595,034) of these people were held under the jurisdiction of state and federal authorities serving sentences of greater than 12 months, leaving around 800,000 individuals housed in local jails, either awaiting trial, pending sentencing, or serving short-term periods of confinement of less than 12 months (Sabol & Couture, 2008; Sabol, Couture, & Harrison, 2007; Sabol, Minton, & Harrison, 2007).[2] Still others were incarcerated by immigration services or under military supervision. Though such figures are large, they pale by comparison with the far greater number of people who move in and out of penal institutions over the course of each year. As the commissioners of the 2006 Vera Foundation report *Safety and Abuse in America's Prisons* observed:

> . . . over 13.5 million people spend time in jail or prison, and 95 percent of them eventually return to our communities. Approximately 750,000 men and women work in U.S. correctional facilities as line officers or other staff. The United States spends more than 60 billion dollars annually on corrections. (Gibbons & Katzenbach, 2006, p. 11)

Such statistical information regularly surfaces in contemporary accounts of incarceration. Yet, it is not entirely clear what such figures signify. As raw numbers, they do seem to be rather large. Without a context, however, what can we make of them? How do they compare, for example, to the prison statistics of other countries? Have they varied over time? Who, in terms of race, gender, age, and geography, are these people confined? Similarly, where are these statistics drawn from in any case? Who compiles them and why? Which populations, if any, do they exclude?

It may be obvious, yet it is worth noting that increases in incarceration, for some—particularly those on the right of the political spectrum—may be approved and celebrated: prison works (Levitt, 1996). For others, such as prison reformers, they indicate a large-scale failure of social policy: prisons destroy families, communities, and individuals (Mauer & Chesney-Lind, 2002; Clear, 2007). For still others, they might signal particular racial problems or biases within the U.S.: prisoners are disproportionately drawn from communities of color (Mauer, 1999). In any case, the raw numbers cannot explain much. To do this, we must ask a series of interconnected questions. What are the causes of mass imprisonment? How have criminologists, prisoners, and other analysts sought to understand the reasons for and effects of confinement? What do current levels of incarceration tell us about the society in which we live? These are the questions that this book seeks to answer.

We already know, for example, that the U.S. heads the world in the rate at which it confines, but how great is its lead? According to the most recent figures compiled by the International Centre for Prison Studies at Kings College London, the U.S. has an imprisonment rate of 750 per 100,000. More than 100 points below it, we can find first French Guyane, with a rate of 630 per 100,000, and then Russia at 628 per 100,000. Cuba comes in at an estimated 503 per 100,000 while South Africa has 335 per 100,000. None of these countries shares much else in common with the U.S., either culturally or economically. Instead, the closest equivalent country, in terms of its economic development and social structure, is England and Wales, with a (relatively) paltry 148 per 100,000. Other, similarly economically developed European nations like Germany (93 per 100,000) and France (85 per 100,000) lie even further behind (www.prisonstudies.org).

America's overwhelming lead in prison rates poses a considerable challenge to those who would explain punitive sentiment and practice as a result of some broad current inherent in the late modern world. Neoliberalism, the risk society, and the "culture of control," though no doubt contributing factors to penal populism in many countries, cannot alone account for America's current love affair with prison (Tonry, 2004, 2007; Pratt, 2007). The explanation must, therefore, lie somewhere else. Yet how we might explain the cause of such American exceptionalism is far from clear; culture, economics, race, gender, geography, and national identity must all play a role, as do their institutional manifestations in laws, sentencing, crime, and the judicial attitudes and actors.

It seems likely that some explanation for the current levels may be found in the recent past, since once a longer historical view is taken, the American primacy disappears. Until the 1970s, the U.S. imprisonment rate had not only been relatively stable at around 110 per 100,000 of its population, but was similar to that of its European allies. So, too, the extent of the racial disparities behind bars consolidated in the 1980s. Yet, focusing on the second half of the 20th century may, in itself, be insufficient, given the grounding of the recent past in the time before, with contemporary events, sentiments, and practices still shaped by the lengthy shadows of colonialism and slavery (Bosworth & Flavin, 2007; Wacquant, 2001a, 2000; Davis, 2003).

The Culture of Control

Over the past two decades, criminologists have spent considerable time examining the rising tide of punitive sentiment in the U.S., and many influential accounts have been made of its causes. One notion in particular that has received much interest from scholars is that of "culture" (see, for example, Garland, 2001a, 2007; Tonry, 2004; Jarvis, 2004). From a variety of perspectives, commentators suggest that current practice reflects a set of ideas and beliefs that have come to characterize U.S. sentiment. Imprisonment rates are not caused by policymakers operating in a vacuum, such figures attest, but are a result of penal populism (Pratt, 2007).

This approach, though useful conceptually, often appears divorced from actual prisons and those confined within them. It is also, as John Braithwaite (2003) trenchantly observed, usually based on a selective view of history that overlooks other mechanisms of social control. Authors more often refer to a general category of "punishment" than to the specifics of imprisonment and, in the process, lose some precision. In addition, the tendency within this field has been to generalize about widespread societal belief systems. Forms of dissent are overlooked and beliefs equated across different segments of the community and varied parts of the country. As a result, not only are differences between states usually elided (although see Barker, 2006; Cavadino & Dignan, 2006), but so, too, scholars have sought to extrapolate from the U.S. to other places. The most influential of such accounts, David Garland's (2001a) *The Culture of Control*, groups England and Wales together with the U.S., while more recently Michael Cavadino and Paul Dignan's (2006) detailed comparative analysis classifies the U.S. with other "neo-liberal democracies" like England and Wales, and Australia, while distinguishing them from "oriental corporatist" Japan, "social democratic" Scandinavia, and "conservative corporatist" continental Europe. Still others argue that "policy transfer" has rendered penal practices in a number of countries essentially alike (Newburn, 2002; Newburn & Jones, 2005).

Such concern with punishment in general rather than with prisons in particular has, however unintentionally, effectively stripped individuals from the analysis. Genealogies of the present, "technologies" of punishment, and the "new penology" proceed with scant attention to the lived experiences of the incarcerated. As a result, issues of race and class are generally glossed over, while in the U.S., outside the work of a few contributors to this body of theoretical work, gender is typically forgotten altogether.

In some sense, then, this book is advocating a more limited analysis of matters of punishment as they strictly pertain to the prison. However, in doing so, I am aiming for something broader. Specifically, by narrowing the field of analysis to concentrate solely on debates about imprisonment, I shall be able to open the space to examine in more detail issues of race and gender and the experience of incarceration. In so doing, I hope to flesh out the culturalist turn and, along the way, identify other conceptual and concrete factors contributing to the enduring practices of incarceration. I shall also spend some time documenting the challenges and alternatives that have been posed by a range of actors, including inmates, prison reform groups, and scholars. For, despite the overweening power of the punitive state, it is important to recall that in all periods, including the present, attempts have been made, and are ongoing, to resist the practices and expansion of confinement. On occasion, such attempts have even been successful. At all times, despite its ubiquity, the prison is contested.

Methodology

In order to understand what prison is for, we must examine what prison is like. The nature of imprisonment includes what the prison does—i.e., the various and sometimes conflicting ways in which it is utilized—as well as how it is experienced. Drawing on historical and contemporary documents written by academics, practitioners, and prisoners, this book builds a textured analysis of imprisonment, in which the reasons for, and legitimacy of, incarceration and the punishment that it entails, are thoroughly probed. As with other sociological studies of punishment (Garland, 1985; Simon, 1993), I draw deliberately and, inevitably, somewhat selectively, from the past to shed light on current practices and beliefs. Though it is based on a variety of primary source material that includes archives, newspapers, legislation, and firsthand accounts, the book cannot pretend to be exhaustive in its historical account. I hope, however, to avoid some of the pitfalls of historical criminology, which all too often selects examples from the past only to further an intellectual argument about the present without acknowledging what has been overlooked.

I began this project with a sense that the dominant narrative about the historical development of U.S. prisons marginalized some groups whose experiences might clarify the dogged legitimacy and vibrancy of such a maligned institution. In my research, I was guided by revisionist feminist and critical race scholars, who pointed out the relative absence of women and minorities in most accounts of the development of the prison (Rafter, 1995; Hannah-Moffat, 2001). As I read further, I came upon other issues, not all of which I had previously considered, from the regular use of prison in wars and conflicts to the frequency with which prisons have been publicly condemned and investigated. Even eugenics, which played such a key role in the early 20th-century expansion of institutions of confinement, had its opponents. Overall, it rapidly became clear that, while a particular set of beliefs and expectations about the form, purpose, and nature of imprisonment may be dominant at any one time, there also coexist many other narratives and viewpoints. The "crisis of penal modernism" (Garland, 1990; Simon, 1993) has, in short, been with us for some time.

Such a view is by no means new. Michel Foucault (1995), after all, argued that penal reformers were born at the same time as the prison. Taking the lead from him, criminologists have for some time observed that, paradoxically, debate over conditions or methods of punishment often shores up the prison. It is as though imprisonment evolves in response to the critique, always promising a new and improved version of itself.

Yet, is that all there is to say? Such a genealogical interpretation of effect is rather pessimistic, leaving the critically minded among us with few hopes or options. Along with others, I bridle against such dystopic views (Zedner, 2002) and, although I am unable to muster much optimism, two additional points about the criticism of imprisonment seem worth making. First, a purely Foucauldian history of the present would have us ignore the intent and sincerity of the prison's many critics. Indeed, although their accounts, however impassioned, have failed to dismantle the prison, their concerns remain valid and, in a longer historical view, surprisingly consistent. We should not dismiss them, but rather look to them for inspiration. These critics remind us that the prison should never be anything other than a measure of last resort.

In addition to recovering such voices of dissent, the historiography of the U.S. prison also reveals the crucial role played by penal institutions and their reformers in nation-building and in maintaining state, civil, racial, and other boundaries. Most obviously, the prison identifies and confines enemies of the state, whether they are hostile combatants or members of the "underclass." In so doing, prisons, in any era, enable the pursuit of war on a different footing, institutionalizing, legitimating, and also disguising quite considerable conflict in our society. In addition to this kind of "enemy penology" (Krasmann, 2007), drawing boundaries of inclusion and exclusion, so, too, more utopian aspirations for the prison at various historical junctures can be interpreted as articulations of an idealized vision of the nation-state (Okun, 2002), inexorably tying the "imagined community" of the prison to that of America.

Despite the existence of a small but robust literature in criminology on the role of the police in forging nations and national identity, connections between imprisonment and nationalism are rarely made (Loader, 2002). Instead, scholars speak more broadly of the relationship between prisons and democracy (Simon, 2007a) or the relationship between mass imprisonment and "statecraft" (Gottschalk, 2006). So, too, although some attention has recently been paid to the use of imprisonment in the War on Terror (Brown, 2005), and there is some theoretical interest in the relationship between war and punishment (Foucault, 2002), the role of prisons as a means of warfare in its own right is rarely discussed outside historical accounts. Yet, just as one of the first acts of any nation is to create a police force to mark out national borders and protect them, so too do states build prisons to discipline their own citizens and to hold their enemies. In moments of revolution and unrest, these places are usually targets of popular anger within and without. In wartime, they expand to hold new populations.

In the following chapters, I shall set out a range of historical and contemporary literature on the prison in order to make sense of the number of people currently incarcerated throughout the U.S. There are, of course, limitations to my analysis. I have relied predominantly on published material, rather than on archival letters and manuscripts—although I use some of those as well.[3] I draw, in particular, on readily available historical print databases such as those of *The New York Times, The Washington Post,* and *Harper's Weekly,* as well as material published in old journals and reports. I also cite published accounts by prisoners. Given the literacy levels of most prisoners and the barriers they face in publishing their stories, such accounts are unlikely to be empirically "representative" of the bulk of those incarcerated. However, as with news reports, academic books, pamphlets from think tanks, and so on, these documents contribute to public debates and explanations of imprisonment. Finally, though I draw on material from a variety of states and the federal system, I recognize that the generalizations about penal policy in America can only ever be partial. As prison statistics demonstrate most obviously, some states appear more reliant on their penal systems than others.

The Structure of Explanation

The first chapter examines the origins and early forms of imprisonment from the arrival of the first colonists to the 19th century. Identifying a number of differences between the North and the South, among women and men, Whites and non-Whites, and between citizens and noncitizens, it uncovers an enormous range of possible histories. The question it then poses is why a certain account of penal development has been prioritized over the others.

Concentrating on the first half of the 20th century, Chapter 2 describes how and why prisons were for so long considered an effective means of reforming social ills. Drawing on contemporaneous literature about rehabilitation, reform, and the medical model, it examines these issues as sources of legitimacy for confinement. In the process, it pays attention to the role of individual reformers in legitimating the nation's penal system. Although most of the ideas from this era have fallen out of favor with politicians, many of its key assumptions remain implicit in the fabric of penal endeavor. A large number of prisons still in use date to this time. Elsewhere, too, in so-called "problem-solving courts" of today, which primarily deal with minor offenses, there has been a recent resurgence of such therapeutic ideas, as judges mandate treatment in lieu of jail time (Nolan, 2001). So too, notions of "dangerous classes" and treatment or rehabilitation continue to abut each other uneasily and inconsistently.

Chapter 3 focuses on the classic sociological studies of prison culture that began with Donald Clemmer's (1940) *The Prison Community.* Usually viewed as the origins of academic sociological inquiry into the prison, these texts shaped the methodology and epistemology of prison studies for decades. In particular, in their failure to address the racial injustices of life behind bars, and the riots that swirled around their research, they depoliticized issues of incarceration in favor of scientific "objectivity." Revisiting these early studies in light of their historical context, this chapter teases out matters of race, gender, and sexuality in mid-20th-century U.S. prisons.

Concentrating on the period between the end of the 1960s and the late 1970s, Chapter 4 documents the failure of the rehabilitative ideal and sketches its replacement. Through newspaper reports and articles from the time, it describes the onset of modern racial tensions within prisons and the impact of prison riots. Although the 1970s began with great hope for reform, as this chapter shows, by the end of the decade, voices from within prison had largely been silenced and the rehabilitation movement was in tatters.

Chapter 5 examines the literature on imprisonment during the 1980s to document how mainstream criminologists, administrators, and legislators became more punitive over this period. Through an analysis of a range of policies introduced by the Reagan administration, it illustrates the shifts in rhetoric about the purpose of incarceration and the supposed responsibilities of the inmate population. In contrast to earlier periods, the language and rhetoric developed during the 1980s continues to resonate within American penal populism today.

Chapter 6 concentrates on the second part of the 1990s and, in particular, on the ideas associated with the writings of David Garland (1990, 2001a) and legislation passed by the Democratic administrations of President Clinton to reduce prisoner access to the courts. It considers the extent to which the prison inadvertently disappeared from view in much of the scholarly literature of this period. It also analyses the studies of women's prisons and modes of resistance that began to flourish in the 1990s, literature that is still frequently ignored within the theoretical debate.

Finally reaching the present, Chapter 7 examines the work of policy-makers and academics who believe that U.S. prisons have reached a tipping point both in numbers and finance (Jacobson, 2005). Through an analysis of legislation and recent penal reform, this chapter considers the promises and pitfalls of the pragmatic approach that characterizes much of the reformist agenda. Some attention will also be paid to the reemergence of inmate and activist writings.

Chapter 8 builds on the previous chapter to appraise the expansion of numbers in immigration detention and the use of imprisonment in the War on Terror. Despite the optimism of some that mass imprisonment in the U.S. may be waning, this chapter suggests that practices of detaining foreigners, enemy combatants, and suspected terrorists effectively reinforced the prison's legitimacy at the moment it was being drawn into question for U.S. citizens. I reflect on why prison scholars have, for the most part, failed to include such matters in their broader research agenda, and what the effect of their silence has been. The deployment of prisons in safeguarding the border, I propose, makes explicit in a manner that has not really been seen since the Second World War, the role of imprisonment in nation-building and armed conflict.

The book concludes by suggesting that a key source of the prison's ongoing legitimacy and vitality relates to its role in shoring up national identity. From the earliest American colonies to the more recent War on Terror, prisons have been put to work defending the (nation) state. In so doing, they act as more than an adjunct to war, effectively becoming sites of conflict themselves. This role of the prison has received scant attention from criminologists and, on the face of it, may seem to be somewhat paradoxical. The majority of penal institutions, after all, exist at the state and local levels, and house U.S. citizen offenders. However, as we have learned from sociologists of punishment, penal practices are more than simply utilitarian responses to crime; they are expressive, cultural forces that serve a number of interests. So too, this book argues, prisons are more than bricks and mortar, but exist as a set of ideas that are continuously debated. It is in these ongoing discussions that the form and nature of our society are articulated; it is here we distinguish the good from the bad, the deserving from the undeserving, and the citizens from the noncitizens. In so doing, we map out no less than our sense of national identity. The question we must ask ourselves, then, is what kind of nation has been formed through the exclusion of so many?

CONCLUSION

When a country like the U.S., committed as it is to the ideals of democracy, and economically developed far beyond many other nations, outstrips the rest of the world in its penal practices and in its punitivism, it is clear that something has gone very wrong. In the absence of persuasive evidence that "prison works," and in light of the considerable cost to individuals and communities that confinement demands, it is more than time to think anew about punishment and incarceration. The prison, despite its apparent ubiquity, has, after all, only been with us for some 200 years, and, only in its present oversubscribed form for the last 20. Once heralded as a more humane method of dealing with lawbreaking, the prison has grown to monstrous proportions, financially and intrinsically. Across the country, it strains state budgets and fractures communities. Many prisons are riddled with violence and most with despair. What, then, explains its ongoing popularity?

Although doubtless there are some individuals who remain such a danger to themselves or others that society can only manage them through incarceration, it is generally the ordinariness of people behind bars—both staff and prisoners—and the disorder of their lives that is most noticeable. Prisons have always been dumping grounds for all sorts of people with social problems—from addiction to poverty—many of whom have been the recipients as well as the perpetrators of violence and suffering. Penal facilities are also often used to house those, including the very old and the mentally ill, to whom society has little else to offer.

The causes of mass incarceration are manifold, yet, always, everywhere, under critique. Though the excesses of popular punitivism are not (yet) safely behind us, voices of moderation are gathering strength. What they lack, however, is a political platform and institutional embeddedness. While courts around the country are demanding improvements within prison, and grassroots activists and policymakers are having some success in their public campaigns, for the most part such activities occur independently of one another. As a result, prisons generally continue to escape accountability. Few states employ prison inspectors or ombudsmen, and it is difficult to learn much about what occurs behind prison walls. Although some of the blame for the silence about day-to-day life in prison lies with the prison researchers who, since the 1970s, have in many cases moved away from the ethnographic project, there are numerous other quite practical barriers to venturing inside. Changes initiated by Reagan and continued by subsequent governments, particularly under the administration of Clinton, have limited prisoners' access to the community, either through courts, visits, or community service.

Since 2001, the world has witnessed what can happen when prisons are allowed to function entirely outside public scrutiny. Guantánamo Bay, Abu Ghraib, and Bagram Air Base jail have shocked millions. Scandalously, however, such places are not alone in their brutality. They are merely more extreme. From staged "gladiator fights" between rival gang members at Corcoran State Prison, to the total sensory deprivation of Pelican Bay State Prison or ADX Florence, both "supermaximum security facilities," or just the everyday humiliation in Arizona county jails, where male detainees are held in tents in the desert, forced to wear women's underwear and work in chain gangs, incarceration continues to be pursued vigorously, and often with an explicit desire to harm and shame offenders. Prisons are places of suffering, punishment, and confinement. Since they are, for the most part, public institutions, they reflect and constitute our national interests. Prisons must be made accountable. In order to be justified, they must also be explained.

NOTES

1. See for example: http://www.kcl.ac.uk/depsta/rel/icps/worldbrief/world_brief.html.

2. Local jails, on occasion, also hold state and federal prisoners and even immigration detainees, depending on space. Sometimes serving inmates of other systems are held in jail if they are facing a further trial or appearing as witnesses in other cases. They might also be brought to a local jail if they need medical care or other service unavailable in their prison area. This more commonly occurs in big urban jails like the Men's Central Jail in Los Angeles or Rikers Island in New York City.

3. For a recent historical account that offers rich archival detail, see Rebecca McLennan's (2008) thorough and vivid account of prisoner protests and political intrigue from 1776 to 1941. See also Mark E. Kann's (2005) thoughtful analysis of penal thought and practice in the early republic, while Blake McKelvey's (1936) book *American Prisons*, an historical text in its own right, provides an unusual amount of detail about penal systems around the country up to 1915.

One

The Origins of U.S. Imprisonment

Beyond the Penitentiary

It is well-known, that in no one place are offered more injurious and vicious examples, than in a prison, where condemned, untried and all other classes of prisoners, are intermingled, without regard either to age, sex, or condition. . . . Accustomed to idleness, debauchery, and practice of frauds upon their keepers, upon visitors and each other, the young and inexperienced criminal is early taught to imitate the dexterity of his elders.

—Turnbull, 1796, p. 19

The prisoner has a right to share in prison, comfortable clothing, wholesome food, pure air, and a free use of water, equally with a humane discipline and ample means of moral instruction.

—Dix, 1845, p. 39

Capt. William Burch, the drunken warden, had come in from his revels, towards midnight; he dragged the sufferers from their beds . . . and was giving vent to his cruelty by putting them to the torture. To hear them scream, and see them writhe and smart under the strap, or the paddle, was to him a rich and sumptuous feast.

—Thompson, 1855, p. 119

Communities have always employed some method of punishment. However, the prison as we conceive of it today as a mechanism of punishment in its own right that is central to the operation of the criminal justice system, only emerged at the end of the 18th century. Modern penal confinement, in this view, is characterized by a series of innovations that include architectural design, systems of classification, reasonably consistent sentencing practices, and a centralized, professionalized administration. Its operation is shaped by the various goals of deterrence, reform, punishment, and rehabilitation (see, for example, Foucault, 1995; Johnson, 1973; Ignatieff, 1978; Rothman, 1971, 1980; Melossi & Pavarini, 1981; Morris, 1995). Before the onset of modernity, institutions known as prisons did exist. Yet they were usually utilized merely as receptacles to hold offenders prior to their "real" punishment or coercively to house debtors. Punishment was almost always physical, and included whipping, branding, and the death penalty. Offenders could also be fined and publicly humiliated by being placed in the stocks.

From the 1770s, such practices in both Europe and America came under sustained criticism, at least when generally applied. Individual reformers, like John Howard in England, or groups such as the influential Philadelphia Prison Society in Pennsylvania headed by Benjamin Rush, commented widely on the evils of corporal punishment and on the inhumane conditions of confinement. The effects of reformers' comments and actions were patchy. For certain individuals and in certain places—most notably for slaves, free Blacks, and their descendants in the South—the foundation of a prison system did not supersede corporal punishment but rather existed alongside it for many years. Indeed, state-sanctioned whipping in U.S. prisons continued in some places well into the 1970s.

One of the first actions of the nascent Philadelphia Prison Society was to lobby successfully against the so-called "wheelbarrow men" who were "employed in cleaning the streets, repairing the roads, &c." Such men, according to the Quaker industrialist and charter member of the Philadelphia Prison Society, Caleb Lownes, had "their *heads shaved* and [were] distinguished by an *infamous* habit" (Lownes, 1794, p. 4). Although the critique of the "long continued, visible, or public punishment, by degrading labour in the streets or upon the highways" (Anon., Brief History of the Penal Legislation of Pennsylvania, 1845, p. 3) is often presented as one that was driven by moral sentiment, documents from the time suggest that prison reformers were dismayed as well by more pragmatic difficulties, such as controlling those set to labor in this fashion. "However well-meant," Lownes laments, such hard labor

> . . . was soon found to be productive of the *greatest evils;* and had a very opposite effect from what was contemplated by the framers of the law. The disorders in society, the robberies, burglaries, breaches of prison, alarms in town and country—the drunkenness, profanity and indecencies of prisoners in the streets, must be in the memory of most. (Lownes, 1794, p. 4)

Existing laws in Pennsylvania were repealed in 1790 and legislation passed to authorize the erection of cells "in order to confine therein the more hardened and atrocious offenders, and for the employment of convicts within the gaol, and not as formerly, in public" (Brief History of the Penal Legislation of Pennsylvania, 1845, p. 4). The refurbished Walnut Street Jail that opened that same year ushered in a new, recognizably modern form of the prison (Teeters, 1955). Confinement in cells, classification, work, education, uniforms,[1] religious instruction, and rehabilitation in the United States all originated at this time. The new penitentiary even separated women and debtors from the rest of the male convicts.

Yet, how useful and accurate is it to trace the origins of U.S. imprisonment to one institution? What of those populations who were not confined either in Walnut Street Jail, or in those institutions that are usually connected to it, namely Eastern Penitentiary in Philadelphia and Auburn Penitentiary in New York?[2] What are some other possible histories of incarceration in the United States and how might they inform our understanding of the system today? As Michael Ignatieff put it in his revisionist account of British prisons,

> The real challenge is to find a model of historical explanation which accounts for institutional change without imputing conspiratorial rationality to a ruling class, without reducing institutional development to a formless *ad hoc* adjustment to contingent crisis, and without assuming a hyper-idealist, all-triumphant humanitarian crusade. (Ignatieff, 1983, p. 77)

In examining the history of U.S. imprisonment, the criminologist must not only find a path between explanation based on agency and structure, but also must appreciate geographical differences and socioeconomic variation in the treatment of many groups within American society. In the South, for example, not only slavery but subsequent practices like convict leasing, chain gangs, and prison farms shaped the historical development of state and local penal systems in ways unlike the Quakers of Philadelphia. The internal variation was, moreover, not limited to a North-South divide. Rather, within each geographical area and state, a number of prison systems and penal practices coexisted uneasily for many years. Whereas convict leasing is typically associated with the Southern states, prisoners all over the country labored for private enterprise. Likewise, even when housed and fed by the state, many, particularly in the West, in places like Arizona, New Mexico, and Montana, worked at building roads and other tasks more typically associated with the convict labor of the South.

Just as today when we must differentiate between federal, state, and local institutions, the British Emissary William Crawford observed in 1834 "three distinct" kinds of prisons in the U.S. First, "County Gaols" confined people before trial as well as convicts whose sentences did not exceed one year, and in some states, two years, imprisonment. These prisons, he declared, fell "under the care of the Sheriffs and magistrates of the respective districts" and were mirrored by the Town Gaols, which "appropriated to the same descriptions of prisoners committed within local jurisdictions, and subjected to the municipal authorities." It was the third class of establishment, "erected at the expense of the State for the confinement of criminals convicted of the higher classes of offences, who are sentenced to various periods, in some cases for life, and in none for less than one year" (Crawford, 1834, p. 3) that primarily interested Crawford. Yet local and county jails, at least in the South, were crucial for the development of the later system of incarceration as they provided much of the labor force for convict leasing and chain gangs.[3]

Colonial Justice

Criminal law and punishment played a key role in the early colonies as the first settlers sought to regulate life, commerce, and property in the New World. The Puritans brought with them a stern moral worldview, along with a commitment to some of the more sanguinary laws of England (Erikson, 1969; Smith, 1961). Court records and descriptions of punitive practices from this period provide a rich seam of analysis for anyone interested in understanding the texture of social life in Colonial America. They also allow a glimpse of power relations, morality, and of the abiding power of religious zealots. Accounts, such as those from the colony of

New Haven, which were transcribed by the Connecticut state librarian in 1857, depict a world shaped by superstition and fear, where confession and capital punishment were thought necessary to rebalance the moral order. To pluck but one example, we may consider the case of George Spencer: Found guilty of "abominable filthyness" [i.e., bestiality] with a sow, Spencer was charged for his crime primarily due to his apparent resemblance to a stillborn piglet "brought forth" from a sow he had acquired (Hoadly, 1857, pp. 62–63). According to the records, the case arose from the following set of circumstances:[4]

> [On] The 14th of February, 1641, John Wakeman a planter and member of this church acquainted the magistrates thatt a sow of his which he had lately bourght of Henry Browning, then with pigge, had now brought among divers living and rightly shaped pigs one prodigious monstter, which he then brought with him to be viewed and considered. The monster was come to the full growth as the other piggs for ought could be discerned, butt brought forth dead. Itt had no haire on the whole body, the skin was very tender, and of a reddish white collour like a childs; the head most straing, itt had butt one eye in the midle of the face, and thatt large and open, like some blemished eye of a man; over the eye, in the bottome of the forehead which was like a childes, a thing of flesh grew forth and hung downe, itt was hollow, and like a mans instrument of generation. A nose, moouth and chinne deformed, butt nott much unlike a childs, the neck and eares had allso such resemblance. This monster being after opened and compared with a pig of the same farrow, there was an apararnt difference in all the inwards. (Hoadly, 1857, pp. 62–63)

Though initially unsure how to interpret this "monster," John Wakeman was soon guided by the "hand of God" in his wife's "speritt," who

> . . . sadly expecting, though she knew nott why, some strange accedent in thatt sows pigging, and a strange impression was allso upon many thatt saw the monster, (therein guided by the neare resemblance of the eye,), that one George Spencer, late servant to the said Henry Browning, had beene actor in unnatureall and abombinable filthyness with the sow . . . (Hoadly, 1857, pp. 62–63)

The ostensible reason for the suspicion of "Goodwife Wakeman" and others lay, then, solely in his appearance, as the record makes clear. He "hath butt one eye for use, the other hath (as itt is called) a pearle in itt, is whitish & deformed, and his deformed eye being beheld and compared together with the eye of the monster, seamed to be as like as the eye in the glass to the eye in the face" (Hoadly, 1857, pp. 62–63).

This case, so strange to the modern eye, occupied the courts of New Haven and Massachusetts for some months in 1642. Held in prison while under interrogation and awaiting his execution, George was frequently questioned by representatives of the church, the magistracy, and fellow inmates. Although he allegedly confessed to another prisoner, Spencer denied his guilt when in the dock. Yet, his testimony was not enough to save either himself or his co-accused—the unfortunate sow. Instead, prior to being hanged, Spencer was forced to witness the sow "slaine in his sight, being run through with a sworde" (Hoadly, 1857, p. 72).

In addition to the strange crimes for which individuals could be punished, justice in the Colonial period also diverged broadly from modern conceptions in terms of the place of the prison in society. Colonial jails fulfilled a number of divergent tasks, most notably holding a range of parties in any legal conflict, including the accused and key witnesses. As historian Mark Kann puts it, jails

> . . . housed debtors, less to punish them than to pry open their purses, and served as detention centers for vagrants, prostitutes, runaway servants and slaves, disobedient apprentices, juvenile delinquents, and the insane as well as prisoners of war, political prisoners, and religious offenders. Some jails also housed inmates' families. (Kann, 2005, p. 123)

Perhaps not surprisingly, in light of this diverse population for which they were responsible, prisons in this period were far removed from the total confinement we expect in our penal institutions today. Rather, inmates were visited frequently by friends and intimates, who brought food and drink. The transcript from New Haven includes a number of descriptions of such meetings, particularly when they involved excessive alcohol (see, for example, Hoadly, 1857, pp. 107–108). In one case, heard at the court at New Haven on 5 April 1644, nine men were found guilty of "a drunken disorderly meeting at the prison on a Lords day att night, where they drunke 3 bottles of sack containing 3 quarts, and 2 quarts of strong water besides" (Hoadly, 1857, p. 133). For this activity, the men were each fined "according to the quallity and aggravation of his offence" (Hoadly, 1857, p. 133).

Throughout the early modern period, prisoners had to pay for the discomfort of being confined.[5] Records from the Essex County witch trials in the late 17th century include a detailed account from the Salem jailkeeper William Daunton for 1692–1693, noting the costs of feeding those accused of witchcraft. One poignant entry reads, "Sarah Good 6 weekes, and for her child Dorih. Good, 1 mo. Dyet 1:01:03." The document includes a 19th-century annotation by "Dr Frank A. Gardner, Antiquarian," which adds that "Sarah Good was executed on Gallows Hill, July 19th, 1692." No mention is made of what happened to her child.

Jailers apparently had some difficultly extracting money from prisoners, which, given the unreliable nature of their wages from the state, could leave them in financial difficulty themselves.[6] Daunton's list, for instance, comprises part of a bill to the state for outstanding pay. Promised 5 pounds per annum, over a nine-year period he received only 23 shillings. Presumably to get around such problems, inmates at the New Haven jail were charged: "a whole yeares rate be forthwith payd within 6 weekes att the most, [a]nd the constant yearely rates to goe on in their halfe yeares course, according [to the] formr order, notwithstanding" (Hoadly, 1857, p. 83). Perhaps because of these costs, and in response to the harsh conditions within jail and the heavy and brutal punishments that awaited inmates, prison escapes seem to have occurred relatively frequently.

By the 1720s, every small town was likely to have a place, sometimes only a single room, hut, or cage, where a runaway slave, convict, or felon could be held until a decision was made about their future. Larger towns and cities had more than one jail, where men and women, adults and children were pent up together in considerable discomfort and in grave danger to their health. There, straw was the only bedding, food was supplied irregularly, and exercise in the open air was usually forbidden. The jail keeper might live on the premises in an annex, or in a house nearby. Such places of confinement were not designed and were not meant to hold people for long. Punishments were generally inflicted on the body. Flogging, branding, and mutilation were common. The stocks and the pillory were also in use, although these were rarely used against free settlers. The slave or the servant could be flogged to death by his owner or employer, almost with impunity.

Under the influence of Enlightenment thinking, conditions in Colonial jails came to be seen as manifestly unjust. Early prison reformers, among them the Quakers of Pennsylvania, understood not only the limits of corporal punishment as a means of altering criminal sensibility but also the evils of congregate living in unregulated detention. The Walnut Street Jail existed long before it became the site of the first American penitentiary in 1790. It was established by an act passed on February 26, 1773, by Richard Penn. The first prisoners were taken there in January 1776, including 105 who had previously been held in "... the old stone jail on High street, which had served the Philadelphia area since 1723" (Skidmore, 1948, p. 168). Despite some improvements in the material fabric of the prisoners' life, the prison was frequently rocked by disturbances, escapes, and illness. The wholesale reforms of the penitentiary still awaited.

The War of Independence (1775–1783)

During the War of Independence, both the British and continental armies made use of a variety of structures to hold prisoners of war. Existing jails and prisons, including Walnut Street Jail in Philadelphia, along with converted warehouses, tents, guardrooms in forts, and ships were put to use. Conditions in most of these prisons were atrocious, and the death rates high. Unlike today, there were no uniformly accepted guidelines dictating treatment of enemy soldiers, and both sides were loath to exchange prisoners in case they would restock their opponent's army. In a letter to General Gage of the British forces published in Philadelphia by the Continental Congress on September 29, 1775, George Washington decried the treatment of American troops:

> I understand that the officers engaged in the cause of liberty and their country, who by the fortune of war have fallen into your hands, have been thrown indiscriminately into a common jail, appropriated for felons—that no consideration has been had for those of the most respectable rank, when languishing with wounds and sickness—that some of them have been even amputated, in this unworthy situation.

On the other side of the hostilities, Captain John Ferdinand Dalziel Smith of the Queen's Rangers met a similar fate. Despite avoiding the ignominity of being clapped in "a very large pair of irons," he could not escape the harshness of confinement:

> I was thrown into a room in the criminal apartment, the door constantly locked, nor person, even in the gaol, allowed to speak to me, in a cold vaulted room, without bed, blanket, or straw, chair or table, obliged to lye on the bare floor, with a log of wood under my head, in the middle of a severe winter, and sometimes three days without a drop of water or any kind of drink. (Smith, 1778, p. 16)

While the ire of both commentators appears to have been roused by the practice of holding soldiers in a "common jail," the real danger of incarceration for troops would have been, as it usually was for most offenders, too, infection, inadequate medical care, or death. Thus, according to a 19th-century account, when a prisoner was first brought on deck HMS *Jersey* moored off Brooklyn, "he was searched for money and weapons, but allowed to retain his clothes and bedding. He was then ordered down in the hold, where he found perhaps a thousand human beings, generally covered with rags and filth, their faces pale with disease and emaciated with hunger and anxiety" (Ellett, 1876, p. 118). Those who perished on board such brigs were either buried in shallow graves alongside Brooklyn Harbor or, on occasion, merely dumped in the river.

Likewise, smallpox was rife in the prison ships used by the British in South Carolina. Although the surgeons were permitted to inoculate captured American troops,

> . . . the wretched objects were still confined on board of the prison-ships, and fed on salt provisions, without the least medical aid, or any proper kinds of nourishment. The effect that naturally followed, was a Small-Pox with a fever of the putrid type; and such as survived the Small-Pox, a putrid dysentery—and, from these causes, the deaths of at least one hundred and fifty of the unhappy victims. (Fayssoux, 1785, reproduced in Gibbes, 1853, p. 118)

Such conditions, Surgeon General Fayssoux suggests, were not the result of poor management, but rather constituted a deliberate attempt by the British to encourage defection of American soldiers to join their ranks. By refusing to provide adequate clothing or food, and by housing prisoners of war in overcrowded, filthy conditions, it was hoped that "their patience would be exhausted and enlistment would ensue." When this strategy failed, the British deputy commissary announced that

> . . . they should be put on board of the prison-ships, where they could not expect anything more but to perish miserably; and that the rations hitherto allowed for the support of their wives and children, from that day should be withheld; the consequences of which would be, they must starve in the streets. (Fayssoux, 1785, as recorded in Gibbes, 1853, p. 120)

The Americans similarly tried to persuade captured British soldiers to join their cause, despite warnings from figures as eminent as Benjamin Franklin over the unreliability of this tactic, given that some former British soldiers betrayed their new colleagues in battle (Franklin, as reproduced in Sparks, 1829; Cogliano, 1998).

On both sides, the prison was used as an ongoing site of the war itself and of a more generalized brutality toward and suppression of the opposition. In so doing, it played an important part in articulating the nation state as well as, more subtly and more diversely, a vision of national identity. Imprisonment is, by nature, an articulation of state power, since only the state has the right to incarcerate an individual—even when it hands over the practicalities of confinement to a private organization. For the Continental troops, in other words, imprisoning British soldiers was more than simply a pragmatic response to an enemy, it was also a powerful statement of American sovereignty. So too, the British practice of transferring (or in contemporary parlance, perhaps, "rendering") American prisoners to be tried in England made clear its sovereign identity.

All told, some 2,400 individuals were sent back to Britain, many of whom were captured on the high seas.[7] They were sent, for the most part, to Plymouth, England, to stand trial for high treason. Here they were held first in prison hulks before being transferred to the local Plymouth jail (Herbert, 1847). Those soldiers who withstood the rigors of smallpox, starvation, or despair were usually found guilty by the British courts and sentenced to prison terms in England.

By placing their opponents in prison, British and American forces labeled them as criminal rather than recognizing them as legitimate foreign combatants. By trying them in England, the British clearly sought to reestablish the authority of the motherland; Americans, this practice averred, had to answer to the British nation-state. Such strategies, however, were only partially successful. Standards of decency—as George Washington's letter made clear—bristled against disrespectful treatment of high-ranking opponents, and indeed, many were released from captivity, often in organized exchanges of prisoners. So too, despite the overweening power of England, studies suggest that many of the American prisoners in Plymouth rejected the authority of Britain, expressing instead a nascent form of national identity and pride as "Americans." Songs and diaries from this time record patriotic impulses as well as organized resistance (Rediker, 1996; Cogliano, 1998). On July 4, 1778, for example, one prisoner by the name of Charles Herbert crowed, "This morning when we were let out, we all hoisted the American flag upon our hats . . . [at] one o'clock . . . we then drew up thirteen divisions [for the thirteen colonies], and each division gave three cheers, till at least we all cheered together . . . We kept our colors hoisted till sunset . . ." (Herbert, cited in Cogliano, 1998, p. 27).

Tellingly, evidence suggests that the American-born prisoners and their burgeoning sense of national identity divided, at least in part, along race lines. Though records do not divulge the number of Black prisoners taken by the British, historian Francis Cogliano recounts a general hostility and suspicion toward the Black prisoners. On April 26, 1778, for instance, one of the White prisoners, Charles Herbert, wrote in his diary that two Black men had been accused of informing to the British and were violently whipped by the White prisoners. Two days later, he wrote, "all the negroes were taken out of this prison, and put into a separate building" (Herbert, cited in Cogliano, 1998, p. 34). Likewise, Cogliano asserts, a greater number of Black prisoners than White sought release from captivity by joining the Royal Navy, suggesting that their affective ties to an American national identity were only loosely felt. While other sources estimate at 20,000 those Black slaves who joined the British on the promise of manumission (Moskos, 1973), such accounts provide a tantalizing glimpse of the racialized nature of American national identity, which was to become so profound, both in the country's prisons as well as in its Civil War.

After the 1783 Treaty of Paris, the newly independent American colonies sought to rationalize the tangle of British models, which had until then informed Colonial legislation and places of punishment. British convicts—who had previously been transported to serve out the terms of their sentences—were no longer welcome. A new Constitution, adopted in 1787, was ratified in each state by June, 1788. The following year, work on a Bill of Rights was hastened when news of the French Revolution arrived. Among the many salutory tales told about revolutionary Paris was that of the storming of the Bastille prison in the center of the city, which was considered to represent the excesses of the Ancien Régime. Less admired, perhaps, were the later attacks on Paris prisons and the slaughter of many of their inmates (Bosworth, 2001). American prisons, overcrowded as a result of the trade depression, which had followed the War of Independence, also periodically stirred waves of anger among the populace. Penal codes began to shed capital punishment for offenses other than murder. Branding and mutilation of the body became outmoded. Flogging remained. Race and slavery emerged as the big questions that the newly enlightened Founding Fathers had to ponder.

Prisons, Slavery, and the Antebellum South

Notwithstanding the ongoing deployment of prison ships today, and the growing salience of prisons as tools of war, the fate of the prisoners of war in the American Revolution is rarely remarked on today in the prisons literature. In contrast, the enduring effect of slavery has been given more attention (Oshinsky, 1997). Within criminology, work by sociologist Loïc Wacquant (2000, 2001a, 2001b, 2002), has been influential, particularly his schematic view of "successive" "peculiar institutions," where he traces a direct line from slavery, through segregation, Jim Crow "justice," and the ghetto to contemporary practices of "mass imprisonment." More broadly, other writers like Jeanne Flavin (2007, 2008) uncover engrained brutality in a whole host of criminal justice, health, and welfare policies targeted at black women. In Flavin's view, "The contemporary struggle over black women's reproductive rights bears a disturbing resemblance to that which took place under slavery, marked as it is by racist stereotyping, paternalism, and insidious forms of control" (Flavin, 2007, p. 95).

Prisons in the South served as an important adjunct to slavery, just as slavery was, in states like Virginia, used as a punishment for "free blacks." Whereas most accounts of slavery have focused on the summary "justice" meted out to slaves by their owners, it is notable that prisons, too, played an important role in controlling slave labor. They were used as holding pens for slaves awaiting sale, as well as places of confinement for runaway and "unruly" slaves. Not only did "hotels, taverns and inns occasionally maintain small jails to contain their customers' human property" (Kann, 2005, p. 204), but prisons (typically county jails) were commonly used to keep slaves awaiting sale. Prisons also held slaves awaiting or undergoing trial (Randolph, 1722; Williams, 1883; Sommerville, 1995). As William Crawford observed in a footnote in his report to the English House of Commons on American Penitentiaries:

> In the Slave States, particularly, the county gaols are truly deplorable. It is the practice to commit a slave to the common gaol whenever it suits the convenience of the owner. Slaves apprehended in endeavouring to escape are also here imprisoned until claimed, or sold to pay the charges incurred by their re-capture and maintenance. In addition to these classes are to be found, with scarcely any means of separation, persons committed for trial, convicts sentenced for minor offences, men, women and children . . . these places of confinement exhibit scenes of great depravity, wretchedness and oppression. (Crawford, 1834, pp. 22–23)

Moreover, Crawford asserted, the number of slaves behind bars was not of little regard. Instead, he claimed,

> Occasionally the number of slaves in custody exceeds all other classes of prisoners. Of eighty-eight prisoners whom I found in the gaol at Baltimore

> seventy-two were slaves, committed not for any offence, but merely for security until they could be sold. They consisted of individuals of all ages, from the old man of seventy to the infant at the breast. Here they were exposed to view previous to sale. (Crawford, 1834, p. 24)

Some states, like Virginia, developed complex procedures to deal with runaway slaves, which not only relied on the prison, but also demonstrated deep interconnections between places of confinement and other social institutions. Thus, the 1722 Act for Amending the Act Concerning Slaves and Servants, drafted by John Randolph, required the law-abiding population to commit to the county jail "every Negro or other person who shall be taken up and brought before any Justice of the Peace and cannot speak English or thro' obstinancy will not declare the name of his or her owner" (Randolph, 1722, p. 3). On imprisonment, it was incumbent on the local sheriff to publicize

> a full description of such Runaway and his cloathing . . . to the clerk or reader of each church or chappell in his county every which church or chappel is hereby required to make publication thereby by setting up the same in some open and convenient place near the said church or chappel on every Lords day during the space of two months from the date thereof. (Randolph, 1722, p. 4)

If the slave was not reclaimed within a two-month period, the law further dictated "the said Runaway to be delivered to the next constable to be by him conveyed to the next Constable and so from Constable to Constable to the public gaol of this Colony" (Randolph, 1722, p. 5). Eventually the jailer was entitled to sell the labor of the slave, providing that he should

> cause a Strong Iron Collar to be put on the neck of such Negro or Runaway with the letters (PG) stamped thereon . . . and that he would agree to deliver the slave to his rightful owner (following payment for costs incurred) should that owner ever claim his property back. (Randolph, 1722, p. 7)

Slaves accused of crime were rarely sentenced to a term of imprisonment, receiving instead immediate corporal or capital punishment.[8] While the likelihood of a slave receiving real justice under such process was not great, some evidence suggests that, on occasion, slaves were found innocent by the courts, particularly if they had supporters within the local White community, or if the "reliability" of their accuser could be successfully impugned. This latter issue was of particular relevance in rape cases involving White working-class women, who themselves often inhabited liminal, and so, vulnerable positions in the social hierarchy (Sommerville, 1995). In this regard, historically informed scholarship suggests, prisons and the broader justice system played dynamic roles in the construction not only of race but also of the gender order (Messerschmidt, 2007; Young & Spencer, 2007).

Southern prisons upheld the "peculiar institution" not merely by confining recaptured slaves or individuals awaiting sale, but also by confining those (Whites) accused of fomenting abolitionism. One such person, Lewis W. Paine (1852), published an account of his years in a Georgia prison, where he was incarcerated for helping a slave escape. Despite legal safeguards, which, according to Paine, in the state of Georgia held that the jailer would provide each prisoner "two pounds of bread, one and a-half pounds of beef, or one pound of pork, with a sufficiency of water, all good and wholesome provisions," while in the County Jail awaiting trial Paine reported being fed "on the coarsest food, the fattest outside of bacon; and the corn bread often contained the print of other teeth than mine" (Paine, 1852, p. 53). Overall conditions were so poor, he wrote, that "even if I had belonged to the family of swine, it would have been hardly just, even to the nature of a hog, that I should be left to wallow in filth, and kept forever in a pent-up sty, without a breath of fresh air!" (Paine, 1852, p. 60). Despite his hopes of improvement, in his first year of confinement, conditions were also poor in the state prison. "There was a great deal of fault found about our clothes. We never got a vest, never but one pair of socks, and sometimes none at all, and never our cotton jackets" (Paine, 1852, pp. 77–78). The warden also failed to provide the prisoners with any blankets. Though matters improved somewhat in his second year, following the appointment of a new warden, most of Paine's book is study of deprivation and mistreatment.

Similar accounts of hard prison conditions, such as George Thompson's 1855 book *Narrative of the arrest, trial, conviction, imprisonment, treatment, observations, reflections and deliverance of Work, Burr, and Thompson, who suffered an unjust and cruel imprisonment in Missouri Penitentiary for attempting to aid some slaves to liberty*, are common. Notable for having been condemned by a jury containing Mark Twain's father, John Clemens, Thompson and his colleagues were sentenced to 12 years hard labor in Jefferson Penitentiary, Missouri. Though none ultimately stayed for the duration of his sentence, being pardoned after four years, all suffered serious health problems. In addition to describing daily prison life, Thompson also depicts in some detail the involvement of private, mercantile interests in incarceration, well before the period of Reconstruction, which is usually associated with the practice of convict leasing. Inmates at Palmyra, as those in Auburn penitentiary in New York State, worked for a whole range of private businesses, both within and outside the prison walls. Unlike Auburn, however, which was run by the state, Palmyra was sold to the highest bidder. Thompson, who happened to be resident when the lease of the institution changed hands, claimed that the new warden, who took control on February 16, 1843, paid the hefty sum of "fifty thousand dollars, for the use and profits of the prison for ten years" (Thompson, 1855, p. 207).

Religious Reform in the North

By far the best known aspect of the history of U.S. imprisonment in the late 18th and 19th century concerns the work of the Quakers in Pennsylvania (Meranze, 1996; Okun, 2002). Champions of solitary confinement, classification, and religious instruction, they are usually viewed as the progenitors of modern American prisons. The early penitentiaries, however, were not without their problems too. "On the first night of the Walnut Street Jail's reopening as a penitentiary," in 1790, historian Rebecca McLennan (2008, p. 43) reports, "The convicts very nearly succeeded in perpetrating a mass escape." In this same institution, "convicts routinely succeeded in enforcing the customary working man's 'rights,' including that of 'Blue Monday,' laying down tools and ceasing work in flagrant violation of the penitentiary's rules" (McLennan, 2008, p. 44). In 1799, one year after inmates at Walnut Street Jail had razed a number of workshops to the ground, an account published by Patrick Lyon, who stood accused of robbing the Bank of Pennsylvania, suggested that many of the reformist goals had been derailed. The promised order was upended by sickness and filth. So too, attempts at work and education had come to little, inmates were bullied by staff, and inadequately fed and clothed:

> I was thrown into an unwholesome prison, where the Yellow fever raged with forcible degree of malignity, there being at the time between twenty and thirty cases of that ravaging disorder then in prison; several of the keepers died . . . during which time, being six weekes under close confinement, and without a bed; I have been twenty-four hours without a morsel to eat, or a drop of water to drink, besides the extreme danger I ran in losing my life, but that terrible, calamitous, and tremendous disorder, nominated the Yellow fever . . . At length, suffering three months of imprisonment, eight weeks of which I was in one pair of stockings; being denied every necessary communication with my friends, and held on suspicion without an oath, (or any ground for an oath), against me. (Lyon, 1799, p. 58)[9]

The yellow fever struck Philadelphia and Walnut Street Jail in particular, again, in 1820. So, too, prisoners repeatedly complained about their living conditions, ensuring that mutinies remained a common part of the confinement experience. In his mid-19th-century account of his life, for example, newspaperman John Binns described a particularly dramatic example of such events that occurred in 1820, when

> . . . the prisoners, in their place of worship, had, on signal given by the clapping of hands, seized and gagged the clergyman and every person in the church, save only the prisoners, many of whom in the conspiracy had come prepared with hammers, hatchets, pickaxes, &c., to break out the wall of the church, on Sixth Street . . . as soon as a few stones were knocked out of the wall, some of the prisoners squeezed their way out, and a few, I think not more than three or four, made their escape. (Binns, 1854, pp. 277–278)

The crowds, who later historians estimate at 400 to 500, were only subdued by the "civil and military authorities" who "fired down upon the most rioutous of the prisoners" (Binns, 1854, p. 278).

Notwithstanding its manifold internal problems, Walnut Street Jail is fondly remembered as the "cradle of the American penitentiary" (Teeters, 1955) and the source of modern penal architecture and administration that reached its apogee at another penal establishment also located in the city of Philadelphia, the Eastern State Penitentiary. Established by an act of the General Assembly of Pennsylvania in March 1821, the Penitentiary, which was not completed until 1829, reflected advanced thinking about prison reform at the time and was specifically designed to hold "two hundred and fifty prisoners, on the principle of solitary confinement of the confict" (*An Act to Provide for the Erection of a State Penitentiary within the City and County of Philadelphia,* as cited in Schmid, 2003, p. 549).

Unlike prisons today, which increasingly resemble one another as states and the federal government utilize the same designs, Eastern State Penitentiary was lavishly decorated by its architect John Haviland.[10] Constructed on a radial plan, Eastern State Penitentiary was a technological marvel of the time, with central heating and water in each cell. According to one impressed visitor, it was "one of the largest buildings in the United States, occupying ten acres of ground," complete with thirty-foot-high walls, towers and a "great gateway . . . twenty-seven feet high and fifteen feet wide . . . filled by a massive wrought iron portcullis, and double oaken gates" (Myers, 1849, pp. 442–443). Coming in at a final cost of $780,000, it was also the most expensive building of its day (Schmid, 2003; see also Johnson, 1994; Dolan, 2007).

Such extravagance by the state legislature, though not without its critics, signaled the seriousness of, and social cachet accorded to, penal reform at the time. Prisons were thought to embody not just the brute strength of the state's rulers, but their wisdom and humanity, too. Elaborate buildings, fitted out with new technologies, pointed to a commitment to the social experiment of reformers and a profound optimism—some might say utopianism (Okun, 2002)—underpinning the penal project. Such institutions not only embodied a particular power configuration but articulated a vision of the nation state in which order, capital, and the sovereign reigned.

As they had with Walnut Street Jail, observers came to Philadelphia from all over the country and beyond to study the Eastern State Penitentiary and its effects. Such figures as Alexis de Tocqueville, Gustave de Beaumont (1833), and William Crawford (1834)—who were among its fans—and Charles Dickens (1996) who was not, brought the debate over solitary confinement, religious instruction, and prison labor to an international stage. Other less luminary figures also wrote of the establishment in their travel accounts of the American version of the grand tour (see, for example, Myers, 1849, pp. 442–444; Kilbride, 2005). Along with Niagara Falls, Eastern State Penitentiary was, for some years, one of the most visited sites in America (Schmid, 2003).

William Crawford, sent out by British government to examine American prisons, was among those who were deeply impressed by Eastern State Penitentiary. His report gave considerable detail about the penitentiary, from an account of its architecture to his musings on the impact of solitary confinement. Describing the appearance of the building, for example, Crawford wrote:

> The penitentiary is situated about a mile from the city of Philadelphia. The site occupies about twelve acres. It is built of stone and surrounded by a wall thirty feet in height. Every room is vaulted and fire-proof. At each angle of the boundary wall is a tower for the purpose of overlooking the establishment. In the centre is a circular building, or observatory, from which several corridors radiate: they are under complete inspection. The cells are ranged on each side of the corridors in the wall of which is a small aperture and iron door to each cell: through this aperture the meals of the prisoner are handed to him without his seeing the officer, and he may at all times be thus inspected without his knowledge . . . (Crawford, 1834, p. 10)

Struck by its technological innovations, he reported admiringly that "a privy is constructed in each cell in such a manner as to preserve the purity of the atmosphere, and prevent the possibility of communication from cell to cell. Heated air is conducted by flues from stoves under the corridors." Somewhere beneath the glowing phrases, he depicted a world controlled to the finest degree, where even during exercise its inmates were kept from contact with each other; "Prisoners are not allowed to walk at the same time in adjoining yards; and when in the yards are inspected by a watchman placed for that purpose in the tower of the observatory" (Crawford, 1834, p. 10).

Unlike its critics, many of whom, like Dickens, believed that total sensory deprivation was cruel and unusual and impeded reform, Crawford approved of total solitary confinement. According to him, "Solitary imprisonment is not only an exemplary punishment but a powerful agent in the formation of morals. It inevitably tends to arrest the progress of corruption . . . The mind becomes open to the best impressions and prepared for the reception of those truths and consolations which Christianity can alone impart" (Crawford, 1834, p. 12).

Notwithstanding such praise, it was to be the regime of another penitentiary, in Auburn, New York, one that eschewed total solitary confinement, which would be adopted across the country and beyond. There, inmates were held in solitary cells overnight, working together in silence during the day in a range of workshops and, from 1824, in a prison factory. Ever loyal to the solitary system, Crawford was quick to criticize Auburn for its reliance on corporal punishment. "It is true," he wrote,

> . . . that the dominion of the lash produces instantaneous and unqualified submission [at Auburn], but this obedience is but of a temporary nature. It imparts no valuable feeling and presents no motive that is calculated to deter eventually from the commission of crime and amend the moral character. (Crawford, 1834, p. 19)

Auburn, indeed, became associated with excessively harsh methods of punishment. The principal keeper, Captain Elam Lynds, a former soldier, ruled the institution with an iron fist. Guards were encouraged to use a variety of corporal punishments such as irons, stocks, the "Crown," or the yoke. Whereas the first two are self-explanatory, the Crown was peculiar to Auburn. Described in *Harper's Weekly* as "a simple helmet of metal, which is worn over the head," it was seen as "rather a badge of disgrace than a method of torture" (*Harper's Weekly*, 1858, p. 809). The yoke, in contrast, was designed to hurt. It was a "bar of five to six feet in length, with a staple at either end to fasten the wrists, and one in the centre to encircle the neck. . . . The pain of the yoke depends on its weight and on the length of time it is worn. They usually vary from thirty-four to forty pounds" (*Harper's Weekly*, 1858, p. 809).

Above all, prison guards used the whip on the inmates, male and female. After one died following a particularly vicious flogging in 1845,

Auburn adopted the "shower-bath" as a means of enforcing discipline. Used extensively throughout mental institutions in Europe and America, this technique was described in some detail in 1858 in *Harper's Weekly* after it, too, led to the death of a black prisoner named More. According to the article, entitled "Torture and Homicide in an American State Prison," there was some variation in the mechanism of the shower-bath. "At Auburn," the author reported, the prisoner

> . . . sits in a chair which reminds one of the old "stocks." His legs and arms are pinioned: his neck fits into a sort of dish, which closes tightly around his throat. As soon as he is fastened therein, a cloth is put into the dish to prevent the water escaping too fast. The string is then pulled, and the stream falls. If the convict does not keep his head well erect, with his mouth as high above water as his position will allow, he will suffocate. Indeed his attitude and the machine are such that he feels perpetually in imminent danger of suffocation.[11] (*Harper's Weekly*, 1858, p. 809)

The unfortunate More, the article claimed, was subjected to this technique utilizing icy water for upwards of thirty minutes in midwinter (*Harper's Weekly*, 1858).

Despite such sadism, it was Auburn that ultimately won out as the favored model penitentiary due, primarily, to its financial success. Even Crawford grudgingly acknowledged that "the labour performed at Auburn is considerable" (Crawford, 1834, p. 16). Listing the work in which inmates were employed, most having been contracted out to private businesses who paid the state per diem amounts per prisoner, he noted: "stone-cutters, smiths, blacksmiths, carpenters, tool-makers, coopers, cabinet-makers, machinists, turners, saddletree-makers, comb-makers, button-makers, weavers, check-weavers, bed-tick weavers, sattinet weavers, tailors [and] shoemakers" (Crawford, 1834, p. 16).

Notwithstanding the considerable differences between these two early penitentiaries, the institutions were united by some common practices. As at Eastern State Penitentiary, for example, the prisoners of Auburn were under constant and invisible observation, even when at work. "A wooden partition, forming a narrow passage, runs down the side of every workshop," Crawford recalled, ". . . by means of small apertures made in the boards, the operations of the convicts can at all times be conveniently inspected, without exciting their observation" (Crawford, 1834, p. 17). Likewise, although they worked in groups, they were prohibited from speaking to one another. Similarly, if not the architectural marvel of Eastern State Penitentiary, Auburn was still a popular destination for tourists, who for a mere 25 cents could visit. One such tourist, young Thomas Mott Osborne, was later to play an important role in reforming the worst excesses of the physical discipline upon which Auburn relied. In his case at least, the visit had an enormous effect. Reminiscing many years later, he asserted that

> no incident of childhood made a more vivid impression on me. The dark, scowling faces bent over their tasks; the hideous striped clothing, which carried with it an unexplainable sense of shame; the ugly close cropped heads and shaven faces; the horrible sinuous lines of outcast humanity crawling along in the dreadful lockstep; the whole thing aroused such terror in my imagination that I never recovered from the painful impression. (Osborne, 1916, p. 1)

The Civil War

Three decades after the musings of Crawford and his contemporaries on the penitentiary, prisons in America were thrust into a new role when, during the Civil War, they held many thousands of men from both sides (Sanders, 2005). Though initially both sides sought to exchange those taken prisoner in battle, numbers, and failures in communication, soon necessitated the erection of prison camps. As in the American Revolutionary War, the imprisonment involved was characterized, on both sides, by great brutality and high mortality rates. Elmira Prison, in New York, for example—a location later to be associated with the reformist work of Zebulon Brockway in the 1876 establishment of a reformatory for young male offenders—was, from April 1864 to July 1865, the place where numerous soldiers from the South died. Elmira Prison Camp, officially known as Camp Chemung, confined over 12,000 Confederate soldiers. One in four of these men died, a death rate much the same as its more notorious Confederate counterpart at Andersonville (Gray, 2001; Horigan, 2002).

Curiously, no hint of the severe conditions can be found in the 1865 *Harper's Weekly* description of "The Camp of Rebel Prisoners at Elmira." The prisoners of war, it said,

> . . . are confined in a space of some twenty acres of ground, with a broad river running in the rear, and high walls on every side. Here about 10,000 of the rebel soldiers who have been made prisoners of war are kept in safe custody, lodging in the wooden huts or in the canvas tents. . . . Sentries are posted all round on the walls, in such a position that they can have a clear view of every thing within the camp, while the movements of the sentries themselves can not be watched by the prisoners. At night the whole place is lighted up with kerosene-oil lamps. (*Harper's Weekly*, 1865, p. 230)

More than that, even, the author continued, "The prisoners at Elmira are well fed and clothed, and there is an efficient medical staff to attend to the sick. They amuse themselves with reading and writing, or making toys and other small articles for sale"[12] (*Harper's Weekly*, 1865, p. 230). Indeed, as at other times and places of institutionalized and state-sanctioned brutality, the problems of Elmira seem to have been willfully ignored. Instead, as in other 19th-century prisons, locals and tourists happily paid to view the confined at Elmira, handing over 10 cents per person to various competing tourist entrepreneurs for the privilege (Gray, 2001).

More notorious than Elmira, Camp Sumter, Georgia, also known as Andersonville, saw the deaths of 225 guards, an unknown number of Black workers, and around 13,000 Union soldiers (Davis, 2007). After the war, its camp commandant, General Henry Wirz, was executed for deliberately maltreating and killing prisoners, though some historians have argued since that the high mortality, at times more than 100 per day, was caused by such mundane factors as insufficient food and medical supplies. The death toll was also, as in the American War of Independence, aggravated by a failure on both sides to exchange prisoners.

At its most crowded, Andersonville held as many as 32,000 prisoners. Altogether, 41,000 men passed through it. The original structure was built on a site of 16.5 acres in 1863 by slaves, and then extended by captive soldiers (Sneden, 1864–1865, p. 14). One firsthand account of Andersonville, written by a 20-year-old Union soldier, John Ransom (1963), described the prison worsening dramatically over time as the prison filled up and the guards became more brutal. Whereas when he arrived on March 15, 1864, he wrote excitedly that rations "consisted of nearly a quart of corn meal, half a pound of beef and some salt. This is splendid" (Ransom, 1963, p. 53), just over one month later, on April 30, those same rations had become "Very small . . . Not more than one quarter what we want to eat and that of the poorest quality" (Ransom, 1963, p. 71). On May 13, he penned a depressing picture of his fellow prisoners: ". . . many have long hair, which, being never combed, is matted together and full of vermin. With sunken eyes, blackened countenances from pitch pine smoke, rags and disease, the men look sickening. The air reeks with nastiness, and it is wonder that we live at all. When will relief come to us?" (Ransom, 1963, pp. 78–79).

In addition to these two massive and notorious prisons, both the Union and the Confederate Army ran many other smaller institutions, pressing all kinds of edifices into use as needed. According to Civil War historian Glenn Robins (2007), for instance, the Confederate authorities ran 32 ". . . principal places for the confinement of Union prisoners" (Robins,

2007, p. 117) in addition to other smaller, temporary sites. Sixteen of these camps were located in the Deep South. On the Union side, Confederate soldiers were held in Point Lookout, Maryland, and in the Old Capital Prison in Washington, D.C., often before being transported farther north to Elmira. On the Confederate side, too, soldiers like John Ransom were funneled through all kinds of places before arriving at Andersonville. As the Union troops ventured farther south, they created new prisons to maintain order, even on occasion, as in Alexandria, Virginia, converting former slave pens to such use.

By now, most of the temporary prisons deployed in this conflict are long forgotten, in favor of more cozily heroic battle sites, favored "heritage" resorts. The graves at Chemung have become part of a National War cemetery, while Camp Sumter is both a National Historic Site under the guardianship of the National Park Service and the location of the National Prisoner of War Memorial and Museum. Such "consecrated sites" were crucial to the recasting of the Civil War conflict in the late 19th and early 20th centuries as one of "tragic fratricide." This rhetorical move not only marginalized the everyday nature of imprisonment in this conflict, but, according to some critics, also covered up the salience of race and inequality in the original conflict; both factors conveniently excised from the myth of national identity (Novkov, 2008; Blight, 2001). The attention given to these institutions overlooks the distinct nature and policies that characterized many of the other institutions, in particular, the racial and class makeup of those imprisoned vis-à-vis those who were exchanged (Robins, 2007).

Reconstruction and Beyond

Although the Southern slave states had leased their penitentiaries to private individuals well before the onset of the Civil War and prisoners there, and in the North, had labored for private profit, the involvement of capital reached new heights in the era of Reconstruction. So, too, did prisoner resistance to enforced labor, with the number of "mutinies" reported in the media escalating dramatically between 1879 and 1892 (McLennan, 2008). Complicating matters still further, many of the Southern penitentiaries had been destroyed during hostilities. In any case, they were not sufficient to house the growing number of convicts, most of whom were former slaves convicted for petty offenses. In the North, decommissioned Union soldiers soon filled the penitentiaries, making up to 90 percent of new entries in some establishments, according to recent estimates

(McLennan, 2008, p. 140). Such former soldiers raised a number of problems for penal administrators, claiming as they did a debt of honor from the state for having defended it. The former slaves were less problematic, as the criminal justice system all too easily replaced slavery, often putting Blacks to work in former plantations.

Despite the range of issues characterizing prisons from this period, it is above all associated with the practice of convict leasing, a penal strategy that, despite being practiced in some form all over the country, became particularly associated with the South, where poor Whites, together with former slaves, were put to work to rebuild the shattered infrastructure and businesses. The brutality of convict leasing was legion, rivaling slavery in its sadism and violence. Under this strategy, according to Frederick Douglass—himself a former slave—convicts were

> . . . leased in bulk in their respective states, to whoever has the political ring, and that party, by paying a small sum to the state, sublets them in gangs to R.R.s [railroads] and other corporations, and to plantations. The State throws off the entire responsibility of caring for her convicts, and turns them over into the hands of the lessee, whose only interest in them is, to secure for himself, what profit he can for their labor. (Douglass, n.d., p. 5)

High mortality and escape rates testify to conditions where women, men, and children toiled for no pay, as do the regular anxious accounts in the newspapers and parliamentary debates of the time (*Augusta Chronicle*, 1874; Cable, 1884; *Washington Post*, 1923; Mancini, 1996). Women were not separated from men, and, as usual, faced a double burden of sexual violence and its result: pregnancy. In one example provided by Douglass, for example, a female convict who had served 14 years gave birth to seven children during her sentence. When queried on this matter, a lessee "testified that 'such irregularities as bastard children occur as long as women were guarded by men.'" His opinion, as recorded by Douglass, nonetheless "was that not much could be gained by separating women from men" (Douglass, p. 20).

In the mid-1990s, historians began to pay more attention to the penal strategies pursued in the South after the war (see, for example, Lichtenstein, 1993, 1995; Oshinsky, 1997; Myers, 1998; Curtin, 2000). They provided detailed and sickening descriptions of the violence of the lease system, as well as of the chain gangs and prison farms that ultimately replaced them. More important, they offered an analytical framework for understanding these strategies and their implication for the later development of punishment in this part of the country.

As Alex Lichtenstein (1993) pointed out:

> The chain gang consisting primarily of black convicts working the roads of the Deep South embodied the brutality of southern race relations, the repressive aspect of southern labor relations, and the moral and economic backwardness of the region in general. But when it originated, the penal road gang was regarded as a quintessential southern Progressive reform and as an example of penal humanitarianism, state-sponsored economic modernization and efficiency, and racial moderation. (Lichtenstein, 1993, pp. 85–86)

Though convict leasing did not completely disappear from the South until well into the 20th century, the precise demise of the practice is surprisingly contested. Concerns about it, in regard to both its brutality and its negative impact on the wages and conditions of free labor, were voiced in some parts of the South as early as 1890, when a constitutional convention in Mississippi called for its abolition (Zimmerman, 1951).

Yet neither of the solutions, chain gangs or prison farms, seems significantly better to the modern eye. Both continued the racialized governance of the South, and both relied extensively on corporal punishment. Prison farms like Angola and Parchman, both in the Mississippi River Delta, were run like former slave plantations, complete with armed White officers on horseback and armed trusty prisoners. Both strategies were "defended as being appropriate to southern conditions because blacks were perceived as suited to the heavy, unskilled labor [they] required and the discipline of coerced outdoor labor was perceived as beneficial to blacks" (Lichtenstein, 1993, p. 106). Despite the supposed progressivism of each approach, however, documents from the time describe conditions of extreme brutality not far removed from convict leasing (Burns, 1932). Indeed, according to Alex Lichtenstein's (1993) summary of media accounts from the time, as late as the end of the 1940s, convicts on the chain gang:

> . . . continued to labor, eat, and sleep with chains riveted around their ankles. Work was done under the gun from sunup to sundown, shoveling dirt at fourteen shovelfuls a minute. Food was bug infested, rotten, and unvarying; rest was taken in unwashed bedding, often in wheeled cages nine feet wide by twenty feet long containing eighteen beds. Medical treatment and bathing facilities were unsanitary, if available at all. And above all, corporal punishment and outright torture—casual blows from rifle butts or clubs, whipping with a leather strap, confinement in a sweatbox under the southern sun, and hanging from stocks or bars—was meted out for the most insignificant transgressions, particularly to African Americans who were the majority of chain-gang prisoners. (Lichtenstein, 1993, p. 93)

Such practices highlight the uninterrupted line that connects slavery to modern practices.

Women's Prisons

If men in early U.S. prisons endured harsh conditions, particularly in the Southern states, those few White women who were incarcerated were doubly affected, while Black women suffered even more. Until the 1980s, however, little was known about the history of women's imprisonment in the U.S. or elsewhere. It was not until the impact of second-wave feminism trickled down to history and criminology that scholars looked into women's experiences (Rafter, 1983, 1985; Freedman, 1981; Butler, 1997; Dodge, 2002). Notwithstanding the influence of 19th-century female reformers like Elizabeth Fry and Dorothea Dix, most accounts of the historical development of imprisonment told only the story of men.

Yet, women were, from the earliest times, sentenced to periods of confinement. Though their numbers were small, their presence can be found in the historical record in a number of ways. Crawford's report to the House of Commons, for example, included detailed plans of the main U.S. penitentiaries and prisons, some of which, like the plan for Auburn, indicate separate women's wings (Crawford, 1834). Some of the firsthand accounts written by men record the treatment of women held in the prison with them (Thompson, 1855). Finally, there are a few examples of memoirs by female prisoners and a few more by female visitors and those who worked with women in prison (Carson, 1838; Perkins, 1839; Dix, 1845; Kirby, 1887). From the early 19th century, female prisoners also were increasingly discussed in the print media.[13]

In his lengthy account of his four years spent in a Missouri prison, George Thompson briefly described treatment meted out to three female convicts. The sexual violence they each encountered makes for unpleasant reading. It was clearly something that Thompson himself condemned and that, according to his testimony, also disturbed some of the other prisoners. Moreover, his account makes clear the different levels of institutional protection the women were accorded, depending on their race and offense. The first woman, whose case he describes in some length, was sentenced to five years imprisonment for killing her husband. Initially put to work in the warden's house, she fell pregnant. Abused by the warden's wife, presumably in retaliation for having been the object of her husband's sexual interest, the woman was forced to give birth assisted only by a male prisoner, nor were any clothes provided for the child. She and her child were released when the woman was pardoned after completing almost two years of her sentence (Thompson, 1835). The next woman Thompson describes "was put in a cell and rivetted fast" rather than employed outside the prison. According to Thompson's account, "Often in the night have we been awakened by her groans and screams for help. After a time the door was unfastened, and the guard could go there whenever they chose" (Thompson, 1835, p. 287). This woman was pardoned after about six months. Naturally, the worst treatment was meted out to the only "colored" woman. Unlike the previous two she was placed in a cell with men and clothed in a prison uniform. She was also forced to work alongside male prisoners and, when in her cell, the door was left unlocked "so that any prisoners could visit her, or any guard by night." When assessing her fate, Thompson writes bitterly, "Now *why* is she treated in this manner? 'O! she is nothing but a *nigger!* And what respect is paid to a *'nigger's'* purity in a slave state?" (Thompson, 1835, p. 288).

In contrast to Thompson's detailed evidence, Dorothea Dix included only two pages on women in her mid-century account of U.S. prisons, suggesting both their small numbers and her relative lack of interest in their plight. Summarizing the situation across a number of states, she observed that

> . . . very few, usually no women convicts, are found in the State prisons in Maine, New-Hampshire, and Vermont. In Massachusetts these are not committed to the State prison, but are sent to the Houses of Correction, severally in Middlesex, Essex, and Suffolk counties; in the other counties they are sometimes detained in the jails. (Dix, 1845, p. 107)

In most of the states she described, women were under the care of a matron within a men's prison, and were eligible for varying amounts of work and activity. In Connecticut prison, for instance, she found 20 women

> . . . under the supervision of an excellent matron. Unfortunately the present discipline of this prison affords for the women no period but Sundays for instruction, except in mechanical labors. In New-York all the women state convicts are sent to a prison at Sing Sing; these average about 72, and are under the direction of a matron, who, with her assistants, are much interested in the improvements of those under their charge. New-Jersey has but two women-convicts, and no matron. The Eastern Penitentiary has 20 women-convicts. This department I have often visited, and always found in order; neatness and good behaviour appear to be the rule and practice of the prison; the exceptions being very rare. The matron is vigilant, and fills her station in a manner to secure respect and confidence. The women are chiefly employed in making and repairing apparel, and have full time for the use of books, and the lessons which are assigned weekly by the ladies who visit the prison to give instruction. (Dix, 1845, p. 107)

That historical literature that does consider 19th-century women's imprisonment tends to prioritize the influence of figures like Dorothea Dix and, before her, Elizabeth Fry, while stressing the paternalism and oppression of the existing system (Rafter, 1981; Freedman, 1980; Butler, 1997). Most also point to the violence many incarcerated women experienced. There were, however, some who challenged these models, such as Eliza Farnham at Sing Sing Women's Prison. Though only matron for a relatively brief period of time from 1844 to 1847, Farnham, in a move prescient of later penal "scientists" and reformers, rejected much of the religious cant of her day and sought to educate the women in her charge. Influenced by a particular strand of phrenology, which proposed that criminal tendencies could be reduced through education, Farnham expanded the prison library, and, most radically, read the women novels. Combining activities of the mind with instruction in traditional middle-class feminine skills such as needlework and flower arranging, she even relaxed the rule of silence and allowed the women to converse with one another.

Farnham's measures were at best controversial. Following the escape of three women under her watch, the rule of silence was reinstated, and Farnham soon resigned. Nonetheless, as a recent article by Janet Floyd (2006) argues, Farnham was not alone in pursuing innovative techniques, but rather was representative of a small group of reform-minded female penologists. Such figures, who included Farnham's deputy Georgiana Bruce; Margaret Fuller, who was a journalist at the left-wing New York publication *The Tribune*; as well as Abby Hopper Gibbons, the first president of the Women's Prison Association, were instrumental in drawing public attention to the plight of female offenders. Ultimately, the work of such women led to the creation of the first reformatory for young women in New York. However, their victories turned out to be bittersweet. As Chapter 2 shall describe in more detail, from a situation of neglect in the 18th and 19th centuries (when most were left to languish in men's prisons) women prisoners in the early 20th century came to be the targets of considerable discipline and intervention.

Debating Imprisonment

One of the striking aspects of the first century of U.S. imprisonment was the vigor with which the prison was debated. Publications from (White and male) former convicts are easy to come by (Harris, 1862; Paine, 1852; Thompson, 1855), while individual reports of concerned citizens and those employed by the state to investigate conditions abound (Crawford, 1834; Dix, 1845). When read in conjunction with related accounts by travelers and diarists (Abdy, 1835; Alexander, 1833), and even alongside more fictional narratives, it seems that prisons and punishment occupied the attention of significant parts of society in ways that are no longer the case. One stark indicator of their attraction to the general public can be found in the records of paying visitors at state penitentiaries like Auburn. According to Dorothea Dix, who, like most reformers, opposed this practice, "visitors' fees at Auburn, in 1842, were $1692.75, and, in 1845, $1942.75,—making $3635.50; at 25 cents each, we have for two years, at one prison, of paying visitors alone, 14542 persons"[14] (Dix, 1845, p. 43).

The implications and effect of such public attention and concern are hard to fathom. On the one hand, they suggest that imprisonment and other forms of punishment like the chain gang provided a public spectacle right through the 19th century. They also show that incarceration remained a contentious topic. When we confine our analysis to prisons in the North, the debate primarily rested on concerns about the efficacy and impact of segregation, as endless documents were produced in favor of and against the Philadelphia and Auburn systems. Texts on the South, largely reflecting the religious and political views of their authors, were more directly critical of the violence of imprisonment and its related mechanisms of social control in leasing and chain gangs.

More recently, a growing number of scholars from a range of disciplines have revisited these early discussions to explain the enthusiasm of the American colonies for adopting particular kinds of punishment and incarceration (Meranze, 1996; McLennan, 2008; Kann, 2005).[15] Such work presents a range of related accounts of American "exceptionalism," which may shed some light on the current manifestation of "mass incarceration." Mark Kann (2005), for instance, relates the punitive orientation of many of the early colonies to the particular political and philosophical notions of "liberty" that lie at the heart of U.S. culture and its Constitution. In a related fashion, Michael Meranze (1996) argues that the penitentiary reflected the aims and limitations of American liberal democracy, in particular that of the individualization of responsibility. Somewhat differently, Anne M. Butler (1997) relates penal policies to the gendered nature of social order on the Western frontier, while Rebecca McLennan (2008) traces the outline of organized labor and political parties in penal policies.

Given the variety of imprisonment in this early period, it seems most likely that its legitimacy and explanation rested on a range of beliefs. Although the reforms famously initiated by the Quakers—first in the

Walnut Street Jail and then extended and developed in the Eastern State Penitentiary and the Auburn Penitentiary—were not the only source of inspiration for imprisonment in the U.S., their form became dominant by the end of the 19th century. Even in the Southern states, where convict leasing and chain gangs were the preferred methods of punishment for Blacks, states did, ultimately, rebuild their penitentiaries. Such institutions, like their counterparts in the North, ostensibly sought to reform their inhabitants through labor and religion.

What the South suggests most clearly is that central to any justification of imprisonment lies an acceptance, even an outright demand, that some people either cannot be redeemed or are not worthy of redemption. Commentators in the North referred to them as "incorrigible" or "feebleminded," whereas in the South the racial and socioeconomic conditions for membership in this group were never in doubt. The debate, ultimately, was not whether there should be imprisonment, but merely for whom and in what fashion.

CONCLUSION

The early history of imprisonment in the United States is typically represented as one of gradual and then thoroughgoing reform. Throughout the 19th century, here and in Europe, "regular diets replaced the fitful provision of food in 18th-century institutions; uniforms replaced rags and personal clothing; prisoners received regular medical attention, and new hygienic rituals (head shaving, entrance examination and bath)" (Ignatieff, 1983, p. 80) did away with the worst of health problems in many establishments. Practices that are now central to incarceration the world over, such as cellular confinement, solitary confinement, education, and prison labor, were all instigated at this time. Such practices not only materially improved prisoners' lives, but also made their confinement more palatable to an increasingly squeamish public. As scholars of punishment from Emile Durkheim to David Garland have demonstrated, the legitimacy or viability of punitive responses stands or falls, at least in part, on public sensibilities. Conditions that were thought appropriate in the 1600s, with the often irrational and violent ends meted out to petty offenders, ultimately became distasteful to many in the 1700s.

However, the history of imprisonment, in the U.S. as elsewhere, is not a Whig story of improvements in humanitarianism. As William Crawford was at pains to point out to his audience back in Britain, the prisons of the early 19th century in America furnished practical solutions to a country in need of low-cost labor. In the South and the North, prisoners were put to work, not so much for their personal benefit or moral development, but for the private individuals who leased their labor. This system, though initially restricted to penal institutions, ultimately spread into the community through convict leasing.

Accounts of imprisonment through the 17th, 18th, and 19th centuries also underline another role of the prison in nation-building. Whether they acted as the safeguards of Puritan and Colonial morality by holding those like George Spencer, accused of violating sexual and moral norms, or whether they were sites of appalling suffering for those from opposing sides in the Revolutionary and Civil Wars, U.S. prisons provided a vision of the nation. For the South, likewise, the use of prisons to house slaves awaiting sale suggests their connection with a view of Southern exceptionalism.

As part of nation-building, and in a manner that resonates eerily with contemporary U.S. policies, prisons were also central to war. More or less at the same time that, in Europe, John Howard was publishing *The State of the Prisons* and in Philadelphia the first Quakers were examining alternative modes of dealing humanely with criminals, vast numbers of Continental and King's soldiers were being held in desperate conditions across a range of penal establishments. Likewise, during the Civil War, prisons were utilized to hold soldiers from both sides in parlous conditions, where many died.

The vast number of local and more celebrated visitors make clear that prisons at this time were also sources of national pride and international interest. Much as it is today, the 19th-century American model of punishment was exported all over the world. Such policy transfer, as those in power today would also have us believe, revealed the superiority of American exceptionalism and democracy.

What such history suggests is that at any one time the prison is fulfilling a variety of social, legal, and ethical tasks. It is an institution that is simultaneously local and real and one that is constituted by and constitutive of larger debates about race, nationalism, gender, justice, and so on. That some of these goals and many of these debates are contradictory is telling. The explanation of imprisonment is, in short, complex, and in its variety rests the institution's ability to persevere. In Chapter 2, I shall examine a shorter period when, even though no wars raged on American soil,

U.S. citizens fought a series of battles in Europe and Asia, to see whether the justifications for incarceration became any more straightforward.

NOTES

1. According to Lownes, the men were "... clothed in woollen jackets, waistcoats, and trowsers in winter, and linen in summer, shirts, shoes, &c. The orderly prisoners, who by their industry can earn a sufficiency for this purpose, are allowed a better suit to attend public worship.... The women are dressed in plain, short gowns, of woollen in winter, and linen in summer. Most of the clothing ... is spun, woven, and made up in the house" (Lownes, 1794, p. 11).

2. For instance, other penal establishments were, however briefly, enormously influential in public discussions of crime and punishment. Though today we mainly celebrate Auburn and Eastern State Penitentiary, both Newgate and Alleghany represented important alternatives at the time.

3. Crawford was quick to point out that the state prisons were notable not only for the relatively long sentences of their confined population, but also because they were the only establishments "under the immediate control of a certain number of Inspectors who are generally paid for their services, and are appointed by, and removable at the pleasure of, the Legislature of Governor of the State" (Crawford, 1834, p. 3). In most states, such inspectors have long since been abandoned.

4. It is worth copying the details of this particular case at some length in order to give a sense of the different set of assumptions under which courts were operating at the time. Such viewpoints also clearly shaped the specific role of the prison. While I have kept the original spellings used in the 19th-century transcription of the case, I have removed, for clarity, its use of superscript letters and shortenings.

5. Recently, some states in the U.S., including California, have seen a return of sorts to this practice, with offenders offered the option of paying for better jail conditions and permission to bring in certain personal items, including cell phones and personal music devices. Short-term prisoners serving under these conditions may also have non-prison-issued food brought to them by family members.

6. It would take over a century for reformers in Pennsylvania to discontinue "this injurious custom [of gaol fees], attended with such a variety of evil consequences." In that state, the Keeper was to be "compensated in a more eligible and permanent manner, by a yearly salary ... for himself and clerk; and as a stimulous to a proper attention to the *employment of the prisoners*, allowed five per cent on the proceeds of their labour" (Lownes, 1794, p. 5).

7. Eventually, most of these individuals returned to the United States under a series of prisoner exchanges in the late 1770s. Others were set free from prison early if they agreed to serve in the British navy (Prelinger, 1975).

8. Typically, before slaves were executed, they were valued first so that their owners could be compensated by the courts. In a letter dated May 12, 1763, one Archibald Campbell informed a slave owner that "your negro Charles has been ... convicted of breaking open a store and is to suffer Death next week. The court have judged him worth £100. I think you are well quit of such a rogue" (MSS 2C 152a1, Virginia Historical Society State Archives).

9. A number of inmates and the male warden of the Walnut Street Jail died during this outbreak of yellow fever. The warden was replaced by his wife, who thereby became the first female warden in the U.S.

10. Haviland also designed the elaborate Halls of Justice, more commonly known as the Tombs, in New York City, ". . . reportedly modeled after an Egyptian mausoleum found in John Stevens's popular travelogue Stevens' Travels" (Gilfoyle, 2003, p. 526).

11. The resonance of this "disciplinary" technique and the contemporary method referred to euphemistically as "waterboarding," which has occurred in CIA prisons and at Guantánamo Bay, is striking and worth noting.

12. Some of these objects can be viewed at the Museum of the Confederacy, which holds numerous such items from Elmira and elsewhere in its prisoner of war art collection. www.moc.org.

13. Near the end of the century, for example, on August 31, 1884, a short entry in *The New York Times* quotes a Mr. Dwyer, referred to as an "olde stager" in the "the Tombs squad," as claiming that the city's "Tombs court was opened in 1838 and this is the first day since the opening that there has not been a female prisoner in the pen. From fifty-odd we have got down to a cipher. What will happen next?" (*The New York Times,* 1884, p. 7).

14. According to Dix, ideally, "none but official visitors, and persons who visit prison for some definite objects connected with the administration of these establishments, and such of the relatives or friends of the prisoner, as by law have the liberty to be admitted, ought to be received. All who go to gratify a mere curiousity, to see the place, and to see how the prisoners look, should be excluded. The effect of this indiscriminate exposure upon the prisoner is bad, or, if it does not injure him, it only proves that he is so hardened in guilt, and so debased, that in being made a spectacle for the gratification of the thoughtless and the curious, he is willing his degredation should be as public as his life has been debased" (Dix, 1845, p. 10).

15. Still other historical studies exist that focus on individual states and facilities within the U.S., describing their development and justification (see, for example, Keith Edgerton's [2004] analysis of punishment in Montana, and Taylor William Banks's [1993] study of Mississippi).

Two

Penal Reform and Prison Science

Engineering Order and Building America

[N]o practically reformative prison system prevails; much doubt of the possibility of such a system exists, and the importance of reforming prisoners seems undervalued.

—Brockway, 1874, p. 144

Science . . . tells us that criminals can no longer be branded as willful sinners possessed of the devil, but classes them as sick individuals who may no more be blamed for their acts than the man who limps because of a broken ankle.

—Beier, 1931, p. 9

The first step in treating any disease is diagnosis. So we try to find out something about the personality of the prisoner, about his family and home surroundings, his school record, work history, social relationships, medical history, his mental rating, the degree to which he can be held responsible for his own conduct.

—Harris, 1942, p. 394

Notwithstanding the benevolent intentions of the early reformers, by the end of the Civil War in 1865, most American prisons, if they were still standing, were forbidding places. The humanitarian impulses championed by the Quakers had long been abandoned and "prisons, intended to be sites of uplift and rehabilitation, [had become] cold, cruel warehouses" (Gottschalk, 2006, p. 167). Prisoners worked under harsh conditions. They were, for the most part, poorly fed, ill-clothed, and subject to routine and often savage corporal punishment. As Chapter 1 attested, non-White inmates and women often suffered most.

It is perhaps surprising, then, that in 1870, just five years after the end of the Civil War, the first national congress of prison professionals, held at Cincinnati, Ohio, called for a radical overhaul of the nation's prisons and the means by which they were being run. This same year, the 15th Amendment to the Constitution was passed, guaranteeing the right to vote to men, "regardless of race, color or previous condition of servitude."

The "Declaration of Principles" that emerged from the National Congress on Penitentiary and Reformatory Discipline called for rehabilitation to become the primary purpose of imprisonment. It "repudiated the silent, lockstep system of punishment, rigid discipline and hard labor accepted as a model for most of the nation's prisons at that time" and called instead for a new era in corrections (Ohlin, 1974, p. 248). In Cincinnati, conference members declared that the ". . . treatment of criminals by society is for the protection of society. But since such treatment is directed to the criminal rather than the crime, its great object should be his moral regeneration." This view was reinforced two years later at the International Prison Congress in London, which drew penal reformers from the U.S. and Europe.

Such regeneration of the offender required not just commitment to reform, but also the time to achieve it. Reformers now advocated indeterminate sentencing instead of fixed terms along with treatment; prisoners should only be released once they could persuade their guardians that they would not reoffend. "No longer was the offender regarded as a morally deficient person, to be controlled by a keeper," it was alleged, instead ". . . he became, for some purposes at least, a 'patient.'" The old rule: "Let the punishment fit the crime"—was replaced by a new maxim: "Let the treatment fit the needs of the individual offender" (President's Commission on Law Enforcement and Administration of Justice, 1967, p. 163). So strong was the reformers' zeal that the first conference members proposed that the responsibilities of the state to offenders should not end "when it has punished him, nor even when it has reformed him." "Having raised him up," they argued,

> . . . it has further duty to aid in holding him up. In vain shall we have given the convict an improved mind and heart, in vain shall we have imparted to him the capacity for industrial labor and the desire to advance himself by worthy means, if, on his discharge, he finds the world in arms against him, with none to trust him, none to meet him kindly, none to give him the opportunity of earning honest bread. (Wines, 1871, p. 559)

For many years, the era of reform ushered in by this first meeting of the National Prison Association was viewed as a high point of penal humanitarianism and as a natural successor to the Enlightenment beliefs of John Howard and his supporters a century earlier. "Widespread interest in humanitarian reforms marked the years closing the nineteenth century and opening the twentieth," historian Jane Zimmerman (1951) asserted, expressing widely held beliefs from her own era. "Individuals and organizations alike showed concern for the ills and needs of society, and state and federal governments, long reluctant to accept responsibility for social betterment, gave in to humanitarian sympathies and passed laws to improve the health, working conditions, and general welfare of the people" (Zimmerman, 1951, p. 462).

Such optimism not only masked the murkier side of the Progressive movement, which found its outlet in eugenics and nearly unfettered intrusion into the lives of the poor (Rafter, 1997), but also gave little sense of the ultimate failure of many of the initiatives from this time. Less than two decades after Zimmerman's article was published, many of the aspirations she lists still awaited fulfillment. The influential report of President Johnson's 1967 Commission on Law Enforcement and the Administration of Justice warned that the progress implemented by the reformers

> . . . has not been uniform or free from complications . . . The old buildings were built in the stoutest fashion, and it has been difficult to secure their replacement. . . . In some States, juveniles are still jailed with adults. In a few, the bulk of the corrections population is still employed on vast farms raising cash crops under conditions scarcely distinguishable from slavery. (President's Commission on Law Enforcement and Administration of Justice, p. 164)

Elsewhere, presaging the penal conflict of the 1970s (see Chapter 4), academic commentators became far more skeptical about the motivations and achievements of the 19th- and early 20th-century reformers

(Rothman, 1971). As Lloyd Ohlin pointed out, "Implementation of the reforms called for in 1870 has had the effect of preserving large penitentiaries as instruments of punishment and incapacitation of offenders rather than their rehabilitation" (Ohlin, 1974, p. 249). Buoyed by a belief in the inherent malleability of the human condition, a view that was reinforced by a growing number of educational, medical, criminological, and other experts, more critical commentators began to emphasize that, despite their best intentions, prison reformers helped legitimate and consolidate incarceration across the country.

Though no wars were fought on mainland U.S. soil over this period, the years under scrutiny, from the late 19th to the mid-20th century, were nonetheless witness to numerous armed conflicts, which deeply affected the wider society. In all of them, the prison played an important role. In some cases, those incarcerated were American citizens, and in others they were foreigners captured on the battlefields of Europe, Africa, and Asia or detained from within the U.S. resident population. Rarely considered in accounts of U.S. imprisonment, such detainees, along with others such as the Puerto Rican nationalists Lolita Lebron, Rafael Cancel Miranda, Irving Flores, and Figueroa Cordero (who were incarcerated for opening fire in Congress in 1954) suggest that in this period, too, prisons were put to work to shore up U.S. national identity and security.[1]

Penal Reformism: The National Prison Association

The National Prison Association still exists. Renamed the American Correctional Association (ACA) in 1954, the organization acts as a bellwether for changes in views about penal practice and legitimacy. Just as in the 19th century, its present members are predominantly correctional officials, and now as then, they include representatives from the worlds of business and education. Originally reformist in nature, the ACA now operates at the interface between private companies and the administration of justice. From its earliest years, the association stressed the utility of technology and expert knowledge in penal governance. These days, private and public sector prisons may apply to it for accreditation for the services that they offer to inmates.

Foreshadowing connections between penal policies and politics, which since the late 1990s have been the objects of much criminological analysis (Beckett, 1997; Simon, 2007a), the first head of the National Prison Association was the future, if undistinguished, U.S. president (1877–1881), Rutherford B. Hayes.[2]

Other leading figures were drawn from business, the military, academia, and medicine. Indeed, until the appointment of Zebulon Brockway, founder and warden of Elmira Reformatory in New York, as president of the association in 1898, many of those most active in the organization were, as one 20th-century commentator put it, "only incidentally connected with the prisons" (Spalding, 1913, p. 724).

Unlike the ACA today, which outside the criminal justice system (and its considerable private investors) operates with a low profile, the views and findings of the National Prison Association were, for a long time, reported and debated. Its annual meetings were reported in a range of sources from *The New York Times* to the burgeoning academic journals of the nascent social sciences. Such dissemination of the views of many of the key penal scholars, and prison wardens, along with prison doctors and other professionals of the day who attended the annual conference, is an invaluable resource for contemporary scholars, while illuminating a public interest in penal matters that has long since dissipated.

From its beginning, the National Prison Association championed a new correctionalism based on "science." In 1893, for example, conference members officially

> . . . deprecated the use of any form of corporal punishment, or other physical torture, and maintained that such punishments hindered, rather than helped, in the maintenance of prison discipline, and advised progressive classification under the working system, with deprivation of privileges, as altogether preferable. (Brinkerhoff, 1893, p. 119)

Classification was key, not just to the maintenance of order, but also to the safeguarding of morals. Like the Quakers before them, penal reformers feared the possible contagion of corrupting forces among offenders. As Rutherford Hayes declared (1886), "Whether we would have it so or not, we must be and are our brothers' keepers. No man's family is intrenched against vice and crime and the shame and wretchedness to which they lead." If "the outcast and criminal" were to be "forgotten or disregarded," he warned, "our whole society will suffer from the taint of human degradation. Like a blood poison it will spread through and through the social system until it reaches the heart" (Hayes, 1886, p. 2).

Such melodramatic phrasing highlights the darker side of the paternalism of the 19th-century reformers, which became more pronounced in the first decades of the 20th century, an approach legitimizing such practices as forced sterilization, medical experimentation, and indefinite detention. These views also lay behind a number of emergent strategies of data gathering, such as Bertillon cards and crime statistics, methods that eventually transformed both prisons and policing. More obviously, they played a role also in the propagation of the Binet intelligence tests, introduced to the U.S. by psychologist Henry H. Goddard in 1910, and to eugenics. In each event, considerable attention was paid to identifying, "treating," and incapacitating the criminal classes, the feeble-minded, and the "morons" for fear they would "taint" the rest of society and weaken the national stock.

"Prison Science": Reformism and Social Engineering

While prisons and other closed institutions proved ideal sites for much early work in prison science (Stanley, 1940), its dissemination occurred in the reams of new journals and study centers that sprang up in the early decades of the 20th century. Like present-day think tanks, organizations like the Eugenics Record Office Cold Spring Harbor Laboratory in New York (1910–1944) and the Human Betterment Foundation in Pasadena, California (1928–1942), provided funds and institutional legitimacy for researchers operating in a number of fields. More broadly, research promoting eugenics could be found across a range of publications, setting the parameters of the nascent disciplines of psychology and criminology. Outlets included the *Journal of Social Science*, the *Journal of Prison Discipline and Philanthropy*, and the *Journal of the American Institute of Criminal Law and Criminology*. In them, as well as in medical publications like *Endocrinology* and in individual research papers, scholars championed the sterilization of criminals and imbeciles (Boston, 1913) and inmate tests for syphilis (Spaulding, 1915), while listing the "physical abnormalities" of criminals (Stanley, 1922) and the health needs of specific subgroups of offenders, including women (Guibord, 1917). Considerable attention was also devoted to discussions of the utility and appropriateness of indeterminate sentencing for "morally and physically impaired" individuals (Lewis, 1903).

Reflecting the contemporaneous influence of eugenics, the writings of Francis Galton (1883), Cesare Lombroso (Rafter and Gibson, 2005), that "founding father" of "forensic anthropology" and criminology,[3] and Alfred Binet[4] and Theodore Simon's belief that intelligence could be scientifically measured, numerous publications from this time describe and analyze the distinguishing physical, mental, and intellectual characteristics of male and female offenders (Healy, 1914; Bryant, 1918). By the end of the 19th century, most states had adopted the Bertillon system of identifying incoming criminals, which had originated in France, where it had become central to policing. Described in detail in a review of the 1888 *Annual Proceedings of the National Prison Association* that appeared in 1889 in *The American Journal of Psychology,* the Bertillon system required prison administrators to take

> . . . the exact measurement of the prisoner on his arrival at the jail or prison. His height, the length and width of his head, the left foot, the outstretched arms, the trunk of the person seated, the four fingers of the left hand, the left arm, and the length of the ear are noted down; and a photograph of the prisoner is taken, both in profile and full-face view. (W. N., 1889, p. 339)

Although primarily a recording device (which was ultimately superseded by fingerprinting), the Bertillon system reflected a widely held belief that, with sufficient research, it would be possible to determine and then treat the causes of crime. "The measurements thus obtained," the reviewer noted approvingly, "are catalogued and systematized in such a manner that it is possible to identify immediately, by reference to a central office, any person whose measurements have been recorded." In so doing, "it promises to shed some light on the existence or nonexistence of the so-called criminal type" (W. N., 1889, p. 339).

Just as many of the new "sciences," including psychology and forensic anthropology, underpinned the legitimacy of 19th- and early 20th-century prisons, so, too, penal institutions played a crucial role in the promotion and development of a range of "scientific" disciplines, from medicine to statistics. "From the standpoint of science," Lee Beier (1931) declared, "all men are not created free and equal, but differ as much in their mental make-ups, judgments and intelligence as they do in their physical appearances" (Beier, 1931, p. 9). While in his case, he concluded that inherent differences among them meant that "the child, feeble-minded, or insane, cannot be considered to the same degree responsible for their actions," others, such as Justice Oliver Wendell Holmes, Jr., in his notorious ruling in the 1927 case *Buck v. Bell,* urged that such differences justified extreme measures: "It is better for all the world, if instead of waiting to execute degenerate offspring for crime or to let them starve for their imbecility, society can prevent those who are manifestly unfit from continuing their kind."

The task, then, became to identify such degenerates. It was here that the prison came into its own in the early 20th century as, simply by being incarcerated, its inhabitants were clearly labeled and identified as social problems. To that end, and in the name of social betterment, the confined provided ample and appropriate cases for a vast array of social and scientific intervention and experimentation, the impact of which can be detected in contemporary society. Vasectomies in the U.S., for example, were pioneered in the Indiana State Reformatory in Jeffersonville as a means of preventing criminals from reproducing. From 1899 until the state passed "a eugenical sterilization statute" on March 9, 1907, Dr. Harry Sharp conducted 225 such operations. Declared unconstitutional by the Supreme Court on May 11, 1921, for failing to provide due process protections, the original eugenicist legislation was replaced six years later by a second statute that provided for an appeal to the circuit court within 30 days after the order for sterilization had been made. The new statute was applicable only to male and female inmates of certain state institutions (including prisons) who presented "hereditary forms" of inadequacy (Eugenical News, 1930, pp. 74–75).

Some thought that with appropriate intervention, some criminals, at least, could be "cured." In California, for instance, Dr. Leo Stanley, the resident physician at San Quentin from 1913 until he retired in 1951, engaged in numerous tests on the testicles of prisoners, purportedly to enhance their testosterone. Attributing crime to inadequate masculinity, Dr. Stanley conducted a series of bizarre and brutal experiments, "transplanting" testicles from recently executed men to healthy prisoners. Given that, on average, only three men were executed each year at San Quentin, Stanley had to seek alternatives. Settling instead on "animal testicular tissue" that he "injected subcutaneously," by 1922 he claimed to have performed 1,000 injections on 656 inmates (Schultheiss & Engel, 2003, p. 357; Stanley & Kelker, 1920; Stanley, 1922; see also Blue, 2009).

Dr. Herbert Goddard, a member of the board of trustees at Eastern State Penitentiary, also believed criminal behavior had its roots in medical problems. He claimed,

> It has long been established that a physical defect of some kind not only affects the entire physical makeup, but the mental reaction as well. We know that school children who are far below the mental standard for their ages and fall far behind in their classes, are changed into bright and energetic pupils simply by the removal of the tonsils and adenoids. There is no reason to believe that similar results cannot be achieved in criminology. Very often some minor ailment will be the thing that really makes criminals. That condition can, I believe, be remedied by correcting the ailment. (*The Prison Journal*, 1924, p. 8)

True to his word, Dr. Goddard removed "large pieces of bone" from the nostrils of a pickpocket who "had never been able to breathe properly" (p. 8), a stone "lodged" in the nose of another, and the tonsils of a short-term prisoner as well. No record is available as to the impact of these operations on their reoffending rates.

Such examples, though strange to the modern eye, are in many ways predictable. Many prisons, after all, continued to use prisoners in medical experiments until the end of the 1970s (Hornblum, 1998; Rusk, 1952), while debate still rages about whether prisoners should participate in drug trials (Gostin, 2007; Lerner, 2007). Also, thanks to the work of Foucault and other sociologists of punishment, the involvement of the early social science practitioners in social control is well known (Simon, 1993). As in any period, however, and despite the considerable impact of eugenics and medical experimentation, there were dissenters. According to Nicole Rafter (1997, p. 152), for example, though New York State passed a law authorizing sterilization of criminals as well as the feeble-minded, insane, and epileptic in 1912, it was never popular, and only one man was ever sterilized under its aegis.

Scholars and reformers were also at odds. In one article, Charles Boston (1913) argued vehemently against laws authorizing sterilization of offenders, while E. A. Doll (1917) called for "caution" when using the term "feeble-minded," if only to maintain the term's legitimacy as a precisely calibrated personality type rather than a purely ideological one. Even Guibord (1917), despite her analysis of the physical characteristics of prisoners, concluded her paper by warning that the "zeal to demonstrate some obscure scientific fact at the base of delinquency" led fellow prison reformers to "swallow the camel while straining at the gnat." According to Guibord, her peers were missing the point:

> We journey about the earth to confer on the historical, the psychological, the philosophical, the eugenic aspect of crime. We, in short, talk all around the edges of the subject meanwhile closing our eyes except for an evasive squint to the one clearly evident fact that at the base of practically all cases sentenced to reform institutions is the one common fact of poverty. (Guibord, 1917, p. 94)

Such poverty, Guibord hastened to add, was not "the empty cupboard and the threadbare garment" but, rather, "poverty in its widest sense," which "conditions from birth inadequate nutrition, dirty and unattractive living quarters, meager education, too early wage-earning, tawdry and vulgar recreational pursuits, absolute lack of aesthetic training and of intelligent human companionship or guidance." It was, in other words, a more general social kind of poverty which, she asserted "prohibits the operation of cultural influences of any sort" (Guibord, 1917, p. 94) Such a view, though tempering a completely prescriptive form of eugenics whereby people were locked into their behavior by their physical characteristics, did not advocate reduced intervention, but wanted such action better linked to ordinary features of American life. Reform, in other words, needed to go beyond individual offenders into their homes, schools, and workplaces.

Thomas Mott Osborne was a particularly influential advocate of penal reform who, for the most part, eschewed eugenics in favor of the virtues of work, education, and leisure activities. A high-profile, weeklong stint in 1913 as an inmate in Auburn Penitentiary in an information-gathering exercise for the Commission on Prison Reform in New York lead Osborne into penal administration. Two years later, he was appointed warden of Sing Sing, a post he followed with a stint as commanding officer at the U.S. Naval Prison in Portsmouth, N.H., from 1917–1920. In both of these institutions, he championed early attempts at inmate self-governance, creating a "Mutual Welfare League," and creating employment, education, leisure, and musical activities. A prolific author and public speaker, he left detailed accounts of his views and practices (Osborne, 1914, 1916, 1924).

Upon arrival at Auburn, Osborne had his "Bertillon measurements" taken and was "photographed front and profile while wearing a white linen shirt-bosom, a very dirty collar of the requisite size, and a black coat and necktie" (Osborne, 1916, p. 48). He was fingerprinted, "twice separately and twice all at once." Then, he reported, "a series of measurements from top to toe" were taken

> . . . and every possible means of identification noted and registered: color of hair and eyes; shape of head; characteristics of eyes, nose, mouth; the scar received at football thirty-four years ago, which I supposed was successfully concealed by my right eyebrow; the minute check on the left ear from a forgotten frostbite; the almost imperceptible bit of smooth skin on the back of my right hand, where a small lump was once removed by electricity; no blemish or defect is overlooked—until I begin to feel like a sort of monstrosity. I derive some satisfaction, however, from the fact that my business-like inquisitor is quite at a loss to account of six peculiar scars upon my upper left arm, familiar to Harvard men of my generation. It is some satisfaction to know that my Alma Mater has not sent many of her sons to take a post-graduate course in this institution. (Osborne, 1916, p. 49)

Osborne was scathing in his attacks on those who suggested that prisoners were less mentally alert and well than others. He was also concerned about the inadequacies of prison management. In his 1924 collection of lectures, for instance, he asserted that:

1. Prisoners are human beings; for the most part remarkably like the rest of us.
2. They can be clubbed into submission—with occasional outbreaks; but they cannot be reformed by that process.
3. Neither can they be reformed by bribery in the shape of privileges.
4. They will not respond to sentimentality; they do not like gush.
5. They appreciate a "square deal"—when they get one.
6. They are not many of them mental defectives; on the contrary, the majority are embarrassingly clever.
7. All of these facts must be taken into consideration, if we want prisons which will protect society. Unless they are taken into consideration, our correctional institutions will continue to be what they have been in the past—costly schools of crime—monuments of wasted effort, of misguided service. (Osborne, 1924, pp. 7–8)

Such attitudes suggest that it would be wrong to view this period as one of unalleviated paternalism and unrestrained social engineering. Yet, even Osborne, with all his reservations about how prisons were run, called on early prison psychologists and psychiatrists to assist him in reducing the great scourge of homosexuality behind bars. Thus, Dr. Bernard Glueck was invited into Sing Sing in 1916 to test nearly all the inmates for mental abnormality. In his subsequent report and academic articles, published after Osborne had been ousted as warden,[5] Glueck (1918) identified 60 percent of the men as belonging to one of three abnormal categories: intellectually defective, mentally diseased, or psychopathic. The benefits of Osborne's reforms were also not equally distributed; as was common practice, Black and White prisoners were segregated in sleeping and work arrangements. Most of the assistance in finding work upon release, as well as many of the education classes inside, were restricted to Whites. Such practice suggests, as with sexuality, a racialized view of innate limitations among Black prisoners and some immigrant groups.

The First World War: Conscientious Objectors and Prison

At the same time that the social science community was locked in debate over the nature of offenders and the best way of treating them, the U.S.A.

once more became embroiled in armed conflict when it belatedly entered the First World War in 1917. As in earlier periods of battle, the First World War altered the form and nature of the criminal justice system. On the one hand, prison populations throughout the U.S., as they did in Europe, diminished when youths were conscripted to fight. On the other hand, a new set of individuals entered the nation's prisons as numerous young men from law-abiding, predominantly religious, but also some political, communities were sent to prison as conscientious objectors. Quakers, Mennonites, and the German Baptist Brethren were all recognized as Pacifist sects under the U.S. Selective Service Act, passed in 1917. Exempted from military service, members of these churches were placed in army camps and put to work in noncombatant roles. A small number, estimated at 350, were court martialed and sentenced to periods of imprisonment up to 25 years or life. In addition to these men, members of the American Socialist Party also refused to serve, as did Jehovah's Witnesses and some followers of other Christian sects, such as the Amish and some Pentecostal groups. Although, usually, the men did not serve beyond five years, and most were incarcerated for far less time, some, like Socialist Eugene Debs, who spoke out against the draft and the imprisonment of those who refused to fight, were sentenced to punitive terms of upwards of 10 years. A small number remained in federal prisons until 1933, when President Franklin D. Roosevelt granted them full pardons (Gooseen, 1997).

Although most accounts of conscientious objectors in the First and Second World Wars (see below) stress the experiences of men from the so-called peace churches, others who were motivated by politics rather than faith also refused to serve and spoke out against the war. Such individuals, who included Communists, Anarchists, and Socialists, were often recent immigrants. Some, like Emma Goldman, criticized the draft, were imprisoned under the 1917 Espionage Act, and eventually deported. Others, like Luigi Galleani and his followers (who included the notorious and ill-fated Sacco and Vanzetti), advocated more radical measures, including bombing. Quite a few people were prosecuted and deported under the 1918 Anarchist Act, which sought specifically to exclude "subversive" foreigners.

In one firsthand account, reproduced in an edited collection published in 2004 (Brock, 2004), Arthur Dunham, who was court-martialed just as WWI ended (2004, p. 130), described life in the largest military prison in the country at Leavenworth Army Barracks, a site that was soon to become pivotal in the creation of a new federal penal system. Upon arrival in 1918,

"... the great iron gates swung open. We passed in, between the two gates, under an archway that reminded one of a medieval castle.... We were rapidly and skilfully searched ... and we crossed a large yard to a great brick building whose immense extending 'wings' loomed towards us out of the darkness." Orientation, which extended over a few days, was a "... long process by which a man [was] transformed into a prisoner" (Dunham in Brock, 2004, p. 134). Due to his refusal to work, Dunham was placed in solitary confinement for 14 days where, he reports, he was handcuffed to the bars of the door and fed bread and water. The cell was "... about 8 x 5 feet and perhaps 8 feet high. The walls were brick; the floor of concrete. The front was, of course, barred. About six inches in front of the steel bars was a wooden partition, shutting out the light and air, except what came through two pieces of screen at the top and bottom of the narrow wooden door.... Within the cell were a washbowl, toilet, three blankets ... and a tin cup" (Dunham in Brock, 2004, p. 139).

Notwithstanding the reformist intentions of the Progressive Era, Fort Leavenworth still practiced measures popular in the 19th century like the "lockstep" and hard labor. Despite operating a classification system of sorts, the camp failed to separate prisoners to any great extent. Serious challenge to such practices at a national level awaited the creation of a formal federal prison system.

The Federal Bureau of Prisons

Although some conscientious objectors and enemy aliens were confined by the federal government during the First World War, at this time the country lacked an extensive web of federal prisons and a federal bureau of prisons. Instead, prisoners were either held in state facilities or, as was the case during the war, the federal government took possession of army camps and similar establishments to house conscientious objectors. Well before it became the maximum-security prison in the federal prison system, for example, the fort on Alcatraz Island in San Francisco Bay held conscientious objectors. After the war, the absence of a national prison system became more problematic. Even so, it took another 12 years before a federal prison system was finally established as part of the Department of Justice on May 14, 1930, by Pub. L. No. 71–218, 46 Stat. 325 (1930). The Federal Bureau of Prisons created by this Act played an important role shoring up penal correctionalism throughout America even in the face of widespread economic downturn. It also offered a locale for incarcerating those designated as threats to national security, thereby more explicitly linking the U.S. nation, rather than individual state sovereignty, to the prison.

The ground had been surveyed for the federal system, both figuratively and literally, 40 years earlier with the passage of the Three Prisons Act in 1891. This legislation initiated the federal prison system by identifying three sites around the country for its first penitentiaries. Development, however, was slow, and six years passed before work commenced on USP Leavenworth, Kansas. Once work began, the prison took a further 25 years to complete. Leavenworth was followed by Atlanta in 1902 and, in 1909, by McNeil Island in Washington State, which had originally been founded as a territorial jail in 1875. The first federal women's prison opened in 1928 at Alderson, Virginia.

Within 10 years of the creation of the Bureau of Prisons, the federal prison population and the number of facilities had almost doubled. Until the repeal of the Volstead Act in 1933, a large proportion of those in federal prisons were sentenced for Prohibition violations and related offenses (National Commission on Law Observance and Enforcement, 1931). When the numbers outstripped the available places, prisoners were held in state facilities or in rapidly converted U.S. military bases. After the Second World War, some of the prisoner of war camps, including the one at Lompoc, California (Cooke POW camp), were converted into federal prisons.

Helpfully for those interested in piecing together administrative views of the purpose of imprisonment, the first two directors of the federal bureau of prisons, Sanford Bates (1936) and James V. Bennett (1970), and the first female superintendant of a federal prison, Mary Belle Harris (1942), published lengthy accounts of their experiences of and hopes for penal administration.[6] Sanford Bates was particularly prolific, both as an author and as a public speaker, throughout his career (see, for example, Bates, 1928, 1930, 1932, 1935). The U.S. Bureau of Prisons also published reports, like its 1942 *Progress in Prisons,* which articulated the goals and the form of federal penal regimes.

From the beginning, Bates advocated a "scientific approach" to crime control. From his demands for more accurate statistics (Bates, 1928) to his support for "scientific penology" (Bates, 1930), Bates articulated an abiding commitment to the potential of "science" to come to the "aid of all our departments of government" (Bates, 1930, p. 2). The *Wickersham Report* into the enforcement of the Prohibition Laws of the United States (National Commission on Law Observance and Enforcement, 1931) had concluded that "the present prison system is antiquated and inefficient. It does not reform the criminal. It fails to protect society." But Bates saw grounds for optimism (Bates, 1932, p. 562). "We have only to look back 50 to 70 years" he argued,

> . . . to discover what significant changes have already taken place. Thousands of "prisoners" are today in honor camps, restrained only by their own sense of honor. The ball and chain, the iniquitous lease system, the shaved head, the water cure and in most instances the striped suit and the dark solitary are things of the past. (Bates, 1932, p. 569)

Imprisonment, he suggested, was a balancing act between punishment and reform.

Such a view of imprisonment was shared by Mary Belle Harris, the first superintendent of the federal institution for women at Alderson, who believed the prison would only protect the public by rehabilitating the offender. Prior to assuming her position at Alderson, Harris had worked at the Reformatory for Women and the State Home for Girls in New Jersey, and before that in the women's workhouse on Blackwell's Island in New York City. Along with a handful of others, including Kathleen B. Davis and Miriam Van Waters, Harris was a part of a small group of highly educated women who were actively involved in prison reform (Freedman, 1998). Such figures were influential in shaping the ideas and practices of the first women's prisons and in championing the beliefs central to correctionalism. They, like Harris (1942), believed that,

> Correctional institutions exist for the protection of society just as hospitals do. But if hospitals, instead of trying to cure the patients sent to them, returned them to the community carrying not only their original disease, but also infected with all the ailments of the other patients, society would rise in its wrath and demand a reform. When it is a question of improving our treatment of prisoners, however, the public scoffs at "prison reform" and allows its jails and prisons to continue to breed and disseminate crime and disease. (Harris, 1942, p. 385)

Like other Progressive reformers, Harris, Bates, and Bennett thought that criminality was caused by social, biological, and psychological factors, which needed treatment rather than punishment. Rehabilitation required "the establishment of new institutions where fresh air, sunlight, work, and responsibility may bring their redemptive forces into play" (Harris, 1942, p. 401). Moreover, the authors agreed, the difficulties facing penal administrators like themselves encompassed more than simply the inmates. They needed well-trained staff. As Harris (1942) put it:

> The new spirit of our time and generation—the spirit of diagnosis and treatment, the spirit of individualization—cannot be poured into the old form of the prison system of past centuries . . . old prison traditions, customs, habits of thought, vocabulary, attitudes, are lurking in the dark corners just as surely as the vermin, and just as difficult to eradicate . . . We must have prison officers—guards, matrons, foremen and teachers—who are intelligent and co-operative in carrying out a rehabilitative program. One of the deplorable by-products of the old prison systems has been the brutalization of the many who have handled prisoners. Mass treatment and restraint by means of walls and guns have imprisoned not only the personality of the prisoner but also that of his keeper. (Harris, 1942, pp. 395–396)

From 1930 until it formally abandoned it in the 1980s, the federal prison system adopted a "correctionalist" approach to incarceration. As articulated in the 1942 document *Progress in Prisons,* such an approach was based on five interrelated elements: social service, classification, education, recreation, and morals and job placement. Education entailed instruction in literacy skills as well as more ambitious programs in health education (first offered at Atlanta Penitentiary in 1930) and vocational training. In her assessment of the federal education offerings in 1945, Margaret Wormley (1945) asserted, "A well rounded utilitarian education is what every prisoner needs, but his mind, as well as his hands, needs cultivation. Books, music, art, and dramatic activities are all complements to his practical training" (Wormley, 1945, p. 427). She then approvingly noted that "in most prisons today there are not only art courses and exhibits, but there is an increasing emphasis on esthetic design and decoration of the institutions themselves" (Wormley, 1945, p. 428). Prisoners, she reported, were also encouraged to enroll in correspondence courses, while ". . . often the university of the state in which a Federal prison is located provides special service for state prisoners. San Quentin, for example, affiliates with the University of California extension service" (Wormley, 1945, p. 428). At Alderson, somewhat predictably, she found that ". . . the household arts are emphasized" although she insisted that "academic training is regarded as important." Classes included the predictable trio of "Cooking, Dressmaking, Needlework," as well as "Laundry Theory" and "Americanization" (Wormley, 1945, p. 429). Dutiful female citizens evidently needed training in the domestic arts as well as in national identity.

That the federal system maintained its commitment to reformist ideals through the Depression and the Second World War is striking, particularly when it championed prison labor in a period when significant pressure was brought to bear on most penal institutions to stop producing prisoner-made goods. Such support at the national level for correctionalist ideals kept them alive in national policy terms, despite numerous practical and ideological forces aligned against them. The federal government, despite state qualms and economic woes, maintained its paternalistic role until social fragmentation and the politicization of crime and victimization proved too much (see Chapters 4 and 5).

The Depression: Prisons, Labor, and Social Structure

The Great Depression and the accompanying New Deal inevitably affected prisons, in terms of both life inside and the rationale for such institutions. Most obviously, despite widespread concern over the deleterious effects of prisoner idleness (Robinson, 1931; Teeters, 1939), legislation was passed to curtail the market for prisoner-made goods (Flynn, 1950). Criticism of idleness was not new, as prison labor had been one of the original planks of the 18th-century penal reformers. Newspapers and reports from any era (including our own) routinely criticize the lack of work and activity behind bars, usually linking it to reoffending and/or prison disorder. Against such views, unions have long asserted that prisoner work competes unfairly on the free market. Although some, including economics professor Louis N. Robinson (1931), argued that the causes of mass unemployment lay elsewhere, and that employing prisoners in state-use programs had little effect on the overall labor market, and others, like the warden at Sing Sing Penitentiary in New York, Lewis F. Lawes (1932), continued to promote its reformative potential, the federal government passed a series of acts in the 1930s that prevented prison industries from competing on the open market. Such policy signaled a radical break with one of the key justifications of imprisonment, which had characterized penal practice since the widespread adoption of the Auburn method (McLennan, 2008).

The Hawes-Cooper Bill, signed by President Hoover in 1929, came into effect in 1934, and was followed the next year by the Ashurst-Sumners Act. Five years later in 1940, the Sumners-Ashurst Act completed the policy reversal on prison labor. Whereas the Hawes-Cooper Bill made it possible for states to bring in laws barring the sale of prison products made in other states, the Ashurst-Sumners Act more explicitly ended interstate commerce of such goods. Private investment declined as it became clear that businesses would be unable to market items produced by prison labor to out-of-state customers, or indeed to anyone other than the state itself. Citing research by James V. Bennett, sometime director of both the federal prison industries and the Federal Bureau of Prisons,

Frank T. Flynn (1950) reported that the shrinking of private investment was already under way by 1934, as "contractors had discontinued work in Alabama, Connecticut, Idaho, Nebraska, New Hampshire, Rhode Island, South Carolina, Tennessee, Vermont, and Wyoming; and only five states retained contracts of any appreciable size—Indiana, Kentucky, Maryland, Oklahoma, and West Virginia" (Flynn, 1950, p. 27). The so-called "factories with fences" were, at least until the outbreak of formal hostilities in the Second World War, left mainly empty.

What, then, can we make of the creation of the Federal Prison Industries (FPI) initiative in 1934? Established under an act of Congress and by President Roosevelt's Executive Order 6917 on December 11, 1934, FPI officially commenced on January 1, 1935. Unlike most of the previous models of prison labor, which had contracted out prisoner labor to private companies and individuals, FPI from its inception was a "state-use" system. Goods produced by prisoners would not be sold on the open market, but rather provided solely to government departments and other federal prisons.[7] Designed to allay the fears of those who were concerned about competition with free labor, this system was shortly adopted elsewhere. By 1940, 88 percent of those U.S. prisoners productively employed in any system—state or federal—were working either in state-use programs or public works, building highways and the like. Some were also working on institutional farms (Flynn, 1950, pp. 31–32). In order to absorb the work of such inmates, many states instituted "compulsory purchase" laws, which dictated that necessary items had to be procured from prison factories. Thus, some states had to purchase license plates from the prison plant, while the U.S. Postal Service had to buy its mail sacks from the federal prison industries.

Once America joined the Second World War, federal prisoners joined the war effort, sewing uniforms and putting together provisions for the troops. At the same time, the question of prisoner idleness assumed a new form, when prisoners across the country requested leave to fight or somehow to engage in the national defense program. In an article published in *The Prison Journal* in 1942, businessman and prison reformer Sam Lewisohn (1942) argued that "... in the prisons of America we have a potential army of defense workers that only needs mobilization to become effective." They could be trained in mechanical engineering to help with the war effort, or give blood, he proposed. "It only needs the Aladdin's lamp of imagination and persistence," he insisted, since "for with all their faults, most prisoners have the patriotic instinct" (Lewisohn, 1942, p. 177). In a rhetorical flourish, he quotes unidentified prisoners writing in a prison publication pleading with free society to let them help:

> We are Americans! Nothing that we did to get ourselves behind bars, nothing that happened in the courts, nothing about our thinking, living or faults has taken this birthright from us. Let us take up this burden. Somewhere in this National Defense Program there are niches for us. Will you help us fill them? (Lewisohn, 1942, p. 182)

Whereas the state happily drew on prisoner labor, more expansive offers to help like this were not taken up. Notwithstanding such claims of citizenship, a prison sentence then, as now, effectively stripped offenders of the rights to and capacity for full participation in civil society.

World War II: Questions of National Security

The outbreak of war in Europe in 1939 had little immediate effect on official policies about U.S. imprisonment. However, once the U.S. officially entered the war on December 7, 1941, the confined male criminal population—as it had done in the First World War—declined, while the number of women behind bars expanded. Whereas young men were siphoned off to fight, women came under increased scrutiny in the justice system, with the police, penal institutions, and early social scientists particularly concerned about their sexual proclivities (Freedman, 1996). Arrest rates for women between 1940 and 1944 doubled, from 8.5 percent in 1940 to 17 percent in 1944, driven in large part by prostitution and prostitution-related offenses (Steffensmeier, Rosenthal, & Shehan, 1980).[8]

In addition to an expansion in the numbers of women behind bars, a parallel yet interconnected web of penal institutions spread as numerous "relocation" and internment camps were established to hold "resident aliens," particularly people of Japanese nationality and descent. From 1942, the U.S. also established a large number of prisoner of war (POW) camps, which, by the war's end, housed an estimated 425,000 men shipped from theaters of war in Africa, Europe, and Asia. Finally, certain conscientious objectors were placed in federal prisons, while some of those permitted to avoid active service were placed in "selective service committee" camps.

The mass incarceration in so-called "relocation centers" of the first of these populations—"persons of Japanese ancestry"—was set in motion two months after the December 7, 1941, attack on Pearl Harbor, when President Roosevelt signed Executive Order No. 9066 on February 19, 1942. Labeled a threat to national security, and stripped of the right to habeas corpus, this group included first-generation Japanese immigrants (or Issei) and their children (Nisei), who had previously worked in high-ranking positions in medicine, the law, and business. Nearly 70 percent were American citizens. Labeled "enemy aliens" by virtue of their Japanese "blood," these American citizens were also denied constitutional safeguards; the Supreme Court ruling in *Korematsu v. United States,* 323 U.S. 214 (1944), held that government policy, based on ethnic identification, was allowable. Some were not released until 16 months after the war ended. A much smaller number of U.S. resident individuals of Austrian, German, and Italian extraction were also incarcerated at this time (Robinson, 2003; Kunioka & McCurdy, 2006).

Most of the Japanese American detainees were held in internment camps in the West, from Washington State to California, although some were housed in the Arkansas Delta and in such places as Laramie, Wyoming (Muller, 2001). Between March 1942 and November 1945, Manzanar Camp, now a National Historic Site like the Civil War prison site at Andersonville, held over 10,000 detainees, more than any other War Relocation Authority (WRA) site. Indeed, so large was the population that, when residents of the camp started their own newspaper, the *Manzanar Free Press,* they were able to attract investment from local businesses, who were keen to advertise their services to this new "market."

In comparison with the massive scale of the Japanese internment, the populations of Italian, German, and Austrian resident aliens and visitors got off rather lightly.[9] Although more than 600,000 Italian citizens, as well as U.S. citizens of Italian descent living in the United States at the time, were labeled by the federal government "internal enemies" and "enemy aliens," only 3,000 were arrested, and 300 were placed in internment camps. In comparison, estimates suggest that 11,000 German residents, quite a few of whom were citizens, were arrested, with just under half of them interned.

For some time, those designated as enemy aliens over 14 years of age were forbidden from entering certain military areas. They were also unable "to leave the country, travel in a plane, change their place of abode, or travel about outside their own communities, without special permission. They were forbidden to own or use firearms, cameras, short-wave radio sets, codes, ciphers or invisible ink" (Rostow, 1945, p. 493). Anyone under suspicion, or who violated the regulations, could be summarily arrested on a presidential warrant (Rostow, 1945). The "basic object of [this] control plan," according to Yale Law Professor Eugene V. Rostow's critical account (1945) was "to keep security officers informed, but otherwise allow the aliens almost their normal share in the work and life in the community" (Rostow, 1945, p. 493). Yet, the regulations were confusing and could be disruptive. For those living in New York City, for example, under the rules agreed on by the two representatives of the federal government in New York City, United States Attorneys Mathias Correa and Harold Kennedy, "German, Austrian, Japanese and Italian aliens" were required to "give notice a week before taking any trip outside the environs of New York. Such notice also must be given before any trip outside the boroughs, lasting overnight or longer, is begun." As the newspaper was at pains to point out, this ruling led to some anomalies whereby ". . . a visit, say, to Jersey City, on which the alien leaves and returns all in the one day, need not be reported. A visit to the same place, if it lasts overnight, must be reported." In addition to this, "Mr. Correa declined to put an exact limit on the distance outside New York contemplated in the term *environs* (*The New York Times*, January 9, 1942, p. 10).

In addition to interning the Japanese and the other suspected "enemy aliens," from 1942 the U.S. government began to send prisoners of war captured in Europe, Asia, and Africa to camps in the United States. As in other periods, some of the POWs were put in institutions that had formerly held convicted criminals. The sheer numbers, however, soon necessitated the construction of numerous additional, temporary places of confinement throughout the country. Like the convict lease system of the 19th and early 20th century, prisoners of war were set to work. Employed predominantly in agricultural labor, but also in such industries as food processing plants, foundries, forest and logging camps, and road building, prisoners were important to the wartime economy of America. As such, they were, for the most part, treated reasonably well, and were even remunerated for their services, even if only at a rate of around 80 cents per day. In the Midwest, which had been settled by German-speaking immigrants, many of these prisoners of war were easily assimilated culturally and linguistically. So useful was their labor that many newspapers reported an anxiety in late 1945, when they began to be repatriated to Italy, Germany, and Japan. As *The Washington Post* declaimed, "Repatriation of POWs is bad news here" (*Washington Post*, 1945a; see also *Washington Post*, 1945b).

As in the First World War, most who claimed conscientious objector status were absorbed by the Civilian Public Service program, often laboring in camps performing agricultural work and other labor for the military (Dahlke, 1945). However, more than 6,000, of whom an estimated 60 to 70 percent were Jehovah's Witnesses, were sent to prison for refusing to agree to the terms of the Selective Service Act (Goosens, 1997; Bennett, 2003). Some served sentences as long as five years, although, in general, their treatment seems to have been far less harsh than that of those who resisted World War I.[10]

The story of conscientious objectors is usually cast as having a religious bent. Yet in both world wars, and in other conflicts since, individuals refused to serve in the military because of their political beliefs in Socialism and Communism as well as in Fascism and Nazism. In the Second World War, an additional group of men were imprisoned for resisting the draft: the Japanese detainees. As Eric L. Muller (2001) describes it, having forcibly interned 120,000 individuals in 1942, already by 1943, the same government turned to this population looking for combat volunteers to serve in the racially segregated 442nd Battalion. By 1944, they were drafting them. Those who refused to fight, on the grounds that their citizenship rights had been denied by their internment, faced stiff penalties. Sent, for the most part, to the federal prison on McNeil Island in Washington State, these men served up to five years in prison, well beyond the period of internment of their family members in the War Relocation Centers.

In the late 1990s, testimonies were gathered from some of those who had been imprisoned, as historians finally turned their attention to those who had refused to fight. One such individual, Edward Burrows, who served two years in federal prison for refusing civilian public service, presented a familiar account of prisoner solidarity and deprivation: "I had problems with officers," he recalled, "but not with prisoners" (Anderson & Burrows, 1996, p. 134). Burrows, like so many before him and since, who had not been in prison before, was appalled by the educational standards among the inmate population. Describing his "amazement" on realizing that ". . . probably out of the 12 or 15 men that were in my cell block, almost half of them were illiterate," he reported that he ". . . spent the first Sunday afternoon writing letters for them" (Burrows, 1996, p. 134). Despite the racial segregation of FCI Tallahassee in Florida, Burrows offered his letter-writing skills to the Black population as well.

Evidence from a range of sources suggests that at least some of the imprisoned conscientious objectors were particularly affected by the racialized nature of their prison experience. In his interviews with formerly imprisoned Japanese American war resisters, Eric Muller (2001, 168) claimed that their jail experience shattered "some of their own preconceptions about race" (Muller, 2001, p. 168). When asked about race relations in FCI McNeil Island, for example, one of the respondents recalled an African American prisoner approaching him soon after arrival and offering, "Any time any of these white guys ever threaten you or give you a bad time, just come to me and I will take care of you" (Muller, 2001, p. 169). Likewise, another respondent states, "I never thought about black people's situation . . . until I heard their stories at McNeil—no money, no jobs, discrimination" (Muller, 2001, p. 169).[11] In three particular establishments—the Danbury Correctional Institution in Connecticut, the Lewisburg Federal Penitentiary in Pennsylvania, and the Ashland Correctional Institution in Kentucky—conscientious objectors led large-scale strikes against racial segregation, downing tools and demanding institutional change. After four months of direct action and agitation, the prison at Danbury agreed to integrate the dining room.

Women's Reformatories

By the end of the 19th century, penal reformers had succeeded, at least in part, in establishing a separate women's prison system across a number of states. The drive for female institutions was reinvigorated in the early 20th century through the work of such middle-class reformers as Josephine Shaw Lovell, Mary Belle Harris, and Abby Hopper Gibbons. Many of the first reformers had been active in the Civil War relief efforts, and before that in a variety of reformist organizations on both sides of the political spectrum, such as the Social Purity and Temperance movements, and the Sanitary Commission, as well as in abolition and suffrage (Colvin, 1997; Freedman, 1984; Waugh, 1997; Rafter, 1997). The politics of such figures varied greatly, as did their views on how best to deal with female offenders.

The first reformatory specifically built for women opened in the U.S. in Indiana in 1873. Prior to this date, and in many states for some time thereafter, women were held in sections of men's prisons. Sing Sing Penitentiary, for example, had since the 1840s contained a separate section for women. New York State opened its first female reformatory in 1901 at Bedford Hills. Still functioning today, Bedford Hills Correctional Facility, although long since redesignated as a maximum-security women's prison, pioneered many reforms in the management of women offenders. Its first inhabitants were required by their superintendent, Katherine Bement Davis, to participate in schoolwork and to learn trades. To the modern eye, Davis cuts a perplexing figure. On the one hand, a fierce proponent of eugenical interventions, advocating indefinite detention of "moral imbeciles" and other social degenerates, Davis believed in more benign interventions for many of the women in her charge, including the salutary and reformatory qualities of fresh air, assigning recreational and work tasks outdoors. Davis also established a nursery in the reformatory to enable women to keep their children with them for up to two years. Although it fell into disuse at some point in the mid-20th century, a nursery was reopened in the 1980s and presently offers one of the few opportunities in the nation for convicted women to maintain direct ties with their children while incarcerated.

Despite considerable endeavors on the part of prison reformers, sex-specific treatment and, in particular, the founding of women's prisons, proceeded only in fits and starts across the country. Notwithstanding early developments in Indiana and New York State in establishing separate reformatories for women, for example, a report in *The New York Times* on July 14, 1897, referred readers to Kansas City, Montana, where the police department began "working women prisoners at breaking stone, the same as the male prisoners." A policy, adopted on the recommendation of the chief of police, who argued that "women prisoners kept in idleness were not sufficiently punished, the women," in order to be able to engage in such physical labor, were provided with "coarse overalls the same as men. They will have no skirts to impede their work" (*The New York Times,* July 14, 1897, p. 3). Similarly, a detailed study of Pennsylvania's jails carried out in 1933 found only limited sex segregation of prisoners. Outside the state's single women's establishment at Muncy, women were routinely mixed with male prisoners. There were almost no female matrons, and those who were employed were roundly criticized (Sanville, 1934a, 1934b).

Occasionally, as today, the treatment of women in prison stood center stage in the public domain when a high-profile individual was sentenced to a period of confinement. One such prisoner was anarchist Emma Goldman, who served one year from 1893 to 1894 at Blackwell's Island Penitentiary in New York City for "inciting a riot" that never materialized. Goldman, who led the 1891 May Day demonstration in New York City, was typical neither in terms of her crime nor in her politicization and education. According to Goldman, the first question that she was asked by the prison authorities on her arrival concerned her religion. Like the 19th-century reformer Dorothea Dix, the warden of Blackwell's Island clearly saw religious faith as integral to convicts' reform. Thus, when Goldman replied that she was an atheist, she was curtly informed that "Atheism is prohibited here. You will have to go to church" (Goldman, 1970, p. 133).

Initially frightened and claustrophobic in her dark, damp cell, Goldman was soon put to work, first as the head of the sewing room and then as a nurse in the hospital wing. When she was placed in the dungeon for punishment, a sympathetic matron opened the cell door for her and provided coffee. Goldman was also not without her own version of middle-class prejudice. Despite believing that "crime is the result of poverty," she stated superciliously that "among the seventy inmates, there were no more than half a dozen who showed any intelligence whatever." The problem for Goldman was not so much that they were resolutely ignorant, but that the prisoners lacked political consciousness. Instead, she remarked with Socialist propriety, their ". . . personal misfortunes filled their thoughts; they could not understand that they were victims, links in an endless chain of injustice and inequality. From early childhood they had known nothing but poverty, squalor, and want, and the same conditions were awaiting them on their release" (Goldman, 1970, p. 136).

Emma Goldman commanded a certain amount of public and media interest. Other unusual cases also occasionally came to public attention. Thus, *The New York Times* described the whipping of "colored woman Nellie White" in Kings County Penitentiary in 1878, reminding its readers on July 10, 1878, that the "Revised Statutes of the State of New-York reads as follows: no *female* confined in *any* prison shall be punished by *whipping* for any misconduct in such prison" (*The New York Times,* 1878, p. 3).

In contrast to the benign, though paternalist, intentions of the late 18th- and early 19th-century reformers, and, countering Emma Goldman's sympathetic if impatient description of them, the female offenders and women's prisons depicted in *The New York Times* were frequently violent. On Independence Day 1883, for example, the paper placed on its front page a description of the case of Virginia Jones, a "colored," who was said to have "created a sensation in court to-day" in Charlotte, North Carolina. "On being told that she must go to jail she flatly refused. She picked up a chair, and striking right and left, cleared the room of its occupants" (*New York Times,* July 4, 1883, p. 1). Six years later, female prisoners again made headlines, this time at Leavenworth Penitentiary in Kansas, where they fatally assaulted a keeper in the course of a riot. "Having secured two hatchets," a group of women sought to free one Mollie Brown, who had been placed on punishment in "the dark cell." On hearing the noise of this attempted liberation, Captain Hanks, husband of the matron of the women's section of the prison, attempted to stop them. Hanks, the newspaper account reported, "is a large, powerful man and made a desperate fight, but while he was warding off the blows, the other women seized his legs and threw him to the floor. Then one of them struck him a fourth time, on the right side of his head, nearly severing the ear and splitting his skull, making a fatal wound, and he now lies in an unconscious condition with no hopes of recovery" (*New York Times,* 1889: 2).

Such accounts underline the paradoxical nature of women offenders. Though seemingly ideal candidates for paternalist reformers, women prisoners in fact posed many challenges to the reform movement. Whether in their capacity to reproduce the next generation of the feeble-minded, their refusal to adhere to appropriate feminine role models, their alarming habit of forming intimate relations, or the overrepresentation of Black prisoners, they were not easy to control or classify. Though some paint the development of penal policy as one of deepening social control over this population of refractory women, it was, at best, always partial (Rafter, 1992, 1995, 1997; Dodge, 2002).

Reform, Science, and Nation-Building

In 1870, the U.S.A. was still recovering from its Civil War. By 1945, it had won two world wars and endured the Depression. Throughout such destabilizing events, public commitment to the goals of reform and rehabilitation remained undimmed. So too did its belief in science. Reformers sought to alter individuals through treatment, not only for their own good, but also for the betterment of society. In so doing, they sketched the shape and boundaries of society itself. In some cases, such as the South, the state was heavily racialized, and so the prison population was disproportionately Black. Everywhere, however, as Guibord (1914) recognized, those in prison were almost exclusively drawn from the poor and the underclass.

In their emphasis on treating the individual, which reached its apogee in the federal vision of correctionalism, the reformers' attitudes are well served by Foucault's observation about power. "One of the first effects of power," he claims, "is that it allows bodies, gestures, discourses, and desires to be identified and constituted as something individual." In this view, the individual is "a power-effect," as institutions and their regimes create expectations and understandings of those they contain. Power then "passes through the individuals it has constituted," transforming and controlling them (Foucault, 2002, pp. 29–30).

At the outset of the Progressive Era, the U.S. was still dealing with the social, economic, racial, and personal fallout from the Civil War. Under such circumstances, the commitment to a paternalistic treatment model appears surprising. However, when considered from a constitutive viewpoint like Foucault's, it seems clear that the ostensibly benign concerns with the individual were effective means of asserting state power. They should, therefore, as others have argued, be considered a mechanism of governance (Rothman, 1980; Simon, 1993). Addressing crime as an individual illness neatly avoided grappling with more complicated and enduring social divisions, while maintaining social control.

Reformers were always somewhat contradictorily concerned with individuals and groups. Notorious studies like the book *The Jukes*, written by one of the members of the Prison Association of New York, Richard L. Dugdale (1877), documented an extended family of criminals over multiple generations. By the early 20th century, this study was viewed as proof of the hereditary nature of delinquency and pauperism. Despite subsequent accounts, which have argued that both Dugdale himself stressed the environmental factors leading to the criminality of his subjects, as well as others, which take issue with his methodology, *The Jukes* was "cited with great frequency as a powerful argument for the permanent custodial care of those members of society who, with a lack of mental equipment, have an increased bent toward crime and immorality, and other practices dangerous to society" (*The New York Times*, December 17, 1911, p. 12). Updated by Arthur H. Estabrook in 1916, this longitudinal study outlined broad characteristics that could identify those most likely to be morally and socially unfit. The prison, and other mass institutions of the time, including mental hospitals, facilitated this way of thinking. By holding and seeking to treat the mass of individuals in an aggregate, they shifted their gaze from the individual to the group and back again.

In this way, the prison marked out the moral boundaries of the nation; always and already, they proclaimed, there is a group outside social norms who must be contained. In the first half of the 20th century, as happened in the first colonies and then again in the War of Independence, the prison also designated the political boundaries of the state. In the incarceration of conscientious objectors, anarchists, enemy combatants, and federal offenders, the prison defended the nation. That the same strategies were deployed against the "criminal classes" suggested, from the earliest moments, that the modern U.S. national identity would be founded on the systematic exclusion of certain (undeserving, dangerous, un-American) groups and individuals.

CONCLUSION

When measured in its own terms, the reform era of U.S. punishment had mixed results. While on the one hand, numerous practitioners, philanthropists, and social reformers agitated for improved penal conditions, their recommendations for change did not always benefit prisoners in the long term. Unlike concomitant attempts to abolish convict leasing, there was no significant move toward prison abolition. Instead, many individuals ended up with longer and even indeterminate sentences, and the prison population grew massively in size.

In 1870, as reported by penal reformer Zebulon Brockway (1874), there were 32,901 individuals in U.S. prisons, "exclusive of those in houses of refuge, houses of correction, and institutions of kindred character" (Brockway, 1874, p. 144). By 1925, when statistics began to be recorded more systematically by the federal government, the sum of sentenced prisoners stood at 91,669, corresponding to a rate of 79 per 100,000 of the population. In 1967, the same year as the report of the President's Commission on Law Enforcement and the Administration of Justice, these totals had become, respectively, 194, 896, or 98 per 100,000 (U.S Department of Justice, 1982, p. 2).

Though many reformers may have been motivated by benign intentions, the long-term impact of their work is far less easy to judge. From those whom history has elevated, like Dorothea Dix, or the Child Savers, to others nearly forgotten, like Kate Barnard, who rose to the highest government post allowed at the time to women in Oklahoma, many worked tirelessly for better pay and conditions for the poor, as well as for penal reform. Echoing the famous statement by Winston Churchill, Barnard asserted in an interview with *The New York Times* that ". . . the care that a people give to their insane, their prisoners, and their helpless men and women and children is the exact measure of their real civilization" (Barnard, 1912, p. SM1). Yet, despite such lofty beliefs and the experimental visions of individuals like Thomas Mott Osborne, prisons remained, for the most part, harsh places that imposed further suffering on their inmates. Furthermore, the paternalism of the reformers, steadfast in their belief in the virtues of indeterminate sentencing, often exacerbated the situation, insisting that they knew better than judges or the inmates in determining when an individual should be released.

As so often in history, "reform" brought negatives as well as positives to those on whom it was visited. Yet, the failures and compromises of the reform period and, above all, the manner in which these failures did not delegitimize the prison, suggest more than a sad story of misguided paternalism. Rather and worse, the reformers' failures ultimately legitimized the prison's place in society by rendering their subjects more culpable and less deserving of sympathy than ever before.

NOTES

1. In 1979, President Jimmy Carter pardoned Lebrun, Miranda, Flores, and Cordero for their attack on Congress, as well as Oscar Collazo, who, in 1950, had attempted to assassinate President Harry Truman.

2. The interconnection between government and criminal justice was not the only characteristic of 21st-century U.S. society that Hayes foreshadowed. His election of 1876 was as close and divisive as that of George W. Bush in 2000 and, as with Bush, hinged in large part on votes cast in Florida. Like Bush, he lost the popular vote to his Democratic rival Governor Samuel J. Tilden but won the Electoral College vote, 185 to 184. Hayes's role in ending Reconstruction in the South, which undermined racial reforms, should also be noted as contributing to the complex and bitter relations between politics, race, and the prison in America.

3. Though see the recent article by Paul Rock (2007) disputing Lombroso's influence in these areas, at least in the UK.

4. Binet originally studied under Jean-Martin Charcot at Hôpital de la Salpêtrière in Paris, a complex institution that combined elements of the workhouse, the prison, and the mental hospital (Bosworth, 2000).

5. For allegedly failing to report homosexual relations among some prisoners.

6. Indeed, there is something of a tradition of this in prison studies, with others like Thomas Mott Osborne (1914) before them producing reflections on their time in charge. Like the federal system, New York State seems, in particular, to have inspired its penal administrators to publish, with Lewis E. Lawes (1932), sometime warden of Sing Sing, also publishing a lengthy account of his days in charge of men behind bars. Others, like Katherine Bement Davis, superintendant at the Bedford Hills prison for women and New York City Corrections Commissioner, was also a prolific author on issues relating to prisons and beyond (see, for example, Davis, 1929).

7. In recent years, legislative changes have enabled increased private involvement in prison labor, though state use predominates.

8. In turn, the incarceration of many of these prostitutes led to growing fears about lesbian relations in prison, a concern that was to be proven right in the sociological studies of the early 1960s (see Chapter 3).

9. As the war progressed, a small number of other foreign nationals were also detained, including Hungarians and other Eastern Europeans.

10. Unlike those in civilian public service, objectors in prison did little to help the war effort, although some participated in medical experiments designed to tackle such conditions as malaria and malnutrition (Bennett, 2003; Peck, 1958).

11. A number of the conscientious objectors, like James Peck (1958, 1962), continued their activism in the Civil Rights Movement.

Three

Prison Culture

Sociology and Social Change

Unable to escape either physically or psychologically, lacking the cohesion to carry through an insurrection that is bound to fail in any case, and bereft of faith in peaceful innovation, the inmate population might seem to have no recourse but the simple endurance of the pains of imprisonment . . . But if the rigors of confinement cannot be completely removed, they can at least be mitigated by the patterns of social interaction established among the inmates themselves.

—Sykes, 1958, p. 82

[T]he old picture of the prison as an inclusive normative and moral community toward which the individual had to take a stance is no longer accurate. The prison is now a conflict-ridden setting where the major battles are fought by intermediate level inmate groups rather than by staff and inmates or by inmates as unaligned individuals.

—Jacobs, 1975, p. 478

Oppressed people cannot remain oppressed forever. The yearning for freedom eventually manifests itself, and this is what has happened to the American Negro. Something within has reminded him of his birthright of freedom, and something without has reminded him that it can be gained. Consciously or unconsciously, he has been caught up by the Zeitgeist, and with his black brothers of Africa and his brown and yellow brothers of Asia, South America and the Caribbean, the United States Negro is moving with a sense of great urgency toward the promised land of racial justice.

—Martin Luther King, Jr., April 16, 1963

The debate on imprisonment in the U.S. altered significantly in the second half of the 20th century, when new ethnographic and statistical methods were employed for the first time in the emerging academic field of prison studies. From the 1930s, sociologists and social psychologists began to conduct detailed analyses of the social organization of relationships in prison. Often employed by the prison administration, these professional social scientists examined role playing, offender groups, and inmate argot with a view to explaining how order in prison was maintained and how a localized prison culture was established. The influence of these studies peaked in the 1960s and 1970s, yet had all but disappeared by the 1980s, just as the prison population began to climb dramatically (see, inter alia, Selling, 1931; Clemmer, 1940; Haynes, 1948; Harper, 1952; Sykes, 1958; Goffman, 1961a; Garabedian, 1963; Ward & Kassebaum, 1964; Jacobs, 1977; Simon, 2000).

The new prison sociologists sought to employ "objective" and "scientific" research methods in compiling their data. Unlike the eugenicists, who also spoke of such notions, however, the new sociologists did not so much wish to alter individuals as to understand them. To that end, they actively engaged in fieldwork, using information that they gathered firsthand through interviews and surveys administered to prisoners and staff. They also examined prison records, rule books, and other written documentation. In so doing, prison sociologists, as well as propounding influential notions of prison culture and the inmate code, laid the foundations of methodological techniques that continue to shape prison studies today. By identifying group patterns and unearthing links between the prison world and the wider society, their work threw into question the correctionalists' narrow focus on individuals and their amelioration.

For many years, prison sociology was dominated by functionalist accounts, which explained prison life as a result of the determining nature of institutional factors (Clemmer, 1940; Sykes, 1958). Early scholars relied on a close working relationship with criminal justice administrators and were frequently employees of the penal system. Mostly, they concentrated exclusively on men's prisons, and within that population, generally on the experiences of White inmates (although see Selling, 1931; Harper, 1952; Ward & Kassebaum, 1965; Giallombardo, 1966a).

From the early 1960s, and more vocally in the 1970s, prison sociology began to change, both in the nature of the researchers and in their findings. No longer so closely aligned to the prison system, sociologists adopted a conflict-based approach promoting the so-called "importation" thesis, which pointed to the influence of external factors on prison culture (Jacobs, 1975). Most of these scholars were openly critical of penal administrators and of incarceration, while one of the primary exponents of the "importation thesis," John Irwin, had served a prison sentence himself (see, for example, Irwin & Cressey, 1962; Irwin, 1970). At the same time, greater attention began to be paid to women's imprisonment and, on occasion, to issues of race and sexuality (Johnson, 1975; Carroll, 1974; Watterson, 1973, 1996). Although scholars of women's prisons remained primarily interested in matters of inmate subculture, they concentrated on different issues from their male counterparts, often seeking a middle ground between explanations that prioritized prison conditions and those that stressed the impact of outside societal beliefs (Heffernan, 1974; Giallombardo, 1966b).

In all cases, the literature on imprisonment was shaped by broader strands of thought and by methodological debates in sociology and criminology. To that extent, quarrels over functionalism and conflict mirrored similar academic discussions occurring elsewhere (Merton, 1957; Parsons, 1951, 1961). Prison sociology, however obliquely, was also responding to the broader transformations occurring throughout society. While the work of writers in the 1940s and 1950s should be viewed in the context of the Second World War and the developing Cold War, by the 1960s their concerns reflected a rapidly changing society and its prison systems that were plunging into disorder and disarray (Adams, 1992). These years marked a period of turmoil in the U.S. Though it had emerged relatively unscathed from the war in economic and material terms, unlike its European and Asian counterparts, the United States had changed. Returning Black GIs, who had fought alongside Whites, challenged racial segregation. Women, who had entered the workforce while the men were away, did not all want to go back to the home. At the same time, government grants to returning servicemen, enabling them to attend university, opened tertiary education to new sectors of the population.

This was also an era of violence. The U.S. shortly went to war again, first in Korea and then, infamously, in Vietnam. The House Un-American Activities Committee (HUAC) hauled people up before it to justify their political views, jailing some, and rendering others unemployable for years for their suspected Nazi or Communist beliefs. Some of these people, like founding member of the American Civil Liberties Union and chair of the American Communist Party Elizabeth Gurley Flynn (1963), were sent to prison. President John F. Kennedy was assassinated, as was his brother, former Attorney General Robert Kennedy, and Black civil rights leader Martin Luther King, Jr. Malcolm X was also gunned down.

As the antiwar movement grew in numbers and in fervor, so, too, did the police response; the state cracked down on students and, in 1969, on gay activists in New York City. Events like the 1960 fire-hosing of university students in San Francisco and the 1968 riot at the Democratic Party National Convention in Chicago all entailed stern displays of state power. Meanwhile, racist violence remained commonplace in large swaths of the country, from the 1955 lynching of Emmett Till in Mississippi to the 1963 firebombing of the 16th Street Baptist Church in Birmingham, Alabama, which killed four young girls. When placed in this context, the overriding concern of prison sociologists in this era to map and understand social order and solidarity takes on new significance. By the same token, the failure of most scholars to address racial conflict and race relations appears even more remarkable.

The Prison Community

Even though there were earlier studies, the creation of a defined field of prison sociology is usually attributed to the 1940 publication of *The Prison Community* by Donald Clemmer (1940, 1958). Based on research that he undertook in the 1930s at the Illinois Southern maximum-security prison at Menard while employed as a sociologist by the Illinois Department of Corrections, *The Prison Community* set the terms of analysis and the research methods for decades to come. Combining interviews with, and observation of, a large total of 2,500 men with the administration of psychometric tests, as well as investigations of prisoners' homes, communities, and "hangouts," plus autobiographical sketches from a selection of the men with whom he built the fullest rapport, Clemmer sought to paint as clear an image as possible of prison life. In particular, reflecting his intellectual debt to early anthropologists like Edward Burnett Tylor and Wilson D. Wallis,[1] he sought to understand the "culture of the prison."

Culture, for Clemmer, as for the anthropologists on whose work he drew, both transcended individuals and could be identified in their actions and beliefs. Like an anthropologist, Clemmer believed that he could "make understandable the extent and degree to which the culture of the penitentiary determines the philosophy of its inhabitants" by focusing on "such phenomena as class stratification, informal group life, leadership, folkways, and various other social controls" (Clemmer, 1958, p. xv). Though nominally focused on the prison, Clemmer, like other functionalists of his time, was concerned with drawing more generalized conclusions about broader society. As one of his later critics, Donald Cressey (1961), put it:

> Clemmer viewed the prison as a laboratory in which some of the conditions and processes in the broader society are observable. His study focused on the inmate community, and was one of the first attempts to examine the idea that the events occurring in social organizations take place because there is an organizational "place" for them to occur. (Cressey, 1961, p. v)

According to Clemmer, "the prison, like other social groups, has a culture" (Clemmer, 1958, p. 85). The book's first two chapters outline the "culture antecedents of the prisoners" (pp. 1–41) and the "composition of the population" (pp. 42–58), including a discussion of inmates' geographical and sociodemographic characteristics as well as their ambition, education, and work experience prior to incarceration. However, in the rest of his study, Clemmer concentrated on those factors within prison which shaped inmates' experience of, and response to, confinement. According to him, prison language (slang or argot), relations among the inmate community, interactions with prison staff, and contact with the outside world were all key components of a penal culture that differentiated life behind bars from outside. Such particularities, in turn, made it difficult for inmates to adjust to life upon release.

In essence, Clemmer identified a troubling paradox of confinement that threw into question most correctionalist goals: in order to survive life behind bars, prisoners must subjugate their pre-prison selves and assimilate to their new world. In this process, they imbibe and perpetuate a specific institutional culture that, in turn, is predicated on the rejection of skills necessary for everyday, law-abiding life. Yet, at the same time, almost all inmates will one day be released back to their communities. How, then, in order to facilitate the successful reintegration of offenders, can prisons minimize the damage they wreak on prisoners' sense of self? What purpose does the overall prison culture serve and how, if it all, can it be altered?

In his research, Clemmer was particularly interested in how prisoners interacted with one another. Through detailed observations and interviews, Clemmer described the variety of ways in which prisoners communicate with one another, how they spend their time, and what social divisions exist among them. He also sought to measure their unity as a group and the extent of their opposition to the penal administration. In contrast to commonplace assumptions at the time, Clemmer found the majority of men in his prison to be unaffiliated with primary inmate groups. There was not, in other words, an obviously united "society of captives," who stood in constant opposition to staff. Yet, at the same time, he argued, all inmates, whatever their primary allegiance, were subject to a force of assimilation or acculturation that he labeled "prisonization."

Despite the many differences he observed among the inmates, most of which were based on factors that they brought in with them, including race, class, education, and the nature of their offenses, Clemmer chose to emphasize this issue of prisonization as definitive of prison culture. During any sentence, he proposed, inmates become assimilated to their life behind bars, "taking on in greater or lesser degree . . . the folkways, mores, customs, and general culture of the penitentiary" (Clemmer, 1940, p. 299), making it difficult for them to adjust to outside life when they were released. They progressively lost contact with others and adopted the cultural norms of institution, key among which was an individual expectation that "the environment *should* administer to him" (Clemmer, 1940, p. 299).

According to Clemmer, there were numerous factors influencing the extent to which an individual became institutionalized, including the number and frequency of the visits that they received, their level of education prior to confinement, and their personal motivation. Prisoners who did not form close bonds with primary social groups of other inmates during their confinement were also less at risk of being acculturated.

He claimed no particular desire "to foster recommendations," but Clemmer clearly viewed prison culture to some degree as invidious, asserting that the ". . . apparent rehabilitative effect which prison life has on some men occurs in spite of the harmful influences of the prison culture" (Clemmer, 1940, p. 313). In the end, he advocated not only more money to improve prison conditions, but greater concentration on a probation system. In an early vision of the "justice reinvestment" and "community corrections" that became popular in the early years of the 21st century, he also called for funds for the study and improvement of service in the communities from which the men in prison were drawn (Clear, 2007).

Importation Versus Deprivation

Nearly 20 years after the publication of *The Prison Community*, Gresham Sykes re-energized prison sociology with his 1958 study, *The Society of Captives*, in which he launched the notion of the "pains of imprisonment." Basing his work on research conducted in the men's maximum-security state prison in Trenton, New Jersey, Sykes identified five areas in which inmates suffer: deprivation of goods and services, of heterosexuality, safety, autonomy, and liberty. Each issue, he claimed, posed a significant challenge to an individual's psychological health and coherent sense of self, implying, once again, that incarceration was inherently at odds with rehabilitative goals. To take just one example, the loss of liberty, for Sykes, referred not simply to the experience of confinement, but also to the psychological impact of the loss of contact with family, friends, and the community. Similarly, being deprived of access to goods and services affected not just the items that inmates could possess, but undermined their sense of control over their own environment. Furthermore, men's inability to engage in heterosexual relations over their prison sentence challenged their sense of self by denying them the emotional release that they craved from sexual and intimate relations with women.

According to Sykes (1958), these "deprivations or frustrations of the modern prison may indeed be the acceptable or unavoidable implications of imprisonment, but we must recognize that they can be just as painful as the physical maltreatment which they have replaced" (Sykes, 1958, p. 64). They are hard to withstand, and deepen the pains of imprisonment, despite the apparent goals of penal reform.

> Deprived of their liberty, stripped of worldly possessions, denied access to heterosexual relationships, divested of autonomy, and compelled to associate with other deviants, the inmates find that imprisonment still means punishment however much imprisonment may have been softened in this modern era by an accent on humanitarianism and reform. (Sykes, 1958, p. 131)

Yet, Sykes's interest in the suffering of prisoners did not lie solely in formulating a critique of incarceration or of the power of the custodians. Rather, like Clemmer, he sought to understand prison life and to probe the foundations of prison culture. What, in other words, he asked, makes penal institutions such distinctive establishments? What can their workings tell us about society at large? In his account of such matters, deprivations and frustrations "play a crucial part in shaping the inmate social system" since inmates must unite in order to lessen their impact (Sykes, 1958, p. 131). More than Clemmer, he depicted a world of inmates pitted against staff, where prisoners constantly looked for ways around the deprivations that a prison sentence imposed.

Sykes expanded many of his original ideas from *The Society of Captives* in an influential article entitled "The Inmate Social System," coauthored with Sheldon Messinger in 1960. According to Sykes and Messinger, prisoners attempted to alleviate the pains of imprisonment by forming what they termed a "solidary opposition" to the guards. United by their suffering, prisoners established a cohesive unit as a form of coping, which was, in turn, governed by an inmate code and articulated through a complex system of prisoner argot. Prisoners, according to the inmate code, must not interfere in the business of other inmates, exploit other inmates, lose self-control, weaken, or trust the guards.

For Sykes, the existence and success of such a code rendered a regime of total power fruitless. Consequently, and despite the apparent supremacy of the guards, Sykes was quick to point out that their ability to govern the "society of captives" was deeply compromised by their lack of authority in the prisoners' minds. Prefiguring later musings on issues of legitimacy and the maintenance of order and control in prisons (Sparks, Bottoms, & Hay, 1996; Useem and Kimball, 1989) and undermining the notion of the "total institution" (Goffman, 1961b), Sykes spent an entire chapter of *The Society of Captives* examining the "defects of total power" (Sykes, 1958, pp. 40–62; see also McCleery, 1957 for a similar analysis). With these words, identified by later commentators (Simon, 2000) as a reflection on the backdrop of the Cold War, Sykes evidently saw his research as illuminating questions about the maintenance of power and control more generally. Thus, he asked:

> In an era when a system of total power has changed from a nightmare of what the future might be like to a reality experienced by millions, questions concerning the theory and practice of total power take on a new urgency. Do systems of total power constrain inherent pathologies, in the sense that there are strains and tensions in the structure which must inevitably crack the monolithic concentration of power? Do types of resistance such as apathy, corruption, and the hard bedrock of informal human ties which are present in every social system curtail the power of the rules? Or is total power a juggernaut capable of crushing all opposition, a form of social organization as viable as more democratic modes? What values are created among the rulers and the ruled? (Sykes, 1958, pp. xv–xvi)

It was not just the Cold War that Sykes may have been imagining, but also the feasibility of maintaining a legitimate order behind bars in the U.S. For though they are rarely mentioned in the contemporary sociological literature, U.S. prisons were strained by inmate dissatisfaction and rocked by riots from the 1940s onwards.[2] Absent from the academic accounts of the time, such disorder was covered in some detail in the popular press around the country. In 1940, for example, *The Chicago Defender* ran a series of articles purportedly told to the journalist "from the lips of a former inmate of one of our state penal institutions" (Bartlett, 1940a, p. 13). On January 27, this unnamed inmate describes a "fracas" involving nearly 200 men who sought "to get better food, more recreation and better consideration in the inmate court." The riot, which was planned ahead of time, ended only after officers fired into the crowd. One youth was killed, and the rest were locked in their cells for 21 days. Those directly involved in the riot were then dealt with summarily by the officers. Taken out of their cells one by one, the former prisoner claims, they were:

> . . . chased down the gallery and, upon reaching the main floor, were beaten down a long line of officers, armed with fire hoses, blackjacks, sticks and anything else they could find. Yells from these helpless inmates reverberated through the entire cell house . . . Trails of blood could be traced from one end of the galleries to another. (Bartlett, 1940b, p. 15)

Similarly, *The New York Times* (1945) reported on its front page an investigation into the June 2, 1945, riot in the Maryland House of Correction at Jessups when "sixteen prisoners were wounded by gunfire, two state guards were maimed and a State Trooper injured when 900 convicts, protesting the lack of meat in their meals, staged a destructive 3½ hour riot in the mess hall and cell block" (*New York Times*, 1945, p. 1).

Finally, in a series of articles published in April 1952, *The New York Times* and *The Washington Post* covered large-scale riots in two New Jersey prisons and one in Michigan. Foreshadowing the better-known Attica Prison riot, prisoners at Trenton State Prison, NJ, took hostages, holding out for a number of days (see Chapter 4). Sanford Bates, the Commissioner of Institutions, offered to meet and negotiate with them, but his offers were rebuffed (*The New York Times*, April 17, 1952, p. 24). In a critical piece published in *The New York Times*, reporter Ira Freeman (1952) attributed the riots to a series of factors, ranging from inmate idleness caused by the restrictions on trade in prison-made goods brought in during the Depression to the length of their sentences and overcrowding. Above all, Freeman argued, the riots illustrated a need for reform: "equal sentences for equal crimes, equitable parole procedure, small institutions with segregated prisoners, adequate work, recreations and educational programs" (Freeman, 1952, p. 24).

In the context of widespread prison unrest, the interest of sociologists in prison culture and the inmate community seems to have more in common than might be expected with the paternalism of earlier reformers, with each being motivated by an abiding concern with the limits of social control. Whereas Sykes and Clemmer provided some hope for the administration, those who followed them painted a picture of a much more divided community that was, as a result, harder and harder to control or manipulate. Just a few years after Sykes published *A Society of Captives,* Donald Cressey and his graduate student, John Irwin, raised anew questions about the maintenance of power and control in prison and, in the process, challenged many of Sykes's claims about deprivation, along with his assumptions about inmate loyalty. Arguing instead that prison life was a direct result of values and identities imported from outside, Irwin, Cressey, and others portrayed a divided inmate community expressed through a variety of prison subcultures (Irwin & Cressey, 1962; Irwin, 1970). Irwin emphasized that the walls of prison were considerably more permeable than prison sociologists had previously acknowledged. People brought ideas and cultural practices and expectations with them, and were influenced while inside by outside forces and ideas.[3] Their pre-prison identities, particularly as they related to offense categories, were crucial, as were their previous experiences of life behind bars. "More specifically," Irwin and Cressey (1962) asserted, ". . . it seems rather obvious that the 'prison code'—don't inform on or exploit another inmate, don't lose your head, be weak, or be a sucker, etc.,—is also part of a *criminal* code, existing outside prisons" (Irwin & Cressey, 1962, p. 145).

Though Irwin and Cressey paid them little attention, the notion of "importation" raised the possibility of including socioeconomic factors into criminological analysis. People arrive in prison not only with experiences of lawbreaking behind them, but also with ideas, identities, and expectations shaped by race, gender, and class. Against the backdrop of the Civil Rights Movement of the 1950s and 1960s, along with the women's movement of the 1970s, the significance of such factors became increasingly apparent within the inmate community. Nonetheless, aside from a few exceptions (see, for example, Bowker, 1983), these topics have generally been omitted from mainstream prison sociology, being ghettoized instead in the more specialized areas of women's prison studies and accounts of race relations.

Gender

The women's movement began in the U.S. in the 1960s. Unlike its later, more radical, manifestations, second-wave feminism had its roots in administrative concerns over equality of the sexes. In 1963, President Kennedy's Commission on the Status of Women, chaired by former First Lady Eleanor Roosevelt, reported discrimination against women in almost every area of life. The 1964 Civil Rights Act, so important to race relations, also prohibited employment discrimination on the basis of sex, while, two years later, that champion of equal rights—the (White) liberal feminist National Organization for Women (NOW)—was founded.

From the early 1960s, sociologists produced a small number of studies that focused exclusively on women in prison. These works, like the first ones on men's establishments, were primarily functionalist accounts of prison culture. Scholars working in this narrow field were, like most penal administrators, influenced by sex role theory positing that women's actions in prison or out could be explained by their social roles as mother, daughter, and wife (Giallombardo, 1966a, 1966b). Three studies characterize the approach of this early, nonfeminist, primarily descriptive literature, respectively: David Ward and Gene Kassebaum's (1965) analysis of "sex roles" in Frontera, work by Rose Giallombardo (1966a, 1966b) in Alderson, and Esther Heffernan's (1974) systems analysis of life in Occoquan. Although each text differed somewhat from the others in its specific focus, they all concluded that women cope with the "pains of imprisonment" in distinct ways from the male inmates described by Clemmer and Sykes. Diverging from the previous analyses of men's prisons, these studies emphasized the private, the domestic, and the sexual.

According to these investigations, women in prison were more needy, more passive, and more domestic than were men. They arrived with their identities formed in relation to their domestic roles. As Ward and Kassebaum (1965) put it, "Women bring to prison with them identities and self-conceptions which are based principally on familial roles as wives, mothers, and daughters, and their related roles (fiancées and girlfriends)" (Ward and Kassebaum, 1965, p. 70). Such backgrounds, unlike the less salubrious identities of male offenders, were thought to be potentially "good." It was unfortunate, then, that they would clearly be undermined by a sentence of incarceration when women were denied access to their family members. Most confoundingly, women did not simply forget their "nature" while confined, but, rather, sought out such affirmation in the women around them. As a result, the authors claimed:

> The overriding need of a majority of female prisoners is to establish an affectionate relationship which brings in prison, as it does in the community, love, interpersonal support, security and social status . . . [t]his need promotes homosexuality as the predominant compensatory response to the pains of imprisonment. (Ward & Kassebaum, 1965, p. 80)

Ward and Kassebaum then spend an entire text quantifying, describing, and analyzing such "homosexuality."

Giallombardo, in her study, came to similar conclusions, but with the added assumption that women's fickle nature was decisive for determining life inside since it made it difficult for them to forge alliances with one another. Instead of uniting against the staff as did the male inmates documented by Sykes and Messinger (1960), they practiced what she terms a "calculated solidarity," "subject to constant interpretation by the inmate as she perceives each situation from the point of view of her own interests" (Giallombardo, 1966b, p. 271). Emulating the research conducted a decade earlier by Sykes, Giallombardo explored conflict and cohesion in a women's prison. Claiming that the "female prison community has been overlooked" (Giallombardo, 1966a, p. 1), she challenged the earlier conclusions drawn by Sykes and Clemmer that "the most important features of the inmate culture emerge as a response to the conditions of imprisonment" (Giallombardo, 1966b, 269). Rather, Giallombardo found that female prison culture was determined by a combination of the roles and statuses in confinement with values and attitudes which the individuals brought into the prison from outside (Giallombardo, 1966b, 288). Moreover, she made explicit that "differences in the informal social structure in male and female prison communities can be understood in terms of the differential cultural definitions ascribed to male and female roles in American society" (Giallombardo, 1966b, p. 270). Although she acknowledged and described disputes between the prisoners, Giallombardo implied that the "generally passive orientation of the female" resulted in a more stable prison environment (Giallombardo, 1966a, p. 102). Similarly, she typecast women as untrustworthy and manipulative, concluding that "the female's self-orientation and the tendency to see one another as rivals both function to decrease expectations of rigid alliance from one another" (Giallombardo, 1966b, p. 275). Like Ward and Kassebaum (1964, 1965), Giallombardo "discovered" the so-called "homosexual dyadic relationship" in American women's prisons to be the most significant structuring factor for daily life and inmate relationships (Giallombardo 1966a, pp. 133–157). Ultimately, then, Giallombardo implied that order and harmony were maintained in women's prisons in much the same way as they would have been, or should have been, in the home.

Heffernan's inquiry was more critical than either of the earlier studies, and many of the issues she raised remain pivotal to an understanding of imprisonment today. They include her sensitive analysis of "time management," trust, and staff-inmate relations (Heffernan, 1974, pp. 66–86, 134–143, 164–187). Initially designed as a "replication of Wheeler's testing of Clemmer's concept of prisonization" (Heffernan, 1974, p. 10), her preliminary research found that different questions had to be asked of the women in prison as the "female social system" did not correspond with that previously identified in the masculine literature; that is, she found, the women rejected the roles typically associated with inmate systems, while still exhibiting sufficient levels of solidarity that neither did the prison collapse into rioting, nor did the women function in complete exclusion from one another (Heffernan, 1974, pp. 10–14).

Heffernan concluded that, in contrast to the propositions of Sykes and Clemmer, there was not one hegemonic inmate system functioning within Occoquan Prison in response to standardized experiences of deprivation. Rather, she identified three different ways of "doing time," which she labeled with characteristic sociological typologies and which form the subtitle of her text: "the cool, the square and the life" (Heffernan, 1974, pp. 16–17). She argued that "the prisoners' 'community of fate' does not produce normative uniformity so much as functional interdependence" (Heffernan, 1974, p. 184), emphasizing that the "inmate system" is both an "adaptive system" as proposed by Sykes and one in which, as Irwin and Cressey claim (1962), "there is constant interplay between normative orientation to prison and the situational framework of each institution" (Heffernan, 1974, p. 184). In order to understand imprisonment, therefore, Heffernan sought to move beyond the binary opposition of visions of deprivation/importation.

Despite the differences between the texts and notwithstanding the challenges that they posed to the male traditions of the sociology of imprisonment, the reliance on sex role theory served to maintain a traditional gender binary between women and men that, in turn, reinforced oppositional notions of domestic (or private)/public and passive/active. Such rigid dualism fitted seamlessly with a broader societal view where women prisoners were thought to need care rather than custody, and medical treatment rather than punishment. With the exception of Heffernan's more nuanced account, such studies did little to disrupt what sometime Civil Rights activist, Communist, and journalist Jessica Mitford

(1973) identified in her brief visit to the Washington, D.C., Women's Detention Center in 1971 as the "essence of women's prisons, the punishment of unchaste, unwomanly behavior, a grotesque bow to long-outmoded nineteenth-century notions of feminine morality" (Mitford, 1973, p. 26). Though traditional views of femininity doubtless saved some women from custody, they rendered those in prison vulnerable to harsh paternalism that saw the overmedication of women in prison and entailed a poor provision of services in comparison with men.

Despite a growing body of troubling firsthand accounts of life in women's prisons, from that of Elizabeth Gurley Flynn in 1963 to Angela Davis in 1974, it was not until the mid-1980s and 1990s that academic studies of women's prisons considered women's imprisonment critically and examined how prisoners resisted authority and its gendered assumptions (see, for example, Bosworth, 1996, 1999; Chesney-Lind & Rodriguez, 1983; Chesney-Lind & Pasko, 2004; Rafter, 1985; Owen, 1998). It was also not until then, either, that much attention was paid to the experiences of women of color. This shift in thinking had to wait for the impact of feminism and critical race theory on criminology, and for the problematization of the relationship between crime and punishment, which emerged in critical studies of men's prisons. Instead, the earliest sociological studies of women's imprisonment, like the first strands of the women's movement, were not particularly radical in either form or content. They sought mainly to direct the scholarly gaze to women, in order to fill in the gaps, rather than to reshape or question relations of inequality.

Race

From the late 1950s, race relations in and outside the prison heavily conditioned prisoner subcultures and inmate organization. As numbers of African American and Hispanic prisoners grew, previous forms of solidary inmate organization fractured. Racism, language barriers, a newly politicized Black population, and a myriad of cultural differences that arose from pre-prison experiences changed American prisons in fundamental ways. Riots swept the country, while inmate-on-inmate violence and hostilities between prisoners and staff escalated (Fraser, 1971; Jacobs, 1975). At the same time, some sought to organize peacefully within prison walls, educating their peers and promulgating new religious and political beliefs. Despite these factors, and notwithstanding the publication of a series of texts in the 1960s that highlighted the experience of minorities in prison (see, inter alia, Fanon, 1967; Cleaver, 1968; X & Haley, 1964; Thomas,

1967), Leo Carroll's 1974 study, *Hacks, Blacks, and Cons,* remains one of the few exceptions to a field that appeared stubbornly inured to difference (see also Jacobs, 1977).

As with the failure to consider women's imprisonment, part of the silence about race was probably a result of the character of the scholars themselves—all were white and most were male. Segregationist policies at the time in most U.S. prisons also made it difficult for researchers to interact with prisoners of color. Nonetheless, the failure to investigate race relations is curious. As James Jacobs (1979) points out, for example, that "even though 50 percent of New Jersey's prisoners were black when Sykes studied [them], his work contained no explicit reference to race relations" (Jacobs, 1979, p. 3). Likewise, although the so-called "importation" model might have directed attention to the communities from which increasing numbers of inmates were arriving, few sociologists thought to include race in their accounts of relevant external factors.

Not just in the South, but also in Northern prisons, Black and White prisoners were routinely separated from one another until the mid-1960s. In some states this practice continued well into the 1970s. As in the wider community, this segregation sparked bitterness within the Black community and institutionalized race-based divisions among the inmate community as a whole. From the late 1950s, Black prisoners began to protest against their treatment at the hands of hostile White inmates and staff. Such resistance became more vociferous and more organized, particularly following the emergence of the Black Muslim movement and, later, the Nation of Islam and early prison-based street gangs (Jacobs, 1977). The impact of these groups, as well as other more long-standing ones like the American Communist Party, was enormous, both on individuals (X & Haley, 1965; Little, 1965; Newton, 1968, Jackson, 1970; Davis, 1974), and on broader penal institutions as a whole (Jacobs, 1979; Johnson, 1975). While some, like Eldridge Cleaver (1968), read Marx in prison, others, like Angela Davis, arrived already politicized. Still others, like George Jackson (1970), inspired thousands with his letters to his friends and family.

Initially, the state responded to the politicization of the Black population by outlawing the Black Muslim movement and punishing prisoners identified with it. In places like Attica, New York, where many of those involved in the uprising of 1971 had been taught by members of the Black nationalist groups, oppression was swift and bloody. Eventually, as will be discussed in more detail in Chapter 4, the resistance of these prisoners and others like them paved the way for radical changes in prison life, particularly in the area of greater religious freedom. Most of these changes, however, did not occur until well into the next decade. It was not until 1969, after all, that the Supreme Court recognized the Black Muslims as a legitimate religion in the case of *Johnson v. Avery*. This same case, which extended many of the protections of the Bill of Rights to all prisoners, including privileged access to jailhouse lawyers, unleashed a torrent of court petitions (Thomas, Keeler, & Harris, 1986; Schaich & Hope, 1977).

The changing sociodemographic nature of the prison community eventually shifted sociological inquiry. Previous accounts emphasizing inmate solidarity came under increased scrutiny and criticism from scholars witnessing the "balkanization of prisoner society" (Jacobs, 1979, p. 8). Instead of unity, subsequent sociologists found fragmentation and division; rather than one inmate code, they identified many (Carroll, 1974; Davidson, 1974; Jacobs, 1977). For some, like prisoner George Jackson, the divisions were fostered quite deliberately by prison authorities, who governed by "divide and rule in its simplest form" (Jackson, 1970, p. 187).[4] Solidarity, in his view, could not withstand the "sense of terror, betrayal and insecurity that resulted from such practices" (Jackson, 1970, p. 187). Others depicted an inmate community that was itself not inured from racism. Piri Thomas, for example, in his autobiography, describes taunting a prison opponent by drawing him "as a funny-book black cannibal, complete with a big bone though his nose" (Thomas, 1967, p. 252). Arming himself in readiness to deal with the man's anger, he relies again on racialized imagery, claiming, "I didn't want to, but if I had to, that mutherfucker was gonna pick cotton in hell" (Thomas, 1967, p. 253).

Sexuality

Despite the transformation of sexual relations that was occurring throughout America in response to advances in, and availability of, contraception, and the women's and gay rights movements, prison scholarship from this era is rarely examined for what it had to say about sex in prison. Nevertheless, concerns over the sexuality of prisoners, particularly of Black men, were a constant theme in prison policy and can be found commented on in the scholarship as well. Thus, from the eugenics movements, through the 1960s and beyond, prurient accounts of lesbian relationships behind bars can be readily located (Otis, 1913; Selling, 1931; Ward & Kassebaum, 1965). Likewise, although there was no equivalent analysis of men's consensual sexual relationships, Gresham Sykes (1958, pp. 70–72) argued that the deprivation of heterosexuality was a defining feature of incarceration.

Widespread belief in the innate sex drive of Black men led some of the Southern states like Mississippi and Carolina to allow "conjugal visitation" among its inmates from the 19th century. Such states were joined by others, including California, New York, Minnesota, Connecticut, and Washington State in the 1970s (Goetting, 1982). For other analysts, the innate (hetero)sexual needs of men served as the basis for advocating penal abolition. Psychiatrist Benjamin Karpman, for example, publishing just after the Second World War, asserted that "the sexual urge is too elemental and instinctive to be completely controlled by confinement" (Karpman, 1948, p. 477). According to him (Karpman, 1948, p. 177), the "more normally sexually constituted prisoner" will attempt to "maintain his heterosexuality." While visits "of female members of the family, even with a screened intervention [i.e., conjugal visit], often ease the tension a good deal, albeit it makes the situation at times more provocative." Prisoners maintained their heterosexuality also through writing letters to women even, according to Karpman, going so far as to address "an imaginary female and himself answer himself for her, using different stationary for himself and for her" (Karpman, 1948, p. 177).

Echoing Clemmer's theory of prisonization, Karpman documented an inexorable slide towards "abnormal sexual practice" (Karpman, 1948, p. 178) depending on the length of an individual's sentence, the strengths of his heterosexual contacts outside the prison, and his moral character. Karpman also seconded Clemmer's institutional explanations, finding causes of men's sexual proclivities in the structure of daily prison life: "Beds are put very close and the sight and smell of naked bodies, the parading and exposure which is unavoidable, charges the atmosphere with excessive stimulation" (Karpman, 1948, p. 479). Linking masturbation to homosexuality, Karpman was equally concerned with both forms of what he labels "paraphilia" or "abnormal sexual practice." Although, he admitted, masturbation in some forms may be a normal outlet of men's sexual desire when their female partner is unavailable, according to him, in prison it quickly became tied to fetishism and abnormality, since "the prison environment . . . constantly forces regression to lower stages of sexual adaptation" (Karpman, 1948, p. 481). In a peculiarly specific hypothetical scenario of such adaptation, Karpman imagined that the prisoner "may improvise a female dress, perhaps even a Hawaiian or

South Sea Island dress, and hula-hula dance himself into a frenzy which is finally relieved by masturbation" (Karpman, 1948, p. 481).

Although he provided no proof for these claims, Karpman suggested that an individual who has engaged in abnormal sex would be forever different. "It could hardly be otherwise," he asserts,

> for the forced redirection of a normal sexual impulse into aberrant channels disturbs and unstabilizes the entire personality. . . . If, previous to confinement he was single and heterosexual, the experiences in prison incapacitate him for normal sexual adjustment. He is more likely to remain single with no urge or capacity for marriage and with a greater possibility for leading a bisexual, rather than only a heterosexual life. (Karpman, 1948, p. 483)

The only solution, for Karpman, was to abolish prisons and replace them with hospitals where criminals could be cured. While heterosexuality failed to generate an extensive abolitionist movement, concerns over inmate sexuality did inspire some administrations to set up conjugal visiting systems. A belief in the "normalizing" effect of women also underpinned those co-correctional facilities that opened up in the late 1960s and early 1970s.

Reflecting the growing interest in matters of prison sexuality, in 1969 Columbus B. Hopper (1969) published a detailed account of Mississippi's "experiment with conjugal visiting." The Mississippi State Penitentiary—more commonly known as Parchman Farm—had allowed its Black male inmates access to women for sex since the early 20th century, "because of the common assumption that Negro men had an insatiable sex drive and therefore had a special need for the sexual outlet provided by conjugal visits" (Goetting, 1982, p. 54). Such women who, Hopper suggests, were often paid for sex, spent time with the prisoners in inmate-constructed shacks known as "red houses." In 1965, however, this ad hoc, racialized arrangement was streamlined and formalized for all men, other than those in maximum security. It was extended to the female prison population in 1972.[5]

Like his sociological contemporaries, Hopper (1969) based his research on "questionnaires, personal interviews, and observation" (Hopper, 1969, p. 15). Probing in a series of questions from the success of the program to the opinions of prisoner wives, Hopper set himself a large task. In practice, most of the book is an account of the historical development of the wider institution and the mechanics of the visiting program. Only in the last two chapters do we get to the heart of his findings. Relying to a large extent on the assessment of "camp sergeants," Hopper found that while Parchman was not inured from the "problem" of homosexuality, prisoners who received conjugal visits seldom engaged in same-sex relations. Even more important, he argued, conjugal visits might mitigate the worst effects of prisonization. "The conjugal visits allow a prisoner to retain a strong identification with his wife. And since he has this right, he is able to keep the self-image of a man who is still important to others" (Hopper, 1969, p. 107). Despite a number of criticisms about the conditions of the conjugal visiting rooms—from the need for fresh sheets between visitors to their similarity to prison cells—most of the wives Hopper interviewed stated their support for the program.

Despite some acceptance, from California to Alabama, of the utility of conjugal visits for men in prison, there was little attempt made to implement such practices in women's prisons. Though sociologists and practitioners had identified and criticized intimate relationships in women's prisons since the early 20th century, they were only occasionally considered as dangerous and threatening as sex between men, and usually only when they breached racial segregation. Predictably in such accounts, the "true" prison lesbian was Black, while for the most part the White woman was merely responding to her otherwise natural feminine need to be loved (Freedman, 1996).

Research Methods, Governance, and Social Control

Many of the early prison classics included brief accounts of the author's research methodology. Commonly, authors utilized a range of methods from "softer" unstructured interviews to what they sometimes referred to as "harder," more "reliable" data drawn from prison records and questionnaires (Irwin, 1970). Unlike most prison scholars today, they tended to interview both staff and inmates, rather than concentrating on one group or the other.

Such accounts resonate with the concerns of contemporary researchers, particularly in the tensions they identify in gathering and analyzing qualitative and quantitative data. As Irwin put it in describing his process of study, "The more 'rigorous' techniques, procedures, and instruments employed in the study produced a rather flimsy and brittle skeleton of 'hard' data upon which 'softer,' but I think 'heavier,' data were draped" (Irwin, 1970, p. 5). Indeed, despite the fact that these early texts were based on large-scale, long-term participant observation, their authors did not rely exclusively on the ethnographic method and its accompanying qualitative ideas. Instead, most, if not all, of the authors were keen to demonstrate their facility with statistical techniques and analysis and were just as concerned with matters of sample size and regression analysis as they were with interviewing technique and building rapport.

In part, such strategies related to the relationship most prison sociologists had with penal administrators. Dependent on them not only for access, but also, as with Clemmer, for their salaries, the first prison researchers had to justify to the state their findings and approach. According to Marxist criminologist Richard Quinney (1978), such strains on prison researchers increased during the 1960s when the "war on crime" gave birth to "a new criminology . . . that has even closer, more explicit ties to the state and its control of threatening social behavior" (Quinney, 1978, p. 279). Such figures, for Quinney, served no less than the interests of the "political economy of capitalism" and needed to be overthrown (Quinney, 1978, p. 290).

While the radicalism of Marxist criminology was yet to influence prison studies (see Chapter 4), and then never particularly strongly in America, some of the early prison sociologists were clearly cognizant both of their relationship to the power structures of the state and of the significance of their research methodologies. Gresham Sykes, perhaps more than many of his colleagues, spent some time musing on his research strategies and techniques. According to him:

> . . . the social system of the prison is a difficult thing to uncover. Criminals in the custodial institution seldom keep written records setting forth the ideology of the inmate population, its myths or its mores. The informant is apt to be defined as a "rat" or a "squealer" and the observer from the free community is viewed with suspicion. Language presents no great barrier, it is true, but there is an argot to be mastered and a misused term marks you off as a pretender. And in this struggle to gain access to the thoughts and life of captives and captors, the social scientist often faces the subtle opposition of the officials, for they too have a stake in the game of acquiring knowledge. (Sykes, 1958, p. xix)

In a statement that prefigured that more famous one made by Howard Becker in his 1967 article "Whose Side Are We On?," Sykes advises his readers that:

> . . . in the polarized society of the prison it is extremely difficult not to become partisan, consciously or unconsciously . . . there is not a single true interpretation but many, and the meaning of any situation is always a complex of several, often conflicting viewpoints. (Sykes, 1958, p. 136)

Nonetheless, unable fully to embrace a subjective approach, Sykes ended up asserting that "... it is only by remaining firmly neutral in one's sympathies that a valid picture of prison life can be uncovered" (Sykes, 1958, p. 136).

CONCLUSION: CONTEXTUALIZING SOCIOLOGICAL ACCOUNTS OF IMPRISONMENT

All too often, the early sociological literature on imprisonment is represented merely as a scholarly debate dominated by a division between proponents of deprivation (Sykes, 1958) and importation (Irwin, 1970). While this debate certainly influenced the development of the broader academic field of prison studies, other aspects of the literature warrant consideration for what they reveal about the justification of imprisonment at the time, as well as about the roots of present academic scholarship. In particular, as with much of the reform discussed in Chapter 2, the early sociological literature is notable for its emphasis on "scientific" method. In conjunction with the ideas and topics stressed by the authors—namely inmate social cohesion for men, and intimate sexual relations for women—this literature laid the foundations not only for the questions asked of the prison, but the methods through which they should be posed.

Moreover, even as prison sociology declined in the 1980s (Simon, 2000), the overall tendency toward prioritizing "science" and "objective" research instruments remained, and continues to structure attempts to explain imprisonment. As a result, much literature takes for granted penal institutions and, however unintentionally, tends to reify and perpetuate them. Finally, the silence of the first sociologists on matters of race and their traditional views on gender continue to limit analyses of incarceration. Thus, despite the vast overrepresentation of racial and ethnic minorities in U.S. prisons and notwithstanding the rapidly growing numbers of women behind bars, these groups are rarely considered in their own right.

Although there are some signs that prison sociology is undergoing a renaissance, particularly in the field of women's prisons (Owen, 1998; McCorkel, 2001), it has yet to recover the position that it occupied in the 1960s and 1970s. Instead, prison scholars remain strangely divorced from inmate life. Whereas the assertion by the first sociologists that prisons had a culture that was shaped by the deprivations inmates endured as well as by the attitudes and identities that they brought with them maintained a focus on inmates as a legitimate topic of research, these days, as any survey of research funding or publications will demonstrate, few studies concentrate solely on life behind bars.

In part, according to Jonathan Simon (2000), the demise of prison sociology occurred once penal administrators and criminologists saw that what had been labeled "inmate society" was no longer an appropriate means through which to maintain order and control. As crime began to surge in the late 1960s, questions about the ability of prisons to secure compliance and reform became more urgent. What needed to be changed? Some scholars argued that demographic shifts in age, race, and crime had altered the confined population, creating a divided "inmate society" that was an unreliable vehicle of social control. Others blamed the pursuit of reformist measures and the growing interventions of the courts for challenging traditional hierarchies in prison. The resultant power vacuum, they said, disrupted the functioning of daily prison life (Jacobs, 1977).

In response to the various social upheavals of the time, President Lyndon B. Johnson created the Commission on Law Enforcement and the Administration of Justice in 1965. Though predominantly concerned with issues of crime and policing, the report of this commission, published in 1967, paid some attention to prisons and correctional settings. When read in conjunction with the sociological literature, it portrays a nation concerned about social order and cohesion that still hoped to find answers in "science." In a strategy not unlike that of previous committees or government departments from the House Un-American Activities Committee to the FBI (both of whom compiled lengthy dossiers on suspected Communists and other activists of the time), the president's commission focused on domestic threats and social problems.[6] No longer at war against a clear external enemy—although in this period the U.S. was still battling the Viet Cong in Vietnam—the dangers emerged from within. The administration of justice needed to be modernized and streamlined in order to serve and protect the law-abiding more effectively. In so doing, the prison would play a central role in securing a disorderly society, as well as in promoting a new vision of change.

Despite the supposed influence of reformers and rehabilitation, the committee found numerous anachronisms in prison architecture, programming, and penal regimes. Instead of a system based on scientific treatment and correctional participation, they paint one dominated by uneasy force, a control in which, as Sykes described, inmates were pitted against guards and united with one another through various articulations of subcultural norms. To counter this situation, the committee advocated the development of a "model institution" that "would be relatively small, and located as close as possible to the areas from which it draws its inmates, probably in or near a city rather than a remote location" (The President's Commission on Law Enforcement and the Administration of Justice, 1967, p. 173). Architecturally, they believed that these institutions should "resemble as much as possible a normal residential setting. Rooms, for example, would have doors rather than bars. Inmates would eat at small tables in an informal atmosphere. There would be classrooms, recreation facilities, day rooms, and perhaps a shop and library" (ibid.). Such a utopian vision, though soon to be dissipated by the demise of the rehabilitative ideal in the late 1970s, sought to involve inmates with staff as near equal participants and to "shift the focus of correctional efforts from temporary banishment of offenders to a carefully devised combination of control and treatment" (ibid.).

The authors of *The Challenge of Crime in a Free Society* believed that ". . . institutions that are small, close to metropolitan areas, and highly diversified in their programs provide excellent settings for research and experimentation and can serve as proving grounds for needed innovations." They would be "accessible to university and other research centers" and would "foster a climate friendly to inquiry and to the implementation of changes suggested by it" (ibid.). Although "[t]he costs of action" involved in implementing their reforms would be "substantial," the committee acknowledged, they warned that "the costs of inaction" would be "immensely greater." More explicitly:

> . . . inaction would mean, in effect, that the Nation would continue to avoid, rather than confront, one of its most critical social problems; that it would accept for the next generation a huge, if now immeasurable, burden of wasted and destructive lives. Decisive action, on the other hand, could make a difference that would really matter within our own time. (The President's Commission on Law Enforcement and the Administration of Justice, 1967, p. 185)

Despite such ominous, and as it turned out, prescient warnings, the social upheavals of the 1960s and 1970s took their toll on inmate solidarity, while prison scholars' interest began to turn to managerialism. In this new vision of prison research, the inmate lost ground to the prison rule book and the administrator. By the 1980s, the locus of power and influence shifted outside the prison walls. Before this transition of power and academic inquiry could occur fully, however, the rehabilitative ideal had to be destabilized. It is to this topic that Chapter 4 shall turn.

NOTES

1. Tylor was the founding professor of anthropology at the University of Oxford, under whom Wallis studied while a Rhodes scholar. Both sought to understand the role of culture in "primitive" societies.

2. So, too, books by prisoners like Caryl Chessman (1954, 1957) and Malcolm Braly (1968, 1976) represented the everyday violence and injustice of life behind bars.

3. Many of Irwin's ideas have recently been resurrected in the school known as "convict criminology," which shall be discussed in Chapter 8.

4. Such divisions, Jackson believed, did not simply characterize relations among inmates, however, but also between prison administrators; whereas "... it is the function of the uniform to hold a man here ... the individual with the tie and white shirt ... determines what we'll eat, what bullshit academic and make-work programs we'll have. ... These two types of cops have been vying for control of the joints ever since the counselor breed came on the grounds" (Jackson, 1970, p. 189).

5. As Hopper makes clear, conjugal visits were just one of a series of reforms that had been introduced in the second half of the 1960s, including the establishment of a vocational education program, and a reception and diagnostic center staffed by a psychologist and offering pre-release counseling. Prisoners stopped wearing the traditional prison stripes in 1967, being clothed instead in "... blue denim shirts and trousers made by female inmates" (Hopper, 1969, pp. 30–31). The lash was still permitted by the laws of the state, but, according to Hopper at least, fell into disuse after 1964 (Hopper, 1969, p. 33).

6. Parts of the FBI files on Martin Luther King, Jr. and Malcolm X can be accessed at foia.fbi.gov/famous.htm, along with the files of other early Black leaders, including W. E. B. DuBois, as well as Albert Einstein and entertainers Lucille Ball, Desi Arnaz, and the Beatles.

Four

An Era of Uncertainty

Riots, Reform, and Repression

To put a person behind walls and not change him is to win a battle and lose a war.

—Chief Justice Earl Warren, quoted in Levinson, 1974, p. 171

To position the "demands" of convicted felons in a place of equal dignity with legitimate aspirations of law-abiding American citizens . . . represents not simply an assault on human sensibility, but an insult to reason.

—Vice President Spiro Agnew, 1971, p. 43

No longer do black prisoners play the sycophant's game of "pleasing the powers,". . . they are in tune with contemporary social and political scenes in the free world.

—former prisoner Clifford Rollins
in Fraser, 1971, p. 49

The social transformations inspired by the civil rights activism of the 1950s and 1960s continued throughout the 1970s, making it a decade of upheaval in the United States. The ongoing antiwar and Civil Rights Movements, along with a weakened economy, generated a sense of societal insecurity while simultaneously raising the possibility of meaningful social change. Across the country, people questioned the legitimacy of key national institutions, from the government to the family. For some, such interrogation was liberating; for others, it was deeply disturbing.

The 1970s was also a decade of confusion in the nation's prisons. Ushered in by two major disturbances—the organized prisoner strike at Folsom in 1970 and the bloody suppression of the prisoner rebellion in New York State's Attica Correctional Facility in September 1971—the decade closed with internecine violence among inmates at the New Mexico State Penitentiary in February 1980.[1] Although the era began with an official reaffirmation of the principles of rehabilitation by the American Correctional Association (1972), it ended with the rehabilitation ideal in tatters.

For a time it seemed that the prison stood "at the center of radical politics" (Jacobs, 1975, p. 480; Cummins, 1994). Institutions experimented with inmate self-governance and prisoner unions (Bloomberg, 1977), while both the popular press and academic journals published searing critiques of punitive practice and sentiment (see, inter alia, Mitford, 1973; Haney, Banks, & Zimbardo, 1973; Nagel, 1973; Reiman, 1979). An organized movement calling for a national moratorium on prison building began, while prisoners became increasingly politicized and vocal (Fraser, 1971; Roberts, 1971; Jackson, 1970). At the same time, however, the 1970s witnessed a massive growth in crime rates not curtailed by a simultaneous expansion in criminal justice administration. Prison numbers grew rapidly and, despite a series of block grants from the federal government to fund solutions through the Law Enforcement Assistance Administration (LEAA), set up in response to the recommendations of Lyndon Johnson's Commission On Law Enforcement and Administration of Justice, institutions were often unable to cope.

As the decade advanced, the left began to splinter, and a more conservative view of punishment, social relations, and race gained greater prominence. State-sanctioned intervention via such organizations as the FBI Counter Intelligence Program (COINTELPRO) fractured some of the more organized resistance within and beyond prison walls, while, despite increased intervention by the courts in a bid to safeguard due process and implement wide-ranging reforms, conditions remained poor in many prisons. Health care, education, and training were usually minimal. Instances of open brutality—particularly towards those designated as "political prisoners"—were not unknown (Shakur, 1987; Jackson, 1970) while everywhere the growing numbers of those jailed strained even the most enlightened of administrations. A time that, in most places, began with a palpable desire for change, ended with the voices of reform all but snuffed out. In the process, the foundations of the U.S. penal landscape of the 21st century were laid.

Attica

Despite the far-reaching influence of the 1970 Folsom uprising, it is the Attica Rebellion for which U.S. prisons in the 1970s are best remembered. On September 9, 1971, after breakfast, a group of prisoners at the maximum-security Attica Correctional Facility in the State of New York refused to proceed to work duty. The rebellion soon escalated, as more than half of the total 2,254 inmates joined in. Over the morning, according to an editorial from *The New York Times,*

> more than 1000 prisoners seized and beat their guards and raced through the corridors and courtyards of the maximum security prison. Bedding and buildings were set afire—six of the buildings were badly damaged; furniture and windows were smashed, and as the pillars of smoke rose above the enclosure, leaders of the riot announced that they were holding 33 guards hostage. (Ferretti, 1971a, p. E8)

Initially, the state responded carefully. Administrators agreed to listen to the prisoners' demands and to allow a group of visitors, including journalists and Black activists, to meet prisoner representatives (Wicker, 1975). The reform-minded New York State Prison Commissioner, Russell G. Oswald, personally talked to prisoners, accepting many of their demands, including a range of administrative and social reforms. From the beginning, it had appeared that Oswald might be sympathetic to the prisoners' cause, since a few days before the riot he had announced at Attica plans for statewide changes long sought by prisoners, including freer access to the media and an end to the censorship of correspondence with their lawyers and public officials. He had also declared that prisoner officers would receive 120 days of training as compared with the existing system of a one- to three-week orientation course. On being appointed state commissioner, Oswald had pledged to move at least 30 percent of the New York State prison population out of maximum-security prisons into new, lower-security facilities that would offer greater educational and rehabilitative options (Kaufman, 1971; Oswald, 1972).

The prisoners at Attica, like the rest of those in the New York State system, were then, as they are today, overwhelmingly (63 percent) Black or Puerto Rican (New York State Special Commission on Attica, 1972). Most had grown up in a few neighborhoods in New York City. Drawn predominantly from these urban enclaves, they were serving lengthy sentences upstate near Buffalo and the Canadian border, where they were guarded exclusively by rural Whites. At the time of the rebellion, there were no Black correctional officers at Attica, nor had there ever been.

After seizing the prison, inmates presented Oswald with a series of demands, the most important of which was a manifesto based on that originally formulated by the prisoners at Folsom. Similar to a list that a group calling itself the "Attica Liberation Front" had championed peacefully a few months earlier, it called for fundamental improvements in living conditions, food, education, and recreation. To reflect the ethnic and religious composition of the prisoner population, the manifesto demanded dietary changes (less pork), Spanish-speaking doctors, and religious freedom. The prisoners also wanted to be paid the minimum wage for their labor, and, despite being unable to vote in any state, federal, or local elections, to be permitted to be politically active behind bars. "We are Men!" they declaimed. "We are not beasts and do not intend to be beaten or driven as such" (Wicker, 1975, p. 315).

The 28 points to which State Corrections Commissioner Russell G. Oswald agreed were reprinted in journalist Tom Wicker's firsthand account of the uprising. Wicker was one of a group of people invited in by the prisoners to negotiate. Other members included Bobby Seale, Chairman of the Black Panther Party, U.S. Representative Herman Badillo of New York, and members of the Young Lords party of New York. The full list is reproduced in Wicker, 1975, pp. 318–319.

1. Provide adequate food, water and shelter for all inmates
2. Inmates shall be permitted to return to their cells or to other suitable accommodations or shelter under their power. The observer committee shall monitor the implementation of this operation.
3. Grant complete administrative amnesty to all persons associated with this matter. By administrative amnesty the state agrees:
   A. Not to take any adverse parole actions, administrative proceedings, physical punishment or other type of harassment, such as holding inmates incommunicado, segregating inmates, or keep them in isolation or in 24-hour lockup.
   B. The state will grant legal amnesty in regard to all civil actions that could arise from this matter.

(Continued)

(Continued)

C. It is agreed that the State of New York and all its departments, divisions and subdivisions, including the State Department of Corrections and the Attica Correctional Facility and its employees and agents, shall not file or initiate any criminal complaint or act as complainant in any criminal action of any kind of nature relating to property damage or property-related crimes arising out of the incidents at the Attica Correctional Facility during Sept. 9, 10 and 11, 1971.

4. Recommend the application of the New York State Minimum Wage Law standards to all work done by inmates. Every effort will be made to make the records of payments available to inmates.
5. Establish by Oct. 1 a permanent ombudsman service for the facility, staffed by appropriate persons from the neighboring communities.
6. Allow all New York State prisoners to be politically active without intimidation or reprisal.
7. Allow true religious freedom.
8. End all censorship of newspapers, magazines and other publications from publishers, unless it is determined by qualified authority, which includes the ombudsman, that the literature in question presents a clear and present danger to the safety and security of the institution.
9. Allow all inmates at their own expense communication with anyone they please.
10. Institute realistic, effective rehabilitation programs for all inmates according to their offense and personal needs.
11. Modernize the inmate education system, including the establishment of a [Spanish-language] library.
12. Provide an effective narcotics treatment program for all prisoners requesting such treatment.
13. Provide or allow adequate legal assistance to all inmates requesting it, or permit them to use inmate legal assistance of their choice in any proceeding whatsoever. In all such proceedings inmates shall be entitled to appropriate due process of law.
14. Reduce cell time, increase recreation time and provide better recreation facilities and equipment, hopefully by Nov. 1, 1971.
15. Provide a healthy diet, reduce the number of pork dishes, increase fresh fruit daily.

16. Provide adequate medical treatment for every inmate. Engage either a Spanish-speaking doctor or interpreters who will accompany Spanish-speaking inmates to medical interviews.
17. Institute a program for the recruitment and employment of a significant number of black and Spanish-speaking officers.
18. Establish an inmate grievance commission, comprised of one elected inmate from each company, which is authorized to speak to the administration concerning grievances and develop other procedures for inmate participation in the operation and decision-making processes of the institution.
19. Investigate the alleged expropriation of inmate funds and the use of profits from the metal and other shops.
20. The State Commissioner of Correctional Services will recommend that the penal law be changed to cease administrative resentencing of inmates returned for parole violations.
21. Recommend that Menenchino hearings be held promptly and fairly. [This concerns the right of prisoners to be represented legally on parole-violation charges.]
22. Recommend necessary legislation and more adequate funds to expand work relief programs.
23. End approved lists for correspondents and visitors.
24. Remove visitation screens as soon as possible.
25. Institute a 30-day maximum for segregation arising out of any one offense. Every effort should be geared towards restoring the individual to regular housing as soon as possible, consistent with safety regulations.
26. Paroled inmates shall not be charged with parole violations for moving traffic violations or driving without a license unconnected to any other crimes.
27. Permit access to outside dentists and doctors at the inmates' own expense within the institution where possible and consistent with scheduling problems, medical diagnosis and health needs.
28. It is expressly understood that members of the observer committee will be permitted into the institution on a reasonable basis to determine whether all of the above provisions are being effectively carried out. If questions of adequacy are raised, the matter will be brought to the attention of the Commissioner of Correctional Services for clearance.

Figure 4.1 The 28 Attica Demands

Oswald agreed to a revised 28-point manifesto (Ferretti, 1971a). He refused, however, to order the removal of Attica Superintendent Vincent Mancusi (Charlton, 1971) or to relocate the rebellion organizers to a "non-imperialistic country." (Mancusi took early retirement some months after the Attica rebellion, in January 1972.) Tragically, the prisoners refused Oswald's compromise offer.

The Attica Rebellion ended at 9:43 a.m. on September 13, 1971, four days after the prisoners seized control of the institution. Despite feverish attempts to negotiate that lasted through the day and night, Governor Nelson D. Rockefeller, early in the morning of September 13, elected to send in the state troopers to take back the prison (Wicker, 1971a). Asserting that ". . . armed rebellion of this type we have faced threatens the destruction of our free society," the state unleashed a military-style attack (Oswald, 1971, p. 28). In the process, nine hostages and 28 prisoners were killed. Despite initial reports that inmates had cut the throats of the hostages during the rebellion, subsequent autopsy reports revealed that all had died from gunshot wounds sustained when the state troopers attacked. Over the next weeks, several more prisoners died from their gunshot injuries. In addition to one guard who had died earlier after being thrown from a cellblock window, the total killed in the Attica uprising rose to 43. Scores of others were hurt.

The New York Times covered the Attica rebellion, its brutal suppression, and its aftermath in great detail. Soliciting commentary from all sides of the political spectrum, ranging from then California Governor Ronald Reagan and Vice President Spiro Agnew on the right to members of the Black Panther party on the far left, overall the paper's editorial line was sympathetic to the reformers. Once it became apparent that the deaths of the hostages were caused by state troopers, the paper seemed to side with the prisoners and with critics of Oswald and Rockefeller (Ferretti, 1971d, p. 1).

In particular, journalists, politicians, and pundits alike were openly concerned about racism, regularly admitting that part of the problem of imprisonment lay in broader conditions of racial inequality. According to the mayor of Newark, for example, ". . . when we look at prison conditions and the brutal use of force at Attica we see the same force of racism which caused and then put down with force civil disturbances in this country's ghettos. This racism cannot be tolerated" (Gibson, 1971, p. 43). Many were also unsure about the rightness of punishment itself.

One day after the violent put-down of the prisoners, the paper published an editorial entitled "Massacre at Attica" in which the author observed:

> Out of yesterday's holocaust must come a recognition that the nation has been living on borrowed time in its failure to correct the abysmal conditions that make life intolerable in Attica and virtually every penal institution. It is as unfair to correctional officers as it is to prisoners to have such conditions continue. (*The New York Times*, 1971b, p. 40)

Similarly, a piece published before the rebellion was over, entitled "Now, Attica Again" (*The New York Times*, 1971a), argued that ". . . there is a crime in present punishment procedures." Prisons, the article asserted, ". . . are schools for lawlessness rather than the reverse" because of poor living conditions and inadequate regimes. "Almost every report investigating prison conditions anywhere in the country," it alleged, "has concluded with a similar set of recommendations for intensifying rehabilitation efforts, expanding job-training programs, liberalizing visiting privileges, increasing educational choices. It is past time to act on them" (*The New York Times*, 1971a, p. 26).

Less than 10 years later, the 1980 riot at New Mexico State Penitentiary received no such compassionate attention.[2] Unlike the careful and detailed analyses of the causes, implications, and responsibility of Attica, New Mexico was presented with brief and peremptory commentary. Perhaps reflecting the geographic distance, *The New York Times* gave it scant notice and, although another newspaper with national circulation, *The Los Angeles Times,* devoted considerably more space to the events, coverage was not sympathetic. Unlike the earlier coverage of Attica, the events at New Mexico were rarely viewed in the mainstream press or anywhere else as an indictment of the overall legitimacy of incarceration or punishment. Instead it became fodder for sensationalist and gory accounts of violence (Morris, 1988; Rolland, 1997).

To be sure, there were significant differences in the riots themselves. While there was enormous fear of inmate violence during Attica, little actually occurred. By contrast, the New Mexico State Penitentiary was notable for the viciousness of the inmate-on-inmate crimes perpetrated during the 36-hour uprising. Inmates held in protective custody were brutally executed after being tortured and, in some cases, dismembered as well. Such behavior could still have been considered through the lenses of race and class, as the actions of the Attica inmates had been. Instead, reporters salaciously lingered on the bestial nature of the crimes, inmate drug use, and the property damage prisoners perpetrated. In their description of events, reporters like Lois Timnick of *The Los Angeles Times* drew direct parallels between prisoners and animals: "Animal studies have shown that when you reach a certain degree of overcrowding, rats will start to attack, and mutilate, each other" (Timnick, 1980, B15). In such a metaphor, of course, the structural nature of the problem—overcrowding—becomes presented as a form of despicable, animalistic (and hence uncivilized, worrying, inexplicable) behavior, action that must be utterly purged from a decent society. "Animal" prisoners had their humanity cut away, wrote the journalist's words.

Although some aspiration for rehabilitation lingered, by 1980 this model for, and explanation of, imprisonment had lost most ground in the United States. As Chapter 5 will demonstrate in more detail, the subsequent decade under Reagan and George Herbert W. Bush furthered the break with past justifications for, and goals of, incarceration. In this era, rather, concerns about racism, and the mixed reaction to the politicization of inmates that characterized many of the journalistic accounts of Attica, were replaced by harsher, purely administrative representations of prisoners and offenders. Lawbreakers above all became depicted as the cause of fear and danger to the community. They needed strict management, and deserved little sympathy and few privileges. In short, as prison historian Charles Bright succinctly puts it:

> The space opened [in the early 1970s] for innovation by the crisis of treatment was soon closed down by the recession and fiscal crisis and by the rising conservative mobilization around issues of law and order that combined a critique of welfare and social service spending with demands for tougher no-nonsense measures against criminals. (Bright, 1996, p. 312)

Reform, in other words, yielded the stage to repression.

Activism Before and After Attica

Two events that predated Attica laid the foundations for much of the prisoner activism of the early 1970s: the shooting of "Soledad Brother" George Jackson[3] at San Quentin by prison guards on August 21, 1971, as he was allegedly trying to escape, and the prisoner strike at Folsom Penitentiary that occurred 10 months earlier. Together, all three events revealed how the increasing demands for prisoner rights and nascent inmate organization, at least within men's establishments, were destabilizing not only the contemporaneous prison administration and the race and gender relations that underpinned them, but also the site and nature of penal reform. Whereas prison reformers traditionally worked outside the walls to ameliorate conditions within, in the 1970s prisoners themselves increasingly sought to define and achieve change on their own definition. Such radical "agency" or independence would prove intolerable.

The Folsom uprising lasted 19 days in November 1970. In a peaceful prisoner strike, all parts of the penitentiary other than emergency medical care were shut down, while prisoners demanded the right to unionize and organize. Although prison administrators refused to grant prisoners' requests, the episode at Folsom led directly to the creation of the California prison union, the nation's first such inmate organization. More generally, the manifesto created by the Folsom prisoners rapidly penetrated other penal institutions across the country, including Attica, where it formed the basis for inmate demands for change. The ease of transmission suggested a commonality of grievance across state and federal lines. The manifesto underscored both the newfound determination of many individuals within prison to seek change, and the considerable public sympathy and support outside, despite the social and economic fractures that lay not far from the surface in American society and in the reform movement (Browning, 1972; Huff, 1974).

Accounts from the 1970s usually stress not only that prisoners were united in their attempts at reform, but also that they were more politically sophisticated and politicized than inmates in previous eras (Fairchild, 1977). As one author put it, prisoners had become aware "... that in an age of instant communication through the mass media, their 'audience' ha[d] widened considerably" (Huff, 1974, p. 176). So too, the mass media became a means of politicization, educating prisoners about their rights and shared experiences (Fairchild, 1977). How do we square activism, however, with the depiction of a fractured inmate group painted by the sociological literature reviewed in Chapter 3 (Carroll, 1974)? Scholars in that field, after all, had claimed that the increasing diversity of the prison population had compromised prisoner subculture, atomizing what was previously a relatively uniform group (Jacobs, 1977). Why, too, would public support for prisoners and inmate solidarity decline so rapidly and completely this decade?

As prisoners became more politicized, and as more politicals were incarcerated, relations between them and their supporters outside could become strained. As one commentator at the time wrote, "... Prison organizers don't speak the same language as the prison reformists. The reason is simple. The reformers went to graduate school, and make a living at reform. The organizers went to prison, and learned to build strikes" (Browning, 1972, p. 134). Though such figures may well have been exceptional, rather than empirically "representative" of the majority behind bars, individuals like Angela Davis (1974), George Jackson (1970), Afeni Shakur (Guy, 2004), and Raul Salinas (1980) reached out to others behind bars and beyond, through their writing and their activism. Their deeply personal firsthand accounts highlighted the relevance and the intersections of race, gender, and ethnicity in prison. As such, their memoirs, poetry, and journalism provide a fruitful source of analysis for contemporary scholars.

Activists, within or beyond jail, who sought to cross racial divisions were often thwarted by institutional barriers. Notwithstanding Huey Newton's claim that ". . . the black prisoners as well as many of the white prisoners identify with the program of the Panthers. . . . by the very nature of their being prisoners they can see the oppression and they've suffered at the hands of the Gestapo [prison guards]" (Newton, as cited in Jacobs, 1975, p. 480), many prisons continued to separate inmates according to race in cells, housing units, and employment well beyond either the 1954 Supreme Court general ruling against segregation in *Brown v. Board of Education* or the 1964 Civil Rights Act. When prisoners challenged this practice in the courts, as they did in *Alabama in Lee v. Washington* (1968), judges were loath to prevent prison authorities from interfering when administrators deemed segregation necessary for maintaining good order and discipline.[4] Even when some states did agree to eliminate segregation in their prison systems, as occurred in the Texas class action lawsuit *Lamar v. Coffield 1977*, it took decades for them to become fully compliant (Trulson & Marquart, 2002; Trulson et al., 2008).

As the prison population diversified racially, gaps among the population opened, which undermined broad inmate solidarity. Such divisions were driven not simply by the enduring segregation behind bars, but by broader hostilities between groups in the community, between Whites and Blacks and Hispanics as well. Nonetheless, from the 1960s onwards, an increasing number of inmates arrived already politicized by their experiences of the Civil Rights Movement and by the increasingly radical Black Power Movement. Just as Malcolm Little had been transformed by his prison experience with such dramatic effect two decades previously to become Malcolm X, other ordinary men and women were influenced by contact with members of groups like the Black Panther Party, the Black Muslims, the Young Lords, and the American Indian Movement (AIM).

Most of the challenges to prisons in the 1970s that are remembered these days occurred in men's prisons and were initiated by male prisoners.

It is important to recall, however, that the 1970s also saw a number of politically active women in prison. High-profile Black Panther activists like Angela Davis, Afeni Shakur, Joan Bird, and Assata Shakur spent time inside. Such figures, along with feminist academics and activists more generally, helped draw attention to the victimization of many female offenders prior to their incarceration, as well as to the "double jeopardy" suffered by women of color (French, 1977, p. 1978). Unlike the paternalism of some of the earlier writing on women's prisons, such accounts identified the intersections of race, gender, and class oppression as crucial to understanding (and resisting) imprisonment.

In the first of what became a multivolume set of personal accounts, Angela Davis spent much of her 1974 autobiography on her experience in prison awaiting trial.[5] Eventually found innocent of all charges, Davis was nonetheless confined for a number of months awaiting trial for murder, conspiracy, and weapons possession. Despite having visited many prisons, Davis appears to have been shocked and frightened when incarcerated herself. As an historical source, her work is particularly rich, not only for its depiction of daily life behind bars, but also, when considered in light of the literature of Chapter 3, for her musings on prison subculture and politics. On arrival at the Manhattan Detention Center for Women in 1971, Davis was subjected, like any other new intake, to a mandatory vaginal and rectal examination (Davis, 1974, p. 22). She describes a bus filled with Black and Hispanic women returning from the courts (Davis, 1974, p. 19), as well as the unsettling image of a pregnant inmate laboring alone and unattended in a prison corridor before being swept off, manacled, to hospital to deliver her baby. Due to her status as a political prisoner, Davis was separated from the mainstream population for much of her time in jail, first on the mental ward, where she movingly depicts the overmedication of inmates with Thorazine, and then in a former doctor's office, alone.

In a firsthand analysis of the kinds of relations identified in Chapter 3 by sociologists, Davis asserts that:

> Two layers of existence can be encountered within almost any jail or prison. The first layer consists of the routines and behavior prescribed by the governing penal hierarchy. The second layer is the prison culture itself: the rules and standards of behavior that come from and are designed by the captives in order to shield themselves from the open or covert terror designed to break their spirits. (Davis, 1974, p. 52)

When considering the impact and nature of this subculture, she suggests that "... in an elemental way [it] is one of resistance, but a resistance of desperation. It is, therefore, incapable of striking a significant blow against the system" (Davis, 1974, pp. 52–53).

At least some resistance seems to have been deliberately accepted by the prison administration as a distraction. This conclusion is, at least, Davis's interpretation of the intimate relations that she observed. Although she initially depicted the organization of prisoners into "... generations of families: mothers/wives, fathers/husbands, sons and daughters, even aunts, uncles, grandmothers and grandfathers" approvingly, as ". . . a defense against the fact of being no more than a number. It humanized the environment with others within a familiar framework" (Davis, 1974, p. 53), she criticized it soon after as a "fantasy life" that was little more than "an easy and attractive channel for escape" (Davis, 1974, p. 55). Like Emma Goldman years before, Davis seemed to be disappointed in the failure of the imprisoned to rise up against their oppressors.

Similar regrets can be heard in Assata Shakur's depiction of life in Rikers Island Correctional Facility while she was a serving prisoner. "Most of the women at Rikers Island," she wrote, "have no idea what feminism is . . . The black liberation struggle is equally removed from the lives of women at Rikers." Unlike the "men prisoners at Rikers Island," she heard no

> . . . revolutionary rhetoric among the women. We have no study groups. We have no revolutionary literature around. There are no groups of militants attempting to "get their heads together." The women at Rikers seem vaguely aware of what a revolution is but generally regard it as an impossible dream. Not at all practical. (Shakur, 1978, p. 12)

Instead of revolutionaries, or even offenders, Shakur depicted the women as victims:

> There are no criminals here at Rikers Island Correctional Institution for Women, (New York), only victims. Most of the women (over 95%) are black and Puerto Rican. Many were abused as children. Most have been abused by men and all have been abused by "the system." There are no big time gangsters here, no premeditated mass murderers, no godmothers. There are no big time dope dealers, no kidnappers, no Watergate women. . . . Most of the women have drug related cases. Many are charged as accessories to crimes committed by men. The major crimes that women here are charged with are prostitution, pick-pocketing, shop lifting, robbery and drugs. (Shakur, 1978, p. 9)

Such figures, unable to resist their captors, hurt themselves:

> . . . the air at Rikers is permeated with self-hatred. Many women bear marks on their arms, legs and wrists from suicide attempts or self-mutilation. They speak about themselves in self-deprecating terms. They consider themselves failures. (Shakur, 1978, p. 12)

Although Shakur (who famously escaped from the Clinton Correctional Center in New Jersey in 1979 and fled to Cuba) may have found scant evidence of the impact of the women's movement or the Civil Rights Movement in prison, outside its walls feminists were active. The 1970s saw the creation of the first battered women's shelters and a growing recognition and condemnation of the endemic nature of violence against women (Brownmiller, 1975). In the courts, *Roe v. Wade* asserted a woman's right to choose (in consultation with her doctor) whether to continue or terminate her pregnancy, while marital rape exemptions began to be struck down in a number of states. Finally, a series of Black and minority feminist groups emerged in the 1970s, including the National Black Feminist Organization, founded in 1973, and the Combahee River Collective, set up in 1974 to address more directly the social problems faced by women of color.

In addition to the racial and ethnic-based identity politics, for which much of the activism within and beyond the prison that is associated with this era is remembered, prisoners also, at times, articulated a fledgling sense of class solidarity. As *The New York Times* journalist Tom Wicker, who was part of the team of independent observers at Attica, put it, the prison uprising there was notable for its ". . . strikingly effective organization, its fierce political radicalism [and] its submergence of racial animosity into class solidarity" (Wicker, 1971b, p. 1). Such class solidarity led prisoners all over the country, from Ohio to New York and California, in women's prisons as well as men's, to unionize (Baunach & Murton, 1973). These inmate organizations lobbied internally and externally to ameliorate prison conditions. In conjunction with other reform groups, including the Black Panther Party, Black Muslims, and outside organizations such as the American Civil Liberties Union (ACLU), which set up its National Prison Project in 1972, they fought for the abolition of censorship of first-class mail, the provision of ministers for the non-Christian population (including Muslims and Native Americans), recruitment programs for minority employees, and higher correctional officer pay to attract more educated workers, as well as standardized grievance procedures. Inmates also wanted expanded visiting rights, furlough programs, the right to have attorney visits conducted in private, expanded education and work offerings, access to law books, and increased levels of autonomy and self-governance. Women desired greater access to their children and better medical care, along with an end to intrusive gendered practices like the mandatory vaginal examinations described by Davis and Shakur.

The Administration of Justice

In response to the rising tide of organized inmate unrest, states and the federal government acted. Post-Attica, many states eased regulations over visiting and mail censorship. Pell grants, which had been approved by Congress in 1972 as part of that year's Higher Education Amendment Act, came into force and, through the provision of federal funds for indigent prisoners, generated a range of prison-based college programs. Similarly, echoing Oswald's initial reservations about the limitations of maximum-security institutions, many states began experimenting with new styles of architecture and lower-security institutions that could, because of their layout, design, and technology, facilitate greater freedom behind bars. Such "campus-style" prisons sought to humanize the prison experience through design. Staff were encouraged to view themselves as "counselors" and to build supportive relationships with their inmate charges.

New penal institutions and practices also spread at this time. Therapeutic communities emphasized group therapy and 12-step programs, while co-correctional facilities sought to "normalize" life behind bars by housing women and men together. Community Service sentences, implemented in New York City in 1978 by the Vera Institute of Justice, whose members had, a decade previously, pioneered the Manhattan Bail Project, sought to divert first-time and low-level offenders from prison altogether. Even those who were confined in regular prisons were to be treated differently. Unlike the ad hoc system of earlier times—when inmates were housed and classified more or less according to the whim of the warden or his deputy—prisoners in many states and the federal system were acclimatized to their new environment through organized admission and orientation processes. Such procedures, which, in the federal system at least, were accompanied by written material and booklets setting out the goals and ethos of the establishment, promised care and assistance for incoming prisoners to mend their ways (Bosworth, 2007a; see, for example, FCI Fort Worth, 1975).

Advocates of correctionalism and rehabilitation had high hopes for these newly designed buildings, believing that the material nature of confinement was central to the likelihood of reoffending. Yet, the optimism of the period in this area, as in so many others, was short-lived. The "campus-style" facilities failed in their bid to reform more effectively than earlier penal institutions and were, in time, abandoned as too costly and insufficiently secure.

It was not just in prison design that the federal government sought to change the culture and practice of criminal justice. When President Lyndon B. Johnson had formed the Commission on Law Enforcement and Administration of Justice to examine public safety in the United States in 1965, he charged it with devising a way to measure and record crime and punishment in the U.S. In its 1967 report, *The Challenge of Crime in a Free Society,* the Commission recommended the creation of two government departments, called today the Office of Justice Programs and the National Institute of Justice, both of which remain central to the gathering and dispersal of criminal justice statistics. These departments originally were known, respectively, as the Law Enforcement Assistance Administration (LEAA), and within it the National Institute of Law Enforcement and Criminal Justice (Feucht & Zedwelski, 2007). Over the course of the 1970s, they proved to be particularly influential in shaping academic and policy discourse about all aspects of the justice system, including the prison. In 1974, for example, the LEAA, in conjunction with the Census Bureau, interviewed 10,400 inmates of state correctional facilities, finally bringing to fruition Sanford Bates's vision of penal science. That same year LEAA also funded the American Correctional Association to establish an accreditation program for prisons around the country.[6]

In 1979, the work of these departments was extended by the foundation of the Bureau of Statistics within the U.S. Department of Justice. Since then, this office, as well as detailing prison and jail statistics, provides regular information about criminal offenders and victims of crime, as well as policing and capital punishment, while reporting on other special topics as needed. Current topics include prisoner reentry and international, comparative crime trends. Information typically differentiates between racial groups, gender, age, region, and types of confinement or jurisdiction. The Bureau also places most figures in a temporal context (i.e., from 1990–1995), demonstrating how such figures have fluctuated over time.

The early 1970s continued gradual court involvement in prisoners' rights cases, which had begun with two Supreme Court rulings in 1964: *Sostre v. McGinnis,* which recognized Muslims as a legitimate religious group who were entitled to the religious freedoms guaranteed by the

Constitution, and *Cooper v. Pate,* which enabled state prisoners to bring allegations of unconstitutional prison policies and conditions against state correctional employees under Section 1983 of the Civil Rights Act. Both decisions ended decades of refusal by the judiciary to intervene in prison-based disputes and signified a recognition of the existence of limited constitutional safeguards behind prison bars (Haas & Alpert, 1989; DiIulio, 1990). In response, prisoners brought cases to the federal courts focusing on all sorts of issues, from the death penalty to their conditions of confinement.

Just as the Supreme Court's decisions on the death penalty in this era shifted practices and ideas about capital punishment, so too, its decisions over prison conditions had profound effects on justifications for and experiences of imprisonment.[7] Rulings in this decade covered such topics as access to jailhouse lawyers, the provision of law libraries, and access to legal counsel (see, for example, *Johnson v. Avery* [1969], *Younger v. Gilmer* [1971], and *Bounds v. Smith* [1977]). Other cases, decided at state levels, dealt with an even broader array of issues, including but not limited to "... privacy, unsanitary conditions, inadequate medical and dental care, overcrowding, nutritionally inadequate food, lack of exercise opportunities, inadequate heating, ventilation, and lighting, and unprovoked physical attacks by prison staff or by other prisoners" (Haas & Alpert, 1989, p. 73).

Legal maneuverings by inmates reaped many benefits and, across jurisdictions, forced state governments and penal administrators to ameliorate conditions. More broadly, prisons became subject to the civil rights legislation of the time, altering staffing as well as inmate services. Although not always fully observed, such laws included the Equal Employment Opportunity Act of 1972, amending the Civil Rights Act of 1964, and officially prohibiting job discrimination on the basis of race, religion, color, national origin, and sex, and Title IX of the Education Amendments of 1972, seeking to end sex discrimination in educational activities. Near the end of the decade, the religious beliefs of Native Americans were finally recognized and protected by the American Indian Religious Freedom Act of 1978. Members of AIM had been particularly involved in a series of court cases on access to religious artifacts and freedom to observe traditional practices, battles which, notwithstanding the federal legislation, continued throughout the 1980s as well (Irwin, 2006).

Despite these reforms, much of the 1970s remained, for many, a period of great hardship behind bars. It was also a decade punctuated by serious civil unrest and violence in the general community.[8] In 1974, 10 states retained statutes that decreed the civil death of anyone sentenced to prison (Bullard, 1974). Inmates in these jurisdictions—Arizona, California, Idaho, Kansas, Montana, New York, North Dakota, Oklahoma, Rhode Island, and Utah—had to overcome enormous legal barriers in their bid to claim much, since they were, by definition, excluded from civil rights. At the same time, women offenders in seven states—Idaho, New Hampshire, Rhode Island, Vermont, Montana, North Dakota, and Wyoming—were "boarded" out of state, making it hard for them to make any meaningful legal demands, since the jurisdiction where they were sentenced had no incentive to alter the conditions in the state where they were held (*Yale Law Journal*, Comment, 1973).

Even as Attica is often remembered for the positive changes to prison administration that it engendered—greater religious freedom, acknowledgment of ethnic differences, and needs in terms of food and language, more visits, an end to mail censorship, development of a range of low-security, campus-style institutions, and so on—it also inspired a series of authoritarian measures, which have become key parts of prison experience. A few weeks after the uprising, for example, the state declared that prison officers would be equipped with riot gear, while New York State Prison Commissioner Russell G. Oswald accelerated plans to set up a maximum-maximum-security prison, which he thought would be an ideal destination for politically motivated prisoners (Kaufman, 1971). Around the same time, Governor Nelson Rockefeller announced his intention to restructure parts of the New York State criminal justice system and, a few years later, presided over the imposition of draconian drug legislation, the effects of which still affect the size and shape of the state's prison population.

Finally, crime continued its inexorable rise through the 1970s. Such disorder, within and beyond the prison, undermined the legitimacy of much penal reform. For as reformers found to their chagrin, prison disturbances and inmate dissatisfaction could be read in more than one way: either the system needed to be liberalized, or perhaps it was not harsh enough. In any case, as crime rates began to escalate, it became more difficult to argue that penal strategies, whether old or new, were being particularly successful.

The Demise of Rehabilitation

Prisons in the 1970s were run, as they had been for most of the 20th century, according to the treatment or correctionalist model. Despite the best intentions of many involved in prison administration, inmate complaints and penal reformers suggested that this system had devolved into one that was marred by grossly disproportionate sentences for similar offenses, as well as by enforced counseling and medical intervention. Not all institutions were uniformly bad, and there were a number of progressive attempts to change penal culture, yet the fact remained that most of what occurred behind bars was left to the discretion of the officers and wardens and that, without specific judicial oversight and regulation, daily prison life and the response to lawbreaking varied enormously across the country.

For many, such apparent randomness in treatment and in sentence length was alarming. Numerous scholarly accounts heavily criticized the capricious nature of decision making and the negative impact of counseling and other supposedly reformative endeavors. From the left, commentators argued that prisons were unjust in themselves and by definition. They held people in terrible conditions, offered few meaningful opportunities for change, and were severely compromised by the erratic system of indeterminate sentencing, which left far too much power in the hands of prison administrators and parole boards to determine whether people were fit for release (American Friends Service Committee, 1971; von Hirsch, 1976). From the right, particularly as crime rates began to soar and as the costs of incarceration rose, there was a countermovement for minimizing reform and rehabilitation deemed ineffective (Wilson, 1975).

Compounding matters for women, a new literature on female offenders hypothesized that the women's liberation movement increased numbers of females behind bars (Adler, 1975; Simon, 1975). "The movement for full equality has a darker side," Adler warned, ". . . in the same way that women are demanding equal opportunity in fields of legitimate endeavor, a similar number of determined women are forcing their way into the world of major crimes" (Adler, 1975, p. 13).[9] Some even blamed the demise of rehabilitation on feminist demands for equality. Requiring women to be treated like men, these critics asserted, undermined the "paternalist logic" of women's treatment programs (Fabian, 1979, p. 6).

Despite their critics, some continued to assert that the system worked, yet, over the course of the 1970s, their voices grew weaker (Carlson, 1974; Levinson, 1974). Two publications were prominent in shaping the outcome of the battle for the American prison. First was the 1974 article by Robert Martinson, "What Works? Questions and Answers About Prison Reform." Equally significant was the Special Committee for the Study of Incarceration in the U.S., which published its report in 1976 (von Hirsch, 1976). Although Martinson later recanted many of his findings, complaining that his article was taken out of context and manipulated by those already opposed to the ideology of rehabilitation, his paper notoriously coined the phrase "nothing works" (Martinson, 1979). In turn, the committee's report, *Doing Justice,* edited by Andrew von Hirsch, outlined the basic tenets of the "justice model," which, however unintentionally, paved the way for a radical restatement of sentencing guidelines that, in turn, led to the introduction of mandatory minimum sentences.

The 1974 article by Martinson presented an overview of literature on the efficacy of rehabilitative programs in a number of U.S. states. In a meta-analysis of education, counseling, medical intervention, and training programs, Martinson found few success stories. Instead, he maintained that techniques commonly touted as central to the treatment model—such as group counseling or vocational training—either had no discernible impact on reoffending rates, or, on occasion, made matters worse. As might be expected, critics of the prison—from both sides of the political spectrum—seized on these findings as proof of the inadequacy of rehabilitation and the medical model. In the process, those from the right also used it to denigrate both prisoner activism and the legitimacy of court intervention in ameliorating prison conditions.

Martinson, however, was less certain about the implications of his findings. In his conclusion, for example, he pointed out:

> It may be simply that our programs aren't yet good enough . . . It may be, on the other hand, that there is a more radical flaw in our present strategies—that education at its best, or that psychotherapy at its best, cannot overcome, or even appreciably reduce, the powerful tendency for offenders to continue in criminal behavior. (Martinson, 1974, p. 49)

Indeed, the major problem for Martinson was the relative paucity of information on which any judgment about the efficacy of prison programs could be based. Not only did few studies exist that measured the success of prison treatment, but those that did were often compromised by poor methodology. When read closely, in other words, Martinson's article offered just as much a call for new research as a critique of rehabilitation.

Though it is Martinson's phraseology that captures best the decline of faith in rehabilitation, in many respects, the report of the Special Committee for the Study of Incarceration in the U.S., published as *Doing Justice* (von Hirsch, 1976), was far more damning. In conjunction with *The Struggle for Justice* (American Friends Service Committee, 1971) and *Punishment and Desert* (Kleinig, 1973), this publication argued that rehabilitation was simply no longer an adequate justification of punishment. Rather, the committee members asserted, "... in everyday thinking about punishment, the idea of desert figures prominently. Ask the person on the street why a wrongdoer should be punished, and he is likely to say that he 'deserves' it" (Hirsch, 1976, p. 45).

Unlike the impassioned response to the Attica rebellion, "desert theory," as it came to be known, sought to downplay the relevance of race, culture, or economics. Such factors, the authors thought, were irrelevant to sentencing. Punishment should simply respond to the criminal act itself. In so doing, their theory stripped the humanity from the legal process. Although the authors of the report called time and again for limited use of incarceration, aiming as they were to do the least possible harm to offenders, their main propositions came to underpin an inexorable shift to the right in penal policy. Criticisms of indeterminate sentencing, which had been inspired by concerns over inconsistency and injustice, were harnessed to unravel judicial discretion and, eventually, to set in place deeply punitive sentencing practices.

Penal Revisionism and Prisoners' Rights: Theory Versus Practice

The story of the demise of rehabilitation is, in many ways, a disheartening one, shaped as it is by unintended consequences and misplaced faith in sentencing reform. Such a pessimistic representation of the penal policy and prisons literature from this decade, however, risks obscuring the multiple ways in which scholars, activists, and prisoners sought to reform or even abolish imprisonment. For the 1970s was a decade marked by energetic and perhaps still unrealized interventions across all sorts of arenas. In criminology generally, Marxist scholars like Richard Quinney (1978, 1979) and Jeffrey Reiman (1979) mounted a sustained critique of the administration of justice, from the police to the prison. The problem, as Reiman (1979) deftly articulated it in his book title, was that the U.S. had become a nation where "the rich get richer and the poor get prison."

Whereas today such radical scholarship is limited to publication in specialist journals like *Critical Criminology* and *Social Justice,* at the time, such authors and other critical commentators appeared regularly in the pages of the mainstream academic journals, including *Criminology, Justice Quarterly,* and *Crime and Delinquency* (see, for example, Bloomberg, 1977; Fairchild, 1977). *Criminology* even dedicated an entire issue to questions about Marxism and the insights of the "new criminology" in 1979 (Quinney, 1979; Toby, 1979).[10] In addition to regular discussions of the political economy of punishment and the relationship between economic deprivation and offending in journals, a steady stream of critical books on prisons were published in the 1970s. Such books ranged in topic from accounts of prisoner protest to prison architecture and inmate unions (see, inter alia, Atkins & Glick, 1972; Nagel, 1973; Berkman, 1979).

In fact, throughout the 1970s, the prison came under sustained and diverse critique from scholars working in a variety of disciplines from psychology to history and philosophy (Haney, Banks, & Zimbardo, 1973; Morris, 1974; Foucault, 1995; Rothman, 1971; Ignatieff, 1978). Moreover, unlike today, many of the academics in question were also active participants in penal reform and in radical prisoners' rights groups.[11] As we have already seen, political prisoners published book-length autobiographies and reached out in radical periodicals and the popular press (Davis, 1974; Shakur, 1978). At this time, too, inmate newspapers flourished in prisons and, on occasion, beyond the prison walls to capture public attention. The best known of these kinds of publications, which is still in production, is the award-winning magazine from Louisiana's State Penitentiary, *The Angolite*. Unlike so many other prison newspapers—such as *The San Quentin* from California, *Joint Endeavor* from Texas, and *The Coming Dawn* from Arizona—which have long since been discontinued, *The Angolite* attained national coverage and notoriety that secured the journal's future. Wilbert Rideau, who was appointed editor in 1976, wrote for many years a column entitled "The Jungle," for which he has received numerous accolades. Much of what he described in it about life behind bars echoes the findings of the prison sociologists discussed in Chapter 3. Life in Angola, according to Rideau, shifted between inmate solidarity and fragmentation. In 1975, for example, Rideau described prisoners and staff working together to rescue inmates from a fire, and for a moment at least, overcoming their institutional(ized) differences. "The crisis over," he wrote, "everyone went their separate ways, resuming their former roles: white and black, powerful and powerless, guard and prisoner, friends and enemies, and so on" (Rideau, 1975).

The violence of life in prison was a constant theme of the newspaper and of Rideau's writing in general, as was the debilitating effect of the prisoners' lack of choice. The inherent constraints of life behind bars intertwine, with the paternalism of prison rules intermingling with the pressures of solitude, to foster fear, frustration, and anger. He reports,

> In prison every day ends the same way—with a key being turned in a door, locking me in for the night. Then we're counted, like things. And a little later

> the lights are cut off and we're sent to bed, like children. As the night creeps slowly by, it gets quieter and quieter. Apprehension hangs heavily in the air, inmates dreading the minutes or hours of solitude before the peace of sleep. This is the hardest time of the day. This is when the walls seem to be closing in on you. During the day, there's work, intrigues, and a thousand little things that keep you moving, stirring, your mind occupied. But at night, there's nothing but the silence . . . and your thoughts. (Rideau, 1978)

Unable to sleep, he writes longingly of his desire to

> . . . quit this ultramasculine jungle, this barbaric dog-eat-dog world where men are deprived of every human need save hunger and thirst, this place where ruthlessness is the rule and mercy, the exception, this vacuum totally devoid of love, charity, brotherhood, beauty, and all of the other things that others take for granted but which are so important to us starved for them. (Rideau, 1978)

Such violence was not always directed at others; prisoners harmed themselves as well. Rarely mentioned outside the medical literature, suicide and self-harm provided the focus of the 1978 July/August edition of *The Angolite*. In it, articles discussed the everyday strains and pressures of life behind bars, concluding bleakly that "any prisoner who has been confined any length of time, has seen his share of death . . . and death in the world behind bars is hideous" (Rideau, 1978).

The everyday and universal causes of the brutality and suffering depicted by Rideau and other inmate authors were dramatically demonstrated in 1971 in the Stanford prison experiment. Fated to become a study piece for American undergraduate sociology students for decades to come, this experiment suggested that incarceration altered not just the character of those in custody but, somewhat alarmingly, also those who kept them. The planned two-week experiment, where graduate students role-played prison guards and prisoners, had to be called off after only six days when the academic coordinators

> . . . witnessed a sample of normal, healthy American college students fractionate [sic] into a group of prison guards who seemed to derive pleasure from insulting, threatening, humiliating and dehumanizing their peers . . . the typical prisoner syndrome was one of passivity, dependency, depression, helplessness and self-deprecation. (Haney, Banks, & Zimbardo, 1973, p. 89)

Insisting that their experiment should be interpreted as a warning about the dangers of power relations in prisons, the authors explicitly linked their study to matters of real-world penal administration. "Shortly after our study was terminated," they observed, "the indiscriminate killings at San Quentin and Attica occurred, emphasizing the urgency for prison reforms that recognize the dignity and humanity of both prisoners and guards who are constantly forced into one of the most intimate and potentially deadly encounters known to man" (Haney, Banks, & Zimbardo, 1973, p. 97).

Another influential text from this decade came from well beyond the social sciences. Michel Foucault's *Discipline and Punish,* originally published in France in 1975, was translated into English in 1977 to great acclaim. In it, Foucault argued that modern forms of treatment were not, as was usually assumed, more enlightened or humane than previous means of dealing with offenders. Instead, they had become more efficient strategies of control. Punishment, he claimed, had simply moved from targeting the body to targeting the mind. Rather than minimizing harm, in his view, prison reformers helped reinscribe the prison in the contemporary landscape. "For a century and a half, the prison had always been offered as its own remedy: the reactivation of the penitentiary techniques as the only means of overcoming their perpetual failure; the realization of the corrective project as the only method of overcoming the impossibility of implementing it" (Foucault, 1977, p. 268). Most provocatively, he asserted, the prison ". . . is not intended to eliminate offences, but rather to distinguish them, to distribute them, to use them" (Foucault, 1977, p. 272).

Foucault's writings continue to be picked over in theoretical discussions of punishment (see for example, Garland, 1990). At the time, however, his work was just one of a number of historical accounts that critically reexamined aspects of the criminal justice and social welfare systems. David Rothman (1971), for example, sketched the failures and disappointments of those who sought to reform the treatment of the mentally ill from the 1820s, while Tony Platt (1969) analyzed the motivations for the "child-saving" movement of the 19th century, which led to the juvenile justice system. So, too, Jacques Donzelot (1979) pessimistically argued that the origins of social welfare systems lay predominantly in a bid to control the poor. Uniting such accounts lay a staunch critique of the paternalist agents of welfare. As Platt (1977) put it in a new preface to the second edition of his book, the

> . . . child-saving movement was not a humanistic enterprise on behalf of the working class against the established order. On the contrary, its impetus came primarily from the middle and upper classes who were instrumental in devising new forms of social control to protect their power and privilege. (Platt, 1977, p. xx)

Prisons and their cognate institutions, whatever the intentions of their administrators or reformers, were powerful mechanisms of enforcing a particular class-based view of social order. Given their imbrications with political elites, such places revealed a necessary relationship between social exclusion (of some) and democracy (for the rest). In a decade like the 1970s, with an organized, racialized, prison-based activism, the reliance of the state on its power to punish was, albeit somewhat briefly, drawn into question.

CONCLUSION

The early 1970s began with great promise in U.S. prisons. Though state violence against prisoners and in prisons was common, the public and the courts had finally become concerned. Starting with the outcry over the shooting of George Jackson at Soledad Prison in August 1971, followed quickly by the abhorrence at the state shootings at Attica, it seemed that the legitimacy of the penal powers was under question. Over the coming years, however, penologists and activists were unable to capitalize on this outrage and, instead, witnessed, and in some cases facilitated, a seismic shift in punitive values from a concern with penal reform to one of punitive deterrence.

The 1980s, which began in prison terms with the bloody riot at New Mexico State Penitentiary, quickly followed by a harsh federal response to the perceived threat posed by the mass exodus from Cuba that became known as the Mariel boatlift (Hamm, 1995), ended with a skyrocketing prison population. Aided and abetted by the Reagan administration's campaign against so-called street crime and drug offenses, such punitive sentiments were, in many cases, nourished by thinly disguised and ill-informed racial animosity. As Chapter 5 will demonstrate, the failures of the 1970s, in combination with the ideologies of the 1980s, created a system that the U.S. is saddled with today.

NOTES

1. The killing of prisoner activist and author George Jackson earlier in 1971 was also a crucial event for prison organizing in the U.S., and is typically understood as a determining factor in the timing of the Attica Rebellion.

2. In contrast, in 1999, a special issue of the *Albuquerque Journal*, designed to address the "social dilemmas" of New Mexico in order to help "determine our future well into 2000 and beyond," lists the 1980 riot as a "black mark on the state's history." Though he describes it as "a rebellion without a plan, without leadership and without goals," the author apportions

blame, at least in part, on the overcrowding, inconsistent prison policies, and prisoner abuse, which, he says, were found by the attorney general's office to have characterized the institution (Gallagher, 1999). Such a critical analysis, closer in tone to those accounts of Attica, did not appear in the mainstream national press at the time of the riot itself.

3. In his assessment of California's radical prison movement, Eric Cummins (1994) suggests that in his lifetime and beyond, Jackson may have been manipulated by the "mythology" surrounding him (though see Bernstein, 2007, for a more sympathetic account of Jackson's politicization and actions in prison). To a great extent, the "real" motivation, experience, and sincerity of any of the prison activists can never be accurately assessed. In any case, such an individualizing of the reform movement would oversimplify the cause and effect of social change. Activist accounts are not to be viewed as some kind of sacrosanct vision, in other words, but rather as texts like any other, which not only capture aspects of the spirit of the times but which were, and remain, influential public documents in the ongoing debate over imprisonment.

4. As indeed, and despite the 2005 Supreme Court ruling in *Johnson v. California* (2005) the State of California continued to do in some form in 2008 (Trulson et al., 2008; Goodman, 2008).

5. Citing an interview with Governor Reagan in the *San Francisco Chronicle* from 1970, Eric Cummins (1994) observes that, at the time of her arrest, "Davis had recently been fired from her post as a philosophy instructor at UCLA by the UC regents at the special urging of Governor Reagan for being 'a member of the Communist Party'" (Cummins, 1994, p. 184).

6. The LEAA was also instrumental in funding and establishing a number of criminal justice programs around the country, to train future criminal justice practitioners, shaping not just penal administration but also scholarly accounts of the justice system.

7. The Supreme Court voted first to suspend executions in 1972 (*Furman v. Georgia*, 408 U.S. 238 [1972]) for being arbitrary, only to reinstate the death penalty in 1976 and then to outlaw it as a penalty for adult rape in 1977 (*Coker v. Georgia*, 433 U.S. 585 [1977]).

8. On November 3, 1979, for example, White supremacists attacked and killed five demonstrators, wounding 10 others, in Greensboro, North Carolina's Black Morningside Homes public housing community in a rally against racism organized by the Communist Workers Party. In 2006, in recognition of the deep wounds caused by these killings, Greensboro City held a "Truth and Reconciliation Project" to try to resolve continuing problems in their community (www.greensborotrc.org).

9. Even though Adler's assertion was demonstrated by a number of authors to be incorrect, it retained its hold on criminological imagination for some time (Steffensmeier & Steffensmeier, 1980; Chesney-Lind & Rodriguez, 1983).

10. Though later criticized by William Chambliss in his Presidential address to the American Society of Criminology (1989) for its biased depiction of Marxist theory, this special issue did place some of the questions about political economy and economic disadvantage at the center of criminological discussion. Chambliss may have been particularly irritated by Jackson Toby's essay, which began by accusing radical criminologists for drawing ". . . upon an old tradition of sentimentality toward those who break social rules" (Toby, 1979, p. 516).

11. David Rothman, for example, was a member of the von Hirsch (1976) committee. Tony Platt took part in demonstrations on the Berkeley campus and subsequently lost his job when the Berkeley criminology department was disbanded, never to be reestablished. Even Foucault worked for the prisoners' rights group GIP in France.

Five

The Punitive Turn

Laying the Foundations for Mass Imprisonment

[The] rise in crime, caused by a hardened criminal class, was fostered partly from a liberal social philosophy that too often called for lenient treatment of criminals. Because this misguided social philosophy saw man as primarily the creature of his material environment, it thought that through expensive government social programs it could change that environment and usher in a great new egalitarian utopia. And yet even while government was launching a rash of social engineering schemes in a vain attempt to remake man and society, it wasn't dealing with the most elementary social problems like rising crime.

—Ronald Reagan, June 20, 1984

Prisons are no more likely to fail than are schools, armies, state hospitals, regulatory agencies, or other important public organizations. If most prisons have failed, it is because they have been ill-managed, under-managed, or not managed at all.

—DiIulio, 1987, pp. 6–7

. . . prison is tearing me up inside. It hurts every day. Every day it takes me further from my life. And I am not even conscious of how my dissolution is coming about. Therefore, I cannot stop it.

—Abbott, 1981, pp. 4–5

The 1980s were a watershed decade for criminal justice and for the nature and justification of imprisonment in the U.S. In 1982, President Ronald Reagan declared a War on Drugs that profoundly altered policing practices and sentencing policy. As a direct result, penal populations soared. Now rehabilitation was abandoned in most states and the federal system as the primary goal of punishment, in favor of ". . . a 'balanced' model of corrections that emphasized instead the 'co-equal' goals of punishment, deterrence and incapacitation" (Roberts, 1994, p. 13). Overcrowding led to a prison boom, and a number of states began to hand over responsibility for running their jails and prisons to private companies for the first time since the 1920s.

In terms of demographics, the 1980s was also a decade of change in the prison population. Not only did the number of minorities behind bars grow rapidly—culminating in 1989, when Black prisoners outnumbered Whites for the first time—but so, too, did the numbers of women in prison. Changes in sentencing practices also brought increased numbers of juveniles into the adult prison system. This era, which began with activist courts seeking to ameliorate prison conditions, ended with greatly reduced federal judicial oversight of state practice.

Although penal activists and reformers continued to operate in this period, academic scholarship on incarceration weakened, as mainstream criminologists became preoccupied with the causes of crime and policing. In particular, few scholars conducted large-scale qualitative research, concentrating on more easily quantifiable information that was often farmed out to them by the prison administration or the government itself in the form of large-scale data sets. Despite some notable exceptions to this drift from in-depth studies of incarceration, particularly in the feminist accounts of the historical development of women's prisons (Rafter, 1985) and the gendered nature of life behind bars (Chesney-Lind, 1986; Chesney-Lind & Rodriguez, 1983), for the most part U.S. criminology turned its back on the incarcerated (Simon, 2000b; Wacquant, 2002). So too, outside the women's literature, influential accounts of life behind bars that were produced at this time sided decisively with the penal administrators, characterizing prisoners as predators and control problems for management (see, for example, DiIulio, 1987; Fleisher, 1989).

Whereas the rhetoric and ideologies of previous historical periods reported so far in this book often now seem quaint, outlandish, utopian, or simply naïve, ideas spawned in the 1980s, if nothing else, usually make for familiar reading. Ideas and idioms that remain in use today, such as "zero tolerance," "broken windows," "get tough," "just say no," "mandatory minimum sentences," and "truth-in-sentencing" date from this period. Central to the War on Drugs—another powerful phrase from the 1980s—other images and terminology were coined that reflected the gendered nature of this policy, and its underlying racism. Frequent terms include the "crack baby," the "crack whore," and the "welfare queen." Likewise, the idea of the "underclass," as an undeserving, urban, Black population of the poor, although predating the Reagan period, also attained widespread popularity from this time in both the media and in the (left- and right-wing) scholarly and government literature (Katz, 1993; Murray, 1984; Wilson, W., 1987). Finally, the notion of victims' "rights" and the field of study known as "victimology," both of which have been harnessed for a range of political expedients and aims, first appeared in this decade (Gottfredson, 1981; Karmen, 1990; Mawby & Walkate, 1994).

That such a wide vocabulary was born in the relatively brief period of the mid-1980s speaks to the radical conservatism and the cultural productivity of that time. That they remain in current use suggests that they continue to structure the collective American imagination about crime and punishment. What might explain their enduring effect?

The Reagan Years

Most accounts of the 1980s describe it as a major break with the past in social, economic, political, and cultural terms (Garland, 2001a; Beckett, 1997). It would be wrong to place all the blame for popular punitivism at the door of a particular presidential administration, since a number of Democrats, including then Senator Joe Biden and Representative Charles Rangel from New York City, criticized Reagan for not tackling crime or drugs enthusiastically enough (*The New York Times,* 1981, 1982). Nonetheless it is fair to say that Ronald Reagan facilitated and then reaped the electoral benefits of penal populism. Rejecting the social and cultural ideals of the New Deal and of the Democratic administration of President Jimmy Carter that preceded him, Reagan sought to reduce government intervention, spending, and controls. His domestic policies were characterized by tax cuts, fiscal deregulation, and a new federalism that reduced funding to the states, and, in principle at least, increased their autonomy to self-govern (Palmer & Sawhill, 1982).

Criminal justice policies stood in notable contrast to most of these changes. Rather than reducing controls over individuals, much of the legislation passed by Congress radically expanded government surveillance, curbed judicial discretion, and strengthened punishment.

Policies also increased federal interests into what had previously been predominantly understood as state matters. At the same time as the doctrine of neoliberalism enjoined individuals to take responsibility for their own health, welfare, and economic security, the federal government promoted harsh, authoritarian government sanctions for those deemed to have broken the law.

In terms of the criminal justice system, Reagan had inherited a nation of prisons in disarray and a society experiencing a dramatic rise in violent and street crime. In 1982, 29 states were "operating either individual institutions or entire prison systems under orders from Federal judges who found conditions in jails or prisons so intolerable as to be unconstitutional" (Rawls, 1982, A1; see also DiIulio, 1990). The national imprisonment rate had hit a 50-year low in 1972, yet a spike in crime in the 1970s had seriously undermined institutional efforts to house offenders, and, by the end of the decade, most penal systems were overcrowded and many were rocked by prisoner unrest. Confronted with this deepening problem, the experts were at a loss. No longer convinced by the promises of rehabilitation (Allen, 1981), scholars, prisoners, and practitioners were searching for a justification for penal practice. Something, clearly, had to be done. But what?

The answer, it seemed, was nothing less than a wholesale readjustment of social expectations and beliefs about crime and punishment, in concert with significant alterations to sentencing practices and conditions of confinement. Officially abandoning rehabilitation as the primary goal of punishment, most states and the federal government now sought to toughen and rigidify criminal justice legislation and policy. In this newly punitive approach to lawbreaking, both the prison and the victim played crucial roles.

The shift in expectations of punishment, and by association of the prison, was a direct effect of the growing concern about visibly racialized forms of street and violent crime. Politicians, academics, and policymakers alike called for harsher sentences for those (predominantly minority youth) who committed such offenses and advocated increased policing of public places and an enhanced concentration on social order (Kelling & Wilson, 1982; Wilson, J., 1983a, 1983b). The rising spirit of the 1980s championed deterrence (Wilson, J., 1983a), selective incapacitation (Cohen, 1983), and new forms of policing that prioritized fixing "broken windows" (Kelling & Wilson, 1982, 1989). In this view, the rehabilitative nature of the prison was drawn into question; convicts were not entitled to individual treatment and reform. Instead, penal institutions became reimagined as society's bulwarks against the selfish, the dangerous, the drug-addicted, and the evil. Inmates, it was asserted, needed strict surveillance and authoritarian rules, not more rights or freedom of expression, in order to persuade them to change their ways (DiIulio, 1987). No longer treatable patients, but "enemies" in a nation at war with itself, they deserved punishment and could only benefit from strict rules and regulations.

In a parallel move that was part of this rhetorical and policy strategy, the debate on crime shifted ground, as politicians and academics began, for the first time in any serious fashion, to concentrate on victims of crime. Announcing on April 8, 1981, that ". . . we need a renewed emphasis on and enhanced sensitivity to the rights of victims," President Reagan established the first national "victims' rights week" and set up a presidential task force on victims of crime. Taking on board most of the suggestions of this body as articulated in its 1982 *Final Report,* the federal government opened the Office for Victims of Crime in 1983, within the Department of Justice.

Whereas previous administrations, most notably that of Lyndon Johnson, had used similar task forces to explore and attempt to address the societal causes of crime and disorder, the Reagan administration, enthusiastically backed by the populist press and cable television news, concentrated instead on the issue of those affected by crime. Recasting the causes of crime from society to the individual, this strategy changed people's expectations about punishment and justice (Wilson, J., 1983b; Beckett, 1997). In the process, the prison and the criminal justice system legitimated, and intertwined with, other economic and social changes that withdrew large-scale government aid in favor of decentralized, smaller governance. Now it all depended on you! Individuals who failed to succeed in this new regime were then effectively deemed responsible for their own difficulties.

Yet, while conventional wisdom has it that the Reagan administration pioneered a new form of populism in which experts were replaced by political pundits, and public opinion polls began to determine and justify policy (Dallek, 1999), others have convincingly argued that what was actually occurring in this period was the successful and ruthless engineering of public opinion. Before polls and pundits could be harnessed, public opinion had to be not only gauged, but also shaped (Young & Perkins, 2005). Evidence suggests that, particularly in relation to matters of crime and punishment, popular feelings were deliberately overstated to legitimate ever harsher policies. Indeed, although the federal government claimed, in developing punitive policies, to be responding to public concerns over crime, particularly in regard to drug offenses, Katherine Beckett (1997) details numerous public opinion surveys from the late 1970s and early 1980s that indicated an ongoing belief in the socioeconomic causes of crime, as well as a general lack of concern over drugs. According to her findings, it was not until after Congress had passed the antidrug legislation that such opinions began to change. Since then, crime has rarely been "off the political agenda," as the phrase goes, and, in the "new bipartisan consensus," all politicians shy away from being labeled as "soft on crime—a failure to talk tough on crime [has become] akin to political suicide" (Newburn & Jones, 2005, p. 74).

So, how was this sea change in popular opinion effected? First, evidence suggests that the public was, to some extent, already receptive to at least some of these ideas. They fell, in other words, on fertile soil. Matters of "crime" and "punishment" also proved to be particularly effective means of governance. Reagan (and subsequent administrations), with punitive rhetoric and frequent iterations of virtuous victims, served to divide communities from themselves and to reentrench forms of intolerance and fear that the New Deal, the Civil Rights Movement, and the welfare reforms of the 1960s and 1970s had sought to overturn.

Equally important was the role played by a growing number of conservative academics, intellectuals, and public figures. In partial response to the decline in the rehabilitative ideal and also in light of the lessening support for Marxist theory within academia, politically conservative scholars became more influential in the late 1970s and 1980s than ever before. In criminology, proponents of rational choice theories of crime became dominant. Authors like Marcus Felson and Ronald V. Clark stressed the situational nature of crime rather than its sociological component, effectively depoliticizing accounts of lawbreaking (Cohen & Felson, 1979; Clark, 1983), while work by James Q. Wilson (1981) and George Kelling on "broken windows" altered policing practices, drawing them away from traditional methods of control to a new focus on street crime and lower-level nuisance activities. In turn, John DiIulio (1987, 1990) transplanted such authoritarian views into prison studies.

Finally, there was the growing impact of the media. More effectively than the prisoners and their reformers, not to mention his political opponents, Reagan was quick to realize the potential of harnessing the press and television, both in his election campaigns and in his daily governance. In doing so, complex matters were grossly oversimplified into marketable sound bites. In an address to the nation broadcast from the Rose Garden on October 2, 1982, Reagan declared War on Drugs. Making his case sound deceptively simple, he said: "Drugs are bad, and we're going after them . . . we've taken down the surrender flag and run up the battle flag. And we're going to win the War on Drugs" (Reagan, 1982). Such rhetoric guilelessly constructed the issue as one of good versus evil, thereby effectively depersonalizing and decontextualizing it. Referring, in the same speech, to drugs as "an especially vicious virus of crime," Reagan creatively deployed a medical metaphor to demonize this activity and thereby effectively redefined the relationship between drug use and health that had characterized previous administrations. In this redeployment of therapeutic terminology, drug use became a problem of morality and individual responsibility, as well as one of "good guys" versus "bad guys." Society must indeed "treat" the "virus" but, because of its "viciousness," the audience was warned that the medicine would not be pleasant. Government intervention will be harsh, this statement implies, but any actions it that takes will be necessary to safeguard the health and well-being of the majority. The needs of the virtuous "silent majority" had to be favored above those of recalcitrant and malign minorities.

While earlier presidents such as Johnson and Nixon had adopted the language of war in their crime and poverty policies and thus in their legitimation of state intervention (and imprisonment), the Reagan administration proved to be particularly effective in popularizing this terminology. Indeed, such combative rhetoric and terminology soon came to characterize most public denunciations of crime. Democratic Senator Joe Biden's critique of Reagan's crime policies drew from a similar source. For Biden, Reagan was insufficiently stern. "Violent crime is as real a threat to our national security as any foreign threat and combating this crime must be as high a priority" (*The New York Times*, 1982, p. A14). (Biden, who at the time of writing is vice president, was to play a crucial role in drafting the Clinton administration's Violent Crime Control Act over a decade later, further entrenching police powers and a reliance on the prison.) Criminals, in this view, fall outside the national polity, and are fundamentally dangerous.

Various explanations exist for the growth of penal populism at this time—from the impact of an inexorably expanding popular media to a growing disenchantment with urban living. While the root causes may be hard to disentangle, what is clear is that the very act of declaring a "war" (whether on drugs, crime, poverty, or more recently on terror) justified (and continues to drive) large-scale government spending and intervention into the lives of certain sections of the community. By defining social problems as ones with bad enemies and good victims, the reference to war destabilized the usual conservative commitment to small government, reduced spending, and cautioned about change, often at the same moment when other forms of government spending on welfare, health, and education were being restricted. More than simply enhancing state control, the language of war rhetorically enhances the dangers of the social problem under fire, and ennobles those who are implementing the social policy. Strangely, too, defining state intervention as a "war" dissociates the individual (in this case the president) from responsibility for ameliorating the social problem. It is only Congress, after all, that can declare war, and they do so only to protect the wider society. The language of war indeed makes conservatives radical.

Although the primary battleground in the War on Drugs was on the streets, the prison occupied an important site in the conflict. As in earlier battles, it functioned as an adjunct, facilitating the broader conflict through housing the (enemy) combatants once they were caught. Morally, too, the prison reaffirmed the need for war, by identifying those within its walls as opponents to the law-abiding majority. Finally, the prison held a front-line place in allegedly protecting those victims of crime, on whose behalf the war was (and continues to be) waged.

The economic dislocation of the 1970s, coupled with the rapid social transformations of the Civil Rights Movement, the women's movement, and the anti–Vietnam War movement, had destabilized, alienated, and alarmed large sections of U.S. society. Despite a lingering concern for matters of social welfare, there was a growing disquiet over issues to do with race and gender, as well as real economic deprivation. In particular, sections of lower-middle-class White America were concerned that Blacks, Hispanics, and Native Americans were being unfairly advantaged. This fear, which, in the Northern states, was evidenced in patterns of urban emigration to the suburbs ("White flight") and, in the South, by more direct and organized racist activity, was easily co-opted into a new, more generalized fear of crime and penal populism that, in turn, relied on an identification with the victim. Offenders were presented in presidential pronouncements and in the media as wicked and deserving of punishment, while society and the victims of crime became the innocent bystanders, in need of protection. In the first year of Reagan's regime, for example, May 1, traditionally that day of trade union celebration, was redesignated "Law Day, U.S.A." Commenting on this decision, then Vice President George Herbert W. Bush (1981) declared on April 6 that ". . . the rule of law represents the civil discourse of a free people. Violent crime is the uncivilized shout that threatens to drown out and ultimately silence the language of liberty." Just two days later, the president himself spoke on the matter, urging "all citizens, from all walks of life, to remember that the personal tragedy of the victim is their own tragedy as well" (Reagan, 1981).

In this narrative, victims became stand-ins for the moral majority, and offenders were reimagined as their opposite. Representative of an approach dubbed by David Garland as "criminology of the other," whereby offenders became viewed as "the threatening outcast, the excluded and the embittered" (Garland, 2001a, p. 137), an ostensibly benign concern for victims inexorably led to increasing punitiveness and a growing intolerance of difference. The offender, in this view, is monstrous and threatening. As Reagan himself put it in the most graphic of terms, suggestive of his own background in movies, the criminal offender is "a stark, staring face—a face that belongs to a frightening reality of our time: the face of the human predator . . . Nothing in nature is more cruel or more dangerous . . ." (Reagan, quoted in Beckett, 1997, p. 47).

Continually referring to victims as "innocent citizens," in contrast to their bestial assailants, who, by implication, were no longer entitled to be full members of the community, Republicans and their supporters promoted a conservative move away from earlier, sociological explanations of crime and, in the process, championed a retributive approach to punishment and imprisonment. Thus, in a presentation to the National Sheriffs Association in Hartford, Connecticut, on June 20, 1984, Reagan scornfully said:

> Individual wrongdoing, they [liberals] told us, was always caused by a lack of material goods, an underprivileged background, or poor socioeconomic conditions. And somehow, and I know you've heard it said—I heard it many times when I was governor of California—it was society, not the individual, that was at fault when an act of violence or a crime was committed. Somehow, it wasn't the wrongdoer but all of us who were to blame. (Reagan, 1984)

No longer were poverty or social exclusion considered relevant, but rather individual responsibility and personal morality explained people's activities. Through such rhetoric, the Republican administration successfully diminished "its duty to provide for the social welfare" while expanding "its capacity and obligation to maintain social control" (Beckett, 1997, p. 10). Crime and punishment, in other words, were used to demonize certain sections of the population—drug users, Blacks, the urban poor—and valorize others: victims.

Legislating Punishment

The expansion of the prison population was not, however, merely an effect of culture or sentiment. Rather, it was an inevitable result of legislation and widespread policy changes in the broader criminal justice system that accompanied such rhetoric at the state and federal levels. In contrast to the Civil Rights of Institutionalized Persons Act (CRIPA), 42 U.S.C. § 1997, which President Carter signed into law in 1980, this decade was characterized by punitive criminal justice–related legislation at the state and federal levels. If CRIPA extended constitutional safeguards and monitoring to all incarcerated persons, including those in jail and prison, by establishing a monitoring mechanism for life behind bars, most of the acts passed subsequently worsened prison conditions by lengthening sentences and sweeping new populations behind bars.

Starting with the Sentencing Reform Act passed in Washington State in 1981 and quickly followed at the federal level by the passage of the 1984 Sentencing Reform Act as part of the Comprehensive Crime Control Act (P.L. 98–473), lawmakers around the country called into question the use of indeterminate sentencing. Driven by diverse and sometimes conflicting beliefs, advocates of sentencing reform sought to ensure that offenders who committed similar offenses received similar punishments. Though on the face of it somewhat unrelated to the prison itself, the newfound anxiety over indeterminate sentencing sprang from widespread concerns over the failure of rehabilitation.

The Comprehensive Crime Control Act overhauled the federal sentencing system, revised bail and forfeiture procedures, and set up the Office of Justice Programs (OJP), which, among its other activities, coordinated the activities of the various research wings of the Bureau of Justice, including the National Institute of Justice and the Bureau of Justice Statistics. The OJP was also given responsibility to administer federal grants to state anticrime efforts. Judges were directed to determine the pretrial detention of individuals based on their purported menace to the community, while federal law enforcement agents were encouraged to confiscate profits and instruments of illegal activity by being allowed to retain proceedings from their actions, rather than having to deposit them in the general fund of the U.S. Treasury, as had previously been the practice. Perhaps not surprisingly, the number of forfeitures rose dramatically, and policing became more aggressive and proactive thereafter.

All parts of the Comprehensive Crime Control Act were significant, but it was the Sentencing Reform Act of 1984 (P.L. 98–473) that had the most dramatic and wide-ranging effect on the nation's penal institutions. This Act created the U.S. Sentencing Commission that, in turn, established the U.S. Sentencing Guidelines. The guidelines took effect on November 1, 1987, and radically changed the nature of sentencing and imprisonment.

The federal sentencing guidelines set out a detailed framework that was held to be mandatory, until the 2005 Supreme Court case of *United States v. Booker* recast them as advisory. For two decades, federal judges, as well as those in many states, were prevented from wielding discretion in determining the response in a case, and were directed instead to follow a fixed grid designed to ensure that they treated all similar crimes the same way.[1] This approach replaced the earlier model of indeterminate sentencing with a so-called "truth in sentencing" approach that, in turn, set out mandatory minimum sentences for a range of crimes. However unintentionally—and members of the Sentencing Commission appear not to have foreseen this result at the time—the guidelines not only withdrew judicial discretion, but they also hardened punitive practice. Many previous sentences of probation were replaced with imprisonment, and sentences overall became longer. Finally, the guidelines also effectively ended parole in the federal system, by requiring offenders to serve their full sentences, minus at best approximately 15 percent time off for good behavior.

Taken together, these policy changes led to an increase in the imprisonment rate and a lengthening of federal sentences. Before the implementation of the act, for example, average federal offenders completed 58 percent of their sentences; after 1987, they served (and continue to serve) 85 percent. When translated into time behind bars, this shift meant that the period that an individual would remain incarcerated in an average 39-month sentence grew from 21 to 34 months (Sabol & McGready, 1999). In the federal system, between 1986 and 1999, prison terms increased from an average of 62 to 74 months, while in the same years, the average time prisoners served more than doubled from 30 to 66 months (Scalia, 2001). Such developments have placed enormous strains on the federal prison system, which it has been unable to manage. Hence, despite contracting out an increasing number of their facilities to private companies and placing some inmates in state prisons, the federal prison system has been operating with an overcrowding rate of around 40 percent for some time (Harrison & Beck, 2005).

In 1986, Congress passed another major piece of legislation that altered the penal landscape in the form of the Anti-Drug Abuse Act (P.L. 99–570). This legislation, which signaled the opening of a new front in the War on

Drugs, increased prison sentences for the sale and possession of drugs, eliminated probation or parole for certain offenders, increased fines, and provided for the forfeiture of assets. As with the eradication of parole, although it began as a series of federal initiatives, states soon took up the antidrug crusade, writing tougher drug laws and imposing stiffer penalties for their violation. At the same time, local law enforcement agencies, whose members were already being encouraged to focus on "street crime," were directed to target low-level street dealers.

The 1986 Anti-Drug Abuse Act notoriously introduced radically disparate treatments for crack and powder cocaine. The resulting legislation, enshrined in the U.S. criminal code (21 USC §841(b)(1)), set up a 100:1 degree of difference between the amounts of crack and powder cocaine that would trigger mandatory minimum sentences. Thus, for a first-time cocaine trafficking offense, an individual in possession of 5 grams of crack was treated the same as someone found in possession of 500 grams of powder cocaine; both would receive a minimum five-year sentence. Likewise, a minimum 10-year sentence without parole was provided for participating in the manufacture, distribution, or conspiracy to manufacture or distribute 500 grams of crack cocaine, in comparison with the same sentence for those found in possession of 5 kilograms of powder cocaine. Despite plentiful scientific evidence that demonstrates no significant difference between the pharmacological effects of powder and crack cocaine, and irrespective of public dissent, critical government reports, academic research, and growing numbers of organizations lobbying the government against the sentencing differential, the 1986 act was not successfully challenged until 2007 (see, for example, Logan, 1999; Sentencing Project, 1998). Finally listening to advice from the Sentencing Commission, from November 1, 2007, Congress amended the 1986 act to reduce the differential, yielding sentences for crack offenses between two and five times longer than sentences for equal amounts of powder. Later that same year, the Supreme Court ruled in *Kimbrough v. United States* that, as in *United States v. Booker,* the sentencing guidelines on drugs could only be advisory rather than mandatory. While some people in prison have benefited from this ruling, scores of others remain serving lengthy sentences for drug possession.

The impact of drug legislation on the prison population was dramatic and immediate. By 1989, after Congress passed another Anti-Drug Abuse Act, state prisons held over 120,000 individuals convicted of drug offenses, more than double the number that had been contained at the beginning of the decade. Likewise, in the federal system the number of individuals serving time for drug offenses more than doubled between 1984 (11,854) and 1989 (29,306). Crucially, their sentences lengthened as well, as changes to federal sentencing guidelines came into effect, and individuals were subject to stringent mandatory minimum terms (Scalia, 2001).

The differential for crack and powder cocaine, as well as the toughened sentences overall, did not merely cause an increase in the prison population, it fundamentally changed the nature of who was incarcerated. Specifically, these pieces of legislation adversely affected minority communities, notably African Americans but also Hispanics. The greater availability and lower price of crack cocaine in urban America, in addition to altered policing practices that targeted street crime and street users, drove large numbers of minority women and men into the nation's prisons. These individuals, who were often serving long prison sentences at a fairly young age, brought with them a host of new viewpoints, experiences, and needs that strained prison relationships and resources. The connection between these issues and the War on Drugs is not always entirely clear, but evidence suggests that the new drug enforcement policies either coincided with, or indeed caused, an upsurge in prison gang membership, as well as the first known cases of human immunodeficiency virus/acquired immunodeficiency syndrome (HIV/AIDS) behind bars. By choosing incarceration over treatment as its favored response for drug use, particularly for those addicted to crack, this legislation and the policing practices that accompanied it unleashed a seemingly unlimited expansion in the prison population, the effects of which continue to shape U.S. prisons today.

Individuals sentenced under the new legislation, particularly those who had been using crack cocaine, were more likely to have been homeless before their incarceration, to have experienced high levels of violence, and, if female, to have exchanged sex for money (Cotton-Oldenburg, Jordan, Martin, & Kupper, 1999; Cohen and Stahler, 1998; Richie, 1995; Maher, 2000). They arrived, in sum, with endemic mental and physical health problems. Drawn from the ranks of the poor, they left behind them fractured families, meaning an upsurge of children in foster care or living with a sole parent or grandparent. The disruption of so many families was accompanied by racialized vilification of single mothers and the children of offenders (Gottfredson and Hirschi, 1990; Herrnstein & Murray, 1994).

The War on Drugs had a particularly pernicious and enduring effect on African American women and Latinas. Not only did their numbers in prison skyrocket but, following a moral panic over so-called "crack babies," many became subject to stringent control over their reproductive freedoms, facing prison terms, forced sterilization, and other punishments (Logan, 1999; Flavin, 2008). To take just one example, an article that appeared in November 1986 in *The New York Times* captures how drug-using women were demonized and racialized. In an account of the "recent explosive increase in the number of abandoned and drug-abused babies," the newspaper opens with a moving description of "Baby L., barely 2 months old" who "frets until a nurse comes to his Plexiglas bassinet and props him up with her hand. His skin, a variegated brown, is dry. His brown eyes, like saucers, lock into those of his rescuer, refusing to notice anyone else for fear he'll lose her attention" (*The New York Times*, 1986, p. 217).

As Logan critically observes, this image of "trembling, helpless infants irrevocably damaged by their mothers' irresponsible actions became a potent symbol of all that was wrong with the poor, the black, and the new mothers in the post-women's movement, post-civil rights era." So-called "crack babies," she asserts, "provided society with a powerful iconography of multiple social deviance (nonmarital sexuality, criminality, drug addiction, aberrant maternal behavior), perpetrated upon the most innocent by the least innocent" (Logan, 1999, pp. 115–116). Thus, despite a lack of consensus within the medical establishment over the long-term implications of a mother's use of crack cocaine for the fetus, added to growing evidence that the problems of children born to mothers using cocaine are often related to a general lack of prenatal care and other forms of addictions (including nicotine) and abuse, women faced (and continue to experience) criminal prosecution for prenatal drug use. Women whose infants were tested positive for drug exposure at birth had (and continue to be at risk of having) their parental rights terminated (Jimenez, 1990; Roberts, 2002; Flavin, 2008).

The changes in sentencing and the harsh new drug laws that characterized this era's approach to criminal justice signified a break with the earlier support for rehabilitation in favor of a combination of retributive notions of desert and incapacitation. Individuals, particularly drug addicts and violent offenders, deserved to be punished, and society—which by this time had become a victim writ large—relied on their incapacitation for protection. Eventually, too, the children of such individuals were labeled as social problems in their own rights. If "crack babies" were initially considered as victims, by the mid-1990s the offspring of (urban, minority) single mothers would become the targets of a new moral panic. Shown to be at risk of participating in illegal activities, disaffected, and undersocialized, predominantly Black, urban youth were dubbed "superpredators" by such conservative commentators as William Bennett and

John DiIulio, and seamlessly swept into the criminal justice system, just as their mothers (and fathers) had been a decade earlier (Bennett, DiIulio, & Walters, 1996). (See Chapter 6.)

Private Prisons

In conjunction with changing justifications of punishment, in the 1980s a number of states turned to the private sector, first to run immigration detention centers, then jails, and eventually, prisons. The private sector had been involved in the prison industry programs of a number of state systems as well as in federal prisons for some time, but only in a piecemeal fashion, employing some prisoners here, running the food service there (Auerbach, 1982). Starting with the Hamilton County Jail in Tennessee in 1984, state governments began to hand over entire penal establishments to private companies, first to run on their behalf, and soon enough to build as well.

As with the War on Drugs and the federal sentencing guidelines, prison privatization received (and continues to attract) bipartisan support. Thus, the federal prison system held out for a long time against privatizing, until, under the Clinton administration, it awarded its first contract to Wackenhut Corrections Corporation to run the minimum-security camp at Taft, California. The federal system, with its endemic overcrowding, along with such hard conservative states as Texas and Oklahoma, is now among the most aggressive proponents of privatization.

The move to privatization generated considerable debate, not only within academia (Auerbach, 1982; Durham, 1989), but also in the press. For some, like Kenneth F. Schoen, the former Commissioner of Corrections in Minnesota, privatization of imprisonment was a cause for concern. According to Schoen, private prisons were a "troubling industry" that had developed "in response to the runaway demand for prison space" (Schoen, 1985, p. A31). "Private investors," he wrote, "are eager to share in the $10 billion-a-year business of imprisoning the nation's almost 750,000 offenders" (Schoen, 1985, p. A31). Such investment, however, was not neutral. Rather, "like the military-industrial complex," he argued, "this industry will capitalize on the public's fears to assure an ever-expanding system" (Schoen, 1985, p. A31).

Others, however, were more enthusiastic. Thus, in an article published in *The Washington Post,* we find a penal administrator, one Paul O'Neill, then Houston district director of the INS, declaiming that "they [Corrections Corporation America] are absolutely fantastic . . . It's a pleasure to do business with people who know what they're doing" (cited in Taylor, 1985,

p. A15). Underpinning much of the debate, whether in scholarly journals or newspapers and magazines, was the overarching question posed by *The Washington Post* staff writer Paul Taylor: "Does anyone other than the state have the right to administer incarceration?" (Taylor, 1985, p. A15).

Although the practice was by no means universally accepted, over the course of the 1980s, states turned in greater numbers to the private sector, as a means of cutting costs and tackling overcrowding. In the process, private prisons both justified themselves and were legitimated by a shifting view on the role of the state. As Republican Senator Stewart Greenleaf of Pennsylvania put it: "Government is better supervising than actually running the operation" (cited in Tolchin, 1985a, p. 78).

Whereas previously states were prepared to pay for their prisons as an investment in social order, and as a representation of their sovereign power, the demise of the correctionalist ethos and its replacement by a more bureaucratic means of managing offenders threw the basic premise of imprisonment into question. Thus, despite vigorous disagreement over the ethics and manner of privatization, *The New York Times* by 1985 reported Democratic New York State Governor Mario Cuomo as saying: "It is not government's obligation to provide services, but to see that they're provided." Interpreting such an assertion as a conclusive sign that ". . . the shifting of government functions to private industry, has transcended its right-wing origins," the article proposed that ". . . the Reagan Administration has gained ground in shifting as many services as possible" (Tolchin, 1985b, p. B12). Prisons, after all, were just one of a number of state services that were now sold.

Prison Building and Supermax

As penal populations began to soar, states and the federal system responded by building more prisons, in what rapidly became a penal housing boom. Unlike the campus-style institutions favored in the 1970s to "humanize" the experience of incarceration, those constructed in the 1980s were usually shaped by little more than a need for space and a desire to keep costs down. When built in urban areas, new high-rise designs were often favored, offering little or no outdoor space and separating inmates on different floors, according to their security classification or sex. Wherever they were built, most new prisons favored "cookie-cutter" designs that were based on prefabricated parts, for cells and security walls, with the result that inmates convicted of vastly different kinds of crimes and held in separate parts of the country began to (and continue to) inhabit essentially the same kinds of spaces. No longer driven by a concern with the individual, such places of confinement became instead, like shopping malls or factories, designed for maximum economic efficiency and order. In addition to such institutions, most states and the federal government brought on line super-high-security institutions often referred to as maxi-maxi or supermax, either by changing practices in existing establishments or by building entirely new facilities (National Institute of Corrections, 1997; King, 1999; Rhodes, 2004).

The so-called "new generation" prisons of the 1980s reflected ideas about prison governance that were initially articulated in the rehabilitation-orientation notions of "unit management" (Levinson, 1999). According to its proponents, the prison population should be divided into smaller groupings and housing units, which could then be more easily monitored through technology and detailed on-the-ground supervision by staff. Despite an initial official commitment to greater staff involvement with inmates, many of the new prisons, particularly at the higher end of the security spectrum, ". . . essentially withdrew staff from the front-line and introduced remote supervision by [closed-circuit television] CCTV of large numbers of cells and big activity areas, access to which was controlled electronically from one or more central control rooms" (King, 1999, p. 171). In supermax prisons specifically, the impact of such views meant that prison social order was reduced to ". . . its lowest possible relevance by increasing the level of isolation of the inmate from both other inmates and the staff toward the theoretical limits points of total segregation" (Simon, 2000b, p. 301)

In their dependence on technology, new-generation prisons of all security levels demanded dramatically altered methods, ideas, and styles of staffing. As a result, they changed prisoners' experiences of confinement. For the most part, they replaced previous, more subjective and discretionary practices, which depended on staff personally knowing the men or women under their care, with a paradoxical combination of anonymity and increased surveillance. Inhabitants of these new institutions are both closely monitored by staff on their housing units and confined in areas that have been designed so that they may be observed from a distance by others in a control room or from various points around the grounds. The "panoptic gaze" of the prison immortalized by Michel Foucault in the 1970s had diversified and multiplied, reducing even further prisoners' capacity for privacy, agency, or autonomy. Whatever their architects' original ambitions for these institutions—and prisons like Oak Park Heights in Minnesota certainly suggest a liberal intent, with its generous regimes and relative freedom within the confinements of its supermax design—the high end of the security spectrum offers places of "total" control and sensory deprivation, with correspondingly high rates of inmate self-harm, psychosis, and other social problems (King, 1991; Simon, 2000b; Haney, 1997).

California led the nation in the prison building boom in the 1980s, opening eight new state prisons in a four-year period between 1984 and 1988, despite having previously built only 12 prisons between 1852 and 1964 (Gilmore, 2007).[2] Such expansion was outpaced by the prison population, which grew by 500 percent between 1982 and 2000, even as crime peaked in 1980 and declined thereafter. Two of the state's most notorious facilities, Corcoran State Correctional Facility and Pelican Bay State Prison, were both constructed in the 1980s. From the beginning, both have been marred by accusations of inhumane treatment and conditions, with Corcoran staff accused of staging "gladiator" fights between rival gang members, and Pelican Bay of subjecting its inhabitants to sensory deprivation.

When it opened in 1989, Pelican Bay State Prison was California's fourth maxi-max (or supermax) prison. Within it was the "first with a high-tech Secure Housing Unit (SHU) which could hold more than 1,000 prisoners" (Krutschnitt & Gartner, 2005, p. 17). Two decades later, the SHU is still the state's most secure facility. Inmates held here live in fully solitary confinement. Inside the cells, the bunks and toilets are molded to the floor. There is no window. The sole natural light enters through skylights in the main area around which the cells are arranged. Inmates stay in their cells for 22 to 23 hours per day and are allowed no contact with others. They emerge only to exercise alone in concrete pens (Weinstein & Cummins, 1996). Despite the documented strains such a regime places on inmates' psychological health, since its inception Pelican Bay has provided a prototype for other states in building isolation units (Haney, 1997).

Like California, the population of the federal system more than doubled between 1980 and 1989. In response, the federal government even more enthusiastically engaged in prison building, opening 20 new facilities between 1987 and 1992. While the majority of these were low- to medium-security federal correctional institutions, the federal system also was not immune to the discourses and practices of "securitization" that began in the 1980s. In 1983, for example, after two inmates killed two guards on the same day, the United States Penitentiary (USP) Marion was redesignated as an unprecedented security level 6 facility and placed on permanent lockdown. Originally opened in 1963 to replace Alcatraz as the most secure federal penitentiary, Marion was never designed to be a supermax prison, but rather, in its design, reflected much earlier views of imprisonment. Galvanized by the brutality of the events in Marion, it nonetheless took the federal system 11 years to open its own purpose-built supermaximum secure facility in Florence, Colorado. Since 1994, ADX has become the primary destination for the most dangerous and recalcitrant of federal offenders, though Marion remains on lockdown. In both places, men are held in solitary confinement for the majority, and in some cases for the totality, of their sentences.

The "toughening" of penal administration that characterized this era was not limited to men, or to adults. Over the course of this decade, an increasing number of states began to waive juvenile offenders to adult courts to receive sentences to adult prisons. So too, supermax conditions were introduced to women's prisons, in the form of smaller control units or "administrative segregation" within larger establishments (Shaylor, 1998). Information about such places is hard to come by, with the exception of the special housing unit (SHU) that existed from 1984 until its closure in 1988 in FCI Lexington. This control unit held primarily politically active prisoners, including a number of Puerto Rican nationalists, and was the subject of a damning public inquiry (Korn, 1988a, 1988b; Zwerman, 1988). Forced to close it, the federal system soon opened a new control unit in 1989 called the Shawnee Unit at FCI Marianna. The Federal Medical Center at Carswell in Texas also includes a control unit for women.

Challenging Imprisonment in an Era of Punitivism

One of the aims of this book is to identify voices about imprisonment that have been forgotten in the dominant narrative. In that regard, the 1980s proves a particular challenge, as it witnessed such a phenomenal growth in prison numbers. Yet, it would be a mistake, as in any period, to imagine that the punitive rhetoric of the time was promulgated without challenge. To be sure, voices of resistance were not very successful in stemming the growth of the prison population, yet attempts were made nonetheless. Though usually depicted as an engine of popular punitivism, the media published some critical accounts of U.S. prisons in this decade, as well as articles in support of rehabilitative programs. In 1987, for instance, *The New York Times* covered the horticultural program at the city's jail, Rikers Island. This program, long since discontinued, sought to reform promising inmates by teaching them how to grow flowers, fruits, and vegetables (Yarrow, 1987, C3). The same paper reported accusations against the special unit for women in

Kentucky (Ayres, 1988), and detailed the challenges posed by the aging population behind bars, directly linking their burgeoning population to the unintended consequences of tough sentencing (Malcolm, 1988).

As in any period, prisoners themselves sought to shed light on their incarceration. Assata Shakur's autobiography, which included searing accounts of her treatment in New York State and New Jersey prisons, appeared in this decade (Shakur, 1987), as did John Henry Abbott's (1981) bestseller *In the Belly of the Beast*. Less renowned, but still in circulation today, are books by Jean Harris (1986, 1988), who was given a life sentence in 1981 for killing her lover, the "Scarsdale diet doctor" Herman Tarnower. So too, Chicano prisoner Raul Salinas's (1980) poetic reflections on his experiences behind bars appeared at this time. Elsewhere, the PEN Prisoner Writing program (founded in 1971) continued to highlight imprisoned authors while, from 1987, the radical journal *Prisoners on Prison* provided another outlet for prisoner-authors and their supporters.

While Shakur and Salinas concentrated on the racism and violence of law enforcement and imprisonment, *In the Belly of the Beast* fiercely attacked the medical model of the rehabilitative era and the unfettered discretion of prison officials. Abbott described how he was incarcerated almost continuously from age 12 to 37, with much of his time in prison spent in solitary confinement. His book, filled with accounts of brutality and dehumanization, confirmed most reformers' concerns with indeterminate sentences and prison conditions:

> . . . I once served five and a half years in a cell in Maximum Security, and for a period of over two years I did not speak to anyone but my sister when she came to visit me twice a month.
>
> When I entered Maximum Security, I was about five feet, nine inches tall. I did not have a beard and did not know basic arithmetic. When I emerged I could not walk without collapsing; I had a full beard and was six feet tall. I had a rudimentary understanding of mathematical theory and symbolic logic and had studied in all the theoretical sciences. I had read all but a very few of the world's classics, from prehistoric times up to this day. My vision was perfect when I was locked up; when I got out, my vision required glasses. (Abbott, 1981, p. 18)[3]

Well beyond the prison walls, the 1980s also witnessed the growth of critical race studies and feminist theory (Davis, 1981; Eisenstein, 1981; Hooks, 1981; MacKinnon, 1982). Although at first glance U.S. criminology seemed little affected by the more radical literature on race, gender, and class, its impact can be sketched. Even as mainstream criminology blamed working, irresponsible, and/or single mothers for juvenile delinquency (Gottfredson & Hirschi, 1990), the 1980s witnessed the emergence of a robust field of feminist criminology (Krutschnitt, 1982, 1984; Mann, 1984; Daly & Chesney-Lind, 1988; Chesney-Lind, 1986; Stimpson, 1989), the first historical accounts of women's imprisonment (Rafter, 1985; Freedman, 1981), and some feminist critique of incarceration (Chesney-Lind & Rodriguez, 1983; Mahan, 1984). Matters of racial inequality within prison and beyond were also considered as scholars sought to account "objectively" for the overrepresentation of minorities behind bars (Petersilia, 1983; Blumstein, 1982). Some more critical depictions of racism behind bars were also published (Jacobs, 1982; Carroll, 1982).

Deeply influenced by the women's movement, feminist criminologists like Meda Chesney-Lind and Nicole Rafter sought to fill in the gaps of knowledge about the birth of the prison and demonstrate the additional burdens suffered by women offenders.[4] Unlike earlier scholars of female offenders and women's prisons, these authors self-identified as "feminists" and as such sought both to understand the "gendered social organization" of the world, and to challenge it (Stimpson, 1989, p. 606). These authors cleared a new path from that laid down in the previous decade by Freda Adler (1975), who had asserted that greater emancipation caused increased female involvement in crime.

Responding to wider debates in women's studies (hooks, 1981), feminist scholars were quick to point out the additional burdens faced by Black women behind bars, from sexual assault to everyday racism. Some even went so far as to suggest that these differences were a constitutive part of the prison itself. Thus, in her historical analysis, Nicole Rafter identified racial differences in the first female penal institutions and in the treatment of minority offenders. "Chivalry" she wrote:

> . . . filtered [white women] out of the prison system, helping to create the even greater racial imbalances among female than male prisoner populations. And partiality toward whites contributed to the development of a bifurcated system, one track custodial and predominantly black, the other reformatory and reserved mainly for whites. (Rafter, 1985, p. 155)

In addition to the critical academic debates on incarceration, the courts, at least initially, continued to play an important role in mitigating the worst aspects of prison life. Even as the federal government sought to reduce prisoners' access to the courts, a growing number of inmates filed legal complaints (Thomas, Keeler, & Harris, 1986; Thomas, 1988). One of the most important legal cases on prison conditions, *Ruiz v. Estelle*, prompted considerable change in the Texas prison system throughout the 1980s, with broader implications for prison systems around the country. Begun in 1972 by prisoner David Ruiz, the far-reaching impact of this case lasted until 2001, when federal oversight of the state's prison system finally came to an end.[5]

The original suit, filed against the Texas Department of Corrections, alleged that prison conditions were unconstitutional. In 1980, the well-named U.S. District Judge William Wayne Justice agreed, issuing a 188-page ruling: Texas prisons, he asserted, were overcrowded and understaffed, medical care was inadequate, and violence was rampant. Judge Justice also singled out the practice known as "building tenders," whereby prisoners were employed as guards, for opprobrium. Justice placed the entire state system under special measures, ordering significant changes to improve conditions. However, the state was slow to meet the conditions set out by Judge Justice, and so, in 1987, he found its government to be in contempt of court and fined it. Later that year, Texas began a concerted program of prison building.

Though conditions in Texas prisons improved in response to *Ruiz v. Estelle,* its scheme of prison building went hand in hand with an overall escalation of the population, leading Texas to its current position in the top three prison populations in the country. So, too, Marie Gottschalk (2006) has argued recently that activists in the 1980s, like sentencing reformers in the previous decade, facilitated the development of harsher penalties. In particular, she suggests, feminist demands for victims' rights and harsher penalties for rapists or pornography played into the hands of the neoconservatives.[6]

In any case, the judicial intervention apparent in *Ruiz v. Estelle* was gradually curtailed in this era by a series of Supreme Court decisions that were widely heralded by conservative commentators (DiIulio, 1990). In a series of cases starting with *Rhodes v. Chapman* in 1981, including *Whitely v. Albers* in 1986, and culminating in *Wilson v. Seiter* in 1991, federal courts were urged to take further into account the perspective of state prison officials and require prisoner complainants to meet higher standards in proving their grounds for complaint. The so-called activist era of the courts was essentially drawn to a close (Feeley, Malcolm, & Van Swearingen, 2004).

CONCLUSION

Globally, the 1980s were defined by a vibrant conservative ideology and the demise of the Communist USSR. In the U.S., there was an effective assault on trade unions that saw membership numbers dwindle and a growing violent crime rate. Divisions between rich and poor grew, while the White flight from urban areas that had begun in the 1960s continued. The neoliberalism of the free market consolidated inequalities, while wrapping them in a guise of popular sentiment, which was, at least in part, upheld by a newly authoritarian approach to law and order. Central to this new sensibility was an invigorated, though not always acknowledged, racial discourse, in which young men of color (and their female partners), were represented as the sources and fundamental arbiters of numerous social problems.

Writers like Ken Auletta (1982) and Charles Murray (1984) popularized an image of the Black underclass existing in a parasitic relationship with mainstream American culture, feeding off the general public's hard-earned taxes and its eager compassion. They—and the treatment they received—were the dystopic inversion of the American dream, a group whose very existence, however problematic, helped constitute the image of the law-abiding. It was no surprise then, that this section of the poor, who also were blamed for their own drug addiction and for threatening law-abiding citizens, deserved no sympathy, but increasingly received harsh punishment. "In this watershed period," David Garland (2001a) claims:

> . . . effective crime control came to be viewed as a matter of imposing more controls, increasing disincentives, and, if necessary, segregating the dangerous sector of the population. The recurrent image of the offender . . . became much more threatening—a matter of career criminals, crackheads, thugs, and predators—and at the same time much more racialized . . . the compassionate sensibility that used to temper punishment now increasingly enhanced it, as the sympathy invoked by political rhetoric centered exclusively on the victim and the fearful public, rather than the offender. (Garland, 2001a, p. 102)

Characterized by a deepening punitiveness and an increased fear of crime and offenders, the 1980s transformed sentencing policy and, in the process, prison populations. The durability—and effect—of penal policies and their accompanying rhetoric can be found in any number of statistical accounts of crime and punishment. All longitudinal (or time series) studies show more or less the same structure, with an ever-increasing confined population serving longer and longer sentences, despite a gradual and then rapid drop in overall crime. Likewise, similar legislative changes governing the criminal justice system that occurred under Reagan have continued in subsequent administrations, no matter their political allegiance.

In defining this era, it is difficult to recall the many attempts made to resist its changes. While in practical terms, the voices of reform that had so dominated the discussion just 10 years earlier lost their power, their ideas did not all die out. Thus, just as supermax facilities came to resemble vast penal gulags of suffering, so, too, some states such as Vermont failed to construct such institutions. Others, like Minnesota, found a middle path, establishing liberal regimes within secure borders at Oak Park Heights. Likewise, while public support appeared to grow for deepening range of punishment, alternative groups grew, decrying their effect. The means by which the radical intolerance of contemporary U.S. penal politics were entrenched, in other words, did not come about solely as a result of state policies. Instead, other more complex and often contradictory forces were in evidence. It is to this topic that Chapter 6 will turn.

NOTES

1. The federal sentencing grid had 258 cells and ranged from sentences of less than six months to life. Though the Sentencing Reform Act of 1984 applied only to the federal system, its main practices were quickly adopted in many states, and, indeed, in the case of Washington State were already current.

2. Excluding prisoner of war camps and war relocation centers.

3. For reformers, Jack Abbott proved to be a mixed blessing. Released on parole in 1981, within a year he had killed a man in a brawl. Jean Harris provided a more domestic picture of imprisonment, describing in some detail intimate relationships among inmates, as well as those between women and staff. In addition to the detail of daily life, Harris considers the causes of women's offending, arguing that in most cases it was driven by poverty. "Sex and drugs pay well," she points out. "Slinging hash and selling ribbons do not" (Harris, 1988, p. 41).

4. In popular culture, too, though it is possible to point to a number of popular examples that celebrated neoliberal economics and dominant race and gender relations, there were also exceptions, examples of resistance and counterattacks. Thus, the 1987 film *Wall Street,* with its notorious line "Greed is good" in conjunction with that other Michael Douglas vehicle of hegemonic masculinity, *Fatal Attraction,* were at least partly offset by Spike Lee's 1989 critical account of race relations in urban America, *Do the Right Thing.* Similarly, Madonna's pseudo-ironical 1985 hit song "Material Girl, coexisted with a burgeoning rap and hip-hop music scene that, at least in some of its guises, challenged race relations while co-opting the celebration of wealth in new and somewhat threatening forms to the dominant White business classes.

5. The impact of Judge Justice's rulings on the Texas prisons was studied throughout this decade by a number of scholars (see, for example, Marquart & Crouch, 1982; Martin & Ekland-Olson, 1987; Crouch & Marquart, 1989).

6. Radical legal scholar and feminist Catherine MacKinnon notoriously worked with Andrea Dworkin in drafting a model antipornography ordinance. Adopted in Indianapolis in 1984, the ordinance defined pornography as inherently discriminatory against women and enabled its victims to sue for damages. It was eventually struck down in 1985 by the Seventh Circuit Court of Appeals in the ruling *American Booksellers Ass'n. v. Hudnut,* 771 F.2d 323 (7th Cir. 1985), a decision affirmed one year later by the Supreme Court in 475 U.S. 1001 (1986).

Six

A Culture of Control

[F]or too long, the debate about crime and drugs in America has been dominated by a relatively small group of anti-incarceration advocates. These advocates have been perpetrating criminal justice myths that have done a great deal to undermine effective law enforcement. What is at stake here is more than an interesting, and somewhat esoteric, academic debate. The body count has risen—lives have been lost—because pernicious ideas have formed an intellectual template for crime and punishment in America.

—Bennett, DiIulio, & Walters, 1996, p. 15

American convicts are subjected to degradation that most people are unable to comprehend and do not want to know about. These are not security technologies, they are the programs. Prisons were built to destroy people.

—Richards, 1998, p. 123

Imprisonment simultaneously serves as an expressive satisfaction of retributive sentiments and an instrumental mechanism for the management of risk and the confinement of danger.

—Garland, 2001a, p. 199

Despite the victory of Democratic presidential candidate Bill Clinton in 1992, and his subsequent successful reelection campaign, the punitive sentiments and practices fostered under the previous 12 years of Republican government continued unabated. In contrast to the widespread economic prosperity of this period, the 1990s were characterized by harsh rhetoric and restrictive policies toward the poor, the foreign, and the criminal. Legislatively active in all these areas, the Clinton administration restricted welfare, lengthened sentences, and reduced opportunities for convicts while incarcerated and after release.

Despite acknowledging biases in drug sentencing every now and again, particularly near the end of his presidency (Wenner, 2000), Clinton ignored the 1997 recommendations of the Federal Sentencing Commission to address the disparities in federal sentencing guidelines over crack and powder cocaine use. Notwithstanding initial attempts at creating some kind of national health care system, which would have offered a safety net to the poor, Clinton failed to deliver on that, too. Instead, opting to focus on those few people who manipulated the welfare system and on violent sexual predators, Clinton, like Reagan so successfully before him, perpetuated what David Garland (2001a) has labeled the "culture of control." Most confoundingly, such punitive sentiment and practice occurred despite a steep national decline in all crime from 1990 to 2000.

Prisons and Politics in the 1990s

Even as crime rates everywhere were falling, imprisonment rates continued to rise throughout the 1990s. Starting at 715,649 in 1990, the total population reached a massive 1,305,253 by 2000. In part due to the impact of the ever-growing base population, the rate of expansion of the confined population declined a little, from a staggering 43 percent increase between 1990 and 1995 to a still elevated 28 percent between 1995 and 2000 (Stephan, 1997; Stephan & Karberg, 2003). Not all states expanded their custodial systems equally, suggesting that no single factor can explain the rise throughout the country (Barker, 2006). It remains the case, however, that everywhere prison numbers grew (Greenberg & West, 2001; Jacobson, 2005).

Within the overall population, there was some variation. The tally of women behind bars expanded at a rate far higher than that of men, while more minority men were incarcerated than White men, and the population of Black and Hispanic women grew fastest of all. Reflecting changes in sentencing practices, more children were imprisoned than in previous periods as many states across the country lowered their maximum age of juvenile court jurisdiction to 15 or 16. By the end of the decade, all states had enacted legislation whereby juveniles charged with certain offenses were sent before adult courts. There, if found guilty, they would be sentenced to adult prison. While the average daily juvenile population in adult prisons in 1992 was 2,527 (representing an increase of 62 percent since 1983), by 1996 it had risen to 8,100 (U.S. Department of Justice, 2001; Strom, Smith, & Snyder, 1998). Finally, the numbers of confined noncitizens also increased substantially through the 1990s. In the federal system, noncitizens made up 25 percent of the total prison population (Stephan & Karberg, 2003).

Despite a continuing "boom" in the prison building industry, construction (up 14 percent) did not keep pace with the increases in the incarcerated population anywhere other than in the private sector, which witnessed a 164 percent growth between 1995 and 2000. As a result, in most jurisdictions overcrowding simply became worse.

In sum, the 1990s, like the 1980s, was a decade characterized by a powerful punitive sentiment. That this mentality was fostered in a period dominated by a Democratic presidential administration challenged received wisdom on the connections between the Republican Party and punitiveness (Davey, 1998). As has been widely noted, Bill Clinton ran in 1992 on a tough-on-crime initiative, cynically taking time out from his campaigning schedule to return to Arkansas to sign the execution warrant of Ricky Ray Rector, a man with diminished mental capacity. Once elected, Clinton continued to use his "hands-on" experience in punishment as political capital, stating proudly to the members of the law enforcement community at the Ohio Peace Officers Training Academy on February 15, 1994, "I know what it means to double the prison capacity of a state, and to sign laws toughening crimes, and to carry out the death penalty, to add to the stock of police officers and try to deal with all the problems that are facing them" (Clinton, 1994b).

To be sure, as with many aspects of his regime, Clinton was a little inconsistent in his punitive rhetoric. In 1992, for example, he argued that "Bush [Sr.] . . . thinks locking up addicts instead of treating them before they commit crimes . . . is clever politics. That may be, but it certainly isn't sound policy, and the consequences of his cravenness could ruin us" (cited in Beckett & Sasson, 2000, p. 70). The following year, Clinton seemed to evince some belief in the sociological causes of crime, asserting that ". . . we have to deal with family, community and education, and find jobs for members of society's underclass to bring structure to their lives" (cited in Beckett & Sasson, 2000, p. 70). Overall, however, state and federal prison systems radically expanded through the 1990s, driven, at least in part, by legislation brought in under Clinton, as well as by previous policies from Reagan and Bush Senior that the Democratic president failed to overturn. His administrations also pursued just as vigorous a War on Drugs as had his Republican predecessors.

Midway through his first term, in 1994 Clinton signed The Violent Crime Control and Law Enforcement Act (P.L. 103–322). This act increased funding for police and prison building and continued to erode parole through the Violent Offender Incarceration and Truth-in-Sentencing Incentive Formula Grant Program, which promised financial incentives to states that made inmates serve at least 85 percent of their sentences.[1] The Violent Crime Control Act further undermined judicial discretion by approving "three strikes" legislation and abolished Pell Grants for prisoners, who, since 1972, had received, along with other impoverished individuals, some financial assistance to pursue tertiary education while incarcerated. Despite the fact that the proportion of such grants allocated to prisoners constituted only 2 percent of the funds distributed to individuals enrolled in full-time tertiary education, and in defiance of overwhelming evidence that education lowers rearrest rates and improves inmate behavior while incarcerated, the Clinton government dismantled it (Tewksbury, Ericson, & Taylor, 2000; Williford, 1994; Simon, 2000a). In 1996, Clinton approved the Personal Responsibility and Work Opportunity Reconciliation Act of 1996 (PRWORA). Claiming to end "welfare as we know it," this act toughened regulations over entitlement to public housing for convicted felons and their relatives, rendering individuals ineligible for Food Stamps and federal housing if convicted of a drug felony (Rubenstein & Mukamal, 2002). This act penalized states that did not establish a similar system in their own public housing laws. The election year of 1996 was busy for criminal justice enforcement, with PRWORA followed by the Anti-Terrorism and Effective Death Penalty Act 1996, which widened the use of imprisonment and detention as a means of border control, and the Prison Litigation Reform Act 1996, which reduced prisoners' access to the courts and undermined their claim to habeas corpus.

The Prison Litigation Reform Act (PLRA) of 1996 was brought in as a rider to an appropriations bill after it failed in a freestanding form in 1994. Based on the theory that prisoners were wasting judicial time with frivolous lawsuits, this act made it much harder for them to seek redress in federal court (Schlanger, 2003). Since 1996, prisoners have had to exhaust the prison's grievance procedures (often referred to as "administrative remedy") before filing a lawsuit. They have also become responsible for their own filing fees. Courts may dismiss any prisoner lawsuit as "frivolous" or "malicious" and, in this case, prisoners may not file another lawsuit unless they are able to pay the court filing fee up front and in full. Prisoners cannot file a lawsuit for mental or emotional injury unless they can show there has been accompanying significant physical injury and, if the judge decides the lawsuit was based on false information or filed in order to harass the people sued, federal prisoners may lose good-time credits (ACLU, 1999).

In much of the crime legislation and in his public pronouncements, Clinton maintained the emphasis on victims and victim rights deployed so effectively by Reagan and George H. W. Bush. As under his predecessors, victims were commonly represented in stark contrast to offenders, as a means of enabling and legitimating more punitive legislation. More broadly, in a number of speeches he tied images of undeserving, dangerous offenders to social policies outside traditional criminal justice areas. In a high-profile example of such legislation, Clinton signed the Jacob Wetterling Crimes Against Children and Sexually Violent Offender Registration Act in 1994. In 1996, this act was amended by Megan's Law, requiring states to initiate programs of community notification (Simon, 2000a). That year at the "One Strike Crime Symposium," Clinton announced that housing projects that failed to fight crime and enforce the one-strike eviction rule for drug dealers would be penalized. According to Clinton, "... this policy today is a clear signal to drug dealers and to gangs: If you break the law, you no longer have a home in public housing. One strike and you're out. That should be the law everywhere in America." Acknowledging that "for some, one strike and you're out sounds like hardball," he unapologetically agreed, "Well it is. It is because it's morally wrong for criminals to use up homes that could make a big difference in the lives of decent families." Warming to his theme, he went on: "There is no reason in the world to put the rights of a criminal before those of a child who wants to grow up safe or a parent who wants to raise that child in an environment where the child is safe" (Clinton, 1996).

Whereas Reagan and Bush Sr. spoke of a shared identity with victims, using those affected by crime to stand metaphorically for all Americans, Clinton conjured up a more specific, gendered victim with great effect. Thus in his speech to the Ohio Peace Officers Training Academy on February 15, 1994, Clinton cited an unidentified "teenage girl" from Shreveport, Louisiana, who allegedly sent him a letter saying: "If I could meet the president, I would ask him to make crime his top priority. Crime is so bad I'm afraid to go outside. I really didn't pay attention to crime until someone shot and killed my friend who was one of my church members." This unnamed, churchgoing young woman was worried, it turns out, not just for her own safety but, in a twist that surely is too good to be true, for her femininity as well: "My concern is,"—listen to this [Clinton exclaimed]—"My concern is I won't have anyone to marry because all the nice young men will have been killed, incarcerated, or in a gang." (Clinton, 1994b). With such a deserving victim, what else could the state do but crack down on crime?

As others have observed, the victim rights movement and the women's groups associated with it often legitimated punitiveness in the eyes of social groups who might otherwise have been doubtful about it (Gottschalk, 2006). The Violent Crime Control and Law Enforcement Act of 1994, for example, which promulgated many measures that drove up the prison population, from mandatory minimum sentences to increased numbers of police on the streets and an expansion of the federal death penalty, brought in the Violence Against Women Act, which, for the first time, sought to make domestic violence a federal issue. Despite some evidence (Brown, 2006) to suggest that the extent to which the middle classes abandoned rehabilitative ideals in this period has been exaggerated, plenty of examples demonstrate a trade-off between the rights of some for the (alleged) protection of others. Unlike earlier discussions of crime and punishment when sanctions were presented as in the best interest of the offenders, calls for more policing of drug and violent offenders along with their harsher punishment were made acceptable through promises of benefits for the potential and actual victims of such individuals. They would be removed for our protection.

From his first State of the Union address in 1993, Clinton included being "tough" on crime as a key part of his strategy to lift "America's fortunes." As it had been under Reagan, this populist approach was effective, notwithstanding its apparent dissonance with core Democratic ideals and its internal contradictions. Crucially, in terms of governance, this rhetoric legitimated the increasing federal encroachment on what had traditionally been understood to be state matters in crime control and policing by elevating them to matters of national concern.

In his 1994 State of the Union Address, Clinton initially asserted that, "while Americans are more secure from threats abroad, I think we all [k]now that in many ways we are less secure from threats here at home. Everyday the national peace is shattered by crime." Violent crime "and the fear it provokes," he ran on, "are crippling our society, limiting personal freedom, and fraying the ties that bind us." Seconds later, however, he acknowledged that "the vast majority of people get up every day and obey the law, pay their taxes, do their best to raise their kids" (Clinton, 1994a).

In reality, the portrayal of an alleged apposition between the "vast majority" of law-abiding people soberly living out their lives and a deepening problem of insecurity was no paradox at all, but rather an effective, if subtle, allusion to an unidentified, undifferentiated criminal underclass, as well as a justification of increased criminal justice activity. Their very lack of defined characteristics differentiated offenders from the moral majority. They were the "others" threatening the "the law-abiding" "us"; they were, in other words, "un-American," who deserved to be excluded from the rights and protections of the polity.

American liberalism almost always privileges the individual, and the individual malefactors come into focus only once they enter the criminal justice system and, especially, once they are behind bars. In an enduring line of reasoning that once motivated eugenic "research" and experimentation, once people are incarcerated, society can finally know them for who they are: dangerous, deviant, and unwelcome. At the same time, however, those in prison are fundamentally "unknowable" to, and different from, society. Locked away and invisible, they remain shadowy figures in a debate about belonging and about good and evil that they can never win.

As he settled into his presidency, Clinton opted in his State of the Union Addresses to present the government's crime control policies as increasingly effective. Despite (or more likely because of) his looming personal problems that would result in impeachment, Clinton took a triumphalist tone in his 1998 speech, claiming victory in his crime policies: "We pursued a strategy of more police, tougher punishment, smarter prevention with crime-fighting partnerships, with local law enforcement and citizen groups, where the rubber hits the road," he claimed, "[and] I can report to you tonight that it's working. Violent crime is down, robbery is down, assault is down, burglary is down for five years in a row across America" (Clinton, 1998). Such assertions, despite far more nuanced and complicated academic evidence, explicitly linked falling crime rates to imprisonment (Zimring, 2007).

Public safety and good management were not the only cheap lessons that Clinton drew from crime control. Crime, or at least violent crime, Clinton (1994a) proposed, was simply "un-American." Like the gathering neoconservatives, who were fated to usurp Clinton's successor Al Gore in the bitterly contested 2000 election, Clinton deployed crime as a means of pushing a particular moralizing and nationalist agenda. Parents, he warned, must take responsibility for their children, stay (or get) married, work, and go to church. In such phrases, Clinton's views became all but indistinguishable from the (heavily racialized) notion of "moral poverty" espoused by his right-wing opponents. Consensus across the shades of political belief, what Americans like to celebrate as "bipartisan" politics, to a large extent remains unchallenged today. Although many date its origins to the 1960s, most commentators agree that the 1990s, with the massive expansion of prison populations throughout the states and dependent territories, took punitive sentiment to a new level. What underpinned such punitiveness, and what forces, if any, sought to resist it?

Punishment and Modern Society: Explaining the Culture of Control

Scholarly accounts of punishment in the 1990s are framed by the publication of two books by David Garland: *Punishment and Modern Society* (Garland, 1990) and *The Culture of Control* (Garland, 2001). Through a close reading of social theory, the former addressed the paradox of penal institutions and punishment, "the rationale for which," Garland (1990, p. 3) claimed, was "by no means clear," while the latter sought to account more descriptively for why the U.S. and the UK, over the course of the 20th century, had become so wedded to punitive sentiment and practice. In conjunction with a series of sympathetic authors across a range of countries (see, for example, O'Malley, 1992; Feeley & Simon, 1992; Simon, 1997; Wacquant, 1999), Garland created a field known as the "sociology of punishment," which reshaped the academic discourse on punishment and, thus, in a related though diluted fashion, on the prison.

Reflecting the vitality of this strand of criminological scholarship, David Garland established the journal *Punishment & Society* in 1999. Whereas at this time most mainstream criminology journals had shied away from theoretical discussions to more positivist, empirical accounts of crime, and were no longer particularly interested in imprisonment, *Punishment & Society* vowed to examine "... the penal field and its various elements—institutions and practices, laws and policies, embedded theories and discourses, representations and rhetorics—as well as the social and political supports upon which these practices depend" (Garland, 1999, p. 9). Today this journal remains at the forefront of theoretical discussions of punishment in the U.S. and elsewhere.

Separate from this body of theoretical work, and for the most part ignored by it, some academics produced accounts of life behind bars in women's prisons (Owen, 1998; Ross, 1998; Rierden, 1997). Even more distant from theory, a handful of former or serving prisoners published firsthand accounts of incarceration (Abu-Jamal, 1995, 1997; Rideau & Wikberg, 1992; Peltier, 1999). Overall, however, while the prison population soared to new heights, the attention of academia lay elsewhere; the majority of experts were (still) "thinking about crime" (Wilson, 1983), and policing (Kelling & Coles, 1996).

According to Garland (1990), "Where once penal institutions appeared to offer a self-evident rationale, in the late twentieth century they increasingly come to seem less obviously appropriate." Their "fit" with the social world and their grounding in the natural order of things, he optimistically asserted "begin to appear less and less convincing" (Garland, 1990, p. 277). Writing at the time from his base in Edinburgh in the UK, where the legitimacy of the prison was significantly less secure than in the U.S. due to a vigorous radical critique of incarceration emanating from universities and penal reform groups, as well as from prisons, Garland appeared to view the penal system as ripe for intellectual reassessment (Sim, 1990; Scranton, Sim, & Skidmore, 1991; Ryan, 1983).[2] The decline of the rehabilitative ideal, he argued, had seriously weakened the prison's grounding myth and rationale. Yet, paradoxically, it had not led to its closure. As a result, the institution appeared to be both "relatively stable and deeply problematic at one and the same time" (Garland 1990, p. 277).

This conundrum had, in various guises, formed the central issue debated by legal philosophers and sociologists for some time. Yet, as David Garland rightly pointed out, it was often ignored by penal practitioners and by the literature that had grown up around prison studies. To that end, part of the purpose of *Punishment and Modern Society* involved a (re)education program where Garland mapped the central ideas of historical theories of punishment. The contributions of Emile Durkheim (1902), Rusche & Kirchheimer (1939), Michel Foucault (1979), Max Weber (1978), and Norbert Elias (1978, 1982) were, thus, all neatly summarized and examined.

Punishment and Modern Society, however, was more than just a literature review, since Garland revisited key texts to garner ideas for developing his own "social approach" to punishment. He asserted "that punishment is a social institution . . . that it is conditioned by an ensemble of social and historical forces, that it has an institutional framework of its own and that it supports a set of regulatory and significatory practices which produce a range of penal and social effects" (Garland, 1990, p. 284). Garland promulgated a more nuanced approach to explaining the paradox of punishment. While he had some sympathy for the Marxist view that the prison's role is to absorb the unemployed when they are not required by capitalism (Rusche & Kirchheimer, 1939; Reiman, 1979; Greenberg, 1977), as well as for Foucault's (1979) belief that the failure of the prison was its purpose in the creation of an unending chain of delinquents, he ultimately criticized both accounts for essentializing the power of the prison. Instead of any reckoning with "power," Garland found Norbert Elias's ideas of culture and sentiment more useful in understanding the appeal and legitimacy of penal practices. "Penal laws and institutions," he argued, "are always proposed, discussed, legislated, and operated within definite cultural codes. They are framed in languages, discourses, and sign systems which embody specific cultural meanings, distinctions, and sentiments." It is these cultural views and artifacts, he asserted, "which must be interpreted and understood if the social meaning and motivations of punishments are to become intelligible" (Garland, 1990, p. 198).

By emphasizing "culture" Garland sought to challenge the dominant approach to penal policy which he thought tended to view punishment in ". . . administrative, means-end ways rather than as a moral or fully social issue"(Garland, 1990, p. 214). Penal measures could ". . . only be considered at all if they conform to our conceptions of what is emotionally tolerable. The matter-of-fact administration of most penal policy is possible because it relies upon measures which have already been deemed tolerable and the morality of which can be taken for granted" (Garland, 1990, p. 214). Likewise, he maintained, "security considerations and the instrumental use of punishment are always in tension with cultural and psychic forces which place clear limits upon the types and extent of punishment which will be acceptable" (Garland, 1990, p. 229). Such cultural expectations may, however, change and, when they do, as with the decline in the rehabilitative ideal, certain penal practices may have to be rethought.

As the decade advanced, and more fully once he moved to the U.S., taking up a professorship at New York University in 1997, David Garland's seeming optimism about the possibility of fundamentally changing the prison evaporated. By the time he published *The Culture of Control* in 2001, he wondered, "Why has prison moved from being a discredited institution destined for abolition, to become an expanded and seemingly indispensable pillar of late modern life?" (Garland, 2001a, p. 199). The answer, he proposed, was multifaceted. On the one hand, the prison had "reinvented" itself, "to serve a newly necessary function in the workings of late modern, neo-liberal societies: the need for a 'civilized' and 'constitutional' means of segregating the problem populations created by today's economic and social arrangements" (Garland, 2001a, p. 199). On the other hand, its expansion was driven by the reemergence of punitive sanctions and of "expressive justice" that appeared to be deliberately harsh and retributive despite the prison's manifest failure to reduce crime and notwithstanding the financial and other burdens they placed on the wider community (Garland, 2001a).

The upswing in crime rates from the 1960s until the 1990s, which seemed not to respond to any interventions, had rattled politicians and administrators, he claimed. "Together with the widely acknowledged limitations of criminal justice agencies," they had "begun to erode one of the foundational myths of modern societies: namely, the myth that the sovereign state is capable of providing security, law and order, and crime control within its territorial borders" (Garland, 1996, p. 448). Not surprisingly then, whereas President Clinton proudly presented his record on crime and punishment as shining proof of his effective governing, Garland suggested that ". . . punitive outbursts and demonizing rhetorics have featured much more prominently in weak political regimes than in strong ones" (Garland, 1996, p. 462).

Linking crime control to governance and state power, Garland argued that expressive and excessive punishments—longer terms, more severe prison conditions—were as much an attempt to disguise the vulnerabilities of the state in power as they were responses to public opinion. In his analysis, governments of high-crime societies like the U.S. engaged in a series of sometimes contradictory efforts in response to crime, demonizing it in punitive strategies and discourses, while at the same time normalizing and lowering people's expectations about the possibility of reducing it. Certain kinds of offenses were merely an unfortunate part of "everyday life." In this view, a wide range of practices from community policing to rational choice theory, which argued that criminals were motivated by utilitarian concerns, were part of a broader "responsibilization strategy" seeking to deflect liability for avoiding victimization to the individual. Citizens had to be careful, crime prevention leaflets warned; women should not walk alone at night; homeowners should install alarms. The sale of private security devices flourished, along with the expansion of private security firms.

It was not just victimization that was redefined, but the causes of crime as well. Whereas crime prevention literature suggested that everyone always was at risk, the same work also sought squarely to blame the offender. Crime was committed by the (rational) individual (Cornish & Clarke, 1986; Clarke & Felson, 1993). It was, thus, the appropriate target of legal sanction and moral outrage. As James H. Warner (1992), then assistant general council of the National Rifle Association of America (the NRA),[3] put it in 1992 at a meeting of the Third Generation, the arch-conservative spin-off from the Heritage Foundation,

> The cause of crime is self evident. Crime is behavior and is controlled by the moral values of the individual. If one's moral values will not permit him to do something, he will not do it. If one's moral values do allow him to do something, no law will restrain him if he believes that he can get away with it. (Warner, 1992, p. 1)

Though somewhat contradictory, assertions that the victim and the offender were responsible for crime conveniently, if subtly, enabled the state to distance itself from the cause and effect of mass incarceration. A similar shift could also be identified in the growing enthusiasm for private prisons. The turn to privatization, which had begun in the 1980s, gathered pace in the 1990s, with the number of prison and jail beds in private facilities increasing more than 35-fold between 1987 and 1998 from 3,100 to 116,626 (Jacobson, 2005). By handing over responsibility for the messy, daily issue of imprisonment to the private sector, the state not only abrogated its own liability, to some extent, but also adhered to the tenets of neoliberalism by involving the market in its governance of crime.

If such strategies represented the victory of neoliberalism, the expressive, punitive rhetoric that still colored much of the political and media discourse revealed the expanding influence of the neoconservatives. Galvanized by Clinton's electoral success, the 1990s was a decade of busy cultural activity on the right in the media, so-called "independent" "think tanks," and academia. Republicans not only took over Congress, but consolidated their control of the television media via Fox News and its affiliates (established in 1986). They were equally energetic in print through large-distribution newspapers such as *The Washington Times* as well as much smaller-circulation journals like *The Weekly Standard.* The number of right-wing think tanks staffed with resident "expert" research fellows expanded considerably, as did lobbying groups and public intellectuals who favored neoconservative ideals.[4]

Neoconservatives, the Culture Wars, and Prison

Evidently, not all these publications, groups, or individuals were equally as concerned about prison matters, nor as influential. Many were busy fighting other fronts in the "culture wars," protecting so-called Christian "family values," seeking to overturn *Roe v. Wade,* and arguing for maintaining the ban on gays in the military. In terms of criminal justice policy, the Brookings Institution, the Heritage Foundation, and the Manhattan Institute[5], along with *The Weekly Standard, The Public Interest,* and *The City Journal,* were particularly influential, in funding and publishing. In this last regard, they issued the work of John DiIulio, Charles Murray, and William Bratton. John DiIulio, a senior fellow at the Brookings Institution for much of this period, published articles on crime and punishment in each of these three magazines in 1995 and 1996. Charles Murray's views on racial differences in IQ were widely debated in the media and academia (Herrnstein & Murray, 1994); his op-eds on crime and punishment were seemingly less controversial, though generally similar in their bent. Finally, as might be expected, William J. Bratton, the former police commissioner in New York City, published in *The City Journal* and was, briefly, based at the Manhattan Institute. Warning of the dangers of overly lenient prison management, "soft" treatment programs, and "liberal" court interventions, such figures crafted an image of super-predators (DiIulio, 1995a) that built squarely on the crime debate of the 1980s. With its barely disguised racial (racist) characteristics, this work dovetailed neatly with populist accounts of race and "intelligence," assertions of a Black "subculture" of violence, and the "moral poverty" purportedly ailing the (Black) underclass that flourished in the press (Bennett et al., 1996; Herrnstein & Murray, 1994).

Political scientists have paid considerable attention to the continuing expansion of the neoconservative movement under Clinton, and also to the role of related think tanks and public intellectuals. Despite the vicious debate such institutions and individuals provoked on crime, criminologists have yet to do more than mention them in passing (Wacquant, 2001b). DiIulio is the best known, whether as an academic, or more recently as a member of the George W. Bush administration, briefly in charge of faith-based initiatives until he resigned his post in somewhat acrimonious circumstances. Previously based at Princeton, before joining the faculty of the University of Pennsylvania, John DiIulio expressed vociferous support for incarceration in general and a particular kind of "tough" management of prisons in particular (DiIulio, 1987). Crowing, in his 1995 piece in *The Weekly Standard,* for example, DiIulio (1995) wrote that "no one in academia is a bigger fan of incarceration than I am" (DiIulio, 1995, p. 28).

DiIulio and his colleagues explicitly wrote of connections between race, crime, morality, welfare, and punishment, calling for harsher prison terms for many offenses. They heaped scorn on "liberals" and academics (usually represented as one and the same, despite their own university affiliations) and their mistaken and dangerous belief in such societal causes of crime as poverty, education, or racism. Instead of structural accounts, these conservative authors developed independently and together a morality tale, in which crime was caused by the breakdown of the modern (Black) family. The implicit racialization of much of the literature from this period can be breathtaking. The so-called "moral poverty theory" espoused by DiIulio, Bennett, and Walters explains crime as a direct result of those who grow up without appropriate adult role models. Such families DiIulio contrasts—just in case you missed his point—with "the churchgoing, two-parent black families of the South" under Jim Crow, who, he says, "never experienced anything remotely like the tragic levels of homicidal youth and gang violence" (DiIulio, 1995a, p. 26). Putting aside his apparent nostalgia for the era of Jim Crow—surely an unintended reading of this piece—DiIulio manages to reveal his hand on matters of race, religion, and family structure. It comes as no surprise to find, then, that elsewhere he recommends the forcible termination of Black parental rights and the White adoption of the resultant parentless Black babies (Bennett et al., 1996), along with various encouragements to marry.[6]

In contrast to such populist figures as DiIulio, the more politically progressive sociologists of punishment largely ignored matters of racial inequality (though see Wacquant, 1999) and failed to reach out to a more general audience, promoting instead a sophisticated but remote theoretical and interdisciplinary account of penal ideologies and practices (Garland, 1990; Feeley & Simon, 1992; Zimring & Hawkins, 1995).[7] Those conducting fieldwork were equally ineffectual. It was left to historians, who, in revisionist and, in some cases, best-selling texts on slavery, unearthed shocking accounts of the violence of convict leasing and plantation prisons. Though such authors usually alluded to the connections between slavery and the current consolidation of the American penal system, for the most part their studies left race safely confined to the past (Oshinsky, 1997; Mancini, 1996; Wacquant, 2001a, 2001b).

Managing Prisons

Given the academic and political debate over punishment, what were prisons in the 1990s actually like? It is, as ever, unwise to generalize about such a diverse system as the U.S. While a number of states and the federal system concentrated on an analysis of risk factors and their classification systems (VanVoorhis, 1994; van Voorhis & Brown, 1996), by 1992 half the U.S. states and the federal system had adopted "shock incarceration" programs that prioritized harsh, physical training, hard labor, and military drill. Others introduced "boot camps" for juvenile offenders. These institutions propagated a "get tough" culture by subjecting relatively minor offenders to discipline that, in its emphasis on the virtues of physical hardship, bordered on corporal punishment (MacKenzie & Souryal,

1994). At the same time, prison systems all over the country constructed in ever greater numbers super-maximum-security prisons to mark out and subdue the "worst of the worst" (King, 1999; National Institute of Corrections, 1997, 1999).

Paradoxically, despite the apparent overweening nature of many penal regimes, prison psychologists regained much of their status and centrality to prison life in the 1990s, designing and implementing classification systems and drug treatment programs. Classification reform in many states, which had begun in the late 1970s following concerns over indeterminate sentencing, became a key vehicle of the actuarial logic of the time. Differentiating inmates according to "objective criteria," classification systems embedded risk-needs assessment into the daily operations of most prisons (see, for example, Jesness, 1996; Hannah-Moffat, 2005). Increasingly, they also distinguished between women and men. In 1993, for example, the federal prison system designed a new classification system for women in recognition that, under the old system, women were being routinely overclassified as security risks (VanVoorhis & Presser, 2001).

Even the 1994 Crime Control Act, which is typically viewed as central to the propagation of punitive sentiment and practice, played a pivotal role in resurrecting prison treatment programs by demanding that the Federal Bureau of Prisons create drug treatment programs in all its establishments. Such programs, which sought to address "inmate drug abuse by attempting to identify, confront, and alter the attitudes, values, and thinking patterns that lead to criminal and drug-using behavior" (Federal Bureau of Prisons, 1999, p. 1), were not, however, a direct return to the past. No longer the basis for any kind of assessment whether the prisoner was ready to be released, they sought instead to encourage the prisoners to reform themselves (Bosworth, 2007a).

Such strategies were representative of "the new penology" identified by Feeley and Simon in an influential article published in 1992. A rare piece on punishment or imprisonment appearing in the academic journal *Criminology,* their article argued that the U.S. was witnessing the evolution of a new approach to dealing with those who broke the law, which was "markedly less concerned with responsibility, fault, moral sensibility, diagnosis, or intervention and treatment of the individual offender" (Feeley & Simon, 1992, p. 452). Earlier discourses of diagnosis or retribution were replaced with discussions of probability and risk as actuarial justice was "concerned with techniques to identify, classify, and manage groupings sorted by dangerousness" (Feeley & Simon, 1992, p. 452). Its task, they said, was "managerial, not transformative," and concerns about rehabilitation and crime control were superseded by anxieties over efficiency and economics (Feeley & Simon, 1992, p. 452).

Actuarial justice, as it was conceived by Feeley and Simon, seemed far removed from the expressive, punitive accounts that had characterized Clinton's various pronouncements on criminals and victims. It would be a mistake, however, to view such justifications of imprisonment as somehow distinct. Rather, they may be more usefully understood as codependent. In this view, the normalization of high incarceration rates (despite a drop in crime) cannot be separated from the growing number of supermaximum secure institutions founded in this era, nor from the ongoing erosion of traditionally rehabilitative prison offerings in education, training, and so on. It was not just that numbers made it harder to deliver services, but that risk management and actuarial justice presented prisons as just another kind of institution to be administered efficiently. In so doing, their particularity and problems receded from view, along with other, loftier goals and limits (Bosworth, 2007a). Like David Garland's notions of a "criminology of the self" and a "criminology of the other," actuarial techniques were appropriate for large numbers of offenders, yet did not, in themselves, rule out punitive responses and rhetoric for the rest. In fact, they may have laid the foundation for harsher responses, both for crimes judged—according to a range of criteria—to be serious, as well as for those who failed to respond to mainstream settings.

Experiencing Incarceration and Challenging the Culture of Control

Despite the development of a vibrant theoretical field about punishment in the 1990s that, in many ways, rescued prison studies from being absorbed wholesale into the administration of justice, many scholars implicitly unhooked the purported object of their study from its reality by marginalizing firsthand accounts and by ignoring the practical and quotidian aspects, let alone the conceptual constructs, of race and gender. Their silence, which was rooted, in part, in methodological divisions, undermined their ability to challenge popular punitivism, since the absence of such firsthand accounts made it difficult to humanize the impact of mass incarceration and challenge the representation of offenders as violent super-predators.

At the same time, overcrowded and overburdened penal institutions became unwilling to allow researchers access, while academic institutional review boards that followed restrictive federal guidelines (designed for biomedical researchers) left many universities, leery of potential lawsuits, uneasy with research in potentially "dangerous" places. The increasing demands of the tenure system may have played a role as well, since young faculty no longer felt free to devote themselves to time-consuming pieces of fieldwork, while the predominance of positivist methodologies within the social sciences, which had sprung up in the previous decade, more broadly favored dataset analysis over qualitative research. All in all, according to Jonathan Simon (2000b), "just when the experience of imprisonment is becoming a normal pathway for significant portions of the population, the pathways of knowledge that made the experience of incarceration visible are closing down" (Simon, 2000b, p. 285).

As suggested in Chapter 5, however, the demise of ethnography has been overstated by many sociologists of punishment. Despite numerous barriers, academics continued to publish ethnographic studies of the prison. In particular, the literature on women's prisons, past and present, blossomed (Krutschnitt & Krmpotich, 1990; Butler, 1997; Owen, 1998; Pollock, 1998; Watterson, 1996). So, too, scholars published the first book-length qualitative studies of Native American prisoners (Grobsmith, 1994; Ross, 1998); articles on long-term inmates (Porporino, 1990); fathers in prison (see, for example, Lanier, 1993); Latino and Latina prisoners (Diaz-Cotto, 1996); and the experience of guards (Conover, 2001). Journalists and prisoners also produced firsthand accounts of life behind bars at this time (Earley, 1993; Rierden, 1997; Abu-Jamal, 1995, 1997; Rideau & Wikberg, 1992; Peltier, 1999).

Most such studies represented life in prison as an ongoing struggle due to overcrowding, institutionalized brutality, and other social inequalities. Institutional life, they suggested, continued to be defined by the "pains of imprisonment" and by a society of captives living in brutal contest with their guards. In her study of counseling in prison, for example, Jocelyn Pollock wrote critically about the numerous difficulties faced by women in prison, as well as the challenges they posed for those who remain committed to rehabilitative endeavors. "How can helping professionals facilitate personal growth and positive change," she asks, "if every message inmates receive—from the first disinfecting shower and rectal search, the barbed wire, and officers yelling at them that they 'ain't shit'—tells them that they are unworthy and unwanted?" (Pollock, 1998, p. 28).

In addition to the academic work on life in prison, a number of national and state lobby groups sprang up in this decade, starting with the organization and publication *Prison Legal News* in May 1990, which sought to cast light on the hidden world of the prison and its effect on individuals and their families. A series of groups, like Families Against Mandatory

Minimums (FAMM) (established in 1991) and the November Coalition (established in 1997), were founded specifically to address the effect of sentencing policies in the War on Drugs. The Justice Policy Institute—a nonprofit organization—formed in Washington, D.C., in 1997 "... to promote effective solutions to social problems and to be dedicated to ending society's reliance on incarceration" (www.justicepolicy.org) has since become highly influential as a source of information on all aspects of the criminal justice system. Another, the abolitionist group Critical Resistance, which began in Oakland, California, in 1998, to lobby for the total abolition of the prison industrial complex, has been particularly effective in mobilizing student groups around the country and in directing their attention to the racial and gender biases of the penal system.

Similarly, the 1990s saw a number of critical publications on U.S. prison conditions from more established human rights and penal reform groups such as Amnesty International (1999), the American Friends Service Committee (1994), and Human Rights Watch (1996, 1997). In addition to such work, a number of accounts of women's imprisonment written by academics and journalists emerged at the end of the decade (Rierden, 1997; Owen, 1998), while others tackled specific problems like mental health in prison (Kupers, 1997). Those behind bars, particularly individuals who self-identified as political prisoners, reached out with firsthand accounts (Abu-Jamal, 1995, 1997; Peltier, 1999) while others told their stories to academic researchers (Girshick, 1999) or had their writings published in edited collections (Franklin, 1998). Inmate-run publications, like *The Angolite, The Journal of Prisoners on Prison, Razor Wire,* and *Prison Legal News,* provided outlets for prisoner-authors, acting as vehicles of social dissent, while some former or serving prisoners produced guidebooks for those entering prison for the first time (Hogshire, 1994; Long, 1990).

Unlike their colleagues in the sociology of punishment, prison scholars were often directly concerned with matters of race and gender and the manner in which such factors structured prison life. In his searing critique of the provision of mental health services in prison, for example, Terry Kupers (1999) found that "... prisoners of color consistently complain that the white officers do not understand them and do not know how to talk to blacks and Latinos. They also feel that most of the staff look down on them and call them derogatory names" (Kupers, 1999, p. 99). Linking such institutional racism to mental health, he went on to claim that "... where racism and interracial tensions are left to fester, inmates of all races are more at risk for attack, harassment, uncontrolled violent outbursts, and mental disturbances of all varieties" (Kupers, 1999, p. 99).

In her study of women in a California state prison, Barbara Owen painted a slightly different picture of race relations, arguing that race was "deemphasized in the everyday life of the prison" and was not "central to prison culture" (Owen, 1998, p. 151). According to one of her research participants, "We are not like the men, because we learn to live with each other. We communicate. It is not a racial thing in here. . . . We all stick together" (Tootie, cited by Owen, 1998, p. 153). It was not that the prison was free from racism, however. Rather, Owen found, much of the racial conflict originated ". . . in the attitude and behavior of staff, often more so than within the prisoner culture" (Owen, 1998, p. 156).

In her ethnography of Native American women in a Montana state prison, Luana Ross accused prison staff in general of a lack of respect for the women under their care and control. Most guards, she said, were "characterized by prisoners . . . as stirring up trouble" (Ross, 1998, p. 161). The Native American women reported particularly poor relations with guards, complaining about being labeled as "troublemakers" (Ross, 1998, p. 164), "racists" (Ross, 1998, p. 165), and denied the right to "practice their religion fully" (Ross, 1998, p. 165). According to Ross, the "image of the 'savage Indian' " thrived (Ross, 1998, p. 166).

Such feminist-inspired literature expanded prison scholarship in other ways as well, by drawing attention to the lives of women before incarceration. Scholars did not limit their analysis to life behind bars, but rather sought to understand the "pathways" to crime and incarceration. Owen's (1998) study of how women negotiated prison life in California and Beth Richie's (1996) disturbing portrait of the sickening violence suffered by many of the African American women she interviewed at the Rose M. Singer Women's Correctional Institution in Rikers Island Jail, New York City, cast stark light on the damaging intersections between race, class, and gender that were otherwise too easily disguised by the populist rhetoric of the time. Such intersections, these studies demonstrated, led women not only into offending, but eventually to prison as well. For such people, prison was "a world that must be lived through and negotiated daily. The women in prison struggle with and accommodate the problems of their outside lives and their lives in prison, solving them through a complex social organization and reconstitution of self." Prison culture, in this analysis, was a result of neither internal factors (deprivations) nor external ones (importation), but rather grew from the interplay between them. It was, in other words, "a dynamic, changing framework" that was "shaped by the struggle to survive" (Owen, 1998, p. 17), a struggle that was determined by intersections of race and gender.

For many, when the Clinton "reforms" of welfare, education, and housing took their toll, life was so difficult on the streets that prison offered a kind of sanctuary. "I probably would have been dead if I had not come to prison" (Owen, 1998, p. 189), said one participant in Owen's study, while another bleakly asserted that prison was "the best thing that ever happened to me" (Owen, 1998, p. 188). Such comments encouraged authors like Lori Girshick to argue that prison had become a "dumping ground for women who have no viable options for self support [and an] institution to which they must turn for drug treatment, job training, or safety from battering" (Girshick, 1999, p. 3). Across the country, from California (Owen, 1998), through North Carolina (Girshick, 1999) to New York City (Richie, 1996), a similar image emerged of women in prison "living at or below the poverty level at the time of their arrest" (Richie, 1996, p. 151) and suffering "acute injury, chronic pain, sexual degradation, and emotional trauma [and] racism" (Richie, 1996, p. 159).

Many of the prisoners who published autobiographical accounts also concentrated on connections between violence, poverty, and racism inside and outside prison. Mumia Abu-Jamal, for example, who was found guilty in 1981 of killing a Philadelphia police officer and has, since then, lived on death row despite having his capital verdict overturned in 2001, published a number of books and articles on racism and violence behind bars. So too, Leonard Peltier (1997), a former leader of the American Indian Movement (AIM) who was convicted and sentenced to prison for life in 1977 for killing two FBI agents, described an ongoing battle with institutional authorities to practice his religious and cultural beliefs. In an account that resonated with Jack Abbott's from almost two decades earlier, Leonard Peltier portrayed the prison environment as claustrophobic and all-encompassing. It could overwhelm a person, he suggests:

> . . . in here, every sound is magnified in your mind. The ventilation system roars and rumbles and hisses. Nameless clanks and creakings, flushings and gurglings sound within the walls. Buzzers and bells grate at your nerves. Disembodied, often unintelligible voices drone and squawk on loudspeakers. Steel doors are forever grinding and slamming, then grinding and slamming again. There's an ever-present background chorus of shouts and yells and calls, demented babblings, crazed screams, ghostlike laughter. Maybe one day you realize one of those voices is your own, and then you really begin to worry. (Peltier, 1999, pp. 5–6)

That so many diverse examples of dissent can be identified—and there are many more, such as those associated with church groups, some of which were founded well before the 1990s—speaks to the contested nature of the "culture of control," despite its apparent hegemony. That so many addressed matters of race and gender in the face of the demonization of much of the minority community in populist rhetoric, the silence on such matters within mainstream and theoretical criminology may be surprising. Together, these counterexamples reaffirm the warning of criminologist Lucia Zedner (2002) against the "dangers of dystopia." Although it is sometimes tempting to view the 1990s as an era of near total consolidation of popular punitivism and as a time when racially motivated criminal justice policies grew unchecked, significant attempts were made to resist it. Activists, prisoners, and academics of all stripes, from historians (Lichtenstein, 1995) to psychologists, argued that "prisons should be deployed very sparingly" (Haney & Zimbardo, 1998, p. 719). In popular culture too, a critique can be identified in a range of Hollywood films, such as *The Shawshank Redemption* (1994), *Dead Man Walking* (1995), and *The Green Mile* (1999), along with more sober documentaries like *The Farm: Angola, USA* (1998).

Given that none of these interventions successfully called into question the reliance on incarceration, are they worth recalling? After all, not even the precipitous drop in crime that began in 1990 and continued throughout the decade undermined political and popular faith in the virtues and need for the prison (Zimring, 2007; Blumstein, 2000). Should we then simply ignore or gloss over challenges to and criticism of imprisonment?

It may be that the counter-discourses were not compelling or considerable enough to outweigh the forces stacked against them. In addition to presidential statements about crime and victims, as well as the divisive policies promoted by right-wing pundits, an enormous volume of misinformation streamed through the popular mind in the 1990s exaggerating the threat of crime, the impact of drugs, and the terrible menace of more lenient sentencing. In such preaching, the media, as ever, often led the way (Donziger, 1996). States and the federal government, also, despite the academic evidence and work by penal reformers, for the most part remained committed to the imprisonment binge. In 1992, the Department of Justice saw no reason to disguise its intent, entitling a report *The Case for More Incarceration.*

It may yet be too early to determine conclusively whether the counter-examples of the 1990s were effective or not. As we shall see, a number of the critiques made in the 1990s have gathered steam in the first decade of the 21st century, particularly once they were rephrased as matters of economics and public safety. Some are cautiously optimistic that mass incarceration may have had its day. If that is the case, then the 1990s may be, eventually, recast as the beginning of the end.

Even so, the failure of robust critique to have much effect on policy should remind us of the sexist and racist logic inherent in much of U.S. society that renders certain sectors of its community expendable. Certainly while prisons have always been used to control the poor and the disorderly, the extent to which incarceration in the 1990s became divorced from any of its historical justifications of justice, crime reduction, or rehabilitation is remarkable.

On another level, the failure of critique suggests that the penal policies and legislation may have been concerned with more than simply punishment. Whereas criminologists have tended to concentrate on the punitive nature of much of the legislation passed in this decade, recently some political scientists have considered the implications of extending the reach of the federal government into what had traditionally been understood as state matters (Gottschalk, 2006; Miller, 2004, 2008). For these scholars, the crime legislation, federal law enforcement, and federal prison policy are vehicles that expand and legitimate federal power. Taken together with David Garland's observations on the connections between punishment and sovereign power, they remind us that any discussion of imprisonment is an analysis of the state of the state and, by implication, the state of the nation.

CONCLUSION

Whereas once penal institutions sought to reform individuals through hard work, discipline, counseling, and/or religion, in the 1990s institutions became little more than warehouses, incapacitating an ever increasing number of women and men. Even as penal administrators and inmates sought to make sense of their lives behind bars and, where possible, make some kind of difference, little trace remained of the reformist optimism once so central to the penal enterprise. Instead, a dystopic vision of America, which had sprung up the previous decade, continued, in which the law-abiding mainstream increasingly criminalized and rejected troubling and troublesome sections of the population. Despite an overall growth in average income and a robust economy, the 1990s was a decade characterized by elaborate and bipartisan calls for ever greater restrictions on and control of the poor, the illegal, and the addicted.

Notwithstanding the immense social and economic costs of such policies and rhetoric, for many, the policies of criminalization were justified by a reduction in crime, as crime fell for the longest period on record. Even as academics failed to agree on the causes of this drop in offending, in his final State of the Union Address in 2000, President Clinton attributed the crime drop to "a national consensus we helped to forge on community police, sensible gun safety laws, and effective prevention." Conveniently overlooking the lumbering behemoth of the overcrowded prison system that such policies had spawned, he left with a parting warning: "Nobody—nobody here, nobody in America—believes we're safe enough. So again, I ask you to set a higher goal. Let's make this country the safest big country in the world" (Clinton, 2000). Tying the nature of the country, as well as its security, to its crime policies, Clinton, in a move prescient of what was to come, made the case for yet more state intervention. War, it seems, whether against crime, drugs, violence, or indeed on "terror," must be endless. If it is, then so too will be the growth of the prison.

NOTES

1. By 2004, only 16 states continued to give their parole boards full authority to release inmates through a discretionary process. The majority of prisoners in America are now released automatically and mandatorily without appearing before a parole board (Petersilia, 1999).

2. Matters in England and Wales, at any rate, culminated in March 1990 with a prisoner takeover of the main prison in Manchester known as Strangeways. Settled peacefully by the state, in marked contrast to the earlier U.S. responses in Attica and New Mexico (see Chapter 4), the Strangeways riot led to a critical report by Lord Justice Woolf, which, in turn, advocated just and fair treatment of those behind bars. Followed by a new Criminal Justice Act in 1991, the UK seemed, for a while, to be attempting some level of decarceration. All this shifted back, however, just a few years later after two high-profile escapes from maximum-security prisons as the Conservative government began espousing the view under then Home Secretary Michael Howard that "prison works." Despite this shift in rhetoric, from justice to punishment, the prison population did not start its rapid escalation until after the 1997 electoral victory of the Labour government.

3. Previously domestic policy advisor in the second Reagan administration.

4. Indeed, the creation of such groups shows no sign of slowing. As of September 2007, for example, there are an estimated 800 such conservative groups and 300 individuals operating in the United States (www.pfaw.org/).

5. Whose slogan, "turning intellect into influence," points to their belief in the power of ideas.

6. In those moments when he was not recommending harsher penalties, DiIulio offered religion as a possible solution to crime. "If we are to have a prayer of stopping any significant fraction of the super-predators short of the prison gates," he wrote, "then we had better say 'Amen,' and fast . . . let our guiding principle be, 'build churches, not jails'—or we will reap the whirlwind of our own moral bankruptcy" (DiIulio, 1995a, p. 28).

7. More recently, figures from this group of scholars, including Jonathan Simon, have begun to use the Internet as a forum for progressive discussions. (See, for example, his blog at www.governingthroughcrime.blogspot.com.)

Seven

Challenging the Culture of Control?

. . . imprisonment is not any longer, if ever it was, a rational response to high levels of crime. Rather, our mass incarceration policy is an historical inheritance, bequeathed to us by wave after wave of crime-fighting at the state and the federal level over the past 35 years. This policy response . . . has now become counter-productive.

—Loury, 2007, p. 2

Locking up criminals for longer periods of time has proven one of America's most effective anticrime strategies.

—Lehrer, 2000, p. 2

After having passed my entire adult life inside, I am convinced that these places of confinement only condition people to fail.

—Santos, 2006, p. 287

As we near the close of the first decade of the 21st century, opinions on the national character, purpose, and legitimacy of U.S. imprisonment are more divided than ever. On the one hand, prisons, in some form, have become ever more entrenched as tools of border control. Immigration detention centers, Guantánamo Bay, military prisons on U.S. soil, and the secret CIA prisons all fit into this category. On the other hand, however, since 2000, there has been a flurry of state and federal commissions, debate, and legislation that has sought to reform elements of the domestic prison system. Examples of national-level commissions and legislation include the 2006 Commission on Safety and Abuse in America's Prisons (Gibbons & Katzenbach, 2006), the October 2007 hearings in the Joint Economic Committee (JEC) on the ". . . social, economic and political costs of mass incarceration in the U.S.," the 2003 Prison Rape Elimination Act, and the 2007 Second Chance Act. Others, at the state level, have concentrated on matters from gender-specific issues in the treatment and needs of female prisoners to the enfranchisement of former felons.[1]

Even before the economic crisis of 2008, some of those states that had been among the fiercest proponents of mass incarceration started to reconsider the wisdom and feasibility of this practice. In Georgia, which expanded its daily prison population by 357 percent between 1980 and 2007, there have been calls to "rebalance" "public safety" and "prison costs" (Welsh, 2008). As the economic recession deepened in late 2008 and early 2009, a number of states from New York to Kentucky began to consider implementing early release programs to avoid budget shortfalls. These states and others, including Texas, Louisiana, and Kansas, have sought also to reduce their penal populations by diverting parole violators. Finally, a range of commentators in criminal justice research centers and think tanks such as the Sentencing Project (Mauer & King, 2007), as well as the expert witnesses to the Joint Economic Committee (JEC) meeting on imprisonment (Western, 2007; Loury, 2007; Jacobson, 2007) and an increasing number of academics (Clear, 2007; Petersilia, 2003) have begun to worry at the collateral effects of mass incarceration, expressing particular concern about the racial disparities in, and effects of, penal policy at the state and federal levels.

To a large extent, anxieties over security and terrorism have replaced issues of crime and punishment as factors galvanizing public outrage and fear. As a result, most of those conservative think tanks and pundits who were so exercised over crime and punishment in the 1980s and 1990s fell all but silent on such matters after 2001, preferring instead to debate Iraq, Al Qaeda, and immigration, as well as the case for eroding civil liberties (see, for example, MacDonald, 2006; MacDonald, Hanson, & Malanga, 2007; Malkin, 2004). The prison is discussed rarely by such figures, and only then approvingly in relation to the drop in crime, or in terms of prisoner reentry (see, for example, Price, 2006; Muhlhausen, 2007; Goldsmith & Eimicke, 2008; MacDonald, 2008).

To be sure, security and imprisonment, particularly in their intersection with justice and civil rights, are deeply inter-connected (see, for example, Feulner, 2006). It may be, however, that the primacy now accorded to security rather than punishment opens the possibility of some systemic change in domestic prisons—if only by shifting public attention. More likely, however, if the past provides any clues to the longevity and ubiquity of the prison, particularly as a tool of, and an adjunct to, warfare, the focus on terrorism will ensure that any reform will be mild at best. In any case, this chapter and Chapter 8 will address these issues separately. Starting with domestic prisons, this chapter documents the various challenges to the culture of control that have bubbled up since 2000. Chapter 8 will concentrate on the prison's role in safeguarding "homeland security" and in controlling immigration.

Prisons in the 21st Century

The prison population, which had accelerated so dramatically in the 1980s and 1990s, began to level off and, in some places, to decline from 2000. Change, however, was short lived. By 2005, though some states—such as New York, New Jersey, and Illinois—either kept their figures stable or saw them continue to retract, the national rate of incarceration began to rise once again.

According to the most recent statistics (West & Sabol, 2008; Sabol & Couture, 2008), ". . . after increasing 2.8% during 2006, the growth of the prison population slowed to 1.8% during 2007" (West & Sabol, 2008, p. 1). The prison population increased in 37 jurisdictions, led by the federal prison system and followed by Florida, Kentucky, and Arizona. It also rose slightly in those states where it had previously been stable or had seen a reduction in confined populations, namely New York, New Jersey, Illinois, and Maryland (West & Sabol, 2008; Sabol & Couture, 2008). As it had the previous year as well (Sabol, Minton, & Harrison, 2007), Vermont experienced one of the largest drops in its penal population, which declined by 3.2 percent in 2007.

Even as the growth of the largest penal systems slowed somewhat, most states and the federal system increased their numbers of beds available during 2007, either by contracting out to private companies or by building new facilities. In 2006, California Governor Arnold Schwarzenegger had attempted a more radical solution, announcing plans to ship 8,000 convicts to private prisons in other states. However, the California Supreme Court overruled this decision, citing the deleterious impact of the distance offenders would be held from their families. The reliance on the private sector was not called into question.

By 2007, 7.4 percent of the total sentenced prison population was held in private facilities, up from 6.5 percent in 2000 (Couture & Sabol, 2008). Even so, most states operated either at the limits of or well above their capacity, led as ever by the federal system, which was overcrowded by 36 percent (West & Sabol, 2008).

Other characteristics of the 21st-century penal population can be gleaned from quantitative accounts produced over this decade. In 2003, for example, a report from researchers at the Federal Bureau of Justice Statistics found that ". . . for women, the chances of going to prison were 6 times greater in 2001 (1.8 percent) than in 1974 (0.3 percent); for men, the chances of going to prison were over 3 times greater in 2001 (11.3 percent) than in 1974 (3.6 percent)" (Bonczar, 2003, p.1). By midyear 2006, women composed 7.2 percent of the total confined population, as compared to 6.1 percent a decade previously. Although men are 14 times more likely than women to be incarcerated, the percentage increase in female prisoners under state or federal jurisdiction has continued to outpace that of men, growing in 2005 and 2006 at a rate that was almost twice as rapid. Similarly, on June 30, 2006, about 1 in 20 Black men were in prison or jail, compared to 1 in 50 Hispanic and fewer than 1 in 100 White men. When attention is turned solely to those within the 25- to 34-year-old age range, the figures for young Black men are particularly grave, with more than 1 in 10 (11 percent) of this group of the Black population in prison or jail.

Such figures depict a prisoner society of considerable racial and gender inequality. Increasingly as well, they suggest that traditional distinctions between inside and out are losing their relevance. If the statistical predictions of Bonczar (2003) come to pass, for example, ". . . about 1 in 3 black males [born in 2001], 1 in 6 Hispanic males, and 1 in 17 white males are expected to go to prison during their lifetime, if current incarceration rates remain unchanged" (Bonczar, 2003, p. 1). The future for minority communities also looks bleak in the forecast of the Pew Charitable Trusts (2007a), according to which, ". . . state and federal prisons will swell by more than 192,000 inmates over the next five years" (Pew Charitable Trusts, 2007a, p. ii). Given that these are merely the figures for imprisonment—and do not include those in jail, nor the far greater number of women and men sentenced to probation or other community-based punishments—it may not be too farfetched to argue that the U.S. is creating its own (racialized) penal archipelago, in ironic parallel with what was once so vociferously condemned in the Soviet Union.

Yet, according to some, this bleak vision of the future does not have to become a reality. Instead, as Michael Jacobson (2005) and others (Clear, 2007; Cadora, 2006) have recently been at pains to point out, there are a number of practical factors that should militate against the U.S. indefinitely expanding its penal state. Primary among their objections, which run the gamut from a decline in public faith in the effectiveness of prison to a growing concern over the unequal racial composition of the prison population, lies money. States simply may no longer be able to afford their habit of incarceration. Having become hooked on the quick fix of punishment, the U.S. is being forced, finally, to take note of its costs—literally and metaphorically. "This is the time," Jacobson (2005) urges, "to develop state-based strategies for penal reform" (Jacobson, 2005, p. 216).

The Costs of Imprisonment: An Emerging Critique

Over the course of the 21st century, an increasing number of scholars and activists have argued that imprisonment in the U.S. has reached, or even surpassed, a tipping point. It is time, such people argue, for "reform" and "downsizing," or even for dismantling the whole system altogether. The U.S. dependency on prison, they assert, is expensive, and worse, ineffective in generating public safety. As the Pew Charitable Trusts (2007a) put it succinctly, "Every additional dollar spent on prisons . . . is one dollar less than can go to preparing for the next Hurricane Katrina, educating young people, providing health care to the elderly, or repairing roads and bridges" (Pew Charitable Trusts, 2007a, p. ii). Or, as Todd Clear (2003) writes more expansively:

> Money that might have been spent on higher education has instead been diverted to pay to open new prisons—at the premortgage cost of about $100,000 per cell. People of color have been the social group hardest hit by prison expansions. About 14 percent of African American males aged 20–45 are locked up on any given day; nearly one-third of African American males born today can expect to serve time in prison on a felony. As many as 2 million people of color are prohibited from voting as a result of felony convictions, a number large enough to have changed the outcome of at least two presidential elections and dozens of congressional elections. (Clear, 2003, p. xiv)

Yet, how new is this critique? The differential impact on minority communities has long been recognized. So too, has the cost of imprisonment.

Neither has significantly undermined the legitimacy of the prison. For example, criminologist Lloyd Ohlin, writing over 30 years ago, noted that:

> The economic costs of [the penal] system constitute an increasingly heavy burden on tax dollars. For example, it is now commonplace in Massachusetts to note that the average annual cost per capita for inmates in state prisons could pay for an academic year at Harvard and a summer of travel and study abroad. (Ohlin, 1974, p. 250)

Perversely, the language of "cost-benefit analysis," which often underpins these critiques, previously justified calls for greater levels of incarceration (Haynes & Larsen, 1984; Gray, Larsen, Haynes, & Olson, 1991; Levitt, 1996). To be sure, the scale of the economic overinvestment in incarceration today is far greater than it was in 1974, as spending has jumped from $9 billion in 1980 to more than $60 billion in 2007. Moreover, the amount spent on corrections has become a dramatic anomaly in relation to other public services, since, over this same period, state and federal legislatures have sought to trim, cut, or even abolish government funding of health, welfare, and education. Even in Alabama, one of the poorest states in the nation, which spends the least amount per inmate in the country, prison expenditures surged by 44 percent between 1990 and 2005. In 2004, when Republican Governor Bob Riley increased the prison budget by 7 percent, he paid for it with a 10–20 percent cut in most other state agencies' budgets (Pew Charitable Trusts, 2007b; Greene & Pranis, 2005).

Until recently, few have been too bothered by these arrangements. States including California and New York long ago decided to spend more of their budgets on corrections than on education, fearing no adverse public reaction. In October 2007, however, the Joint Economic Committee (JEC) held hearings on the "costs" of mass incarceration. Charged with reporting on the current economic condition of the U.S., the JEC is meant to make suggestions for improving the economy. Yet, despite the committee's primary interest in economic efficiency, the expert witnesses and the senators concentrated especially on the social burdens of mass incarceration for the U.S. as a whole, and for specific minority communities in particular.

In his opening remarks, Democratic Senator Jim Webb of Virginia articulated an unusually stiff critique (for a politician) of U.S. prisons. Referring to the strategy of mass imprisonment as "... one of the largest public policy experiments in our history" that had "test[ed] the limits of our democracy and push[ed] the boundaries of our moral identity," he asked the assembled experts whether there were "... ways to spend less money, enhance public safety, *and* make a fairer prison system." Evidently concerned with the broader moral, social, and economic implications of the country's penal policy,[2] he observed that:

> America's incarceration rate raises several serious questions. These include: the correlation between mass imprisonment and crime rates, the impact of incarceration on minority communities and women, the economic costs of the prison system, criminal justice policy, and transitioning ex-offenders back into their communities and into productive employment. Equally important, the prison system today calls into question the effects on our society more broadly. (Webb, 2007, p. 1)

Those called to advise the committee—three academics and two criminal justice practitioners—followed Webb's lead with equally stern warnings. Starting with the sheer cost of incarceration, Glenn C. Loury, the Merton P. Stolz Professor of the Social Sciences in the Department of Economics at Brown University, informed the committee that "... spending on law enforcement and corrections at all levels of government now totals roughly a fifth of a trillion dollars per year. In constant dollars, this spending has more than quadrupled over the last quarter-century" (Loury, 2007, pp. 1–2). His criticism, however, did not stop with the expenditure involved, but, rather, like Senator Webb's, addressed the more general social costs of mass incarceration for U.S. society. In particular, along with Bruce Western, Professor of Sociology at Harvard University, Loury condemned the "wide racial gap" in the opportunities and punishment of U.S. citizens.

Western stressed the far-reaching impact, or what he called "collateral consequences" (Western, 2007a, p. 6), of a prison sentence on an individual's ability to find employment, adequate housing, and education after release. Putting in a plug for the Second Chance Act of 2007 that would address the resettlement needs of former prisoners in the community, Western advocated the creation of "... criminal justice social impact panels in local jurisdictions that can evaluate unwarranted disparities in juvenile and adult incarceration." This strategy, he suggested, could go some way towards eliminating "disproportionate incarceration in poor and minority communities" (Western, 2007a, p. 7). Such ideas were echoed in the testimony of the other witnesses, as each repeated the importance of helping prisoners after release.

Other than Loury's and Western's discussion of racial imbalance, the overarching thrust of the JEC's hearings was concerned with the relationship between state expenditure and effectiveness. As the director of the Vera

Institute of Justice in New York City, Michael Jacobson (2007) bluntly put it: "What do we get for that money?" (Jacobson, 2007, p. 3). In articulating his critique of prisons in such terms, Jacobson reflected a growing tendency in U.S. policy and scholarship to import the language and techniques of cost-benefit analysis to the debate over imprisonment. Such attitudes, apparent not only in the Vera Institute of Justice but also in those promoting "community justice" (Clear, 2007) or "justice reinvestment" (Cadora, 2006), seek quite deliberately to recast the relationship between incarceration and crime. Instead of making the (unpopular) academic argument that crime and punishment are largely unrelated, and steering clear of a grassroots-style "social movement" critique of imprisonment founded on social justice, self-styled "pragmatists" like Jacobson use "evidence-based research" to make their case that prison is expensive and ineffective, and that alternative sanctions are cheaper and better. In this view, the conditions of economic recession can be seized as an opportunity for change, in order to champion penal moderation.

In contrast to the dystopic views of the sociologists of punishment, who remain pessimistic about the likelihood of positive reforms, the pragmatism of Jacobson has been widely adopted in discussions of prisons and parole. Thus, authors of the Pew Charitable Trusts (2007a) report *Public Safety, Public Spending,* claimed that alternatives to incarceration "... can lead to better public safety outcomes while saving money," a situation that they define as "the dictionary definition of win-win" (Pew Charitable Trusts, 2007a, p. v). Driving home the economic critique, the Justice Mapping Center, headed by Eric Cadora, took statistical information about offenders to draw detailed maps of the local impact of state imprisonment. He used the same technology to reveal the inefficient use of criminal justice practitioners' time, showing the illogical distribution of parole and probation caseloads. Though crime may be dispersed across a city, prisoners tend to concentrate in particular neighborhoods. Just one area of Brooklyn in New York City, for example, known as Brownsville, which has 3.5 percent of Brooklyn's population, accounts for 8.5 percent of the state of New York's prison population. According to research conducted by the Justice Mapping Center in 2003, it cost $11 million to incarcerate people from just 11 city blocks in 2003 (Cadora, 2006; see also www.justicemapping.org).

Recasting the issue in econometric language, experts such as Cadora, Clear, and Jacobson have sought—with some success—to persuade states and the federal government to spend their money on alternative sanctions. Not only does overcrowding lead to diminishing returns as a crime control mechanism, they argue, but there is growing evidence that, once imprisonment rates cross a particular threshold, crime rates actually increase (Stemen, 2007; Clear, 2007; Clear, Rose, Waring, & Scully, 2003). It is not only the case that "... reforms can occur at the same time that public safety is protected" (Jacobson, 2005, p. 13), but that society will be better protected with fewer people behind bars. Public safety, which is meant to be a "benefit" of incarceration, is actually damaged by the imprisonment binge.

Prison Conditions and Public Safety

In 2006, the Vera Institute of Justice published *Confronting Confinement*, a far-reaching report on conditions in American prisons. Chaired by former U.S. Attorney General Nicholas deBelleville Katzenbach,[3] the Commission on Safety and Abuse in America's Prisons conducted public hearings and prison visits over a 15-month period. Through interviewing current and former correctional staff, as well as some family members of prisoners and academic experts, the commission presented an unusually complex and nuanced vision of life behind bars.

Structuring their analysis around the twin issues of safety and violence, the commission devised a series of recommendations that included: eliminating overcrowding, providing meaningful activity and rehabilitation, improving health care behind bars, limiting the use of segregation, professionalizing the career paths of prison guards, establishing independent oversight, and creating a nationwide data collection service on imprisonment generally. In each case, as in the cost-benefit argument, improving safety behind bars was primarily justified as a means of protecting the law-abiding community outside. "What happens inside jails and prisons," the authors of the report asserted, "does not stay inside jails and prisons. It comes home with prisoners after they are released and with corrections officers at the end of each day's shift. We must create safe and productive conditions of confinement not only because it is the right thing to do, but because it influences the safety, health, and prosperity of us all" (Gibbons & Katzenbach, 2006, p. 11).

A similar concern for public safety had been articulated three years earlier in the bipartisan support for the 2003 Prison Rape Elimination Act. This law, which for the first time publicly acknowledged the existence and problem of sexual violence behind bars, aimed both to generate information about the extent of prison rape and to encourage penal systems to devise methods of best practice for minimizing such violence. Correctional administrators are required to monitor, record, and address prison rape. In its emphasis on "data gathering" and its prioritization of costs and benefits, the Prison Rape Elimination Act, 2003 (P.L. 108–79), makes public safety its main concern (s2 (8)), followed by secondary issues such as institutional order (s2 (10)) and the ability of victims of sexual assault to reintegrate successfully into the community upon release (s2 (11)). Economic costs are also stressed in (s 2(14)), which describes the negative impact the level of prison rape has on the "effectiveness and efficiency of the United States Government expenditures through grant programs." In Section 3 of the Act, which details the purposes of the legislation, protecting "the Eighth Amendment rights of Federal, State, and local prisoners" comes in third last in significance, well behind techniques of data gathering and definition. Somewhat surprisingly, such constitutional safeguards appear only before the goals of "efficiency and effectiveness of Federal expenditures" (s (8)) and the rather opaque desire to "reduce the costs that prison rape imposes on interstate commerce" (s3 (9)).

A desire to diminish the potential victimization of the public and the cost to the government, rather than a concern over the human rights of prison victims or prison offenders, is also apparent in the words of the chairman of the National Prison Rape Elimination Commission, federal judge Hon. Reggie B. Walton. He thought it necessary to link explicitly the financial impact of incarceration with public safety to argue against sexual violence in prison, asserting that:

> The high incidence of prison rape undermines the effectiveness and efficiency of United States Government expenditures through grant programs such as those dealing with health care; mental health care; disease prevention; crime prevention, investigation, and prosecution; prison construction, maintenance, and operation; race relations; poverty; unemployment and homelessness. (www.nprec.us/about.html)

Such representation of the impact of sexual assault, as a set of "costs" to the state, has peculiar implications, denying the status of "victim" to the very individuals it is purporting to protect. The real, albeit as yet unrealized, victim is the community, which must, as ever, be protected. The harrowing depictions of victimization published by the prisoner support group Stop Prison Rape (www.spr.org) and others who have been affected by sexual violence are kept out of sight, and any dissonance that might arise from labeling prisoners (offenders) as victims is (narrowly) avoided.

A similar sleight of hand can be found in many of the discussions of the high rates of recidivism, or the failure of ex-prisoners to adjust to the community, which underpinned bipartisan support for the Second Chance Act 2007 (H.R. 1593). Signed into law by President Bush on April 9, 2008, this act amended the Omnibus Crime Control and Safe Streets Act of 1968 to improve existing reentry programs for adult and juvenile offenders while also developing new ones. It called on correctional systems to create more and better drug treatment services for those in prison and upon release, and to develop mentoring programs to help prevent reoffending. Such reforms will be funded by the usual system of block grants to states at an estimated cost of $400 million over the proposed 2008–2012 period.

According to Bush (2008b), the act will ". . . give prisoners across America a second chance for a better life" while also supporting "the caring men and women who help America's prisoners find renewal and hope." In an unexpected return to his original rhetoric of "compassionate conservatism" that had so swiftly dissipated upon his acquiring office, he spoke approvingly of the "acts of mercy that compassionate Americans are making the nation a more hopeful place." Oddly, he referred to a particular vision of American exceptionalism that had not been applied to offenders for many a year: "The country was built on the belief that each human being has limitless potential and worth. Everybody matters." Invoking a Christian metaphor, he articulated a shared vision of human frailty that interpreted offenders more gently than the dangerous animalistic figures popularized by Reagan and perpetuated across the political spectrum ever since. "I tried to remind them that the least shall be first," he says, in reference to a visit he made to a program for addicts in Baltimore, Maryland. "I also reminded him [sic] I was a product of a faith-based program. I quit drinking—and it wasn't because of a government program. It required a little more powerful force than a government program in my case" (Bush, 2008b).

The Second Chance Act, according to Bush (2008b), is a "work of redemption"; it "reflects our national interests" in lowering recidivism rates. In a radical articulation of the war metaphor that, throughout his presidency, served to divide Americans from one another, he described those who help former offenders as "members of the armies of compassion." Then, in what was surely a deliberate echo and inversion of his November 6, 2001, speech about the War on Terror, he characterized the act as an assertion of unity: "We're standing with you, not against you" (Bush, 2008b).

Bush's speech seems distant from the demonization of offenders—particularly of drug users—which has dominated public discourse in the U.S. since the 1980s. Yet, in certain key respects his words do not move him far from the traditional approach to offenders. As in the Prison Rape Elimination

Act, 2003, it is the community in his speech that is being protected and that is thus the victim, rather than the offender. By engaging the private sector in service provision, particularly faith-based groups, the act and its surrounding discourse about cost and safety resonates with neoliberal values of the Republicans, according to which individuals, working with compassionate helpers, must help themselves. Those who fail presumably deserve to be punished and further excised from the community.

Even as concerns over public safety and spiraling costs generated change in the operation of some penal systems and thus in the experiences of those incarcerated, they did little to challenge the punitive rhetoric that has characterized penal policy for so long. Instead, under their rubric, many states in this decade expanded their post-sentence measures. California, for example, began to tag all its released sex offenders with Global Positioning System (GPS) devices, while a number of states set up indefinite civil detention orders, permitting them to hold forever those designated as too dangerous for release. More generally, cost-cutting measures continued to chip away at education and training behind bars. Pragmatism, in the absence of a normative argument about (social or legal) justice, can serve many masters. A more robust, principled critique emerged from the courts.

The Courts: An Alternative Source of Critique

After coming to power in January 2001, the Bush administration appointed two new Supreme Court justices, Justice Samuel Alito and Chief Justice John Roberts,[4] along with numerous federal and district circuit judges. Concerns ran high in a number of quarters over the ideology behind such appointments, and their long-term effect on matters of social justice and cohesion in the U.S. It is perhaps surprising, then, that in regard to the prison at least, the first decade of the 21st century witnessed a considerable amount of court intervention and legislative activity over a whole range of aspects of life there. In particular, across a number of states, class action lawsuits by prisoners have won considerable amelioration of prison health care. With most dramatic effect, in 2005, the entire prison health care system of California was placed under receivership by U.S. District Judge Thelton Henderson of San Francisco, who determined that ". . . the state killed one inmate per week through medical incompetence or neglect" (Human Rights Watch, 2006, p. 508).[5] The state, which provides health care to around 175,000 prisoners in the 33 state prisons through services that have been contracted out to a range of providers, was accused by the judge of acting with "outright depravity" (Sterngold, 2005, p. A1).

Judge Henderson had originally heard the case against California in 2001 in *Plata v. Schwarzenegger.* At that time the court found that the state was in violation of the Eighth Amendment of the U.S. Constitution, which forbids cruel and unusual punishment. Though the suit was initially settled in 2002, when the state agreed to a range of remedies, by 2005 it had become apparent that insufficient improvements had been made. The administrator of the health care system reports directly to Judge Henderson, who was empowered to make improvements irrespective of the cost to taxpayers. At the end of 2008, the prison health care remained under the governance of the California Prison Health Care Receivership Corporation (www.cprinc.org), despite a number of appeals by the state. The costs of running the system have skyrocketed since long-term unpaid bills have finally been paid and substandard medical care is slowly improved. Following an investigation, California State Controller Steve Westly (2006) estimated the costs of running the health system in the financial year of 2006 at a massive $1.48 billion. In August 2008, the state was ordered to pay $8 billion over the next five years. As part of this ongoing case, the District Courts for the Eastern and Northern regions put the state of California under a tentative ruling on February 9, 2009, to reduce its overcrowding in order to facilitate prisoner access to health care; if it is followed through, up to 57,000 people may be disgorged.

The class action suit on behalf of California state prisoners is not the only one of its kind either currently in the courts or recently decided. The Ohio Justice Policy Center, for example, settled *Fussell v. Wilkinson* in October 2005, after two years of litigation. The settlement of this case, which also centered on prisoner health care, required the State of Ohio to hire 300 new, licensed medical staff, including 21 new physicians, to improve "quality control measures, and to revise all medical policies and protocols" (www.ohiojpc.org/main.html). In 2006, the U.S. Department of Justice informed Delaware, too, of its ". . . intent to investigate the adequacy of medical and mental health care services in five facilities operated by the State's Department of Corrections pursuant to the Civil Rights of Institutional Persons Act (CRIPA), 42, USC § 1997 to determine whether the services violated inmates' constitutional rights" (Delaware Department of Corrections, 2006, p. 3). On December 29, 2006, the state entered into a memorandum of agreement with the Department of Justice to improve its prison conditions, six months later appointing a monitoring team to ensure compliance. A number of other states, from Michigan to Nevada, have also been under investigation since 2006 for the health care and treatment of their inmates.

Other significant legislative reforms introduced after 2000 also affected the nature of and justification for imprisonment as well as its impact, even though many of them have not actually addressed the prison itself. In 2005, for example, Iowa and Nebraska both adopted measures that enabled former felons to vote, while in 2006 and 2007, Florida, along with Connecticut and Tennessee, reenfranchised many of those with felony convictions. In 2000, California voters passed Proposition 36, which mandated treatment rather than imprisonment for first- and second-time drug offenders. Other states, including Hawaii (SB 1188, 2002); Washington State (SB 2338, 2002); Kansas (HB 2309, 2003); Maryland (SB 194, HB 295, 2004); as well as Washington, D.C. (Proposition 62, 2002) followed suit, with similar legislation for diversion and treatment of drug offenders. Arizona had passed legislation four years earlier, in 1996 (Proposition 200), while, in a series of other states, including Michigan, Ohio, Florida, and Massachusetts, there were unsuccessful attempts at bringing in similar initiatives (Rinaldo & Kelly-Thomas, 2005). Such reforms reflect the growing influence of "therapeutic jurisprudence," a movement that has also led to the creation of drugs and community courts in most states that divert low-level, nonviolent offenders from jail (Nolan, 2001).

Most dramatically, in the federal system, on May 1, 2007, the U.S. Sentencing Commission proposed an amendment to the U.S. Sentencing Guidelines to reduce the sentencing range of crack cocaine offenses. Passed on November 1, 2007, this amendment applies to about 70 percent of crack cocaine users found guilty in federal courts, and should reduce sentences by an average of 15 months. As of year end 2008, Congress was still considering whether to make the ruling retroactive. On a smaller scale, but also suggesting some shift in public—or at least political—sentiment, in 2005 California legislators introduced a bill permitting condom distribution in state prisons, which passed the Assembly but not the Senate, while prisons in Mississippi and Vermont and jails in New York, Philadelphia, Washington, D.C., San Francisco, and Los Angeles have all permitted some condom distribution (Human Rights Watch, 2006).

Such examples are but some of the interventions that have been occurring in recent years in the penal administration and treatment of (ex-)convicts. When considered in tandem with the growing concerns over public safety and fiscal responsibility, they beg the question of whether these reforms represent a waning faith in prison as a whole, or merely exhibit a periodic readjustment of practice that may be driven by a number of overlapping forces, from overcrowding to good order and management. The sheer range of reforms that have been introduced since 2000, in addition to the shifting terminology that has dampened down some of the more punitive rhetoric that had previously dominated penal matters, is notable. However, as earlier chapters of this book have demonstrated, penal reforms have yet to dismantle the prison in any era. Instead, they have usually reentrenched it in a new form.

There are other factors, too, that make it hard to be optimistic. Not only are prison numbers rising once again, but there has been very little principled or normative public debate over the legitimacy of prisons per se, outside the more radical abolitionist movement (Davis, 2005). Thus far, most reforms merely tinker with the machinery of imprisonment, rather than questioning its purpose per se. The limitations of this approach were demonstrated most vividly when Hurricane Katrina devastated New Orleans in 2005, and city authorities abandoned the residents of the local jail to the rising floodwaters. So, too, the highly racialized, and inaccurate, accounts of a breakdown in law and order more generally suggested an ongoing groundswell of hostility toward the poor and disenfranchised.

Hurricane Katrina

On August 29, 2005, the Category 4 Hurricane Katrina hit the Gulf Coast area, passing close to New Orleans and, even though its arrival had been anticipated for some days, caused severe loss of life and property damage. A week after the hurricane had passed, the New Orleans levee system failed, and much of the city was flooded. The storm also devastated large swaths of Mississippi and Alabama. The results were soon obvious, when thousands of predominantly poor African Americans were left behind in New Orleans while their wealthier neighbors escaped. Despite claims in the media that ". . . tens of thousands of people *chose* to remain in the city" (Treaster & Kleinfield, August 30, 2005, p. 1), many were unable to leave in advance of the storm, because they lacked access to transportation. The more fortunate among those who did stay behind congregated at the New Orleans Convention Center (the Superdome) hoping for promised assistance. Others were left inside their houses or on the roofs of their dwellings, awaiting rescue. Some drowned.[6]

While commentators on the left decried the social inequalities and institutionalized racism unearthed by the differential impact of Hurricane Katrina, scholars and pundits on the right crafted familiar and deeply racialized accounts of lawlessness and violence among those who stayed behind. For

Anthony D. Romero, the Executive Director of the American Civil Liberties Union, Hurricane Katrina "... thrust a national spotlight on the persistence of racism in the context of American poverty and American Privilege" (Romero, 2007, p. 4). In contrast, Nicole Gelinas (2005), writing in The Manhattan Institute's publication, *The City Journal*, described the "... looters, rapists, and murderers who have terrorized New Orleans" (Gelinas, 2005, p. 1) as part of the city's preexisting "black criminal class" (Gelinas, 2005, p. 3). Rebecca Hagelin, a senior communications fellow at the Heritage Foundation and luminary in the conservative evangelical movement, suggested that nobody should have been surprised that the underclass became vicious: "In a culture where many people dress like gangstas, talk like gangstas, and strut like gangstas, should we be shocked and horrified that they start engaging in gangsta crime when given the opportunity?" (Hagelin, 2005a, p. 1).[7]

Almost from the beginning of the flooding, sensational newspaper reports depicted spiraling crime and disorder. Staff reporters from *The New York Times*, for example, referred to "opportunistic thieves," citing the city's director of homeland security Colonel Terry Ebert, who claimed that "these are not individuals looting . . . they are large groups of armed individuals" (Treaster & Kleinfield, August 30, 2005, p. 1).[8] Soon the reports became shriller, with comments from reporters and state officials, including the New Orleans mayor, stating that civil order had broken down and that violence was resulting, particularly at the Superdome. The city and those covering the disaster, it was claimed in a familiar evocation, must as a result stand on "war footing" (Carter, 2005). Charles Murray (2005), in an editorial in *The Wall Street Journal*, took such accounts to their logical conclusion, asserting that the hurricane revealed the growing numbers of the underclass and the (unspecified) dangers they pose to the rest of society. Differentiating between the deserving and undeserving poor in a rhetoric that was scarcely new, he characterized the latter as "the looters and thugs, and . . . the inert women doing nothing to help themselves or their children. They are the underclass." As the subtitle to his analysis proclaimed: "The poverty Katrina underscored is primarily moral, not material" (Murray, 2005, p. 11).

In fact, it seems that the reports of violence were groundless, and much of the "looting" appears to have been aimed at finding food and water rather than stealing material goods. As the authors of the American Civil Liberties Union (ACLU) report put it, "hungry white victims 'found' the food they needed to survive, while blacks doing the exact same thing were said to have 'looted' it" (ACLU, 2007, p. 11). The scale and impact of the misinformation, which has never fully or effectively been rebutted, was such, Jonathan Simon (2007b) observes, that "one of the major cultural memories and civic lessons that Americans seem to have taken from the story of New Orleans after Katrina is that law and order must be enforced at all costs as a chief priority of government at all levels" (Simon, 2007b, p. 1). And indeed, in an article published one year after the hurricane struck, Nicole Gelinas, a Manhattan Institute scholar and contributing editor to *The City Journal,* commented: "It's an enduring mystery why Bush hasn't used the Katrina disaster to show the world that America can rebuild a major city using a bedrock conservative principle: law and order first" (Gelinas, 2007, p. 3). Faced with an extreme example of state incompetence and insouciance, the media and the public turned instead to a more familiar, and, despite the fear it spawned, therefore, perhaps more reassuring narrative about crime, risk, and the urban (and minority) poor. Nowhere did this response have a more adverse effect than on the population of the city jail whom the authorities abandoned to the rising floodwaters.

Louisiana, like most Southern states, has a large penal population. Notwithstanding a recent dip in its overall rate of imprisonment, it had long been a leader in the area, locking up 1 in 100 of its residents at the end of 2005, well before the national tally rose to that level. Whereas, in terms of its prisons, Angola Penitentiary is probably the best known, boasting the state execution chamber, the annual rodeo, and *The Angolite,* Angola was, for once, not the penal institution that revealed most starkly the harshness of punitive sentiment in the state. Instead, that was left to a much more banal institution: the city jail.

At the time of the hurricane, this place—known as the Orleans Parish Prison (OPP)—held around 6,500 men, women, and children, of whom 2,000 were state prisoners and 200 were federal prisoners (Roman, Irazola, & Osborne, 2007; see also ACLU, 2006). The rest were local offenders awaiting trial or sentence. Like other jails, much of its population were illiterate, suffering from mental health problems, and coming off drugs. A certain proportion would also have been found innocent.

As the waters rose, most of the guards of the Orleans Parish Prison simply left, abandoning their charges to the deluge. After the flood, both the ACLU via the National Prison Project and Human Rights Watch interviewed numerous detainees (National Prison Project, 2006a). Their accounts chime with that of "Inmate #1," who

> . . . says her dorm quickly filled with chest high water. She states she was next moved to a smoke-filled dorm where she was housed with male prisoners. She says that the deputies locked her and the other prisoners inside the

> dorm. . . . She says she was not fed or given water for three days. Inmate #1 says she was next moved into a room filled with water and made to stay there for 24 hours prior to being moved onto the Interstate 10 overpass. On the overpass, she states she was ordered not to move on threat of being shot by the guards. While on the overpass, she states that fellow prisoners were losing consciousness from hunger and dehydration; she herself was pepper-sprayed. (National Prison Project 2006b, p. 1)

Another described being made ". . . to wait in line in water up to his/her neck," while struggling toward the overpass for collection. When on the overpass, such detainees were prevented from walking around. Upon finally boarding a bus to be taken to Angola, they were "pushed and verbally abused by Angola deputies" (National Prison Project, 2006b, p. 1).

The ill treatment continued once OPP inmates were shipped to other institutions. Not only were these other facilities often inadequate, but they were also violent. Four hundred were sent to the former prison facility at Jena, which was hastily reopened.[9] Here, many allege, they were kicked, beaten, and taunted with racial and sexual slurs (Human Rights Watch, 2005 p. 511; ACLU, 2006). At least 500 were held well beyond the duration of their original sentences. Contact with family members was difficult to establish, and many who were interviewed by Human Rights Watch (HRW) and the National Prison Project of the ACLU spoke of their anxiety about what had happened to their relatives during the storm.

The failure to evacuate the city jail, as well as the difficulty in rendering aid to those sheltering in the Superdome or in their homes revealed a fragile (federal, state, and local) government that, on the one hand, was unwilling to govern, and on the other, unable to do so properly. Under such circumstances, the hurricane did more than simply expose the "deep racial divisions that have long existed in New Orleans" (ACLU, 2006, p. 17),[10] it drew into question the political state's very purpose and legitimacy. In a state like Louisiana where social and racial control have been so deeply intertwined for so long, the racialization of fears about the breakdown in law and order should come as no surprise. So, too, apocalyptic visions of "no-go areas" and "war zones" were inevitable in a city without a fully functioning criminal justice system. Unable to govern, what else could it do but declare war on itself?

Governing Through Crime

In a major theoretical contribution to the debate over punishment that was published immediately after Hurricane Katrina, Jonathan Simon (2007a) asserted that mass imprisonment should not be viewed as ". . . a social strategy to reconfigure the domination of African Americans or discipline the margins of the labor force to support the increasing demands for exploitation of the neoliberal economic order, although it may well have these effects, but as a policy solution to the political dilemma of governing through crime" (Simon, 2007a, p. 159). According to Simon, the war on crime, which has been ongoing since Nixon, has altered "... the way political authority of all sorts and at all levels has been exercised" (Simon, 2007a, p. 261). Crime control has leached into many unrelated areas, and has, in the process, transformed the relationship between citizens and their government. Paradoxically, state power has been simultaneously strengthened and dispersed, as individuals have been constantly enjoined and/or forced to police themselves to avoid (seemingly inevitable) victimization.

By recasting crime policy as a means of "governance," rather than as a straightforward mechanism of social control, or as a mere statistical phenomenon, Simon directed criminological attention to the politically constitutive nature of criminal justice strategies and rhetoric. Along with a series of other authors in this decade, Simon also reminded us to think about the role of the state and federal governments in any analysis of imprisonment (see also Gilmore, 2007; Miller, 2008). Crime control, in this view, has undermined democracy itself, on the one hand, by enabling the fierce expansion of government intervention strategies and, on the other, by a parallel and concomitant retraction of state responsibility for safeguarding its own citizens. "Mass imprisonment," Simon (2007a) wrote, "... and the girding of public and private space against crime reflect an ongoing struggle by Americans and their public and private organizations to manage the relationship between security and liberty" (Simon, 2007a, p. 16). Those who are arrested or appear before the courts are not the only ones being "governed" in other words, but rather, as in Garland's (1996, 2001a) depiction of "responsibilization strategies," all citizens are expected to govern themselves to avoid victimization.

Although Simon spends relatively little time examining the prison itself, penal institutions have become central to "governing through crime." The prison, in this analysis, is "... a space of pure custody, a human warehouse or even a kind of social waste management facility, where adults and some juveniles distinctive only for their dangerousness by society are concentrated for the purposes of protecting the wider community." It "... promises no transformation of the prisoner through penitence, discipline, intimidation, or therapy" (Simon, 2007a, p. 142), but draws its legitimacy from the threat that it poses to lawbreakers and the security that it promises to victims. "Prisons provide a public good," he argues, "that is directly aimed at insecurity, the form of public need that crime legislation has made both visible and compelling" (Simon, 2007a, p. 157). As a result, the ". . . prison has become even more central to political order than it was to earlier styles of rule" (Simon, 2007a, p. 154).

Somewhat tempering Simon's bleak view of the prison as warehouse, most penal systems continue to pay lip service to rehabilitation. Thus, even as most prisoners remain idle due to cuts in services and overcrowding, penal administrators urge inmates to learn from their confinement to beat their addictions, eschew crime, and act responsibly (Bosworth, 2007a). They must, in other words, govern themselves.

A quick glance at the Web sites of a selection of state departments of correction reveals how the language of responsibility dovetails with concerns over efficiency and public safety in a familiar managerialist rhetoric. The "mission" of the Utah Department of Corrections, for instance, is to ensure public safety

> . . . by effectively managing offenders while maintaining close collaboration with partner agencies and the community. Our team is devoted to providing maximum opportunities for offenders to make lasting changes through accountability, treatment, education and positive reinforcement within a safe environment. (www.cr.ex.state.ut.us/)

Meanwhile, prisoners in Alaska ". . . will be treated in a safe and humane manner, and will be expected to enhance their ability to reform every day," while those in Mississippi are urged to ". . . be smart, choose freedom," and reject offending altogether (www.correct.state.ak.us/; www.mdoc.state.ms.us/).

Despite being, second to the death penalty, the most extreme articulation of the state's power to punish, prisons have also become a strategy of "governing at a distance." In so doing, they too "govern through crime," reflecting the contours and nature of the state and its sovereign power, while, in their calls for inmate responsibility, denying the extent of their control. Such paradoxical display and denial of power is facilitated by the ongoing absence of actual prisoners in most accounts of U.S. prisons. In addition to such administrative tools as mission statements, much academic and policy literature fails to include the experiences of the convicts. As a consequence, prisons have become a kind of dystopic "imagined community" (Anderson, 1984), just as mythologized as the idealized victims of criminal legislation so well identified by Jonathan Simon. Prisoners become demonized as the "worst of the worst," or romanticized as "political prisoners" and "intellectuals" (James, 2003; Rodríguez, 2006). Such polarized views not only grossly overstate the nature of the vast majority of rather ordinary people behind bars, but also maintain a strict binary between victims, or law-abiding citizens, and offenders that, in turn, inextricably requires the law-abiding citizens of the polity to reject and distance themselves from those behind bars. Inclusion, in other words, depends on exclusion.

Opening the Prison: Convict Voices

In fact, despite their absence in the mass media and in theoretical analysis, since 2000, there has been a resurgence of firsthand accounts of prison life in the U.S. (see, for example, Baca, 2002; Rodríguez, 2006; Johnson, 2003; James, 2003; Santos, 2006), prison teaching (Tannenbaum, 2000; Moller, 2003; Trounstine, 2001) and, despite various declarations of their "curious eclipse" (Wacquant, 2002), prison ethnography as well (Rhodes, 2004; McCorkel, 2003; Conover, 2001; Dermody Leonard, 2003). Such depictions appear in a number of formats, some more academic than others. Increasingly, for example, current and former prisoners are utilizing the Internet to publicize their views and experiences. Others are publishing firsthand accounts of life behind bars. Finally, and relatedly, the 21st century has seen a consolidation of a field known as "convict criminology" written by (predominantly male) former prisoners who now work in universities (Ross & Richards, 2003).

Even though serving prisoners remain, for the most part, unable to access the Internet themselves (although some prisons, like FCC Victorville, have recently introduced an e-mail system by which certain prisoners can send and receive e-mails from specific, approved individuals), the Internet, nonetheless, has become an important site of debate over the effectiveness and aims of incarceration. Web sites include personal ones, maintained by family friends in the community (see, for example, www.freedebicampbell.com, and www.michaelsantos.net), and those that promote "networking," and dating, between prisoners and those outside (www.prisonerlife.com). Most prison reform or activist groups operate Web sites (such as www.criticalresistance.org; www.famm.org; www.thefortunesociety.org), and there are a small number of blogs that address prison issues (see, for example, www.texasprisonbidness.org and gritsforbreakfast.blogspot.com).[11]

If the 1990s was characterized by a growth in right-wing think tanks and their accompanying publications, the first decade of the 21st century has witnessed a more general explosion of political and social commentary online. As the state with one of the largest prison systems, it is fitting that

California is also home to many of the most vocal critics of incarceration, both online and elsewhere. Umbrella organizations like the Prison Activist Resource Center (PARC) (www.prisonactivist.org) and Critical Resistance (www.criticalresistance.org), which organize grassroots groups around the country and provide educational resources and an outlet for prisoners' voices, publish much of their work online. California even has its own prison moratorium project, which, among other issues, provides explicit guidance in the form of a handbook for *How to Stop a Prison in Your Town* (California Prison Moratorium Project, 2008). Of course, the impact on policymakers of such testimonies is unclear, and, when emanating from former or serving prisoners, is unlikely to be great. Nonetheless, the sheer volume of such literature, whether published in more traditional areas or online, reveals a vibrant counterculture of penal critique that challenges many of the justifications of imprisonment.

Firsthand accounts usually resonate more with earlier sociological writings on the deprivations of imprisonment than with the recent theoretical literature on punishment. They also cast some doubt on the commitment of the state to facilitate personal growth or transformation behind bars. Michael Santos, for example, who is serving a 45-year federal sentence for his involvement in the distribution of cocaine, has written extensively on the everyday difficulties facing men in prison.[12] Much of his work calls into question the institutional commitment to helping prisoners reform:

> As soon as gates lock a man inside, the prisoner learns that the goal of the corrections system is to store his body until his sentence expires. There is no mechanism within the system to recognize efforts a prison may make to redeem himself. Consequently, few commit to such a path. Prisoners learn to live inside and forget, or willfully suppress, the characteristics of life in normal society. In so doing, they simultaneously condition themselves further to fail upon their release. (Santos, 2006, p. 280)

Despite the hopes of those who crafted the Second Chance Act, for instance, Santos suggests that the failures of former prisoners are written into the penal institutions themselves as prisoners and prison staff exist in uneasy conflict:

> Despite what corrections professionals may publish or profess, those of us who live in prison are convinced that administrators implement few programs with the interest of preparing offenders for law-abiding lives upon

> release. There is no authentic interest in motivating or encouraging prisoners to distinguish themselves with excellence. Programs exist purely for inmate accountability. They are tools administrators use to maintain security. To believe otherwise is akin to believing that the tobacco companies have an interest in helping people to stop smoking. (Santos, 2006, p. 283)

In any case, according to Santos, the inability of prisoners to control the basic elements of their daily lives—from their work details to their cell-mates and the prisons in which they are held—makes it difficult to do anything much. "Minutes after I finished the draft of this manuscript," Santos writes:

> . . . an officer announced an order over the loudspeaker at the federal prison camp. He wanted me to me report to the control center. Expecting bad news of some kind, I addressed and stamped an envelope. Then I sealed my manuscript pages inside and dropped the package into the outgoing mailbox before reporting. It was a good move, because soon after I presented myself, officers locked me in steel cuffs for placement in solitary confinement . . . At the following morning . . . officers unlocked the cell door and ordered me into chains. They marched me onto a bus that drove me to an airport in a neighboring community. In small steps because of the chains binding my ankles, I boarded an airplane full of convicts. We began a long flight that would keep me in transit for six weeks. (Santos, 2006, pp. xxv–xxvii)

Such modes of internal governance, whereby prisoners can be moved without warning, unavoidably (and perhaps deliberately) disrupt families, education, and training. In the federal system, they can result in individuals being moved thousands of miles.

In addition to accounts by prisoner authors like Santos, two other kinds of academic literature have sprung up this decade, which also stress the importance of individualized, highly personalized experiences of incarceration. Both, though located within academia, present themselves in (partial) opposition to it. The first body of literature, known as "convict criminology," describes how prisoners seek to defy or at least mitigate the culture of control under which they reside (www.convictcriminology.org). It seeks ". . . to create realistic criminology that impacts the reader in ways typical academic research and writing fails to do." Professing to be ". . . shocked by the number of criminologists who although they claim to be experts have little or no firsthand experience with how human beings experience the criminal justice system," the founders of Convict Criminology,

Jeffrey Ross and Stephen Richards (2003), maintain that such unconvicted authors "... simply do not comprehend the profound impact that imprisonment has on many individuals" (Ross & Richards, 2003, p. 349). "Adequate instruction in criminology, criminal justice, and corrections," they state, "requires field experiences to supplement what is learned in university classrooms" (Ross & Richards, 2003, p. 503).

Despite professing to be a new contribution to debates about imprisonment, on at least one axis, convict criminology remains remarkably familiar to more traditional studies of the prison, specifically in its failure to engage critically with race and gender. Even though some women contribute book chapters or articles to convict criminology publications, none, at the time of writing, are former prisoners. Likewise, the male contributors rarely address issues of either race or gender.

The second body of prisoner accounts makes up for these absences in convict criminology, focusing directly on matters of race, and to a lesser extent on gender as well (Stanford, 2004). This body of radical scholarship corresponds to a looser body of scholars, few of whom self-identify as criminologists, who are for the most part located in ethnic studies departments (Rodríguez, 2006; James, 2003; Johnson, 2004). These writers refer to prisoners as "political," "intellectuals," and "activists," constructing an histor(iograph)y of radicalism behind bars, from George Jackson to the present. Within this body of literature, there is considerable debate over "who 'qualifies' as a U.S. political prisoner." Spelling out the debate, Joy James (2003) rejects an "overly inclusive and simplistic" definition that would include "any incarcerated individual who self-defines [as a political prisoner]; anyone the state labels as a 'criminal' or 'terrorist'; and anyone the state politically discriminates against through differential enforcement of laws, racially and economically driven sentencing regimes, and prison treatment" (James, 2003, p. xi). In contrast, Dylan Rodríguez argues for a broader remit that would include " 'commonly' imprisoned people," who are "overwhelmingly poor, black, and brown ..." (Rodríguez, 2006, p. 5).

Reflecting institutional arrangements and intellectual allegiances, as well as methodological and political beliefs, these authors work closely with abolitionist reform groups, particularly with Critical Resistance. Like the "convict criminologists," they reject the possibility of a "neutral" standpoint on matters of incarceration. The prison, for them, embodies state brutality, and, in the disproportionate numbers of African Americans behind bars, can be linked directly to the institution of slavery. Despite addressing prison conditions and the justification of incarceration, prison activist literature rarely draws on mainstream or theoretical criminological literature, preferring instead an alignment with literary or ethnic studies to one with criminal justice. So, too, criminologists and policymakers fail to engage with such accounts, cordoning off "race studies" and gender into a specialized—and overlooked—body of work.

CONCLUSION: GOVERNING THROUGH IMPRISONMENT?

An optimistic reading of the various publications on prison suggests that there is a growing dissatisfaction with the institution. Some states are waking up to its economic and social costs. The flurry of commissions, court intervention, and legislative activity, and the marked decline in histrionic media verbiage about "super-predators" and the like, along with diversion initiatives such as Proposition 36 in California, and even the growing nationwide dissent over mandatory minimum sentences, seem to indicate a potential for a shift away from an overreliance on incarceration. However, for all that potential for reform, actual decarceration has been minimal, and there has been little movement to close prisons. New York City, for example, has kept its average daily jail population more or less stable, since 2001, at around 14,000 men, women, and children behind bars at any one time, down from 23,000 in 1993. So too, it has 9,000 fewer state prison inmates than it did 10 years ago, representing a drop of 12 percent. Yet, despite assurances from then Governor Eliot Spitzer that the state would close four of its upstate prisons, at a savings of $70 million, in April 2008, Spitzer's successor, Governor David Paterson, abandoned this plan. It may well be that economic surplus enabled mass incarceration, but thus far economic deficit has been slow to change that.

Indeed, though economic and, to a lesser extent, safety arguments seem to be effective in generating a national, if muted, critique of current incarceration policies, the failure of such strategies to engage in any depth with more complicated normative or rights-based arguments about incarceration made elsewhere suggests that penal moderates remain cautious about their likelihood of success (see, for example, Lazarus, 2004). Presenting their findings as "neutral," scientific, and "un-partisan" (see, inter alia, Austin et al., 2007; Cadora, 2007; Pew Charitable Trusts, 2007b), many authors cede the fiery rhetorical territory to their opponents, who, as Hurricane Katrina demonstrated, remain ready to pounce on the undeserving poor (Murray, 2005; Gelinas, 2005).

It may seem strange to quibble over the motivation for and language of penal reform, when, in the case of prison rape, for example, shamefully little had been done until it was presented as a financial and public safety issue that could be resolved, in large part, through objective data gathering. Nonetheless, arguments couched in this terminology can only with difficulty provide a means of critical reflection on the longevity of the prison, let alone establish a basis for developing a tougher analysis of its practices and beliefs. It cannot explain why, when recidivism rates have been high for a long time, concern over public safety has only recently been articulated. Likewise, unless their attitude hinges on a question of degree, why now should the public balk at paying for its prisons? Since cost savings and lower reoffending rates are presented as ends in themselves—that are somehow separate from thornier matters of human rights, morality, or justice—what is to protect against practices that might be extremely harsh, but reduce overheads or recidivism?

The weaknesses, or at least the limitations, of this approach were rendered most obvious, as they so often are in criminal justice matters, in the State of California. California operates one of the most overcrowded and most rapidly growing prison systems in the country, currently holding more than 175,000 prisoners in a system designed for about half that number. It is also a state where the lobbying power of the correctional officers union has been (and remains) notoriously influential (Gilmore, 2007). In this environment, fiscal and public safety arguments have been either overridden or transformed into a hardly recognizable form. Thus, faced with the possibility of a federal takeover of the state prison system, Governor Schwarzenegger signed the "bipartisan" Assembly Bill 900 or Public Safety and Offender Rehabilitation Services Act of 2007, committing $7.7 billion to add 53,000 prison and jail beds, while expanding drug treatment programs and developing secure "reentry" facilities. These practices, which could expand the prison system by one-third, were presented both as penal "reform," and as targeted at reducing reoffending and thus improving public safety.

Without an emphatic commitment to decarceration as a principled measure in itself, or indeed, to placing offenders into community penalties instead of prison, the economic- and public-safety-based arguments provide ineffective challenges to the legitimacy of imprisonment. They may even provide ballast for a radical expansion. In short, despite the reformist intentions of many authors, their reports, commissions, and legislation fail to break sufficiently with the punitive sentiments of the 1990s, which greatly reduced prison programs.

In any case, as Chapter 8 will detail, just as some popular opinion was starting to grow in opposition to the reliance on incarceration for drug offenders, another group of people were judged to be appropriate subjects for confinement: noncitizens. Much of the federal government's response post-9/11 reaffirmed the vitality of imprisonment, at the precise moment it was being called into question. Not only have scores of noncitizens been held in immigration service detention centers and federal prisons, but the U.S. has exported its high-security, no-frills imprisonment in the War on Terror. Under the two Bush administrations, military prisons and detention centers were presented as fundamental to U.S. national security. While there are some signs that policy may shift on these matters under President Obama, it is, as yet, too early to predict. The prison is dead. Long live the prison.

NOTES

1. See, for example, the October 2005 report from the Commonwealth of Massachusetts's Department of Correction Advisory Council, the 2005 commentary from the Vermont Agency of Human Services, and the 2004 findings of the Oklahoma Special Task Force for Women Incarcerated in Oklahoma.

2. In this, Webb (2007) cited Winston Churchill's famous statement of 1910, that "... the mood and temper of the public in regard to the treatment of crime and criminals is one of the most unfailing tests of the civilization of any country."

3. Previously U.S. Attorney General under President Lyndon Johnson.

4. Samuel Alito replaced Sandra Day O'Connor, and John Roberts replaced Chief Justice William Rehnquist.

5. After the prison health care system was under receivership for more than a year, prisoners in California in 2006 were still dying from common and treatable medical conditions such as asthma. Prison doctors were also continuing to fail to identify or treat preventable conditions that included perforated ulcers and hernias. One prisoner even died of hypothermia (Imai, 2007).

6. Strangely, the number killed remains unclear. Unlike those victims of 9/11, about whom the state sought to be as precise as possible, the figures of those killed by Katrina are hotly contested. According to the Web site of the Louisiana Department of Health and Hospitals, which stopped recording figures on August 1, 2006, 1,464 people died and 135 remain missing.

7. Hagelin is better known for her commentary and publications on the alleged demise of heterosexual family values. She has been a regular commentator on FOX News and along with her colleagues from right-wing think tanks like the Heritage Foundation publishes with conservative, Evangelical presses like Thomas Nelson and Regnery Publications (see, for example, Hagelin, 2005b).

8. The same quote was cited in a different article the following day as well (Treaster, August 31, 2005).

9. Jena itself became the subject of national attention in 2007 when a group of six Black teenagers were arrested and charged with attempted murder for their assault on a White teenager, Justin Barker, that landed him in the emergency room of the local hospital for three hours. The violence followed an earlier racially charged incident, in which three White students hung nooses from a tree at the local high school after a Black student asked if he could sit under it. The only member of the six youths to be tried, Mychal Bell, was convicted of aggravated battery and conspiracy. Though his convictions were overturned on appeal on the grounds that he should have been tried as a juvenile rather than as an adult, he was incarcerated for almost 10 months and was kept incarcerated while awaiting a retrial in December 2007 (*The New York Times*, September 27, 2007).

10. Such divisions continue to hamper reconstruction efforts, as the failure of the government to protect the most vulnerable New Orleans residents prior to the hurricane or in its immediate aftermath has been matched by a patchy response in the longer term. Certainly, sections of the city have been rebuilt, and tourism is clawing its way back. Yet, more than four years later at the time of writing, significant problems remain. Large swaths of the city have been left to molder, with their (Black) residents still in Federal Emergency Management Agency (FEMA) housing or out of state. The city has rushed to rebuild OPP, yet has succeeded in opening only one quarter of the original bed space, so it is more overcrowded than ever, with detainees routinely sleeping on the floor. Medical and mental health care have been stretched well beyond the institution's capacity (ACLU, 2008).

11. In contrast, those political blogs from both sides of the political spectrum (which became so influential in the 2008 presidential election) rarely discussed imprisonment or criminal justice matters, choosing instead to focus on the wars in Iraq and Afghanistan, and on other matters of U.S. politics.

12. His work can be found online and in print, where his books appear with academic and more popular trade presses (Santos, 2001, 2006; www.michaelsantos.net).

Eight

The New Detention

Securing the Border

Securing our border is essential to securing the homeland.

—George W. Bush, November 28, 2005

Humans have human rights simply because they are humans. Hence even terrorists have rights that they cannot be denied. A liberal society is committed to respect the rights of those who have shown no respect for rights at all, to show mercy to those who are merciless, to treat as human those who have behaved inhumanly. This commitment to observe obligations even when they are not reciprocated is a defining characteristic of any society under the rule of law. Why else do we believe that even the most odious criminal is entitled to a fair trial and proof of guilt beyond a reasonable doubt?

—Ignatieff, 2004, p. 34

I woke up last night when I heard the keys of someone returning to their hotel room. I woke up in a fright and thought one of the guards was coming to put on my chains. I then realized that the light in the room was on. When locked up in our cages, the lights were on as well, and I thought to myself: "You can sleep in the dark now"—and I switched it off.

—Former Guantánamo Bay detainee Jamal al-Harith,
cited in Human Rights Watch, 2004b, p. 23

Despite some evidence that the enthusiasm for mass imprisonment of domestic offenders in the U.S. may be waning, there remain significant reasons to be skeptical about the long-term success of the strategies and arguments described in Chapter 7. Not only did aggregate imprisonment rates start to rise again in 2005, but, under the Bush administration, a host of new penal institutions sprang up as part of the War on Terror. Immigration detention centers, Guantánamo Bay, military prisons on U.S. soil (or in its seas),[1] and the as yet unknown number (or location) of secret CIA prisons for alleged terrorists all suggest that, notwithstanding some concerns over the legitimacy and efficacy of mass imprisonment for American citizens, incarceration retained its grip on the imagination of policymakers in the U.S. throughout the first decade of the new century. Even as President Obama (2009a) signed his first Executive Orders to close Guantánamo Bay within 12 months, and to devise "lawful" ways of managing enemies caught in battle (Obama, 2009b), imprisonment per se was not called into question as a tool of warfare and security; those remaining prisoners of war will most likely be relocated into the federal prison system.

Prisons have always held noncitizens, particularly in times of war. However, after September 11, 2001, the number of foreigners incarcerated for civil and criminal matters, as well as for terrorism, rose considerably. Although detention is applied in the criminal justice system only for suspected or actual illegal activity, for noncitizens it may be used as a "preventative" measure in a number of different circumstances, even in the absence of an actual criminal event (Cole, 2005). At the most extreme end, those accused of terrorism have, since 2001, been detained in a web of facilities, most of which are offshore; anyone suspected of terrorist activity in the U.S. may be held preventatively, either in a U.S-based facility or, until recently, in Guantánamo Bay. Foreigners convicted of a criminal offense, who have completed their periods of confinement, are detained pending deportation, while incarceration has become mandatory for all asylum seekers who arrive without proper documentation, as well as for some who do. Finally, even those people on U.S. soil who have committed what are otherwise civil offenses regarding their immigration status—by failing to renew their visas or to inform the Department of Homeland Security when they relocate to a new home—may be detained prior to their removal.

To manage this growing (and diverse) population, the federal government has had to open a number of new custodial facilities throughout the country and beyond. For some of these institutions, limited data and details are available. For others, however, it is far more difficult to grasp what is going on. Private contractors, who have built some of the detention centers in Iraq and Afghanistan, offer crumbs of information on their Web sites, while think tanks also publish some rudimentary statistics (see, for example, www.globalsecurity.org). Similarly, government agencies such the Department of State (www.state.gov) and the Multi-National Force-Iraq (www.mnf-iraq.com), provide detailed descriptions of detention facilities. However, despite President Bush's acknowledgment on September 6, 2006, that the CIA operates secret prisons abroad for holding "key suspects" in the War on Terror, little official information about such places has been provided. Instead, nongovernmental organizations and journalists, in concert with former detainees, attempt to paint a portrait of what such closed institutions are like (Reprieve, 2008; Human Rights Watch, 2004, 2007).

In the asylum and immigration context, U.S. Immigration and Customs Enforcement (ICE)—formerly known as the U.S. Immigration and Naturalization Service (INS)[2]—has, in recent years, opened a network of new custodial institutions. Even so, detainees continue to be housed in federal, state, and local correctional facilities along with U.S. citizens and so-called "criminal aliens" awaiting trial or following conviction. As with the war prisons, much of the available information about such places is produced by journalists and human rights groups.

This chapter considers whether immigration centers and facilities holding terrorist suspects are entirely different from those jails and prisons with which this book has been concerned, or whether they are merely new versions of the American prison. Such places are designed to hold noncitizens, secure the border, and protect the homeland. In so doing, they are suffused with, and reinforce, a powerful rhetoric of nationalism and belonging; their inhabitants are unwelcome, unknown, and threatening. In practice, however, their populations can be quite indistinct from those in regular prisons, and the threats they pose unclear.

Those who hold American citizenship have ultimately been relocated to the regular penal system, whatever their crimes. Thus, John Walker Lindh (who was captured in Afghanistan and dubbed the "American Taliban" by the media) and José Padilla (who was arrested at a Chicago airport and accused of planning to detonate a "dirty bomb") were initially labeled enemy combatants and placed in military detention, but now live out their sentences in federal penitentiaries. In the immigration system, some U.S. citizens have been mistakenly identified as foreign and even, on occasion, deported.[3]

Context

Although it is tempting to imagine that immigration detention and the so-called "new war prisons" (Butler, 2004) are post–September 11 developments, in fact both predate it. As earlier chapters have shown, not only has the U.S. imprisoned enemy soldiers and suspected citizens in all its military conflicts, but the number of foreigners in detention has been growing rapidly since the mid-1990s (Welch, 1996, 2003; Dow, 2004). While terrorist suspects have mainly been located offshore, foreign offenders and asylum seekers are held in state and federal prisons and in local jails. They are also placed in a network of institutions run by the ICE, as well as in private facilities contracted to ICE. Wherever these detainees are held, by virtue of their nationality they are denied many constitutional protections that citizens take for granted. Until June 2008, those held in Guantánamo Bay were denied that most basic legal safeguard, habeas corpus.

Given the range of foreigners in confinement, it is impossible to generalize about their numbers. For example, even as the population of Guantánamo fell from a high point of 536 in June 2002 to 270 in June 2008 (Human Rights Watch, 2008; www.globalsecurity.org), reports estimate that elsewhere, the number of detained "enemy combatants" or "ghost prisoners" was surging (Human Rights Watch, 2007; Grey, 2007).[4] Similarly, on March 23, 2008, U.S.-led forces in Iraq recorded more than 23,000 individuals in their custody (Stone, 2008), at the same time that at least 630 were confined in the secretive and controversial Bagram "theater internment facility" in Afghanistan.

Reliable statistics about those held on U.S. soil for immigration offenses or as asylum seekers are similarly hard to obtain. Figures are presented in varied formats from one year to the next, and are also from a range of jurisdictions. They are not published as regularly as are other prison statistics. While, in principle, almost all foreigners subject to detention and imprisonment should become the responsibility of ICE, in practice, and despite multiple security initiatives, they may not always be reported to the immigration services. Foreigners serving sentences in state or federal prisons will be made subject to the Institutional Removal Program, whereby, at the end of their sentences, they are detained prior to deportation, only if their citizenship details are passed on to ICE. In any case, different states count noncitizens in various ways. In their annual reports, for example, New York State differentiates between "foreign-born" and "native-born" irrespective of their actual citizenship status.

For all these reasons, the recorded statistics on foreigners probably underestimate their presence in the American prison system. With this caveat in mind, on June 30, 2007, the year for which the most recent figures are available, 96,703 so-called "criminal aliens" were identified in the custody of state or federal correctional authorities, representing 6.32 percent of the total population of convicted offenders in such facilities (Sabol &

Couture, 2008, 8).[5] In 2005, the U.S. Government Accountability Office (GAO) reported an increase of 15 percent in foreigners in federal custody between 2001 and 2004, the majority of whom were Mexicans. The foreign tally, which, over the years under analysis cost the federal government an estimated $5.8 billion, made up 27 percent of that system's total incarcerated population (GAO, 2005). Just five state prison systems—Arizona, California, Florida, New York, and Texas—incarcerated 80 percent of the total number of foreign prisoners, accounting for 74,000 individuals in fiscal year 2003. That same year, according to the GAO, a further 147,000 noncitizens were held across 698 jails (GAO, 2005; Harrison & Beck, 2004).

In addition to these foreign actual or suspected offenders, in mid-year 2007 there were over 27,500 men, women, and children in U.S. Immigration and Customs Enforcement detention, the majority of whom had no criminal history. Over the course of a year, this figure translates to 300,000 people passing through about 400 institutions, scattered all over the country. This population of immigrant detainees has been growing rapidly and alongside the national prison population, from 1,593 in 1985 to 13,676 in 2000 to 27,634 in 2006 (Sabol, Couture, & Harrison, 2007; Scalia & Litras, 2002). Of those held by ICE in 2006, just over half (50.7 percent) were detained on immigration law violations, 40 percent for criminal offenses, and the remaining 9.3 percent "pending charges or disposition" (Sabol, Couture, & Harrison, 2007, p. 9). Reflecting for the most part policy changes about the policing of the U.S.-Mexico border, which have made detention mandatory, those held for immigration law violations had increased by 79 percent over the previous year.

As part of a raft of border control initiatives brought in by the Bush administration, ICE opened more of its own facilities and/or directly contracted out with greater enthusiasm to private companies. Even as the number of ICE detention centers grew rapidly, with yet more planned or currently under construction, there were insufficient numbers of institutions to hold the vast numbers of people being detained.[6] Thus, in June 2007, according to the ICE Web site, the immigration detention system consisted of seven contract detention facilities (CDFs), eight service processing centers (SPCs), and more than 350 local and state facilities operated under "intergovernmental service agreements" (IGSAs), for which the ICE Office of Detention and Removal (DRO) pays as needed.[7] In January 2000, all facilities holding individuals for ICE became subject to the *ICE National Detention Standards* which, according to ICE, "reflect current American Correctional Association (ACA) standards, which are the national benchmark for all varieties of detention operations"

(U.S. Immigrations and Customs Enforcement, 2007, p. 5). The detention standards were subsequently revised in 2008 (U.S. Immigration and Customs Enforcement, 2008).

Although there are important reasons to consider those held purely under immigration act powers separately from those convicted of criminal offences or detained as a result of U.S. military action in Afghanistan and Iraq, there are, as the DRO's reliance on ACA standards suggests, also multiple overlaps and interconnections between such figures and the places that hold them. Whether they are held in federal, state, or local correctional facilities or by ICE, the majority of so-called "criminal aliens" have been convicted of drug-related offenses. Within this group, too, as in the native population, women have often received particularly harsh treatment, caught by mandatory minimum sentences for their first offenses, even though such laws were originally intended to punish drug "kingpins."

More generally, as with drug offenders, noncitizens confined for criminal offenses, immigration law violations, actual or suspected terrorism, or while their asylum cases are pending, tend to be drawn overwhelmingly from communities considered to be non-White. Other than John Walker Lindh, the vast majority of U.S. citizens convicted of terror-related offenses have been African American. Typically Muslim converts, many were radicalized in prison or influenced by those who had been. Such young men—like Gregory Patterson and Levar Washington, who were caught in Los Angeles robbing a gas station, and subsequently found to be members of the outlawed, prison-based group Jam'iyyar Ul-Islam Is-Saheeh (JIS)—resemble more than they differ from the majority of domestic prisoners (Glover, 2007; Reza, 2008; Sanchez, 2007). So, too, Mexicans represent the largest group of foreign nationals in immigration detention, and in the U.S. more generally.

The range of activities for which noncitizens may be incarcerated suggests that (certain) foreigners may be peculiarly vulnerable to confinement and to other forms of state control. Such a claim may seem initially somewhat counterintuitive, since the U.S. has traditionally boasted a fairly open immigration policy and celebrated its multicultural identity. According to the tenets of the American Dream, all who could work and contribute to the construction of the new society were welcome. In practice, however, the history of immigration control has been one of fluctuating levels of restriction and welcome. Strict limits have always existed, at least for some, from the Chinese in the 19th century to Southern Europeans in the early 20th century, and Black and Hispanic populations in most eras (Tichenor, 2002; Calavita, 2007). In allowing some populations access while restricting others, immigration policies have created, both legally and symbolically, the persona of the "illegal" immigrant itself. In turn, such subordinated figures have been crucial to the construction of the U.S. citizen, serving to identify those who belong set against those who do not (Ngai, 2004).

When viewed in this light, the current crop of legislation governing the treatment of refugees, asylum seekers, immigration offenders, criminal aliens, enemy combatants, and terrorists may be no more than the most recent manifestation of a long history of population management. To be sure, counterterrorism has influenced practice since 2001, if only by fueling a populist imagery about the dangers of (certain) foreigners (see, for example, Malkin, 2004; MacDonald, Hanson, & Malanga, 2007). Yet such ideas are not new. What is novel and demands explanation, however, is the harshness of recent legislation, and the zeal with which it has been enforced. As immigration policies and military action draw increasingly on a penal model in their governance of risk and security, they reveal once more the active role of imprisonment in securing and constituting the nation.

The Law[8]

Well before announcing its War on Terror, the U.S. had begun to use detention as a primary means of dealing with certain foreigners under particular circumstances. For example, the Immigration Act of 1990, which modified much of the Immigration and Nationality Act of 1952, enabled the INS to detain aliens pending a decision on whether or not they were to be deported. The recent growth in numbers behind bars was facilitated by legislation passed since the mid-1990s that expanded the capacity of the state to incarcerate (and deport) immigrants, refugees, and other foreigners. Immigration law dovetailed with the punitivism of the times, often complementing the more narrow criminal justice legislation brought in under Presidents Bill Clinton and George W. Bush. In particular, although different in their scope and focus, a series of acts between 1996 and 2001 expanded the use of mandatory detention for a vast array of issues associated with noncitizens. These laws included the Illegal Immigration Reform and Immigrant Responsibility Act of 1996 (IIRIRA), the Antiterrorism and Effective Death Penalty Act of 1996 (AEDPA), and the U.S.A. Patriot Act of 2001, which was renewed in March 2006.

Until the passage of the U.S.A. Patriot Act in 2001, it was Title III of the Illegal Immigration Reform and Immigrant Responsibility Act of 1996—implemented in 1997—that most radically expanded the use of detention as a means of managing noncitizens. In addition to changing the way in which asylum seekers were dealt with at the border, Section 321 of IIRIRA introduced a number of new offenses for which permanent resident aliens and those on work or tourist visas could lose their residency and be deported. Legal resident aliens, or those in possession of a "green card," who were convicted of crimes known as "aggravated felonies," would, from that time, be detained prior to removal proceedings, even if they were ultimately found eligible to stay in the country. As a category of immigration law, "aggravated felonies" are not the same as criminal felonies, and include a wide range of misdemeanors that would not result in prison terms. In addition to expanding powers to imprison residents, the act also allowed immigration officials to detain asylum seekers while ascertaining the veracity of their claims. Anyone found to have overstayed a visa or attempting to enter without one can also be held. All immigrants and asylum seekers have to be detained prior to deportation or removal.

IIRIRA reflected a hardening of views toward immigrants that occurred against the backdrop of a deepening punitive sentiment that also targeted offenders and the poor (see Chapter 6). At the same time, economic and work-based restrictions on employers and the state began to loosen. Just two years before the act, for example, the North American Free Trade Agreement (NAFTA) came into being and, at the same time, the INS launched "Operation Gatekeeper" in San Diego, and California approved Proposition 187, which, until it was deemed unlawful in 1997, denied health, welfare, housing, and education to illegal immigrants and their children. In 1996, Clinton signed into law the Antiterrorism and Effective Death Penalty Act (AEDPA) and the Personal Responsibility and Work Opportunity Reconciliation Act (PRWORA) (P.L. 104–193. 110 Stat. 2105). While AEDPA began the process of criminalizing activities that the Patriot Act continued with such effect, PRWORA not only denied federal benefits to most legal and illegal immigrants and their children, but also threw thousands of American citizens, predominantly women, off the welfare rolls and back to "work" or starvation (Potocky-Tripodi, 2002; Rubenstein & Mukamal, 2002). Taken together, these acts created an environment where immigration, poverty, and criminality become closely associated with one another in a manner that amplified their alleged risk and social costs to the state. Unlike the market, such rhetoric made clear, these populations needed regulation.

Since the 1990s, then, the U.S., along with many other industrialized, liberal democracies, has successfully labeled undocumented immigrants as "illegals." This labeling has occurred legislatively and symbolically at all levels of government, and in media representations, too (Welch & Schuster, 2005). As President George W. Bush put it in November 2005, "America has always been a compassionate nation that values the newcomer and takes great pride in our immigrant heritage; yet we're also a nation built on the rule of law, and those who enter the country illegally violate the law" (Bush, November 28, 2005). Much of the response to the events of 9/11 furthered this rhetorical shift, away from multiculturalism and the great "melting pot" of American national identity, toward fear, suspicion, and "security." Culminating in the passage of the Patriot Act, which was signed into law just six weeks after the attacks on the Pentagon and the World Trade Center in New York City, allegations about imminent threats and terrorism spawned a startling range of judicial and extrajudicial practices by the U.S. military, the CIA, and the Department of Justice that only recently have been called into question.[9]

Renewed and expanded in March 2006, the Patriot Act greatly increased the U.S. government's capacity to monitor and detain noncitizens, and the FBI's ability to watch U.S. citizens as well. Section 215, for example, permits the government to obtain

> . . . any tangible things (including books, records, papers, documents and other items) for an investigation to protect against international terrorism or clandestine intelligence, provided that such investigation of a United States person is not conducted *solely* on the basis of activities protected by the First Amendment to the Constitution [italics added]. (Public Law 107-56, 2001)

The FBI, in other words, does not have to establish probable cause or have any reason to look through people's possessions. A telling example of the erosion of constitutional safeguards that came to characterize the Bush administration's treatment of terror suspects, the Patriot Act enabled the investigation of foreigners simply for exercising what were previously understood to be their First Amendment rights of freedom of speech and association, by, for example, logging onto specific Web sites that the government was monitoring.[10] Prisoners are the only other group of people in the U.S. whose First and Fourth Amendment rights are similarly curtailed.

In terms of detention, Section 412 broadened the capacity of the state to hold noncitizens suspected of terrorism for lengthy periods without legal assistance and without charge. Like Section 215, this part of the Patriot Act denied constitutional protections to noncitizens while greatly expanding the powers of the attorney general. With no more than his or her unreviewed certification that there are reasonable grounds to believe that a noncitizen is ". . . engaged in terrorist activities or other activities that threaten national security," a foreigner may be detained by ICE for up to seven days without charge (Chang 2002, p. 64). If the persons certified by the attorney general as "terrorists" have committed any immigration violations, however minor and unrelated to terrorism, they may be detained for as long as immigration proceedings take, with renewed certification from the attorney general every six months. The Fourth Amendment standard of "probable cause" is no longer required. Like those "enemy combatants" held in Guantánamo Bay, noncitizens certified as terrorists had, until 2008, no rights to be informed of the nature of the evidence against them.

Other than the Patriot Act, the federal government had little success in introducing further legislation on such issues. Particularly in the field of immigration, where Bush frequently articulated a desire to reform current practice, such legislative failure was not for want of trying, as a slew of bills were presented to both houses.[11] In relation to the War on Terror, the government passed two pieces of legislation, the Treatment of Detainees Act of 2005 and the Military Commissions Act of 2006, following public outcry over the torture of detainees at Abu Ghraib prison in Iraq in 2004 and in response to the Supreme Court decision of *Hamdi v. Rumsfeld,* which criticized the military tribunals at Guantánamo Bay.

Importantly, the failure to introduce new immigration legislation did not prevent significant policy development. Rather, a range of administrative changes were instituted on an ad hoc basis that expanded the numbers in detention and those employed in policing the border. More broadly, in its dealings with noncitizens and enemies, the federal government also ignored considerable legislative and normative restraints with no ill effect. Until President Obama reversed the policy on January 22, 2009, the U.S. refused to observe the 1949 Geneva Conventions governing the treatment of prisoners of war for those captured in Iraq or Afghanistan, according to which

> . . . prisoners of war must at all times be treated humanely. . . . [they] must at all times be protected, particularly against acts of violence or intimidation and against insults and public curiosity. . . . In no case shall disciplinary punishments be inhuman, brutal or dangerous to the health of prisoners of war. (Geneva Convention III, 1949)

It also violated international law and intruded on the sovereignty of its allies by snatching individuals from their streets and transporting them to detention.[12]

Even apparent compromises, like the Detainee Treatment Act of 2005, appear to have had little effect in reversing the culture and expectations of punishment. Included in that year's defense appropriation bill, this act officially prohibited (in facilities run by the Department of Defense) various forms of "enhanced interrogation techniques" that had become commonplace. The following year, the government published the document "Human Intelligence Collector Operations" from the *U.S. Army Field Manual on Intelligence Interrogation,* which explicitly repudiated such techniques. Though important and welcome developments, these policies on detainees have been widely criticized, particularly for their failure to regulate the CIA in any detention or interrogation (Suleman, 2006). As the Director of the CIA, General Michael V. Hayden, acknowledged, in a televised discussion over the definition of "enhanced techniques," and their relation to torture, ". . . enhanced techniques . . . are in that range between the *Army Field Manual* . . . and the limits that U.S. law and U.S. treaty obligations allow. *No one has ever claimed that the Army Field Manual exhausts all the lawful interrogation techniques that the American Republic can use to defend itself*" [italics added] (Hayden, 2007). In any case, in defiance of international laws and treaties, former Attorney General John Ashcroft, testifying to a Congressional panel on such matters on July 17, 2008, refused to accept that the simulated drowning or "waterboarding" carried out by the CIA on Al Qaeda suspects had constituted torture. Such opponents, Ashcroft and his colleagues asserted over and over again, were not prisoners of war, but rather "enemy" or "unlawful" combatants. Until President Obama's Executive Order of January 22, 2009 such figures, it was asserted, existed outside legislative safeguards and deserved and should have expected different treatment.

Despite being a signatory to the 1951 UN Convention on Refugees and its 1967 Protocol, which promise to enable those in need to seek asylum and to avoid sending anyone to a place where he or she may be tortured, the U.S. has, along with most other liberal democracies, brought in a raft of restrictions to its immigration and asylum rules that make it harder for individuals to claim refugee status and more likely that they will be deported, even if they face real risks of being killed or tortured as a result. In both these policy areas, the U.S. has relied increasingly on a network of penal institutions, some purposely built, others simply sections of existing establishments. Still others, far beyond the reaches of the country, are hidden from any serious examination.

Other than the usual critical voices from organizations like Amnesty International and Human Rights Watch, it is difficult to identify much of a coordinated campaign against immigration detention or the mistreatment of detainees. Despite numerous congressional hearings about matters ranging from FBI eavesdropping on citizens to "waterboarding," the Bush administration remained committed to the same policies throughout his tenure. In practical terms, too, the absence of a fresh legislative framework did not prevent policy development in either area. As Bush made clear in his final State of the Union Address in 2008, despite failing in its bid to introduce legal reforms, his administration had been active in immigration policy.

> America needs to secure our borders—and with your help, my administration is taking steps to do so. We're increasing worksite enforcement, deploying fences and advanced technologies to stop illegal crossings. We've effectively ended the policy of "catch and release" at the border, and by the end of this year, we will have doubled the number of Border Patrol agents. (Bush, 2008a)

From changing the questions on the citizenship naturalization test, to increasing funding for border controls, more border police, and physical barriers along the border with Mexico, the federal government pursued a tough-on-immigration approach that resonated powerfully with the earlier language about and policies on domestic offenders. They erected more barriers for legitimate visitors, mandating fingerprinting at the border for all noncitizens. Everyone, it seems, is already under suspicion, with mobility just another arena that needs securing. Under such circumstances, it should come as no surprise that the detained population surged.

Detaining Immigrants

Although the immigration detention system has been expanding at a great pace since the mid-1990s, little is known about conditions in immigration detention centers. As with the more secretive war prisons, accounts of immigration detention are produced almost exclusively by human-rights organizations like Amnesty International, Human Rights Watch, and the American Civil Liberties Union (ACLU), as well as through the efforts of some investigative journalists (Dow, 2004; although see Welch, 1996, 2003). Such a relative dearth of information is usually interpreted as reflecting a general lack of public interest in the fate of those there confined (Welch & Schuster, 2005). Whereas there have been large-scale demonstrations over the rights of immigrants to work or stay in the U.S., those in detention have attracted few public supporters, outside individual cases. Unlike other detainees, asylum seekers and those being held prior to removal following a prison sentence do not publish firsthand accounts of their time behind bars. The scarcity of literature on detention centers may also reflect simpler barriers to empirical research, including linguistic ones, a rapid turnover in detainees, and the unwillingness of such institutions to allow entry to academic researchers.

In so many practical and symbolic ways, immigration detention centers resemble state, federal, and local correctional facilities (Simon, 1998). Detainees share characteristics and experiences with U.S. citizen prisoners. They are, for example, predominantly Black or Hispanic, they receive inadequate medical care, have poor access to educational programs, and insufficient contact with their families (Goldstein & Priest 2008a, 2008b; ACLU, 2006; Human Rights Watch, 2007, 2008). According to journalist Mark Dow, one of the few to document life inside immigration detention centers, noncitizens, like prisoners, are

> . . . regularly transferred from jail to jail without warning, usually in the middle of the night. Transfers are used to punish detainees who seek media attention, to break up peaceful hunger strikes, to isolate detainees from legal help, and more generally, as part of a nationwide system of intergovernmental service agreements, private contracts, available bed space, and ad hoc human warehousing. In the course of transfers and processing into new jails, detainees' essential legal paperwork commonly disappears, their personal property is stolen, and families lose track of their loved ones since the immigration agency explicitly disclaims responsibility for informing family of the unannounced moves. (Dow, 2007, p. 539)

In most senses, however, noncitizens are in a worse, and more vulnerable, position than are domestic offenders. The U.S. immigration complex does not encounter the constraints that face the criminal justice system. Not only is there no automatic judicial oversight of immigration detention centers, there is no independent review of ICE decisions to detain arriving asylum seekers either. There are also no absolute restrictions on the time noncitizens may be detained, even without proving that they pose a flight or security risk. Even though immigration detainees should be deported within a 90-day period, once this period is over, ICE can extend it. In a report published in 2002 on worldwide immigration detention, the Lawyers Committee for Human Rights (2002) cited investigative research conducted by *The Dallas Morning News* which "had obtained statistics revealing that over 851 noncitizens in detention had been detained for over three years, and that 361 of these detainees were asylum seekers or other detainees who had not been convicted of any crime" (Lawyers Committee for Human Rights, 2002, p. 122).

Unlike citizen offenders, noncitizens detained by ICE have no access to government-funded legal aid. Those who have already served time in a correctional facility endure a kind of "double jeopardy" when they are detained again prior to their removal, rather than being deported immediately following the completion of their criminal sentences (Dow, 2007). Moreover, after September 11, 2001, habeas corpus for such individuals was, like those accused of terrorist activity, severely restricted.

Although the untrammeled power of ICE was curtailed by the 2001 Supreme Court decision *Zadvydas v. Davis,* which limited the conditions under which detainees could be held indefinitely; three years later, the Government Accountability Office found that ICE was still holding hundreds of detainees for longer than they should have been (Dow, 2007; GAO, 2005). In March 2009, an investigative report from the Associated Press found more of the same. Of a total detainee population of 32,000, there were 18,690 immigrants with no criminal conviction. More than 400 of those without a criminal record had been incarcerated for at least a year, 12 had been held for three years or more, and one man from China had been locked up for more than five years. Nearly 10,000 of those in custody had been held for longer than 31 days. In contrast to calls for fiscal restraint in domestic prisons, the costs of immigration detention have soared, doubling to $1.7 billion since 2003 (Roberts, 2009).

In 1998, firsthand accounts in a Human Rights Watch report depicted the confusion of asylum seekers routinely detained while their case was considered. One man, from Iran, who had been placed in Nacogdoches County Jail in Texas, complained impotently, "I have not committed any crime. I have never been in any type of prison system but when I came here they locked me up like I'm some kind of criminal . . . they locked me up along with inmates, people that have committed crimes . . . I fear for my life. . . ." (Human Rights Watch, 1998, p. 4). Long-term legal residents of the U.S., with families and jobs in the community, also end up in such places, while they await deportation to countries where they have long since lost any meaningful ties.

From accounts of the rapes of female asylum seekers at Krome Avenue Detention Facility in Florida (Welch, 1996), to the inmate at Virginia Beach Detention Center who told Human Rights Watch that "here it is normal for officers to beat detainees without reason . . ." (Human Rights Watch, 1998, p. 4), immigration detention centers and those who staff them are dogged by accusations of violence and aggression. So too, at Orleans Parish Prison—that same institution where guards abandoned detainees to the rising waters caused by Hurricane Katrina—journalist Mark Dow (2007) found "... prison guards had provided U.S. citizen inmates with weapons and sent them to beat down a group of nonviolent Cambodian and Vietnamese INS detainees" (Dow, 2007, p. 540). For Dow, this violence was more than simply the actions of a few corrupt guards, it had become the point of such places. "Despite reports of brutality at OPP, or perhaps because of the brutality and despite the reports," he observed, "INS had a continuing contract with the jail" (Dow, 2007, p. 541).

Investigations in a number of states have uncovered institutionalized brutality, from denial of everyday medical care to a refusal to provide life-saving retroviral drugs, even when they had previously been allowed in the jails or prisons from which detainees had been transferred. There are also cases of individuals forcibly sedated for deportation, and, perhaps most shocking in its indifference, a woman simply forgotten in a county jail cell, left without food or water for four days in Arkansas (Human Rights Watch, 2007; Goldstein & Priest, 2008a, 2008b; Nossiter, 2008). Such cases suggest a widely held view that detainees are less than human. As a former correctional officer at Union County Jail, where he and a number of his colleagues were convicted of assaulting detainees, put it, "There's a lot of dark side to this country ... The word *foreign* makes them despise you. People have a lot of hatred" (Eric Mensah, cited in Dow, 2004, p. 52). Such behavior exists on an even more extreme level in that other penal system for dealing with noncitizens—the war prisons.

The War on Terror

Just as it has in immigration policy, detention has played a crucial role in the U.S.-led campaigns in Afghanistan and Iraq. Since 2001, the U.S. has placed an unknown total number of suspected terrorists in Guantánamo Bay, Cuba; in Abu Ghraib, Camp Cropper, and Camp Bucca in Iraq; at Bagram Air Force Base in Afghanistan; in naval brigs; and in undisclosed secret locations around the world. The U.S. grabbed many of the people in these detention centers from the streets of their allies and illegally transported them in a process that has become euphemistically referred to as "rendition" or "extraordinary rendition" (Grey, 2007).

Due to the secrecy surrounding this process, it has been difficult to determine how it has affected those caught up in it. Recently, however, a number of authors and organizations—none academic—have begun to piece together accounts of life within these secret prisons (Rose, 2004; Grey, 2007;

Stafford-Smith, 2008; Kurnaz, 2008). As many former detainees have been released, evidence has mounted of routine torture, humiliation, and degrading treatment at the hands of American servicemen and women, as well as from foreign intelligence and police services working in concert with the CIA (Begg & Brittain, 2006; Human Rights Watch, 2004). The American government, these accounts allege, transported detainees to prisons in other countries to be tortured.[13] Some were eventually flown to U.S.-controlled territory in Cuba or to Afghanistan, while the fate of the majority is unknown.

Over time, Guantánamo Bay attracted increasing criticism from Congress and the public. Similarly, there was considerable outcry in 2004 when photographs emerged of torture by U.S. military personnel at Abu Ghraib Prison in Iraq. For the most part, however, concern about such places within the U.S. was limited until the 2008 Democratic Primary and the subsequent election campaign of then Senator Barack Obama.[14] Part of the reason for the muted concern no doubt relates to the widely accepted premises of the War on Terror—that the U.S. is at profound risk and must be allowed to defend itself. Also, the sheer lack of publicly available information has impeded much critical commentary; as Lisa Sanchez (2007) has argued, the war has been constituted from the start by a series of absences—no Osama Bin Laden, no pictures of the wounded and the dead, and, we might add, no information about detention.

Such a deliberate absence has been particularly clear in regard to Guantánamo Bay, which, until sustained legal challenge, existed not just out of sight as an offshore American institution, but also beyond the reach of constitutional safeguards (Kaplan, 2005). Somewhat paradoxically, however, in many ways Guantánamo Bay is a penal institution like any other. Previously the site of an immigration detention center used in the 1980s and 1990s to exclude Haitian asylum seekers, Guantánamo Bay sprang into popular consciousness in 2002, when the first "enemy combatants" from Afghanistan arrived "soaked in their own urine, ear-muffed, masked and unable to see," and clothed in bright orange jumpsuits. These men were placed in Camp X-ray: ". . . a dozen rows of steel-mesh cages, open to the elements, ringed by a razor-wire fence" (Rose, 2004, pp. 1–2). For many, this image—released by then U.S. Defense Secretary Donald Rumsfeld—remains the enduring one of Guantánamo Bay. Yet, according to visitors from the British House of Commons Foreign Affairs Committee, who went to Cuba in September 2006, such a view of Guantánamo may be unhelpful. Rather than a place of exception, it is, they argued, a far more familiar institution: the maximum-security prison. "The facilities at Guantánamo," they concluded, "are broadly comparable with those at the United Kingdom's only maximum security detention facility, *but the conditions are not*" (House of Commons Foreign Affairs Committee, 2007, p. 3; emphasis added). While the institution "scores highly on diet and on health provisions"—notwithstanding its policy of force-feeding noncompliant detainees—it failed to achieve "minimum United Kingdom standards on access to exercise and recreation, to lawyers, and to the outside world through educational facilities and the media" (ibid). Many U.S. penal institutions—from supermaximum secure facilities to the overcrowded jails throughout the country—would fail the same test. Guantánamo, this report implies, should be considered a regular prison used for an irregular purpose.[15]

Although it is usually referred to in the singular, when visited by the British delegation, Guantánamo Bay was made up of six subcamps numbered I to VI. According to the Foreign Affairs Committee (2007):

> Camps I to II are of predominantly wire cage construction, but with concrete floors, hard roofs and protection from the elements. Each block houses up to 48 detainees, in two rows of 24 cells. At the end of each block are showering and basic exercise facilities. The cells are small, about 2 metres by 1.5 metres. They are equipped with a fixed bunk and basic sanitation. An arrow set into each bunk points to Mecca. (House of Commons Foreign Affairs Committee, 2007, p. 10)

Camp IV, they went on, "... is classed as medium-security and houses 'compliant detainees.'" As in many domestic prisons, detainees are accommodated in dormitories. They eat and pray together and wear different uniforms. This is the only facility in the complex where the lights are dimmed (but, it would seem, not extinguished) at night. (House of Commons Foreign Affairs Committee, 2007, p. 11)

Camps V and VI were both modeled on specific U.S. prisons. Camp V, which was designated as "maximum security," followed the "Indiana model," housing 100 prisoners in four, two-story wings. "All walls, floors and doors are of solid construction," the committee reported, "which greatly reduce the scope for detainees to converse without being overheard. Guards look into each cell every few minutes, and also monitor them using cameras" (House of Commons, Foreign Affairs Committee, 2007, p. 11). This camp also houses the "interrogation facilities." Camp VI, which was originally designated as a medium-security facility, was based on the "Michigan model" U.S. penitentiary. Since opening, it was reconfigured as maximum security. As in Camp V, detainees were continually monitored.

Despite vigorous attempts by neoconservatives to defend it (Feulner, 2006), Guantánamo Bay was, from the outset, heavily criticized by human rights organizations (Human Rights Watch, 2008), the courts, and journalists (Rose, 2004; Horton, 2007). Over time, these voices of dissent were joined by former detainees (Begg & Brittain, 2006) and academics (Butler, 2004; Kaplan, 2005). "The evidence," David Rose (2004) bitterly asserts:

> . . . suggests that large numbers of the Gitmo prisoners, running into the hundreds, were absolutely innocent of the least involvement in anything that could reasonably be described as terrorist activity. They ended up there as a result of military-intelligence screening procedures in Afghanistan and elsewhere that were flawed and inadequate, made still worse by the use of woefully poor and virtually untrained translators. (Rose, 2004, p. 9)

In June 2008, the Supreme Court finally acted on such critique, ruling in *Boumediene et al v. Bush* that enemy combatants held in detention at Guantánamo Bay had the right to challenge their captivity in domestic courts. In delivering the opinion of the Court, Justice Anthony Kennedy admonished the Bush administration. "The Framers [of the Constitution]" he said, "viewed freedom from unlawful restraint as a fundamental precept of liberty, and they understood the writ of habeas corpus as a vital instrument to secure that freedom" (Kennedy, in *Boumedienne v. Bush,* 2008, p. 9). Returning them their habeas corpus rights in one fell swoop, the court enabled detainees to demand the reason for their detention and some amelioration of their condition. Notwithstanding the fulsome praise from the director of the Heritage Foundation, Edwin J. Feulner (2006), who asserted that "a tour of Guantánamo Prison Shows America at its best," by midyear 2008 even Secretary of State Condoleezza Rice (2008) admitted that "Guantánamo is a detention center that . . . we would very much like to close." According to Obama's Executive Order of January 22, 2009, "The detention facilities at Guantánamo for individuals covered by this order shall be closed as soon as practicable, and no later than 1 year from the date of this order" (Obama, 2009a).

For some, however, such a statement may be of cold comfort. According to Clive Stafford-Smith, for example, who has acted as legal counsel for a number of the detainees, closing Guantánamo Bay alone would have little impact on U.S. practices elsewhere.[16] It has been easily surpassed in significance by the war prisons in Iraq and Afghanistan, not to mention those secret CIA detention centers located throughout the Middle East and beyond, which are also set to be closed down. Such places have for the most part escaped large-scale controversy, with the exception of Abu Ghraib, which, in April 2004, was revealed as the site of endemic torture and humiliation at the hands of U.S. military personnel. Previously notorious under Saddam Hussein, Abu Ghraib was used by the U.S. until August 2006 to hold suspected "insurgents." Staffed by low-level U.S. soldiers, a number of whom had worked in the field of corrections in the U.S., the jail was the site of a number of human rights abuses, some of which the military jailers photographed. When the sadistic images surfaced on the television program *60 Minutes,* the U.S. government belatedly sprang into action, appointing a military commission of inquiry and, ultimately, sentencing a number of the staff who had brutalized the detainees to lengthy terms in military prisons.

The Taguba report (Taguba, 2004) itemized the ". . . intentional abuse of detainees by military personnel." Illegal actions included:

a. (S)* Punching, slapping, and kicking detainees; jumping on their naked feet;
b. (S) Videotaping and photographing naked male and female detainees;
c. (S) Forcibly arranging detainees in various sexually explicit positions for photographing;
d. (S) Forcing detainees to remove their clothing and keeping them naked for several days at a time;
e. (S) Forcing naked male detainees to wear women's underwear;
f. (S) Forcing groups of male detainees to masturbate themselves while being photographed and videotaped;
g. (S) Arranging naked male detainees in a pile and then jumping on them;
h. (S) Positioning a naked detainee on a MRE Box, with a sandbag on his head, and attaching wires to his fingers, toes, and penis to simulate electric torture;
i. (S) Writing "I am a Rapest" (sic) on the leg of a detainee alleged to have forcibly raped a 15-year old fellow detainee, and then photographing him naked;
j. (S) Placing a dog chain or strap around a naked detainee's neck and having a female Soldier pose for a picture;
k. (S) A male MP guard having sex with a female detainee;
l. (S) Using military working dogs (without muzzles) to intimidate and frighten detainees, and in at least one case biting and severely injuring a detainee;
m. (S) Taking photographs of dead Iraqi detainees. (Taguba, 2004, pp. 16–17)

In addition to these practices, many of which were represented in the photographs, Taguba also reported several additional "credible" acts of abuse reported by detainees. These included:

---

*NOTE: (S) refers to abuse claims that have been substantiated by investigation.
(U) refers to abuse claims that are unsubstantiated but credible.

a. (U) Breaking chemical lights and pouring the phosphoric liquid on detainees;
b. (U) Threatening detainees with a charged 9mm pistol;
c. (U) Pouring cold water on naked detainees;
d. (U) Beating detainees with a broom handle and a chair;
e. (U) Threatening male detainees with rape;
f. (U) Allowing a military police guard to stitch the wound of a detainee who was injured after being slammed against the wall in his cell;
g. (U) Sodomizing a detainee with a chemical light and perhaps a broom stick.
h. (U) Using military working dogs to frighten and intimidate detainees with threats of attack, and in one instance actually biting a detainee. (Taguba, 2004, pp. 17–18)

Despite the extensive coverage of the prisoner abuse in the mass media, the Department of Defense investigations (Taguba, 2004; Ryder, 2003), and some academic analysis (Brown, 2006; Philipose, 2007; Ehrenreich, 2004), little information is available about the general conditions of the facility and about what happened after the jail was closed. There is not much to go on. The International Red Cross, which visited detainees fairly early on, does not make their accounts public, and, in part because of the photographic evidence, attention has tended to focus on the violence meted out to those held captive, and the culpability of the staff who did it. Yet, as with Guantánamo Bay, Abu Ghraib shared a common bond with other more everyday facilities in the U.S. According to former soldier Aidan Delgado (2007), who was posted for a while at Abu Ghraib until he obtained conscientious objector status and a discharge, detainees lived ". . . in canvas tents set on wooden platforms on the ground, each cluster of tents hemmed in by a razor-wire barrier. It's freezing cold outside and they never have enough blankets or coats. They're packed sixty or so people to a tent, in cramped quarters, so sickness spread rapidly throughout the camp" (Delgado, 2007, p. 169). "It's so filthy," he remarked, "that, if you saw it, there's no way you would believe it was the product of U.S. ingenuity" (Delgado, 2007, p. 170).

Delgado was, it would seem, not familiar with other U.S. prisons. Despite his claim that "Abu Ghraib is nothing like any prison I've ever seen or even read about" (Delgado, 2007, p. 170), considerable similarities can be identified between it and more humdrum institutions. Arizona, for example, holds county detainees in large canvas tents, subject to the intense desert temperatures. So, too, filth is a common complaint of many domestic prisoners. In any case, as Taguba (2004) pointed out, at Abu Ghraib, "Brigade personnel relied heavily on individuals within the Brigade who had civilian corrections experience, including many who worked as prison guards or corrections officials in their civilian jobs" (Taguba, 2004, p. 37). While the nation and the world were scandalized by accounts of sexual abuse, aspects of that, too, seem familiar (Gordon, 2006) as such activities remain common in many U.S. prisons. Likewise, Taguba found that in common with many domestic prisons:

> The Abu Ghraib and Camp Bucca detention facilities are significantly over their intended maximum capacity while the guard force is undermanned and under resourced. This imbalance has contributed to the poor living conditions, escapes, and accountability lapses at the various facilities. (Taguba, 2004, p. 25)

Just as the British delegation that visited Guantánamo Bay commented on the similarities between that institution and domestic prisons, so, too, the American Civil Liberties Union (ACLU) laments that "U.S. violations of the Convention Against Torture are not limited to actions by military personnel overseas in the 'war on terror,' but in fact are far too ubiquitous at home." From the mistreatment of detainees during Hurricane Katrina to the "prolonged solitary confinement, extreme temperatures, intimidation by dogs, painful restraints and electro-stun devices" that are commonplace in many U.S. penal facilities, the ACLU finds examples "chillingly similar to those experienced by detainees abroad" (ACLU, 2006, p. 1; see also Human Rights Watch, 2005).

In March 2006, the U.S. transferred 4,500 inmates to other coalition-run sites, such as Camp Cropper at the Baghdad airport, and finally handed Abu Ghraib back to Iraqi authorities. Currently, two prison systems exist in parallel in Iraq, one run by the Iraqi Ministry of Justice, and the other by the U.S.-led coalition forces. So, too, in that other often forgotten war zone, Afghanistan, U.S. forces operate a military internment center at Bagram Air Base, alongside national prisons staffed by Afghanis and other detention centers run by North Atlantic Treaty Organization/International Security Assistance Force (NATO/ISAF). Only the International Red Cross is able to visit those imprisoned in such places (ICRC, 2007). While numbers have been dropping in Guantánamo, they have been growing steadily at Bagram, resting at year end 2008 at 630. Unless the Obama administration changes course dramatically in this area, such numbers seem set to rise even further, with plans announced in May 2008 for considerable expansion. According to an article in *The New York Times*, ". . . the United States will build what officials described as a more modern and humane detention center that would usually accommodate about 600 detainees—or as many as 1,100 in a surge—and cost more than $60 million" (Schmitt & Golden, 2008, p. 1).

In early 2008, the main U.S.-run prison in Afghanistan hit the headlines, appearing in a front-page article in *The New York Times* (Golden, 2008), aspects of which were taken up by other national and international media outlets (Horton, 2008). Part of the confidential memorandum to the U.S. government from the International Red Cross was leaked, complaining "... that detainees in the isolation area were sometimes subjected to harsh interrogations and were not reported to Red Cross inspectors until after they were moved into the main Bagram detention center and formally registered—after being held incommunicado for as long as several months" (Golden, 2008, p. 2). Despite some expansion and renovation, "... the detention center," article author Golden notes, "remains a crude place where most prisoners are fenced into large metal pens" (Golden, 2008, p. 2). More ominously, according to Scott Horton (2008) from *Harper's Magazine* online, "... it's been well established for some time that the intelligence community has its own independent operations at the site, and at other sites in Afghanistan" (Horton, 2008, p. 1).

The facility at Bagram, according to some, demonstrated the deep interconnections between the public face of the War on Terror and its illicit practices of secret prisons and torture that have, only since January 2009, been officially repudiated (Fletcher & Stover, 2008; Obama, 2009b). That such practices were legitimated at the highest level of government is not contested. It is some time since the classified presidential directive, issued on September, 17, 2001, less than a week after the attacks on the Pentagon and the World Trade Center, on authorizing a secret detention and interrogation program to be run by the CIA has been public knowledge. So too, in a televised address on September 6, 2006, Bush "... acknowledged that the CIA had been secretly detaining suspected terrorists in facilities outside of the United States" (Human Rights Watch, 2007, p. 27).

What the government has never made clear, however, is the manner in which such detainees were treated while incarcerated, nor what happened to them subsequently. As Human Rights Watch puts it:

> The fate of the missing detainees is one of the main unanswered questions about the CIA's secret prison program, but it is not the only one. Much is still unknown about the scope of the program, the precise locations of the detention facilities, the treatment of detainees, and the cooperation and complicity of other governments. Although confidential sources, including CIA personnel, have described some aspects of the program to journalists, and a small number of former detainees have recounted their experiences, many details of the program remain hidden. (Human Rights Watch, 2007, p. 3)

Given the absence of official accounts, we must turn instead to the growing evidence put forward by nongovernmental organizations (NGOs) and by former detainees themselves. In 2007, Human Rights Watch published the testimony from Marwan Jabour, who was arrested in Pakistan, and then beaten by the Pakistani intelligence services, before being held by the CIA in Afghanistan for two years. During his confinement by Americans, Jabour claims, he was subject to stress positions, kept naked for long stretches, and shackled in a cell with no window. His only contact with others was with his interrogators. The prison, in his words, "was a grave" (Jabour, cited in Human Rights Watch, 2007, p. 13). This man estimated, Human Rights Watch reports,

> . . . that in the more than two years he was held at the prison, he saw a total of about 70 staff, consisting of some 25 guards and 45 civilians, including interrogators, supervisors, three or four doctors, and a few psychologists. He said everyone was American except for the translators, who, he said, were mostly Arabs. (They could have been Arab-Americans.) He said there was an Iraqi translator, three Egyptians, and a Lebanese woman. (Human Rights Watch, 2007, p. 20)

Jabour's account meshes with others that have been published since 2006. Briton Moazzam Begg, for instance, passed through Bagram on the way to Guantánamo. Here, he alleged, he was threatened with "rendition" to Egypt to be tortured. He also witnessed others being abused such as a ". . . young pale-looking Arab boy who . . . for refusing his meals . . . was taken to cell one, alone, and made to stand shackled and hooded" (Begg & Brittain, 2006, p. 146). Another prisoner, he claimed, was chained to a ". . . giant circular steel bracket . . . His movement was restricted to a 180-degree arc around the bracket. As he was unable to reach the toilet, he used the area where he slept to relieve himself" (Begg & Brittain, 2006, p. 147).

If Begg, at Bagram, was spared torture, at Kandahar, German permanent resident Murat Kurnaz alleged that he was not. In his memoirs, published in 2007 one year after his release from Guantánamo Bay without charge, Kurnaz described a litany of institutional abuse over a five-year period. At Kandahar, Americans placed electrodes to the soles of his feet. They also forced his head under water, while hitting him in the stomach. They strung him from a chain suspended from the ceiling for five days (Kurnaz, 2007). Kurnaz claimed also to have witnessed the deaths of other detainees at Kandahar.[17]

There is, of course, no way to verify such claims. And some would doubtless call into question the wisdom of relying on the alleged memories of detainees. However, without a body of official or academic literature in their place, they, and the publications of their advocates, are all we have. At the very least, the similarities in these men's experiences reaffirm the point that such facilities were operating in clear contravention of international laws and norms. When conducted by other countries, extrajudicial detention has been roundly criticized by the United States. "International human rights law prohibits enforced disappearance," as Human Rights Watch (2007) points out, but "... such persons, who remain 'disappeared' until their fate or whereabouts become known, are also more likely to be subjected to torture and other cruel, inhuman or degrading treatment" (Human Rights Watch, 2007, p. 4). Yet, despite the alleged commitment of the U.S. to resist and condemn human rights abuses, until President Obama's Inaugural Address, in which he condemned the previous administration's actions, there had been little official challenge of such practices. So, too, has the criminological community been slow to comment.

Scholarly Accounts of the War on Terror: A Failure of the Criminological Imagination?

Outside the work of a few (Welch, 2003; Bosworth, 2007b; Sanchez 2007), most critical academic analysis of the detention of foreigners and terrorists has been produced by legal scholars (see, for example, Cole, 2005, 2007; Fletcher & Stover, 2008), and those writing in cognate disciplines like international relations, ethnic studies, and social theory (e.g., Mathur, 2006; Butler, 2004). As with domestic prisons, most of the changes to detention conditions have been forced through by the courts.

Within criminology, it is particularly regrettable that prison scholars have failed to engage with these issues. A survey of *The Prison Journal* from 2001 to 2008 elicits not one piece on immigration detention, foreign nationals in prison, or other related matters. While *Punishment & Society* and *Theoretical Criminology* yield a few articles on immigration control,[18] none is based on empirical research conducted in a detention center (see, for example, Welch & Schuster, 2005; Krasmann, 2007). Those who work on policing in the U.S. seem to have been more interested in border control, while, in broader terms, criminologists working in Canada, Australia, and the UK have also paid some attention to such matters (Deflem, 2002; Pratt, 2005; Guerette, 2007; Brotherton & Kretsedemas, 2008; Pratt & Valverde, 2002; Pickering & Weber, 2006; Bosworth, 2007b, 2008; Bosworth & Guild, 2008).

When scholars have written about war prisons, whether from within criminology or from disciplines such as sociology or social theory, most have been interested in their symbolic meaning, rather than in the actual experiences of detainees and their guards. As a result, many have favored highly complex theoretical language and approaches over empirical research. While such choices are surely influenced by the significant barriers to interviewing serving or former detainees, particularly those held by the U.S. military or the CIA, others from beyond the academy have managed both to consult former detainees and to visit some of the establishments in which they are held (Rose, 2005; Stafford-Smith, 2008; Foreign Affairs Committee, 2007).

It is, in short, not simply an empirical problem but an epistemological one, too. Can criminologists speak on such matters as torture and terrorism? Does the administrative language of crime control illuminate such complex areas, or do they require a new "criminological imagination"? Can a subject so often bound to the state speak on such transnational matters? For some, the old imagination will do just fine; ". . . criminology and criminal justice can be of direct assistance in the fight against terrorism," Gary Lafree and James Hendrickson (2007, p. 782) assert. Criminology, in their view, can devise ". . . best practices for processing those who commit terrorist acts" (ibid), while also illuminating the ". . . etiology of terrorist behavior" (ibid). Thus, in recent years, scholars associated with that most pragmatic school of criminological scholarship, rational choice theory, have touted academic techniques for ". . . outsmarting the terrorists" (Clarke & Newman, 2006).

For others, however, criminologists must think anew about such matters in order for the discipline to maintain its relevance (Morrison, 2006). Insisting on existing categories, particularly those drawn from the literature on rational choice, sidesteps complex questions about justice, morality, and power. Such an approach, while perhaps seeking to narrow and defuse some of the populist rhetoric in favor of a "criminal justice approach" to terrorism, can only oversimplify matters (Lafree & Hendrickson, 2007).

Those few scholars who have attempted to analyze war prisons or immigration detention centers more expansively have drawn on Foucault, particularly on his writings on governmentality (Welch, 2008). A growing number also cite the writings of Giorgio Agamben with his ideas about sovereign power and "bare" life (Agamben, 1998, 2005; Sanchez, 2007). According to Agamben, the state deliberately uses moments of conflict and uncertainty to extend its sovereign power by declaring a "state of exception," which requires freedom from the restrictions of the rule of law and government by decree. "Because the sovereign power of the president is essentially grounded in the emergency," which, Agamben points out, is typically "linked to a state of war, over the course of the twentieth century the metaphor of war becomes an integral part of the presidential political vocabulary whenever decisions considered to be of vital importance are being imposed" (Agamben, 2005, p. 21). In providing for exceptional powers in states of emergency, he suggests, the liberal state is a good deal less liberal than it claims.

Despite the appeal and utility of Agamben's ideas, his work and that of his followers has been harshly criticized by the somewhat unexpected figure of Judith Butler (2007), who argues that it had led people to make "the same description time and again" (Butler, 2007, p. 43). This repetition not only confuses different examples of suffering and abuse into "undifferentiated instances of 'bare life' " but, as Butler (2007) points out, "ends up taking on the perspective of sovereignty and reiterating its terms" (Butler, 2007, pp. 42–43). Above all, it directs attention away from lived experience of incarceration.

In a similar vein, in their enthusiasm to theorize the abuses at Abu Ghraib, some scholars seem to forget the lived experiences of this penal institution. Instead, Abu Ghraib is deployed metaphorically, to inform us about the "state of feminism" (Ehrenreich, 2004) or, even more absurdly, about the nature of Western art (Eisenman, 2007). For Barbara Ehrenreich, for example, "What we have learned once and for all from Abu Ghraib is that a uterus is not a substitute for a conscience" (Ehrenreich, 2005, p. 69), while art historian Stephen Eisenman (2007) views the photographed detainees as reminiscent of ". . . defeated warriors from Hellenistic Greek Sculptures . . . posed (as in a tableau vivant) like the bound slaves of Michelangelo" (Eisenman, 2007, p. 11).

Not only do such writers fail to understand Abu Ghraib as a prison, but also they make no attempt to include the perspectives of those subject to incarceration in such places. In the absence of such voices, not only is political criticism rendered less effective, but so, too, our common bonds of humanity disappear. Predictably then, in many of their discussions, the authors have produced an unending replication of the abusive images, in which they, however unintentionally, revictimize the detainees time and again (Philipose, 2007). As Liz Philipose (2007) observes in her thoughtful account of the analysis of the Abu Ghraib images, such thoughtlessness reached its apogee in the U.S. when the images were displayed in two art galleries. Still available online, the faces of the detainees are perfectly visible, captured forever in perpetual humiliation and available to anyone with an Internet connection.

The body of work that may be the most useful conceptually for understanding both the reliance on the prison in this decade and some of its implications may be found in the interdisciplinary field of "security studies." Though this is not an area particularly associated with American criminology, with some notable exceptions (Cole, 2005), scholars working in this field routinely debate the limits and effects of "securitization" through analysis of policing, surveillance, criminal law, and so on. Whereas "security" is a social good—we all desire to feel secure, and indeed, can only flourish if we do—increasingly, such authors demonstrate, "our" security is being presented as a zero-sum game in conflict with the liberties and rights of others (Zedner, 2004; Loader & Walker, 2007). That is to say, though security and liberty are, to some extent, basic human rights, in practice our ability to claim them has been significantly reduced as states have appropriated greater powers of intervention into the lives of all of us.

In the conflict over security, states and communities identify those who belong and those who do not by setting out entitlements and responsibilities. As the benefits of security have become increasingly restricted to citizens or long-term residents, states effectively divide up diverse populations into more manageable parts. Immigrants become recast as drains on the economy or as threats to social order. The political allegiance of noncitizens or their commitment to democracy is cast into doubt. In such discussions, which have occurred with depressing frequency this century, the legitimacy of detention is reaffirmed as a place to hold such risky populations. So too, a vision of national identity has emerged that is based on exclusion (Guild, 2007).

CONCLUSION

Since September 11, 2001, the United States government has been widely criticized for violating basic human rights in the fight against terrorism. The Bush administration, according to one particularly stringent critique:

> . . . authorized interrogation techniques widely considered torture, including by its own Department of State in its annual human rights reports. It has held an unknown number of detainees as "ghosts" beyond the reach of all monitors, including the International Committee of the Red Cross. And it has become the only government in the world to seek legislative sanction to treat detainees inhumanely. (Human Rights Watch, 2006, p. 501)

As this chapter has outlined, the first decade of the 21st century witnessed the detention of an increasing number of vulnerable people seeking refuge in the U.S., the separation of family members of U.S. residents, and a widespread denial of basic human rights to immigration detainees, actual and alleged terrorists or combatants. In each instance, the state relied on the prison, both figuratively and literally, to administer and identify such people.

Used to hold enemy combatants as well as failed or pending asylum seekers and "criminal aliens," prisons and detention centers were set to work to secure the "homeland" by holding (and thus defining) those of uncertain origin and suspicious intent. Such institutions both relied on, and invigorated, a harsh and simplistic security discourse that divided the world into those who were "with" the United States and those who were "against" it. In this political vision, the U.S. government claimed the right to define many people in the world as hostile and unlawful, men, women, and children undeserving of human rights–based safeguards. Despite initiating military aggression in Afghanistan and Iraq, the U.S. presented itself as vulnerable—by constantly reiterating the "security" threat against it and by locking up would-be immigrants and refugees in order to ascertain their dangerousness.[19]

Under these circumstances, it is not surprising that the prison—whether in the form of immigration detention centers, or war prisons—should have become the place to hold so many. Penal institutions offer a physical and symbolic exclusion zone, while actively constructing parallels between foreigners and offenders. Detention centers provide not just utilitarian sites for states, but also symbolic ones. They offer an appealingly circular logic—those behind bars must deserve to be so confined, since otherwise they would not be imprisoned. They also suggest an orderliness to the process. Despite evidence of their significant violence, brutality, and disorder, prisons remain synonymous with discipline and regulation. They are part of a "justice" system. Even as the public cannot see within them, we are assured that all is well; it is a prison, not a holiday camp. Finally, and somewhat paradoxically, these two aspects of imprisonment are underpinned by a third view, which is that even if prisoners do suffer a little, at the hands of overzealous guards, this is acceptable. After all, as the saying goes: "If you can't do the time, don't do the crime."

The paradox posed by both the War on Terror and immigration detention is that the methods deployed have been both novel and familiar. There are numerous overlaps among immigration detention centers, war prisons, and American correctional facilities, from the actual individuals who staff them to their physical layout and design (Brown, 2005; Human Rights Watch, 2008). At the same time, however, the scope of the state's power and the extent of its discretion have been breathtaking. The War on Terror does not break with traditional modes of U.S. governance and penality. Instead it has rearticulated and expanded them. In so doing, at least under the Bush administration, it established a new standard of guilt and untrammeled power to punish. Although it is unlikely that the numbers of foreigners will ever match those of U.S. citizens incarcerated for drug offenses, their population is large enough to fill some cells that might otherwise be left empty. Moreover, due to the similarities in race, gender, and class of the noncitizens with drug offenders, their incarceration proceeds down a well-worn path. In addition to the "surrogate ghetto" role identified by scholars like Loïc Wacquant (2000), prisons in the 21st century became the new borderlands, protecting us not just from the trouble within United States society, but also from beyond.

NOTES

1. José Padilla and Yasser Hamdi were both initially held in the Naval Consolidated Brig in North Charleston, South Carolina.

2. In 2003, the former Immigration and Naturalization Service was absorbed into the new Department of Homeland Security and divided into two separate agencies. The Bureau of Citizenship and Immigration Service now deals with visas and other everyday issues facing foreigners in the U.S. while, according to its mission statement, the Bureau of Immigration and Customs Enforcement (ICE) "is responsible for identifying and shutting down vulnerabilities in the nation's border, economic, transportation and infrastructure security" (U.S. Immigration and Customs Enforcement, 2005).

3. Pedro Guzman, who is unable to read at more than a second-grade level, was mistakenly deported to Tijuana, Mexico, even though he was a U.S. citizen, born and raised in Los Angeles. He spent nearly three months homeless in Mexico until he was found and returned to his mother's care. According to his lawyers, Mr. Guzman had informed the ICE officials that he was a U.S. citizen (Brosnahan & Rosenbaum, 2008).

4. While it is impossible to verify how many are held in such illegal institutions, estimates range from less than 50 to as many as 27,000 (Human Rights Watch, 2008; Stafford-Smith, 2008; Grey, 2007).

5. It is unclear whether the federal government under President Obama will reduce its reliance on immigration detention. On the White House Web site's listing of the administration's "agenda," under "Immigration," is listed a 2007 speech to the Senate, in which Obama called for "stronger enforcement on the border" (Obama, 2007).

6. That financial year, ICE claimed on its Web site to have identified for removal 164,296 people incarcerated in federal, state, and local facilities.

7. Others, such as those 500 or so individuals held in the federal detention center at Oakdale, Louisiana, though part of ICE's remit, are in a legal limbo. Most of them are from Cuba, and were part of the 1980 Mariel boatlift. Since the U.S. has no repatriation agreement with Cuba, they cannot be returned, but due to their criminal convictions the U.S. government is not prepared to let them settle in the U.S.A. Their criminal conviction also, has meant that they have not benfitted from the Supreme Court's decision in *Zadvydas*. In 1987, a number of those in Oakdale rioted, setting the prison ablaze and taking hostages (Hamm, 1995).

8. The first Immigration Act, passed in 1875, barred prostitutes and criminals from entering the U.S. Subsequent acts were passed over the next two decades, such as the Chinese Exclusion Act of 1882, the Immigration Act of 1882, and the Contract Labor Act of 1885, which sought both to control labor and to regulate the entry of Chinese nationals, while preventing the arrival of convicts, lunatics, and "idiots." A federal immigration bureaucracy was established by the Immigration Act of 1891, which also authorized the deportation of illegal aliens. Through much of the 20th century, the U.S. favored a quota system to maintain a stable ethnic constitution, while, depending on its foreign policy of the moment, easing barriers for refugees and others fleeing opponents (e.g., the communist regimes in the former USSR and Cuba) abroad. These days, as with other countries, U.S. law gives preference to skilled immigrants, who can fill certain employment needs, while also being bound by its international responsibilities to accept refugees (Tichenor, 2002; Calavita, 2007).

9. One popular exception can be found in the blogosphere, where a number of authors mounted a consistent opposition to such practices and institutions (see, for example, thedailykos.com).

10. As many predicted it would (Cole, 2003), this section of the act increased the FBI's ability to monitor anyone residing in the U.S. In contrast to the indifference that greeted this treatment of foreigners, there was considerable public outcry when the extent of phone interceptions of citizens became known.

11. For example, the Border Protection, Antiterrorism, and Illegal Immigration Control Act of 2005 passed the House of Representatives on December 15, 2005, but failed in the Senate, as did the Comprehensive Immigration Reform Acts of 2006 and 2007, and the Securing America's Borders Act (S. 2454) of 2006.

12. Ominously, and in contrast to his actions on Guantánamo Bay and the Geneva Conventions, President Obama has not promised to end the practice known euphemistically as "rendition."

13. According to Grey (2007), the U.S. government relied on "rendition" in previous eras and under previous regimes. However, such "rendered" figures were rarely taken to be punished or interrogated by U.S. officials, but rather were sent back to their countries of origin (to be dealt with summarily). It is not just the purpose of rendition that has changed, he claims, but also its frequency as, since September 11, 2001, the U.S. government has come to rely on it increasingly often.

14. While neither he nor his opponent, Senator John McCain, addressed the human rights concerns in the immigration detention system (or, indeed, in the wider detention system), nor did they mention the secret CIA prisons, Obama was implacably opposed to Guantánamo Bay from the start. He was also committed to drawing down U.S. troops from Iraq and thus, presumably, from the military prisons they operate in the region as well. As this chapter demonstrates, since his inauguration, President Obama has in fact acted decisively on war prisons, though he has (yet) to address immigration detention or domestic prisons in any consolidated fashion.

15. And, some would argue, an illegal purpose (Rose, 2004; Stafford-Smith, 2008).

16. Demonstrating yet another overlap between Guantánamo Bay and the regular justice system, Clive Stafford-Smith has also been particularly active as a legal representative for defendants on death row. A dual UK–U.S. national, he has been admitted to the bar in the U.S. and has devoted much of his career to death row cases.

17. In a report published in November 2008 by the University of California at Berkeley, a number of former Guantánamo detainees reported having been subjected to similar physical and psychological abuse at both Kandahar and Bagram, which included enforced nudity, stress positions, being chained upside down from the ceiling, and frequent beatings. One respondent claimed to have "witnessed the violent death of a young Afghan detainee in Bagram" (Fletcher & Stover, 2008, p. 23).

18. These included a special issue in 2001 devoted to an international comparison of such matters (see, inter alia, Melossi, 2003; Young, 2001; Asale-Adjani, 2001).

19. And by way of unending referral to the events of September 11, 2001.

Conclusion

Where To From Here?

Recourse to the penal apparatus in advanced society is not destiny but a matter of political choices, and these choices must be made in full knowledge of the facts and of their consequences.

—Wacquant, 2001b, p. 409

The infliction of punishment by a state upon its citizens bears the character of a civil war in miniature—it depicts a society engaged in a struggle with itself. And though this may sometimes be necessary, it is never anything other than a necessary evil.

—Garland, 1990, p. 292

The great penal gulag being constructed in the United States has taken liberal democracy to its limits.

—Young, J., 1999, p. 190

At year end 2008, the U.S. incarcerated more than 2.4 million men, women, and children in more than 5,000 prisons and jails, as well as very many others in war prisons and immigration detention centers. More than one in 100 American adults was under some form of confinement. State, federal, and local systems together accounted for an annual expenditure of over $60 billion, a figure that jumped nearly 600 percent between 1982 and 2004 (Loury, 2007).[1] Despite an increasing number of calls for reducing the confined population, both the federal government and many states were forging ahead, investing in new establishments and forecasting rapid future growth.

Since the establishment of the Walnut Street Jail, the U.S. has been mass exporting its penal models across the world. From the mid-1980s, such transfer of penal practices and ideologies was facilitated by the global reach of many of the U.S.-based private prison companies. After 2001, both were joined in pursuit of the War on Terror by the continual deployment of new kinds of incarceration, whether on U.S. soil for citizen combatants to immigration detention centers for those who would claim asylum or enter the country without documentation. Still more sinister forms appeared in those prisons that the U.S. military and the Central Intelligence Agency (CIA) established throughout the world to detain terror suspects.

The prison, it seems, is in rude health. Yet, in every era, including our own, it has been dogged by criticism. From the first penal reformers in Philadelphia, who found that overcrowding undermined the reformative goals of their cherished new style of management in the Walnut Street Jail (Skidmore, 1948; Teeters, 1955), to contemporary hand-wringing about violence behind bars and rates of reoffending of domestic prisoners (Gibbons & Katzenbach, 2006; Petersilia, 2003), to the debate about state-sanctioned torture abroad (Stafford-Smith, 2008), the prison has been the target of intense and ongoing criticism.

Critique has been made from a range of quarters: serving and former prisoners, penal reformers, academics, and justice practitioners all express concern. In 1924, New York penal reformer Thomas Mott Osborne (1924) bluntly asserted that "our prison system has been a failure" (Osborne, 1924, p. 14), while a quarter century later, the Russian émigré and psychiatrist Benjamin Karpman (1948) despaired that "whatever motive or motives society might have had originally in using imprisonment as a means of handling the criminal, they all have seemingly failed of their purpose and promise" (Karpman, 1948, p. 475). At about the same time, economist Louis N. Robinson (1942) poetically characterized prisons as ". . . eddies in the current or stream of progress, collecting rubbish in the form of outworn ideas and whirling it around and around for years before finally letting it pass on" (Robinson, 1942, p. 184). In 1967, President Johnson's commission agreed, conceding that the promises of penal reformers were unfulfilled and the nation's prisons in disarray (President's Commission on Law Enforcement and Administration of Justice, 1967).

Sometimes, concerns about imprisonment seem to hinge closely on questions of efficacy. The rising crime rates in the 1970s, for example, were cited by many as proof of the manifest failure of incarceration (Wilson, 1975).

Yet, such utilitarian concerns usually mask murkier anxieties over social cohesion, race relations, and justice. Many have argued that, since the 1960s, crime control—and the prison—has become a favored mode of governance in the U.S. because governments felt they could do (or at least be seen to be doing) something about it. As Jonathan Simon (2007a) puts it, "... Alone among the major social problems haunting America in the 1970s and 1980s, crime offered the least political or legal resistance to government action" (Simon, 2007a, p. 31). Notwithstanding the recent disquiet over the domestic prison system concerns that have only increased since the economic crisis of 2008, not all forms of confinement have (yet) been drawn into question. There has, for example, only been muted criticism of immigration detention centers, which seem to have been accepted as a necessary evil, safeguarding the border and the homeland. While the notorious prison at Guantánamo Bay should be closed by year-end 2009, and the U.S. government has declared its intention to apply the Geneva Conventions to foreign combatants and end unlawful forms of CIA interrogation, for as long as the U.S. remains at war, war prisons, in some form or another, are here to stay.

In short, notwithstanding the litany of laments about its virtue as well as the reiterated charges of ineffectiveness and injustice leveled at it, the prison has become increasingly entrenched in U.S. society, in its cultural imagery, in its criminal justice systems, and, increasingly, in its mechanisms of border control and warfare. In many respects, then, the persistence of the prison, in the face of critique, has been one of its most impressive and defining characteristics (Mathiesen, 2006). What can we make of this paradox? What, after all this time, explains imprisonment?

Prisons, History, and Paradox

For some, like legal scholar Michael Tonry (2004), prisons have simply become self-perpetuating. "American policy makers, having grabbed hold of current [penal] policies, are stuck and do not know how to get loose" (Tonry, 2004, p. 11). So, too, criminologist Todd Clear (2003) finds some explanatory utility in expectations. The "... upsizing of the penal system has been one of the signal characteristics of contemporary American culture," he writes, and "we are used to the idea that politically and socially, a prison term is seen as a solution to a social problem" (Clear, 2003, p. xiv). Yet, what kind of "solution" does the prison actually offer? To which "social problems" does it respond? How is it that, in both of these accounts, the U.S. is so passive? Who, in the terminology of former President Bush, is the "decider" of criminal justice policies?[2]

Whereas once it might have seemed self-evident that prison was a (sensible) response to crime, the "great American crime drop," where the infraction rate fell largely independently of the rise in prison numbers, has undermined the credibility of that belief (Blumstein & Wallman, 2000, 2006; Zimring, 2007). Likewise, as a "solution," the prison remains frustratingly evasive; ineffective in reforming most of its targets and unsuccessful at their deterrence, it seems that at best it operates as a "punishment." Yet, even in this regard, its frequent application may be diminishing its effect, since an increasing number of writers argue that the prison is little more than a rite of passage for certain young men. In some communities, these authors suggest, a custodial sentence has become a formative part of a man (Roberts, 2004; Wacquant, 2001b).

For a long time, the history of imprisonment was put forward as reason enough for the institution's legitimacy. The prison, proponents of this narrative from the late 18th century onward claimed, is a humane, effective, rational, and modern response to crime. However, plentiful counter-examples can be found to contradict each of those beliefs. From its origins, the prison has been the site of inhumane treatment. Just as ". . . it is a truism well worth remembering that behind all forms of law, public or private, lurks a background threat of violence within the law" (Simon, 2007a, p. 14), so, too, the consistent levels of violence and suffering within (some) penal institutions across all historical periods suggest that harm may be a constitutive part of a sentence of confinement. Prisoners, it would seem, should suffer, at least a little.

The efficacy of imprisonment is likewise easily challenged, whether through reference to reoffending rates, the collateral damage visited on family members and the communities from which prisoners come, or the failure of punishment to do much to assuage the victims of crime. Without these two justifications, claims about the "rationality" of the prison are far less convincing. Further evidence against its reasonableness can also be found in sentencing disparities, and in the idleness and the everyday frustrations of most serving prisoners, while penal institutions are neither particularly orderly nor predictable. Even the "modernity" of the institution can be called into question. Not only does historical research date the institution earlier (Bosworth, 2000), but distasteful and reactionary contemporary penal practices, from the use of unmuzzled dogs in removing prisoners from their cells to everyday humiliations at the hands of their keepers, call into question the commitment of the state to a civilized, modern worldview.

How should we interpret such manifold failures of this institution, particularly when they seem to have such little effect on the fate of prison itself (Mathiesen, 2006; Christie, 1981)? For some, they represent no less than the total control of the state over, and its abuse of certain segments of, its population. Serving prisoners in any era write of the custodians' unfettered power over their every action (Paine, 1852; Cleaver, 1968; Abbott, 1981; Santos, 2006), while activist scholars portray those behind bars as victims of state brutality and conspiracy (Rodriguez, 2006). For others, like Michel Foucault (1977, 1980), the institution's undeniable inadequacies are its very *raison d'être*. It was never meant to succeed on any of the parameters listed above, but to hold those whom society viewed deviant and, in so doing, to create more "delinquents." In his view, well-meaning penal reformers constantly tinker at the edges of the institution, only to embed it more deeply into social structures and imaginations; historical figures like Thomas Mott Osborne, as well as contemporary organizations like Families Against Mandatory Minimums (FAMM), are complicit in shoring up the health of the institution.

Perhaps, some assert, we should be bolder. All the evidence points in one direction. Prisons are "obsolete" and ripe for demolition (Davis, 2003). Yet, even in those states like New York where numbers have dropped and stayed down, no prisons have (yet) been dismantled. Simply recounting their inadequacies has not undermined their standing. Rather, according to David Garland's more dispassionate view, ". . . the prison simultaneously pursues a number of objectives and is kept in place by a range of forces" (Garland, 1990, p. 289). Under such circumstances it would be naïve to assume that the prison was designed to "succeed" in any single task. This is not to say, of course, that thousands of criminal justice and prison staff have not been motivated to help, punish, deter, or, in some way, influence those who commit crime. It is hard to see how any social institution could continue without some aspiration for effect.[3] The point, however, is that their success or failure seems to have little impact on the prison itself. Therefore, the purpose and legitimacy of the institution must rest elsewhere.

For some, the longevity and robustness of the prison lie somewhere in the slippery constructs of sentiment, culture, and governance (Garland, 1990, 2001a; Simon, 2007a). For others it springs from the racialized inequalities that continue to structure U.S. society (Wacquant, 1999) and in the web of state and financial interests that uphold the "prison industrial complex" (Davis, 2003; Gilmore, 2007). Still others stress the gendered dynamics of penal institutions and their role in constructing (racialized) notions of masculinity and femininity (Sudbury, 2005; Bowker, 1980), while increasingly there have been attempts to explain imprisonment with reference to political structures and democracy (Gottschalk, 2006; Barker, 2006; Miller, 2008). All these approaches, which exist uneasily side by side in current American scholarship, are persuasive. Yet, in their epistemological differences and disciplinary distinctions, they leave certain questions about the vitality and longevity of the prison unanswered. What, for example, are the structural and institutional forces underpinning "culture"? What, in other words, is the relationship between culture and diversity? How do views and belief change over time? What historical, cultural, and democratic processes enabled the racist logic of imprisonment to survive and flourish? What forces resisted it?

As is well established, the dominant historical narrative of U.S. prisons is primarily the story of the treatment of White men and, for that matter, is largely based on their experiences in one particular part of the country. Women's prisons evolved differently, while, depending on where they were located in the continental United States, Black and Native American prisoners were also treated distinctly. The history of U.S. prisons has other absences, which are less defined by identity politics and more by a penological taxonomy that characterizes some penal institutions as relevant and many others as not. Hospital prison wards, closed mental institutions, and even jails, for example, are rarely considered in the literature on prisons or punishment. For the most part, juvenile detention centers are examined separately, even as the numbers of children incarcerated in adult state prisons have risen dramatically, recasting the relationship between juvenile and adult corrections.

Military prisons and penal institutions utilized in times of war are also, generally, overlooked, as are immigration detention centers. These days, Camp Sumter (Andersonville) and the cemetery where Confederate detainees from Elmira, New York, were buried (Woodlawn National Cemetery) are typically interpreted and linked to the tourist story of the Civil War, rather than as part of the history of U.S. imprisonment. Reflecting the same logic, documents on Civil War prisons are not held alongside material on "regular" prisons, but are instead kept centrally in the National Archives under military topics. Similarly, the Nisei and those prisoners of war brought in from Europe, Asia, and Africa do not make it into many criminological accounts of the prison, even though some of the places they were confined were converted into federal correctional institutions and, while they were in operation, most followed the logic of mainstream prisons. Instead, they are considered only in histories of the "home front" in the Second World War. While human rights organizations have focused their attention on more recent war prisons and on immigration detention centers, neither has been incorporated into the penological scholarship.

Still other lacunae in the explanations of U.S. imprisonment can be identified. There remains a geographical bias in much prisons scholarship that prioritizes certain states over others. While there is a healthy body of work on prisons in the Southern states (see, for example, Ward & Rogers, 2003; Lloyd, 2000; Banks, 1993; Yackle, 1989), which maps their historical and contemporary nature, such texts are often overlooked in broader accounts of confinement, their explanatory utility somehow limited only to understanding the South. More generally, the deeper historical roots of prisons remain outside much criminological analysis, with most scholarship focused either on contemporary events or on those that date to the 1970s.

What, if anything, can we conclude from the broad sweep of prisons literature and the ongoing debates within it? Do any of the overlooked penal institutions help explain imprisonment today? Does the "presentist" orientation of much prisons scholarship blind us to longer-term characteristics of penal institutions?

To some extent, the forgotten war camps seem most obviously relevant at a time when the War on Terror has revitalized imprisonment in the face of considerable domestic critique. In a similar fashion, the relationship between immigration detention and the protection of national interests is worth reconsidering as the number of noncitizens behind bars grows considerably each year. The geographical divide in knowledge reminds us to be ever cautious of generalizations, while at the same time providing compelling examples of context-rich analysis.

Together, all the missing topics remind us that prisons literature, like prisons themselves, is based on exclusion; some factors are relevant, some matters are not. It is only by leaving out certain issues, voices, and places that a generalization of the role, purpose, and nature of imprisonment can unfold. Yet, by excluding war prisons, immigration detention centers, and the South from the mainstream narrative, not to mention firsthand accounts, historical periods before the 1970s, jails, juveniles, and so on, only a partial explanation of the prison emerges. Prisons, in this view, are explained primarily by their role in recent historical events and in response to recent views on and levels of domestic crime.

Taking a longer historical perspective and including a more diverse set of places and establishments illuminates other roles played by the prison. In particular, it becomes clearer that prisons have always had a part to play in securing national and more local and state borders and identities.

This is not to argue that prisons reflect an essentialized view of American exceptionalism (Whitman, 2005; Garland, 2005) since, as this book has shown, the justifications of the prison have changed over time. Rather, it is to raise a set of new questions about the role of prisons in practices and rhetoric of nation building. If prisons in the South reveal certain widely accepted views on race, could prisons more generally inform us of such sentiments on a national scale? What can be deduced from the similarities between immigration detention facilities and state and federal prisons? War prisons are explicitly designed to secure the nation; do prisons in peace operate in a similar fashion?

Securing the Nation in Troubled Times

Since the 1960s, politicians have declared "war" on a range of social problems, including crime (Nixon), drugs (Reagan and Bush Sr.), and violence (Clinton). At the same time as these conflicts raged at home, the U.S. also fought abroad, whether in Vietnam, Latin America, or alongside the North Atlantic Treaty Organization (NATO) in the Balkans. Most recently, America's involvement in fronts at home and abroad has been dramatically expanded by the War on Terror (Bush Jr.).

Wars, historians and political scientists tell us, are the means by which states either defend their territorial integrity or seek to expand their spheres of influence. Not only does conflict rewrite geopolitical maps, but it also inspires and generates particular accounts of ethnicity and national identity (Smith, 1981, 1986). In the War of Independence, for example, an American nationalism was forged in opposition to Colonial rule from Britain, just as participants in the Civil War sought to articulate and justify Southern exceptionalism in the face of Northern intervention. Wars also drive social change and technological developments (Marwick, 1978).

In such conflicts, political leaders typically deploy ". . . good-versus-evil rhetoric to mobilize their citizens." Such "demonization," political scientist Peter Liberman (2006) asserts, "makes enemies appear more dangerous," binding citizens together in fear, and freeing the state to pursue more radical strategies (Liberman, 2006, p. 687). Judicial safeguards are often relaxed, and state power expanded. Governments demand, and usually are granted, freedom from legislative restrictions and rule increasingly by decree (Agamben, 1998, 2005). War, in other words, goes with authoritarian government.

In periods of war, nationalism is also heightened, in calls for (military) sacrifice, justifications of aggression, and depictions of threat, vulnerability, and victimization. In this regard, the U.S.-led conflicts in Iraq and Afghanistan have been no exception. Since their advent, at least until the 2008 financial crisis, such passions drew attention from domestic issues like poverty and race relations (Aretxaga, 2001). They also deflected concerns about the failings, costs, and impact of the expanding criminal justice system.

As the historical overview in this book has demonstrated, armed conflict in any era dramatically expands the penal population, extending the prison's reach into the lives of people in the U.S., be they citizens or not. "Total wars," as do civil ones, seem to call for "total institutions" to hold and identify their enemies (Goffman, 1961a). Numerous penal institutions sprang up during the American Revolution, as they did again in the Civil War, to hold the enemy of the moment, somehow defined. In both the First and Second World Wars, the U.S. set up prisoner of war camps, going to great lengths in the latter conflict to bring prisoners over from Europe, Africa, and Asia. In light of this history, the exportation of the U.S. prison system to deal with suspected terrorists, and to maintain order in Afghanistan and Iraq, can be viewed as merely the most recent manifestation of a lengthy tradition.[4]

In each of these battles, prisons are meant to safeguard the nation. In this guise, they house menacing individuals and, if only for the duration of a sentence, neutralize their danger. By grouping such people, prisons help to identify—and enable the state to gather information about—the threats to the nation. Those confined are, for the period of their detention and often well beyond it, excluded from the rights and opportunities afforded to the rest.

Prisons in times of peace work with similar effect. It is not just the liberty of offenders that is curtailed, but during their confinement and in some states afterwards as well, they cannot vote. Depending on their crimes, they are banned from certain jobs, from drawing on federal welfare support, and, in some states, from residing in public housing. Such modes of exclusion both rest on and reinforce beliefs that those in prison are dangerous, undeserving, not like "us."

The prison, in other words, in war or peace, identifies those who threaten the majority in an affective sense, not just as an actuarial risk. In so doing, they legitimate and depend upon widely held punitive sentiment. More than that, however, this book has suggested, prisons contribute to discourses of (national, state, and local) identity and belonging. By excluding noncitizens and offenders, they symbolically define citizens and the law-abiding. In more practical ways, too, prisons articulate and rearticulate the boundaries of the (nation) state. Just as one of the first acts of war is to establish a place to hold captured enemy combatants, so, too, nascent states usually establish prisons. Notwithstanding the move to privatization, prisons remain, at their very base, articulations of the state's power and its right to punish.

In building a prison, as they do with their police (Loader, 1997; Loader & Mulcahy, 2003), states establish a particular narrative of national identity that is based on forces of inclusion and exclusion. However, whereas the police are presented as noble figures engaged in the pursuit of social order, security, and the "American way," we tend to be far more ambivalent about the "virtues" of the prison and its custodians. Despite the prison boom, there have been few public representations celebrating those who lock up others. There are no correctional officer heroes on prime time television or erstwhile heads of corrections celebrities like former chief of the New York Police Department (NYPD) William Bratton called on to take credit for the drop in crime.[5] Instead, prisons and their inhabitants occupy an uneasy, partly hidden yet ever more central, part of U.S. society.

Whereas the first prison sociologists considered penal institutions as communities in their own right, existing separate from society (Clemmer, 1939; Sykes, 1958), such views were soon challenged by others, who argued that prison culture was shaped by wider social forces (Irwin, 1970; Heffernan, 1974). These days, when one in 100 adult U.S. residents is incarcerated, and others are held in immigration detention centers, war prisons, and elsewhere, it makes little sense to imagine that such figures exist somehow outside or beyond the nation. Those who are incarcerated, even many noncitizens, have family and friends in the community. Though physically excluded from society, they maintain ties with it. Even those, such as long-term prisoners, inhabitants of supermaximum secure facilities, the seriously mentally ill, and detainees of the War on Terror, who may be effectively completely divorced from the wider community, lost in solitary, or in the vagaries of their own minds, can still call on the rest of us morally. As inhabitants of institutions, which explicitly represent the state and its power, they are always a part, however despised, of the national collectivity and its moral conscience. Prisons, in short, are constitutive of the whole; they are deeply imbricated in national and state economies, as well as in local communities and in individual lives: ". . . in the minds of each lives the image of their communion" (Anderson, 1984, p. 6).

Prisons and the State

Since the events of September 11, 2001, social theorists and those working in political science and international relations have focused their attention on issues of war, terrorism, and torture. These, we are told, are the issues of our times. Yet many old problems remain unresolved: racial inequalities, gender, and class. Outside a small body of work on Guantánamo Bay and Abu Ghraib—most, in any case, written by those in other disciplines—prison scholars have been silent about the role of the prison in war, just as they often continue to overlook its complicated entanglement with race and gender, too.

As this book has shown, prisons are put to use most enthusiastically in times of trouble, when the state is seeking either to define itself—as in the American Revolution and the Civil War—or when it is defending its interests and its way of life—such as during the Second World War. In their ever-expanding size, prisons institutionalize war, whether it is waged on the streets of U.S. cities or farther afield. In so doing, they reinscribe the power of the (nation) state. So too, in a point of convergence, as the numbers of incarcerated criminals, foreigners, and combatants stay high, and as new forms of imprisonment are continually devised, national identity and security become ever more closely linked to, and dependent on, the prison.

The "crisis of penal modernism" and the decline of the rehabilitative ideal, so the familiar argument goes, called into question the limits of the sovereign state (Garland, 1996). The inability of the state to deliver its promises of security and crime control caused it to abrogate its previously cherished monopoly on punishment in favor of "governing at a distance." Paradoxically, however, such neoliberal ideology increased state intervention into people's lives by expanding the prison system and by feeding a punitive discourse that legitimated enhanced surveillance and legislative control. In a similar fashion, the War on Terror has facilitated a vast growth in state power and in restrictions on mobility. There has also been an upsurge in nationalist sentiment and in its fellow traveler xenophobia, especially when targeted at the domestic "other," new immigrants.[6]

At present, the U.S. remains locked in a war without end. If history is any guide, such a battle promises not only an ongoing mass imprisonment, but also a national identity that increasingly denies the common bonds of neighbors, sons and daughters, and friends. Is that to be the future of the United States?

NOTES

1. In 2007, state expenditure on corrections alone totaled just over $50 billion, consuming $1 in every 15 discretionary dollars of state budgets (Pew Charitable Trusts, 2009, p. 1).

2. On April 18, 2005, when criticized for standing by then Secretary of Defense Donald Rumsfeld in the face of steep opposition from the military, Bush replied, "I'm the decider, and I decide what is best."

3. As Franklin Zimring and Gordon Hawkins put it, "Although it is logically and legally possible to continue both to administer prisons and to use imprisonment as a punishment without the support of any specific justification or ideology of imprisonment, it would be difficult in a political democracy to do so without any positive sense of purpose or function for them. Those who work in prison, those who sentence offenders to prison, and those who support the institution in less palpable ways all need some paradigm of imprisonment, a sharp image of what prisons are needed for and may achieve" (Zimring & Hawkins, 1995, p. 5).

4. Prisons were not the only criminal justice system affected by military rhetoric and reality over this period. It was the National Guard, for instance, who opened fire on demonstrating students at Kent State University in 1970 and again, in concert with state troopers, who put down the Attica Rebellion in 1971. Less dramatically, though with possibly greater effect, the Coast Guard and the Navy have played key roles in interdicting drugs at sea, just as they were deployed to prevent the safe landing of undocumented migrants fleeing Haiti (Kraska, 2001). In New Orleans, the National Guard replaced the city's police department after Hurricane Katrina, pulling bodies from the water and detaining those suspected of crime.

5. Notwithstanding attempts from individual corrections departments to "brand" their work as akin to that of the police, those who work for New York City's Department of Corrections are the "city's boldest," as compared to the NYPD, who are the "city's finest."

6. The turmoil of the markets in September 2008 also led to the federal government effectively nationalizing mortgage provision in the U.S., by taking control of Fannie Mae and Freddie Mac, which underwrote 80 percent of American mortgages. That same month, the government also nationalized American International Group (AIG), the nation's largest insurance provider. It appears in many respects that the retreat of the state may be over.

References

Cases Cited

Buck v. Bell, 274 U.S. 200 (1927)
Skinner v. Oklahoma ex rel. Williamson, 316 U.S. 535 (1942)
Korematsu v. United States, 323 U.S. 214 (1944)
Cooper v. Pate, 378 U.S. 546 (1964)
Sostre v. McGinnis (1964) Cert. Denied 379 U.S. 892, 85 S. Ct. 163, Bl. ed. 2d. 96 (1964)
Lee v. Washington, 390 U.S. 333 (1968)
Johnson v. Avery, 393 U.S. 483 (1969)
Holt v. Sarver 309 F. Supp. 362 (E.D. Ark. 1970), *Aff'd by,* 442 F.2d 304 (8th Cir. 1971)
Younger v. Gilmer, 404 U.S. 15 (1971)
Furman v. Georgia, 408 U.S. 238 (1972)
Roe v. Wade, 410 U.S. 113 (1973)
Coker v. Georgia, 433 U.S. 585 (1977)
Pugh v. Locke, 406 F. Supp 318 (1976), *Aff'd by,* 559 F.2d 283 (11th Cir. 1977)
Bounds v. Smith, 430 U.S. 817 (1977)
Ruiz v. Estelle, 503 F.Supp. 1265, 1385-1390 (S.D.Tex.1980)
Chapman v. Rhodes, 452 U.S. 337 (1981)
American Booksellers Assn., Inc. v. Hudnut, 475 U. S. 1001 (1986) 98 F. Supp. 1316 (S.D. Ind. 1984), aff'd. 771 F.2d 323 (7th Cir. 1985), aff'd, 475 U.S. 1001 (1986)
Whitely v. Albers, 475 U.S. 312 (1986)
Wilson v. Seiter, 501 U.S. 294 (1991)
Ruiz v. Estelle, 161 F.3d 814, 833 (5th Cir. 1998)
Hope v. Pelzer, 536 US 730, 122 S. Ct. 2508 (2002)
Hamdi v. Rumsfeld, 542 U.S. 507 (2004)
Rasul v. Bush, 542 U.S. 466 (2004)
United States v. Booker, 543 U.S. 220 (2005)
Johnson v. California, 543 U.S. 499 (2005)
Kimbrough v. United States, 552 U.S. ___ (2007)
Boumediene v. Bush, 553 U.S. ____ (2008)

Acts

Act to Encourage Immigration, 1864 (13 Stat. 385)
Chinese Exclusion Law, 1882 (22 Stat. 58)
Immigration Act, 1882 (22 Stat. 214)
Contract Labor Act, 1885 (23 Stat.332)
Immigration Act, 1891 (26 Stat. 1084)
The Espionage, Act 1917, 18 U.S.C. §2388 (repealed by Act of Mar. 3, 1921, ch. 136, 41 Stat. 1359)
The Anarchist Act, 1918 also known as the Immigration Act 1918, (Stat. 1012)
The National Prohibition Act, 1919 (P.L. 66–66, 41 Stat. 305)
The Emergency Quota Law, 1921 (42 Stat. 5)
Immigration Act, 1924 (43 Stat. 153)
Hawes Cooper Act, 1929, 49 U.S.C. 60
Pub. L. No. 71–218, 46 Stat. 325 (1930)
Ashurst-Sumners Act, 1935, 18 U.S.C. 1761
Oklahoma's Habitual Criminal Sterilization Act. Okla.Stat.Ann. Tit. 57, §§ 171, *et seq.;* L.1935, pp. 94 *et seq.*
Sumners-Ashurst Act, 1940, 18.U.S.C. 1761
Civil Rights Act of 1964 (Pub. L. 88–352, 78 Stat. 241, July 2, 1964)
Omnibus Crime Control and Safe Streets Act, 1968 (Pub. L. 90–351, June 19, 1968, 82 Stat. 197, 42 U.S.C. § 3711)

Higher Education Amendment Act, 1972 (Pub. L. 92–318, § 1, June 23, 1972, 86 Stat. 235)

Civil Rights of Institutionalized Persons (CRIPA) Act, 42 U.S.C. § 1997

The Comprehensive Crime Control Act, 1984 (P.L. 98–473)

The Federal Sentencing Reform Act, 1984 (P.L. 98–473)

The Anti-Drug Abuse Act, 1986 (P.L. 99–570)

The Anti-Drug Abuse Act, 1988 (P.L. 100–690)

The Violent Crime Control and Law Enforcement Act, 1994 (P.L. 103–322)

The Personal Responsibility and Work Opportunity Act, 1996 (P.L. 104–193)

Anti-Terrorism and Effective Death Penalty Act, 1996 (P.L. 104–132)

Illegal Immigration Reform and Responsibility Act, 1996 (P.L. 104–208)

Prison Litigation Reform Act, 1996 (P.L. 104–134)

Megan's Law, 1996 (P.L. 104–145)

Death in Custody Reporting Act, 2000 (P.L. 106–297)

The Mentally Ill Offender Treatment and Crime Reduction Act, 2000 (P.L. 108–414)

U.S.A. Patriot Act, 2001 (P.L. 107–56)

Prison Rape Elimination Act, 2003 (P.L. 108–79)

Detainee Treatment Act, 2005, 119 Stat. 2742

Military Commissions Act, 2006 (P.L. 109–366)

Second Chance Act, 2007 (P.L. 110 – 199)

State of California "Public Safety and Offender Rehabilitation Services Act of 2007" (AB 900)

Archives and Facsimiles

Douglass, Frederick. (n.d.) The convict lease system. *The Frederick Douglass Papers at the Library of Congress.* Retrieved August 1, 2008, from http://memory.loc.gov/cgi-bin/ampage.

Dounton, William. (n.d.) *William Dounton's account for the keep of the witches, Salem Witchcraft Papers from the Essex Institute, 1692–1713.* Retrieved December 28, 2007, from http://etext.lib.virginia.edu/salem/witchcraft/archives/essex/eia/large/015_0002.jpg.

Eugenical News. (1930). The second Indiana sterilization law. *Eugenical News* (vol. 15), pp. 74–75. Cold Spring Harbor, ERO, Eugenical News, 15. Accessed February 22, 2008, from http://www.eugenicsarchive.org/html/eugenics/static/images/1889.html.

Espy, M. Watt, & Smykla, John. (1987). *Executions in the United States, 1608–1991: The Espy File* (machine-readable data file). Ann Arbor, Michigan: Inter-University Consortium for Political and Social Research. Retrieved December 20, 2007, from http://www.icpsr.umich.edu/cocoon/ICPSR/STUDY/03465.xml.

FBI files on Martin Luther King, Jr. and Malcolm X. Retrieved May 5, 2008, http://foia.fbi.gov/famous.htm.

FCI Fort Worth. (1975), *Resident handbook, 1971–1975.* Fort Worth, TX: FCI Fort Worth.

Gibbes, R. W. (1853). *Documentary history of the American Revolution, Consisting of letters and papers relating to the contest for liberty, chiefly in South Carolina, in 1781 and 1782, from originals in the possession of the editory and from other sources.* Columbia, SC: Banner Steam-Power Press.

Hayes, Rutherford B. (1886). Speech to the National Prison Congress, Atlanta, Georgia, November 6, 1886. Manuscript available at the Rutherford B. Hayes Presidential Center, Spiegel Grove, Fremont, OH.

Hening, William Waller. (1819). *The statutes at large: being a collection of all the laws of Virginia, from the first session of the Legislature in the year 1619.* Richmond, VA: The Franklin Press.

Herbert, Charles. (1847). *A relic of the Revolution, containing a full and particular account of the sufferings and privations of all the American prisoners captured on the high seas, and carried into Plymouth, England, during the Revolution of 1776.* Boston: Charles Pierce.

Hoadly, Charles J. (1857). *Records of the Colony and Plantation of New Haven, from 1638 to 1649. Transcribed and edited in accordance with a resolution of the General Assembly of Connecticut with occasional notes and an appendix.* Hartford, CT: Case, Tiffany and Company.

King, Martin Luther, Jr. (1963). *Letter from Birmingham Jail,* April 16, 1963. Retrieved May 2, 2008, from www.kingpapers.org.

Lownes, Caleb. (1794). *Account of the alteration and present state of the penal laws of Pennsylvania, containing also an account of the gaol and penitentiary house of Philadelphia and the interior management thereof.* Lexington. Available at Early American Imprints Series 1, University of Oxford.

Lyon, Patrick. (1799). *The narrative of Patrick Lyon, who suffered three months severe imprisonment in Philadelphia gaol; on merely a vague suspicion, of being concerned in the robbery of the Bank of Pennsylvania: with his remarks thereon.* Philadelphia: Frances and Robert Bailey. Early American Imprints, Series 1, no. 35752. University of Oxford, Archive of Americana.

Randolph, J. (1722). An Act for Amending the Act Concerning Servants and Slaves and for the Better government of convicts imported and for the further preventing the clandestine transportation of persons out of this Colony. P.R.O. Colonial Office Class 5. Vol. 1387. (Act 5 of year 1722). Virginia. MSS 13: 1722 June 7:1, Virginia Historical Society State Archives.

Ransom, John. (1963). *John Ransom's Andersonville diary.* Middlebury, VT: Paul S. Eriksson.

Smith, John Ferdinand Dalziel. (1778). *Narrative or journal of Capt. John Ferdinand Dalziel Smith, of the Queen's Rangers, taken prisoner by the rebels in 1775, lately escaped from them, and arrived here in the* Daphne. New York: Gaine. Early American Imprisons, Series 1, no. 16072. University of Oxford.

Smith, Joseph H. (Ed.). (1961). *Colonial justice in western Massachusetts (1639–1702): The Pynchon Court record.* Cambridge, MA: Harvard University Press.

Sneden, Robert Knox. (1864–1865). Plan of Andersonville Prison. In *The Robert Knox Sneden Diary* (Mss5:1 Sn237:1 v. 6, p. 14). Virginia Historical Society State Archives.

Sparks, Jared. (Ed.). (1829). *The diplomatic correspondence of the American Revolution* (Vol. 1). Boston: N. Hale and Gray & Bowen.

Turnbull, Robert. (1796). *A visit to the Philadelphia Prison; Being an accurate and particular account of the wise and humane administration adopted in every part of the building; containing also an account of the gradual reformation, and present improved state of the penal laws of Pennsylvania with observations of the impolicy and injustice of capital punishment in a letter to a friend.* Philadelphia: Budd and Bartram. 31321. University of Oxford: Archive of Americana.

Washington, George. (1775). *Letter to General Gage.* Philadelphia, September 29, 1775. The following Letters are published by order of the Honourable Continental Congress. Early American Imprints Series 1, no. 14558. University of Oxford: Archive of Americana.

Web Sites

www.aclu.org/prison/index.html
www.amnesty.org
www.calipmp.org
www.clintonpresidentialcenter.org
www.convictcriminology.org
www.criticalresistance.org
www.curenational.org
www.detentionwatch.org
www.eugenicsarchives.org
www.famm.org
www.thefortunesociety.org
www.freedebicampbell.org
www.globalsecurity.org
www.hrw.org
www.justicepolicy.org
www.michaelsantos.net
www.prisonactivist.org
www.prisonstudies.org
www.spr.org

Newspaper and Magazine Articles

Agnew, Spiro. (1971) The "root causes" of Attica. *The New York Times*, February 17, p. 43.

A. P. Tabert was beaten on head, guard says work starts at 4 a.m. Held heel on his neck. (1923). April 18, 1923. *The Washington Post*.

Augusta Chronicle (1874). The convict-lease system in Georgia. *Augusta Chronicle*, August 1, 2.

Ayres, B. Drummond. (1988). Prisoner charges poor conditions are U.S. "pyschiatric experiment." *The New York Times*, June 8, A18.

Barnard, Kate. (1912). "Miss Kate," livest wire in prison reform, visits us. *The New York Times*, December 8, 1912, SM1.

Bartlett, Alexander. (1940a). Inside Bartown: Story of prison life. *The Chicago Defender*, January 20, 13–15.

Bartlett, Alexander. (1940b). Inside Bartown: Story of prison life. *The Chicago Defender*, January 27, 13–15.

Cable, George Washington. (1884). The convict lease system in the southern states. *The Century: A Popular Quarterly*, *27*(4), 582–599.

Carter, Bill. (2005). Television finds covering area hit by storm is like working in a war zone. *The New York Times*, September 1, 1.

Charlton, D. (1971). School teacher turned warden, Vincent Ralph Mancusi. *The New York Times*, September 13, 71.

DiIulio, John, Jr., (1996). My Black crime problem and ours. *City Journal*, *6*(2), 14–28.

DiIulio, John, Jr. (1995a). The coming of the super-predators. *The Weekly Standard*, *1*(11), 23–28.

DiIulio, John, Jr., (1995b). White lies about Black crime. *The Public Interest*, *118*, 30–44.

DiIulio, John, Jr., (1994). The question of Black crime. *The Public Interest*, *117*, 3–32.

Ferretti, Fred (1971a). Men from Bed-Sty and Harlem guarded by "farmers." *The New York Times*, September 12, E8.

Ferretti, Fred. (1971b). Attica prisoners win 28 Demands, but still resist. *The New York Times*, September 13, 1.

Ferretti, Fred. (1971c). "Like a war zone." Air and ground attack follow refusal of convicts to yield. *The New York Times*, September 14, 1, 28.

Ferretti, Fred. (1971d). Autopsies show shots killed 9 Attica hostages, not knives. *The New York Times*, September 15, 1, 32.

Feulner, Edwin. (2006). A tour of Guantánamo prison shows America at its best. The Heritage Foundation, November 9, 2006. Retrieved August 4, 2008, from http:// www.heritage .org/ Press/Commentary/ed110906b .cfm.

Fleisher, Mark S. (1997). Can we break the pattern of a criminal lifestyle? *USA Today*, May 1, 1.

Fraser, C. Gerald. (1971). Black prisoners embrace new view of themselves as political victims. *The New York Times*, September 16, 49.

Freeman, Ira Henry. (1952). Prison revolts dramatize need for various reforms. *The New York Times*, April 27, E7.

Gallagher, Mike. (1999). 1980 prison riot, a black mark on state's history. *Albuquerque Journal*, September 19, 1999. Retrieved November 16, 2008, from http://www.abqjournal.com/2000/nm/future/9fut09-19-99.htm.

Gelinas, Nicole. (2005). A perfect storm of lawlessness. *City Journal*, September, 1–4. Retrieved March 14, 2009, from http://www.city-journal.org/html/eon_09_01_05ng.html.

Gibson, Kenneth. (1971). The unnecessary deaths. *The New York Times*, September 17, 43.

Gilmore, Gerry J. (2008). Iraq detention centers give glimpse into al-Qaida, general says. American Forces Press Service, June 9, 2008. Retrieved August 11, 2008, from http://www.defenselink.mil/news/newsarticle.aspx?id=50153.

Glover, Scott. (2007). Two plead guilty to southland terror plot. *Los Angeles Times*, December 15, 2007.

Golden, Tim. (2008). Foiling U.S. plan, prison expands in Afghanistan. *The New York Times,* January 7, 2008, 1.

Goldstein, Amy, & Priest, Dana. (2008a). System of neglect: As tighter immigration policies strain federal agencies, the detainees in their care often pay a heavy cost. *The Washington Post,* May 11, A1.

Goldstein, Amy, & Priest, Dana. (2008b). Some detainees are drugged for deportation: Immigrants sedated without medical reason. *The Washington Post,* May 14, A1.

Hagelin, Rebecca. (2005a). *Throwing out the thugs.* Washington, DC: The Heritage Foundation. Retrieved March 14, 2009, from http://www.heritage.org/Press/Commentary/ed090605a.cfm?RenderforPrint=1.

Harper's Weekly. (1858). Torture and homicide in an American state prison. *Harper's Weekly,* December 18, 808–810.

Harper's Weekly. (1865). The camp of rebel prisoners at Elmira. *Harper's Weekly, 4*(15), 230.

Hayden, Michael V. (2007). Transcript of Director Hayden's interview with Charlie Rose. Retrieved March 25, 2009, from https://www.cia.gov/news-information/press-releases-statements/press-release-archive-2007/interview-with-charlie-rose.html.

Hayes, Rutherford B. (1886). Prison reformers. The national association listen to various audiences (Atlanta, Ga). *The New York Times,* November 6, 2.

Horton, Scott. (2008). More incommunicado detentions in Afghanistan. *Harper's Magazine* online. Retrieved January 7, 2008, from http://harpers.org/archive/2008/01/hbc-90002102.

Horton, Scott. (2007). State of exception: Bush's war on the rule of law. *Harper's Magazine,* July, 74–81.

Kaufman, Michael T. (1971a). Time ran out for Oswald as he planned reforms. *The New York Times,* September 15, 32.

Kauffman, Michael T. (1971b). Oswald seeking facility to house hostile convicts. *The New York Times,* September 29, 1.

Kelling, George, & Wilson, James Q. (1982). Broken windows: Police and neighborhood safety. *The Atlantic Monthly, 249,* March, 29–38.

Kelling, George, & Wilson, James Q. (1989). Making neighborhoods safe. *The Atlantic Monthly, February, 263*(2), 46–52.

Lehrer, Eli. (2000). The left's prison complex: The case against the case against jail. The Heritage Foundation. October 9. Retrieved August 4, 2008, from http://www.heritage.org/Press/Commentary/ed100900.cfm.

MacDonald, Heather. (2005). How to interrogate terrorists. *The City Journal, 15*(1), 1–5. Retrieved March 16, 2009, from http://www.city-journal.org/html/15_1_terrorists.html.

MacDonald, Heather. (2006a). Illegal immigration myths. *City Journal,* February 5. Retrieved March 13, 2008, from http://www.city-journal.org/html/eon2006-05-01hm.html.

MacDonald, Heather. (2006b). Seeing today's immigrants straight. *City Journal, 16*(3), 1–5. Retrieved March 16, 2009 from http://www.cityjournal.org/html/16_3_immigration_reform.html.

Malcolm, Andrew. (1988). Aged inmates pose problem for prisons. *The New York Times,* December 24, 1, 6.

Murray, Charles. (2005). The hallmark of the underclass: The poverty Katrina underscored is primarily moral, not material. *The Wall Street Journal,* October 2. Retrieved July 5, 2008, from http://www.opinionjournal.com/extra/?id=110007348.

New York Times. (2007). Beating case will remain in juvenile court. *The New York Times,* September 27, 31.

New York Times. (1986). Who will care for the border babies? *The New York Times,* November 30, 217.

New York Times. (1982). Democrat asserts Reagan shortchanges crime war. *The New York Times,* September 5, A14.

New York Times. (1981). Reagan lax in War on Drugs, House is told. *The New York Times,* November 19, A2.

New York Times. (1971a). Now, Attica again. *The New York Times*, September 11, 26.

New York Times. (1971b). Massacre at Attica. *The New York Times*, September 14, 40.

New York Times. (1952). Peace offer made to prison rebels. *The New York Times*, April 17, 24.

New York Times. (1945). Investigation of prison riot is ordered. *The New York Times*, June 4, 1–2.

New York Times. (1941). U.S. attorneys give rules for aliens. *The New York Times*, January 9, 10.

New York Times. (1915). Prison cells fill as idleness grows; Superintendent Riley notes a regular winter increase of inmates of penal institutions. Predicts 5,500 by April 1. State in all has only 4,800 cells—cost of maintenance of institutions increases. *The New York Times*, February 8, p. 5.

New York Times. (1911). Degenerate family costs state heavily. *The New York Times*, December 17, 12.

New York Times. (1897). Women to break stone. *The New York Times*, July 14, 3.

New York Times. (1889). Female prisoners rioting. *The New York Times*, December 10, 2.

New York Times. (1884). Not one female prisoner. *The New York Times*, August 31, 7.

New York Times. (1883). A female prisoner's exploit. *The New York Times*, July 4, 1883, 1.

New York Times. (1878). The whipping of female prisoners. *The New York Times*, July 10, 3.

Nossiter, Adam. (2008). Arkansas woman, left in cell, goes 4 days with no food or water. *The New York Times*, March 12, 2.

Oswald, Russell. (1971). Statement by Commissioner Oswald. *The New York Times*, September 14, 28.

Price, Hugh B. (2006). Transitioning ex-offenders into jobs and society. Washingtonpost.com. April 10, 2006. Retrieved November 25, 2008, from http://www.washingtonpost.com/wp-dyn/content/article/2006/04/07/AR2006040701179.html.

Priest, Dana. (2006). The wronged man: Unjustly imprisoned and mistreated, Khaled al-Masri wants answers the U.S. government doesn't want to give. *The Washington Post*, November 29, C01.

Priest, Dana. (2005). CIA holds terror suspects in secret prisons. *The Washington Post*, November 2, A01.

Rawls, W., Jr. (1982). Judges' authority in prison reform attacked. *The New York Times*, May 18, A1.

Reza, H. G. (2008). Man sentenced to 22 years in L.A.-area terror plot. *Los Angeles Times*, June 24, 1.

Rice, Condoleezza. (2008). Interview with press, Kings Park, Perth, July 25, 2008. Retrieved August 1, 2008, from http://www.state.gov/secretary/rm/2008/07/107457.htm.

Rideau, Wilbert. (1978). The jungle. *The Angolite.* Retrieved August 8, 2008, from http://www.wilbertrideau.com/notes/8.html.

Rideau, Wilbert. (1976). The jungle. *The Angolite.* April 14, 1976. Retrieved August 8, 2008, from http://www.wilbertrideau.com/notes/8.html.

Rideau, Wilbert. (1975). The jungle. *The Angolite.* March 30, 1975. Retrieved August 8, 2008, from http://www.wilbertrideau.com/notes/9.html.

Roberts, Michelle. (2009). AP: Most immigrants in detention did not have criminal records. Retrieved March 29, 2009, from http://thehispanicinstitute.net/node/1359.

Roberts, Steven V. (1971). Prisons feel a mood of protest. *The New York Times*, September 19, 1.

Rusk, Howard, M. D. (1952). Prisoners play vital role in scientific experiments. *The New York Times.* May 11, 73.

Schmitt, Eric, & Golden, Tim. (2008). U.S. planning big new prison in Afghanistan. *The New York Times*, May 17, 1.

Schoen, Kenneth. (1985). Private prison operators: The benefits promised are dubious. *The New York Times*, March 28, A31.

Stafford-Smith, Clive. (2008). U.S. holding 27,000 in secret overseas prisons: Transporting prisoners to Iraqi jails to avoid media & legal scrutiny. *Democracy Now,* May 19. Retrieved August 3, 2008, from http://www.democracynow.org/2008/5/19/clive_stafford_smith.

Sterngold, James. (2005). U.S. seizes state prison health care. Judge cites preventable deaths of inmates, "depravity" of system, *San Francisco Chronicle,* July 1, A1.

Stone, Major General Douglas. (2008). Press conference on detention in Iraq, March 23, 2008. Retrieved August 3, 2008, from http://www.mnf-iraq.com/images/stories/Press_briefings/2008/march/080323_transcript.pdf.

Taylor, Paul. (1985). Should private firms, build, run prisons? *The Washington Post,* May 7, A15.

Timnick, Lois. (1980). *The Los Angeles Times,* February 7, B15.

Tolchin, Martin. (1985a). Privately run prisons dividing Pennsylvania legislators. *The New York Times,* December 15, 78.

Tolchin, Martin. (1985b). New momentum in the selling of government. *The New York Times,* December 18, B12.

Treaster, Joseph B. (2005). Life-or-death words of the day in a battered city: I had to get out. *The New York Times,* August 30, 1.

Treaster, Joseph, & Kleinfield, N. R. (2005). New Orleans is now off limits; Pentagon joins relief effort. *The New York Times,* August 31, 2005, 1.

Washington Post. (1945a). 3674 POWs to lose jobs in this area. *The Washington Post,* September 29, 5.

Washington Post. (1945b). Repatriation of POWs is bad news here. *The Washington Post,* December 11, 5.

Washington Post. (1923). Tabert was beaten on head, guard says. *The Washington Post,* April 18, 1.

Wicker, Tom. (1971a). 4 days of talks in Attica end in failure. *The New York Times,* September 14, 1.

Wicker, Tom. (1971b). "Unity!" A haunting echo from Attica. *The New York Times,* September 15, 1, 33.

Wilson, James Q. (1983a). Thinking about crime: The debate over deterrence. *The Atlantic Monthly, 252*(3), September, 72–88.

Yarrow, Andrew. (1987). From "big house" to greenhouse. *The New York Times,* April 2, C3.

Texts

Abbott, John Henry. (1987). *My return.* New York: Prometheus Books.

Abbott, John Henry. (1981). *In the belly of the beast: Letters from prison.* New York: Random House.

Abdy, E. S. (1835). *Journal of a residence and tour in the United States of North America, from April 1833 to October 1834* (Vols. I, II & III). London, UK: John Murray.

Abu-Jamal, Mumia. (1997). *Death blossoms: Reflections from a prisoner of conscience.* New York: Plough Publishing House.

Abu-Jamal, Mumia. (1995). *Live from death row.* New York: Harper Perennial.

ACLU. (1999). Prisoner's rights. Retrieved February 8, 2007, from www.aclu.org/FilesPDFs/prisonerrights.pdf.

ACLU. (2006). *Enduring abuse: Torture and cruel treatment by the United States at home and abroad.* Retrieved July 4, 2008, from http://www.aclu.org/safefree/torture/torture_report.pdf.

Adams, Robert. (1992). *Prison riots in Britain and the USA.* London, UK: Macmillan.

Adler, Freda. (1975). *Sisters in crime.* New York: McGraw-Hill Book Company.

Agamben, Giorgio. (2005). *State of exception.* Chicago: The University of Chicago Press.

Agamben, Giorgio. (1998). *Homo sacer: Sovereign power and bare life* (Trans. Daniel Heller-Rozen). Stanford, CA: Stanford University Press.

Alexander, Capt. J. E. (1833). *Transatlantic sketches, Comprising visits to the most interesting scenes in North and South America and the West Indies with notes on Negro slavery and Canadian emigration* (Vols, I and II). London, UK: Richard Bentley.

Allen, F. A. (1981). *Decline of the rehabilitative ideal: Penal policy and social purpose.* New Haven, CT: Yale University Press.

American Friends Service Committee. (1994). *The rise of control units in the U.S.* Philadelphia: Author.

American Friends Service Committee. (1971). *Struggle for justice: A report on crime and punishment in America.* New York: Hill & Wang.

Amnesty International. (2005). *United States of America/Yemen: Secret detention in CIA "black sites."* New York: Amnesty International. AMR 51/177/2005. Retrieved July 4, 2008, from http://www.amnesty.org/en/library/asset/AMR51/177/2005/en/dom-AMR511772005en.pdf.

Amnesty International. (1999). *Not part of my sentence: Violations of the human rights of women in custody.* New York: Author.

Anderson, Benedict. (1984). *Imagined communities* (2nd Ed.). London, UK: Verso.

Anderson, Brent, & Burrows, Edward. (1996). From CPS to prison. In Heather Frazer & John O'Sullivan (Eds.), *We have just begun not to fight: An oral history of conscientious objectors in civilian public service during World War II.* New York: Twayne Publishers, Inc.

Anderson, Lloyd. (2000). *Voices from a Southern prison.* Atlanta: University of Georgia Press.

Anon. (1845). Brief history of the penal legislation of Pennsylvania. *Journal of Prison Discipline and Philanthropy.*

Aretxaga, Begoña. (2001). Terror as thrill: First thoughts on the "War on Terrorism." *Anthropological Quarterly, 75*(1), 139–150.

Artemel, Janice, & Parker, Jeff. (1985). Alexandria slave pen archaeology: Public profits from private efforts. *Fairfax Chronicles, IX*(1), 1–4.

Asale-Adjani, Angel. (2003). A question of dangerous races? *Punishment & Society, 5*(4), 433–448.

Atkins, Burton M., & Glick, Henry R, (Eds.). (1972). *Prisons, protest, and politics.* Englewood Cliffs, NJ: Prentice Hall.

Auerbach, Barbara. (1982). New prison industries legislation: The private sector re-enters the field. *The Prison Journal, 62*(2), 25–36.

Auletta, Kenneth. (1982). *The underclass.* New York: Random House.

Austin, James, Clear, Todd, Duster, Troy, Greenberg, David F., Irwin, John, McCoy, Candace, Mobley, Alan, Owen, Barbara, & Page, Joshua. (2007). *Unlocking America: Why and how to reduce America's prison population.* Washington, DC: The JFA Institute.

Baca, Jimmy Santiago. (2002). *A place to stand.* New York: Grove Press.

Banks, Taylor William. (1993). *Brokered justice: Race, politics, and the Mississippi prisons, 1798–1992.* Columbus, OH: Ohio State University Press.

Barker, Vanessa. (2006). The politics of punishing: Building a state governance theory of American imprisonment variation. *Punishment & Society, 8*(1), 5–32.

Bates, Sanford. (1936). *Prisons and beyond.* New York: Macmillan.

Bates, Sanford. (1935). Federal prisons. *The Prison Journal, 15,* 143–144.

Bates, Sanford. (1932). Have our prisons failed? *Journal of Criminal Law and Criminology, 23*(4), 562–574.

Bates, Sanford. (1930). Scientific penology. *The Prison Journal, 10*(1), 1–4.

Bates, Sanford. (1928). Criminal records and statistics. *Journal of the American Institute of Criminal Law and Criminology, 19*(1), 8–14.

Baunach, Phyllis, & Murton, Thomas. (1973). Women in prison: An awakening minority. *Crime and Corrections, 1,* 5–13.

Beaumont, Gustave de, & de Tocqueville, Alexis. (1833). *On the penitentiary system in the United States and its application in France.* Philadelphia: Carey, Lea & Blanchard.

Beck, Allen J., & Karberg, Jennifer C. (2001). *Prison and jail inmates at midyear 2000.*

Bureau of Justice Statistics Bulletin. Washington, DC: U.S. Department of Justice. NCJ 185989.

Beckett, Katherine. (1997). *Making crime pay: Law and order in contemporary American politics.* New York: Oxford University Press.

Beckett, Katharine, & Sasson, Theodore. (2000). *The politics of injustice: Crime and punishment in America.* Thousand Oaks, CA: Pine Forge Press.

Beckett, Katharine, & Western, Bruce. (2001). Governing social marginality: Welfare, incarceration and the transformation of state policy. *Punishment & Society, 3,* 43–59.

Begg, Moazzam, & Brittain, Victoria. (2006). *Enemy combatant: The terrifying true story of a Briton in Guantánamo.* London, UK: The Free Press.

Beier, Lee C. (1931). Reformation as a science. *The Prison Journal, 11,* 9–11.

Bennett, James V. (1970). *I chose prison.* New York: Alfred A. Knopf.

Bennett, Scott. (2003). *Radical pacifism: The War Resisters League and Ghandian nonviolence in America, 1915–1963.* Syracuse, NY: Syrcause University Press.

Bennett, William, DiIulio, John, Jr., & Walters, J. P. (1996). *Body count: Moral poverty . . . and how to win America's war against crime and drugs.* New York: Simon & Schuster.

Berkman, Ronald. (1979). *Opening the gates: The rise of the prisoners' movement.* Lexington, MA: Lexington Books.

Bernstein, Lee. (2007). The age of Jackson: George Jackson and the culture of American prisons in the 1970s. *The Journal of American Culture, 30*(3), 310–323.

Binns, John. (1854). *Recollections of the life of John Binns: Twenty-nine years in Europe and fifty-three in the United States. Written by himself with anecdotes, political, historical and miscellaneous.* Philadelphia: Parry and Macmillan.

Blight, David. (2001). *Race and reunion: The Civil War in American memory.* Cambridge, UK: Cambridge University Press.

Bloomberg, Seth A. (1977). Participatory management: Toward a science of correctional management. *Criminology, 15*(2), 149–164.

Blue, Ethan. (2009). The strange career of Leo Stanley: Remaking of manhood and medicine at San Quentin State Penitentiary, 1913–1951. *Pacific Historical Review, 78*(2), 210–241.

Blumstein, Alfred. (1982). On the racial disproportionality of U.S. prison populations. *Journal of Criminal Law and Criminology, 73*(3), 1259–1281.

Blumstein, Alfred, & Beck, Allan J. (1999). Population growth in U.S. prisons, 1980–1996. In M. Tonry & J. Petersilia (Eds.), *Prisons: crime and justice—A review of research* (Vol. 26) (pp. 17–61). Chicago: The University of Chicago Press.

Blumstein, Albert, Cohen, Jacqueline, & Nagin, Daniel. (1978). *Deterrence and incapacitation: Examining the effects of criminal sanctions on crime rates.* Washington, DC: National Academy Press.

Blumstein, Alfred, & Wallman, Joel. (Eds.). (2006). *The crime drop in America* (Rev. Ed.). New York: Cambridge University Press.

Blumstein, Alfred, & Wallman, Joel. (Eds.). (2000). *The crime drop in America.* New York: Cambridge University Press.

Bonczar, Thomas P. (2003). *Prevalence of imprisonment in the U.S. population, 1974–2001.* Bureau of Justice Statistics Special Report. Washington, DC: U.S. Department of Justice. NCJ 197976. Retrieved March 14, 2009 from http://ojp.usdoj.gov/bjs/pubpdf/piusp01.pdf.

Boston, Charles. (1913). A protest against laws authorizing the sterilization of criminals and imbeciles. *Journal of the American Institute of Criminal Law and Criminology, 4*(3), 326–358.

Bosworth, Mary. (2008). Border control and the limits of the sovereign state. *Social and Legal Studies, 17*(2), 199–215.

Bosworth, Mary. (2007a). Creating the responsible prisoner: Federal admission and orientation packs. *Punishment & Society, 9*(1), 67–85.

Bosworth, Mary. (2007b). Identity, cititzenship and punishment. In Mary Bosworth and Jeanne Flavin (Eds.), *Race, gender, and punishment: From colonialism to the War on Terror* (pp. 134–148). New Brunswick, NJ: Rutgers University Press.

Bosworth, Mary. (2002). *The U.S. federal prison system*. Thousand Oaks, CA: Sage Publications.

Bosworth, Mary. (2001). Anatomy of a massacre: Gender, power and punishment in revolutionary Paris. *Violence Against Women, 7*(10), 1101–1121.

Bosworth, Mary. (2000). Confining femininity: A history of gender, power and imprisonment. *Theoretical Criminology, 4*(3), 265–284.

Bosworth, Mary. (1999). *Engendering resistance: Agency and power in women's prisons*. Aldershot, UK: Ashgate.

Bosworth, Mary. (1996). Resistance and compliance in women's prisons: Towards a critique of legitimacy. *Critical Criminology, 7*, 5–19.

Bosworth, Mary, & Flavin Jeanne (Eds.). (2007). *Race, gender and punishment: From colonialism to the War on Terror.* New Brunswick, NJ: Rutgers University Press.

Bosworth, Mary, & Guild, Mhairi. (2008). Governing through migration control: Security and citizenship in Britain. *The British Journal of Criminology, 48*(6), 703–719.

Bowker, Lee. (1980). *Prison victimization*. New York: Elsevier.

Braithwaite, John. (2003). What's wrong with the sociology of punishment? *Theoretical Criminology, 7*(1), 5–28.

Braly, Malcolm. (1976). *False starts: A memoir of San Quentin and other prisons*. Boston: Little, Brown.

Braly, Malcolm. (1968). *On the yard: A novel*. London, UK: Hutchinson.

Bright, Charles. (1996). *The powers that punish: Prison and politics in the era of the "Big House," 1920–1955: Law, meaning, and violence*. Ann Arbor, MI: University of Michigan Press.

Brinkerhoff, R. (1893). The National Prison Association. *Annals of the American Academy of Political and Social Science, 4*, 118–119.

Brock, Peter. (Ed.) (2004). *"These strange criminals": An anthology of prison memories by conscientious objectors from the Great War to the Cold War.* Toronto: University of Toronto Press.

Brockway, Zebulon. (1874). Reformation of prisoners. *Journal of Social Science, 6*, 144–154.

Brosnahan, James J., & Rosenbaum, Mark D. (2008). Written statement for a hearing on "immigration & customs interrogation, detention and removal" submitted to the Subcommittee on Immigration, Citizenship, Refugees, Border Security, and International Law of the House Judiciary Committee, Wednesday, February 13, 2008. Retrieved July 28, 2008 from http://www.aclu.org/images/asset_upload_file36_34132.pdf.

Brotherton, Mark, & Kretsedemas, Philip (Eds.). (2008). *Keeping out the other: A critical introduction to immigration enforcement today*. New York: Columbia University Press.

Brown, Elizabeth. (2006). The dog that did not bark: Punitive social beliefs and the middle classes. *Punishment & Society, 8*(3), 287–312.

Brown, Michelle. (2005). Setting the conditions for Abu Ghraib: The prison nation abroad. *American Quarterly, 57*(3) (Special Issue: Legal Borderlands: Law and the Construction of American Borders), 973–997.

Brown, Wendy. (2006). *Regulating aversion: Tolerance in the age of identity and empire.* Princeton, NJ: Princeton University Press.

Browning, Frank. (1972) Organizing behind bars. In Burton M. Atkins & Henry R. Glick (Eds.), *Prisons, protest, and politics* (pp. 132–139). Englewood Cliffs, NJ: Prentice Hall.

Brownmiller, Susan. (1975). *Against our will: Men, women, and rape.* New York: Simon & Schuster.

Bryant, Louise Stevens. (1918). The women at the house of correction in

Holmesburg, Pennsylvania. *Journal of the American Institute of Criminal Law and Criminology, 8*(6), 844–889.

Bullard, Rockwood Wilde III. (1974). Prisoners' rights to unrestricted use of the mails. *New England Journal on Prison Law, 1*, 80–102.

Burns, Robert E. (1932). *I am a fugitive from a Georgia chain gang!* New York: Vanguard.

Bush, George H. (1981). *Remarks of the Vice President Concerning Law Day, U.S.A., 1981,* April 6, 1981. From the Presidential Papers. Retrieved August 12, 2008, from www.presidency.ucsd.edu.

Bush, George W. (2008a). State of the Union Address, January 28, 2008. Retrieved August 12, 2008, from http://www.whitehouse.gov/stateoftheunion/2008/index.html.

Bush, George W. (2008b). Speech on the signing of the Second Chance Act. Retrieved July 28, 2008, from www.whitehousegov/news/releases/2008/04/20080409–2.html.

Bush, George W. (2006). President discusses creation of military commissions to try suspected terrorists. The East Room, The White House, September 6, 2006. Retrieved December 2, 2008, from http://www.whitehouse.gov/news/releases/2006/09/20060906–3.html.

Bush, George W. (2005). President discusses border security and immigration reform in Arizona, Davis-Monthan Air Force Base, Tucson, Arizona, November, 28, 2005. Retrieved July 28, 2008, from http://www.whitehouse.gov/news/releases/2005/11/20051128–3.html.

Butler, Anne M. (1997). *Gendered justice in the American West: Women prisoners in male penitentiaries.* Urbana, IL: University of Illinois Press.

Butler, Judith. (2004). *Precarious life: The power of mourning and violence.* New York: Verso.

Cadora, Eric. (2006). Open society. *Criminal Justice Matters, 64*(1), 20–23.

Calavita, Kitty. (2007). Immigration, social control, and punishment in the industrial era. In Mary Bosworth and Jeanne Flavin (Eds.), *Race, gender and punishment: From colonialism to the War on Terror* (pp. 117–133). New Brunswick, NJ: Rutgers University Press.

California Prison Moratorium Project. (2008). *How to stop a prison in your town.* Retrieved January, 12, 2009, from http://www.calipmp.org/media/docs/2011_pmphdbk1–22.pdf.

Carlson, Norman. (1974). Behavior modification in the Federal Bureau of Prisons. *New England Journal on Prison Law, 1*(2), pp. 155–166.

Carroll, Leo. (1982). Race, ethnicity, and the social order of the prison. In R. Johnson & Hans Toch (Eds.), *The pains of imprisonment* (pp. 181–203). Beverly Hills, CA: Sage Publications.

Carroll, Leo. (1974). *Hacks, Blacks, and cons: Race relations in a maximum-security prison.* Lexington, MA: Lexington Books.

Carson, Ann. (1838). *The memoirs of the celebrated and beautiful Mrs. Ann Carson: Daughter of an officer of the U.S. Navy, and wife of another, whose life terminated in the Philadelphia prison* (2 Vols.). New York: Greenwich Street.

Cavadino, Michael, & Dignan, James. (2006). *Penal systems: A comparative approach.* London, UK: Sage Publications.

Chambliss, William J. (1989). State organized crime. *Criminology, 27*(2), 183–208.

Chang, Nancy. (2002). *Silencing political dissent: How post–September 11 anti-tterrorism measures threaten our civil liberties.* New York: Seven Stories Press.

Chesney-Lind, Meda. (1986). Women and crime: The female offenders. *Signs, 12,* 78–96.

Chesney-Lind, Meda, & Pasko, Lisa. (2004). *The female offender: Girls, women, and crime* (2nd Ed.). Thousand Oaks, CA: Sage Publications.

Chesney-Lind, Meda, & Rodriguez, Nancy. (1983). Women under lock and key. *The Prison Journal, 63,* 47–65.

Chessman, Caryl. (1957). *The face of justice.* Englewood Cliffs, NJ: Prentice Hall.

Chessman, Caryl. (1954). *Cell 2455, death row.* New York: Prentice Hall.

Chevigny, Bell Gale (Ed.). (1999). *Doing time: 25 years of prison writing.* New York: Arcade.

Christianson, Scott. (1998). *With liberty for some: 500 years of imprisonment in America.* Boston: Northeastern University Press.

Christie, Nils. (1981). *Crime control as industry.* London, UK: Routledge.

Clarke, Ronald V. (1983). Situational crime prevention: Its theoretical basis and practical scope. In Michael Tonry & Norval Morris (Eds.), *Crime and justice: An annual review of research* (Vol. 4) (pp. 225–256). Chicago: The University of Chicago Press.

Clarke, Ronald V., & Newman, Graeme. (2006). *Outsmarting the terrorists.* New York: Praeger.

Clarke, Ronald V., & Felson, Marcus. (1993). *Routine activity and rational choice.* New Brunswick, NJ: Transaction Press.

Clear, Todd. (2007). *Imprisoning communities: How mass incarceration makes disadvantaged communities worse.* New York: Oxford University Press.

Clear, Todd. (2003). Foreword. In Jeffrey Ian Ross & Stephen C. Richards (Eds.), *Convict Criminology* (pp. xiv–xvi). Belmont, CA: Wadsworth.

Clear, Todd, Rose, Dina, Waring, Elin, & Scully, Kristen. (2003). Coercive mobility and crime: A preliminary examination of concentrated incarceration and social disorganization. *Justice Quarterly, 20*(1), 33–64.

Cleaver, Eldridge. (1968). *Soul on ice.* New York: Dell.

Clemmer, Donald. (1940/1958). *The prison community.* New York: Holt, Rinehart & Winston.

Clinton, William Jefferson. (2000). State of the Union Address. Retrieved August 27, 2008, from http://www.presidency.ucsb.edu/sou.php.

Clinton, William Jefferson. (1998). State of the Union Address. Retrieved August 27, 2008, from http://www.presidency.ucsb.edu/sou.php.

Clinton, William Jefferson. (1996). Remarks by the President at One Strike Symposium, The White House, Office of the Press Secretary, March 28, 1996. Retrieved August 27, 2008, from http://clinton6.nara.gov/1996/03/1996–03–28-president-remarks-at-one-strike-crime-symposium.html.

Clinton, William Jefferson. (1995). State of the Union Address. Retrieved August 27, 2008, from http://www.presidency.ucsb.edu/sou.php.

Clinton, William Jefferson. (1994a). State of the Union Address. Retrieved August 12, 2008, from http://www.presidency.ucsb.edu/sou.php.

Clinton, William Jefferson. (1994b). Remarks by the president to members of the law enforcement community, Ohio Peace Officers Training Academy London, Ohio. Retrieved September 24, 2008, from http://www.clintonpresidentialcenter.org/archives/.

Clinton, William Jefferson. (1993). State of the Union Address. Retrieved August 12, 2008, from http://www.presidency.ucsb.edu/sou.php.

Cogliano, Francis. (1998). "We all hoisted the American flag": National identity among American prisoners in Britain during the American Revolution. *Journal of American Studies, 32*(1), 19–37.

Cohen, E., & Stahler, G. (1998). Life histories of crack-using African-American homeless men: Salient themes. *Contemporary Drug Problems, 25,* 373–397.

Cohen, Jacqueline. (1983). Incapacitation as a strategy for crime control: Possibilities and pitfalls. In Michael Tonry & Norval Morris (Eds.), *Crime and justice* (Vol. 5). Chicago: The University of Chicago Press.

Cohen, Lawrence E., & Felson, Marcus. (1979). Social change and crime rate trends: A routine activity approach. *American Sociological Review, 44,* 588–605.

Cohen, Mark. (2005). *The costs of crime and justice.* New York: Routledge.

Cole, David. (2007). *Less safe, less free: Why America is losing the War on Terror.* New York: New Press.

Cole, David. (2005). *Enemy aliens: Double standards and constitutional freedoms in the War on Terrorism.* New York: New Press.

Colvin, Mark. (1997). *Penitentiaries, reformatories, and chain gangs: Social theory and the history of punishment in nineteenth-century America.* London, UK: Macmillan.

Conover, Ted. (2001). *Newjack: Guarding Sing Sing.* New York: Vintage Books.

Cornish, David, & Clarke, Ron V. (1986). *The reasoning criminal: Rational choice perspectives on offending.* New York: Springer-Verlag.

Cotton-Oldenburg, N., Jordan, K., Martin S., & Kupper, L. (1999). Women inmates' risky sex and drug behaviors: Are they related? *American Journal of Drug and Alcohol Abuse, 1,* 129–140.

Crawford, William. (1834). *Penitentiaries (United States) Report of William Crawford, Esq., on the Penitentiaries of the United States, addressed to His Majesty's Principal Secretary of State for the Home Department.* London, UK: House of Commons.

Cressey, Donald (Ed.). (1961). *The prison: Studies in institutional organization and change.* New York: Holt, Rinehart & Winston.

Crouch, Ben, & Marquart, James W. (1989). *An appeal to justice: Litigated reform of Texas prisons.* Austin, TX: University of Texas Press.

Cummins, Eric. (1994). *The rise and fall of California's radical prison movement.* Stanford, CA: Stanford University Press.

Curtin, Mary Ellen. (2000). *Black prisoners and their world, Alabama, 1865–1900.* Charlottesville, VA: University of Virginia Press.

Dahlke, H. Otto. (1945). Values and group behavior in two camps for conscientious objectors. *The American Journal of Sociology, 51*(1), 22–33.

Dallek, Robert. (1999). *Ronald Reagan: The politics of symbolism* (2nd Ed.). Cambridge, MA: Harvard University Press.

Daly, Kathleen, & Chesney-Lind, Meda. (1988). Feminism and criminology. *Justice Quarterly, 5,* 497–538.

Davey, Joseph Dillon (1998). *The politics of prison expansion: Winning elections by waging war on crime.* Westport, CT: Praeger.

Davidson, R. T. (1974). *Chicano prisoners: The key to San Quentin.* New York: Holt, Rinehart and Winston.

Davis, Angela. (2005). *Abolition democracy: Prisons, democracy, and empire.* New York: Seven Stories Press.

Davis, Angela. (2003). *Are prisons obsolete?* New York: Open Media.

Davis, Angela. (1981). *Women, race, and class.* New York: Random House.

Davis, Angela. (1974). *Angela Davis: An autobiography.* New York: Random House.

Davis, Katherine. (1929). *Factors in the sex life of twenty-two hundred women.* New York: Harper & Brothers Publishers.

Davis, Robert Scott. (2007). Near Andersonville: An historical note on Civil War legend and Reality. *The Journal of African American History, 92*(1), 96–105.

Deflem, Mathieu. (2002). *Policing world society: Historical foundations of international police cooperation.* New York: Oxford University Press.

Delaware Department of Corrections. (2006). Memorandum of Agreement between the United States Department of Justice and the State of Delaware Regarding the Delores J. Balor Women's Correctional Institution, the Delaware Correctional Center, the Howard R. Young Corrections Institution and the Sussex Correctional Institution. Retrieved September 16, 2008, from http://doc.delaware.gov/pdfs/delaware_prisons_moa_12-29-06.pdf.

Delgado, Aidan. (2007). *The sutras of Abu Ghraib: Notes from a conscientious objector in Iraq.* Boston: Beacon Press.

Department of the Army. (2006). *FM 2–22.3(FM 34–52). Human Intelligent Collector Operations.* Headquarters, Department of the Army. September 2006. Retrieved August 1, 2008, from http://www.army.mil/institution/armypublicaffairs/pdf/fm2-22-3.pdf.

Dermody Leonard, Kathleen. (2003). *Convicted survivors: The imprisonment of battered women.* Albany, NY: SUNY Press.

Diaz-Cotto, Juanita. (1996). *Gender, ethnicity, and state: Latina and Latino prison politics*. Albany, NY: SUNY Press.

Dickens, Charles. (1996). *American notes*. New York: Modern Library.

DiIulio, John, Jr. (1991). *No escape: The future of American corrections*. New York: Basic Books.

DiIulio, John, Jr. (Ed.). (1990). *Courts, corrections, and the Constitution: The impact of judicial intervention on prisons and jails*. New York: Oxford University Press.

DiIulio, John, Jr. (1987). *Governing prisons: A comparative study of correctional management*. New York: The Free Press.

Dix, Dorothea. (1845). *Remarks on prisons and prison discipline in the United States* (2nd Ed.). Philadelphia: Joseph Kite & Co.

Dodge, L. Mara. (2002). *"Whores and thieves of the worst kind": A study of women, crime, and prisons, 1835–2000*. DeKalb, IL: Northern Illinois University Press.

Dolan, Francis X. (2007). *Eastern State Penitentiary*. Chicago: Arcadia Publishing.

Doll, E. A. (1917). On the use of the term "feeble-minded." *Journal of the American Institute of Criminal Law and Criminology, 8*(2), 216–221.

Donzelot, Jacques. (1979). *The policing of families*. New York: Random House, Inc.

Donziger, Steven R. (1996). *The real war on crime: Report of the National Criminal Justice Commission*. New York: Harper Perennial.

Dow, Mark. (2007). Designed to punish: Immigration detention and deportation. *Social Research, 74*(2), 533–546.

Dow, Mark. (2004). *American gulag: Inside U.S. immigration prisons*. Berkeley, CA: University of California Press.

Dugdale, Richard L. (1877). *"The Jukes": A study in crime, pauperism, disease and heredity*. New York: Putnam and Sons.

Durham, Alexis III. (1989). Origins of interest in the privatization of punishment: The nineteenth and twentieth century American experience. *Criminology, 27*(1), 107–140.

Durkheim, Emile. (1902). Two laws of penal evolution. Originally appeared in *Année Sociologique, 4*, 65–95. Reprinted in D. Melossi (Ed.), (1990), *The sociology of punishment: Socio-structural perspectives*. Aldershot, UK: Ashgate.

Earley, Pete. (1993). *The hot house: Life inside Leavenworth*. New York: Bantam Books.

Edgerton, Keith. (2004). *Montana justice: Power, punishment, & the penitentiary*. Seattle: University of Washington Press.

Ehrenreich, Barbara. (2004). Feminism's assumptions upended. In David Levi-Strauss & Charles Stein (Eds.), *Abu Ghraib: The politics of torture* (pp. 65–70). Berkeley, CA: North Atlantic Books.

Eisenman, Stephen. (2007). *The Abu Ghraib effect*. London, UK: Reaktion Books.

Eisenstein, Zillah. (1981). *The radical future of liberal feminism*. Boston: Northeastern University Press.

Elias, Norbert. (1982). *The civilizing process: State formation and civilization*. Oxford, UK: Blackwell.

Elias, Norbert. (1978). *The civilizing process: The history of manners*. Oxford, UK: Blackwell.

Ellett, Elizabeth F. (1876). *Domestic history of the American Revolution*. Philadelphia: J. B. Lippincott & Co.

Emsley, Clive. (1997). Introduction: Political police and the European nation-state in the nineteenth century. In Mark Mazower (Ed.), *The policing of politics in the twentieth century: Historical perspectives* (pp. 1–25). New York: Berghahn Books.

Erikson, Kai. (1969). *Wayward Puritans: A study in the sociology of deviance*. New York: John Wiley & Sons.

Fabian, Sharon. (1979). Towards the best interest of women prisoners: Is the system working? *New England Journal on Prison Law, 6*(1), 1–60.

Fairchild, Erica. (1977). Politicization of the offender. *Criminology, 15*(3), 287–318.

Fanon, Franz. (1967). *Black skin, White masks*. New York: Grove Press.

Federal Bureau of Prisons. (1999). *Substance abuse treatment programs in the Federal Bureau of Prisons: Report to Congress, as required by the Violent Crime Control and Law Enforcement Act of 1994.* Washington, DC: U.S. Department of Justice.

Feeley, Malcolm, & Simon, Jonathan. (1992). The new penology: Notes on the emerging strategy of corrections and its implications. *Criminology, 30*(4), 449–474.

Feeley, Malcolm, & Swearingen, Van. (2004). The prison conditions cases and the bureaucratization of American corrections: Influence, impacts and implications. *PACE Law Review, 24*(2), 433–475.

Feucht, Thomas, & Zedlewski, Edwin. (2007). *The 40th Anniversary of the Crime Report.* Washington, DC: National Institute of Justice. NCJ 218261. Retrieved March 15, 2009, from http://www.ojp.usdoj.gov/nij/journals/257/40thcrime-report.html.

Flavin, Jeanne. (2008). *Our bodies, our crimes: The policing of women's reproduction in America.* New York: New York University Press.

Flavin, Jeanne. (2007). Reproducing racism: Slavery's legacy in Black women's struggle for reproductive rights. In Mary Bosworth & Jeanne Flavin (Eds.), *Race, gender and punishment: From colonialism to the War on Terror* (pp. 95–114). New Brunswick, NJ: Rutgers University Press.

Fleisher, Mark S. (1989). *Warehousing violence.* Thousand Oaks, CA: Sage Publications.

Fletcher, Laurel, & Stover, Eric. (2008). *Guantánamo and its aftermath: U.S. detention and interrogation techniques and their impact on former detainees.* Berkeley, CA: University of California Press.

Floyd, Janet. (2006). Dislocations of the self: Eliza Farnham at Sing Sing Prison. *Journal of American Studies, 40*(2), 311–325.

Flynn, Frank T. (1950). The federal government and the prison-labor problem in the states. I. The aftermath of federal restrictions. *Social Service Review, 24*(1), 19–40.

Foucault, Michel. (2004). *Society must be defended: Lectures at the College de France, 1975–1976.* London, UK: Penguin.

Foucault, Michel. (2002). *The order of things.* London, UK: Routledge Classics.

Foucault, Michel. (1977, 1995). *Discipline and punish: On the birth of the prison.* New York: Vintage Books.

Foucault, Michel. (1980). *Power/knowledge: Selected interviews and other writings, 1972–1977.* London, UK: The Harvester Press.

Franklin, Bruce (1998). *Prison literature in America: The victim as criminal and artist.* New York: Oxford University Press.

Freedman, Estelle B. (1998). *Maternal justice: Miriam Van Waters and the female reform tradition.* Chicago: University of Chicago Press.

Freedman, Estelle B. (1984). *Their sisters' keepers: Women's prison reform in America, 1830–1930.* Ann Arbor, MI: The University of Michigan Press.

French, Laurence. (1978). The incarcerated Black female: The case of social double jeopardy. *Journal of Black Studies, 8*(3), 321–335.

French, Laurence. (1977). An assessment of Black female prisoners in the South. *Signs, 3*(2), 483–488.

GAO. (2005). *Information on criminal aliens incarcerated in federal and state prisons and local jails.* GAO-05-337R. Washington, DC: U.S. Government Accountability Office. Retrieved July 17, 2008, from http://www.gao.gov/new.items/d05337r.pdf.

Garabedian, Peter. (1963). Social roles and processes of socialization in the prison community. *Social Problems, 11,* 139–152.

Garland, David. (2006). Concepts of culture in the sociology of punishment. *Theoretical Criminology, 10*(4), 419–447.

Garland, David. (2005). Capital punishment and American culture. *Punishment & Society, 7*(4), 347–376.

Garland, David. (2001a). *The culture of control: Crime and social order in contemporary society.* Chicago: The University of Chicago Press.

Garland, David. (Ed.). (2001b). *Mass imprisonment: Social causes and consequences*. Thousand Oaks, CA: Sage Publications.

Garland, David. (1999). Editorial: Punishment and society today. *Punishment & Society, 1*(1), 5–10.

Garland, David. (1996). The limits of the sovereign state: Strategies of crime control in contemporary society. *The British Journal of Criminology, 36*, 445–471.

Garland, David. (1990). *Punishment and modern society*. Oxford, UK: Clarendon Press.

Garland, David. (1985). *Punishment and welfare: A history of penal strategies*. Aldershot, UK: Ashgate.

Gellner, Ernest. (1983). *Nations and nationalism*. Oxford, UK: Blackwell.

Geneva Convention III. (1949). *Convention III relative to the treatment of prisoners of war* (August 12). Retrieved March 25, 2009, from http://www.icrc.org/ihl.nsf/7c4d08d9b287a42141256739003e63bb/6fef854a3517b75ac125641e004a9e68.

Giallombardo, Rose. (1966a). *Society of women: A study of a women's prison*. New York: John Wiley.

Giallombardo, Rose. (1966b). Social roles in a prison for women. *Social Problems, 13*(3), 268–288.

Gibbons, John J., & Katzenbach, Nicholas de Belleville. (2006). *Confronting confinement: A report of the Commission on Safety and Abuse in America's Prisons*. New York: Vera Institute of Justice.

Gilfoyle, Timothy J. (2003). "America's greatest criminal barracks": The Tombs and the experience of criminal justice in New York City, 1838–1897. *Journal of Urban History, 29*(5), 525–554.

Gilmore, Ruth Wilson. (2007). *Golden gulag: Prisons, surplus, crisis, and opposition in globalizing California*. Berkeley, CA: University of California Press.

Girshick, Lori. (1999). *No safe haven: Stories of women in prison*. Boston: Northeastern University Press.

Glueck, Bernard. (1918). A study of 608 admissions to Sing Sing Prison. *Mental Hygiene, 2*, 85–51.

Goetting, Ann. (1982). Conjugal association in prison: Issues and perspectives. *Crime and Delinquency, 28*, 52–71.

Goffman, Erving. (1961a). On the characteristics of total institutions: The inmate world. In D. Cressey (Ed.), *The prison: Studies in institutional organization and change* (pp. 15–67). New York: Holt, Rinehart and Winston.

Goffman, Erving. (1961b). *Asylums: Essays on the social situation of mental patients and other inmates*. London, UK: Penguin Books.

Goldman, Emma. (1970). *Living my life* (Vols. 1 and 2). New York: Dover Publications.

Goldsmith, Stephen, & Eimicke, William B. (2008). *Moving men into the mainstream: Best practices in prisoner reentry assistance*. Manhattan Institute, Civic Bulletin, No. 51. March 2008. Retrieved November 25, 2008, from http://www.manhattan-institute.org/pdf/cb_51.pdf.

Goodman, Philip. (2008). "It's just Black, White, or Hispanic": An observational study of racializing moves in California's segregated prison reception centers. *Law and Society Review, 42*(4), 735–770.

Gooseen, Rachel W. (1997). *Women against the good war: Conscientious objection and gender on the American home front, 1941–1947*. Chapel Hill, NC: University of North Carolina Press.

Gordon, Avery. (2006). Abu Ghraib: Imprisonment and the War on Terror. *Race & Class, 48*(1), 42–59.

Gostin, Lawrence O. (2007). Biomedical research involving prisoners: Ethical values and legal regulation. *Journal of the American Medical Association, 297*(7), 737–740.

Gottfredson, Michael. (1981). On the etiology of criminal victimization. *Journal of Criminal Law and Criminology, 72*, 714–726.

Gottfredson, Michael, & Hirschi, Travis. (1990). *A general theory of crime*. Stanford, CA: Stanford University Press.

Gottschalk, Marie. (2006). *The prison and the gallows: The politics of mass incarceration in America*. New York: Cambridge University Press.

Gray, Michael P. (2001). *The business of captivity in the Chemung Valley: Elmira and its Civil War prison.* Kent, OH: Kent State University Press.

Gray, Tara, Larsen, Clark R., Haynes, Peter, & Olson, Kent W. (1991). Using cost-benefit analysis to evaluate correctional sentences. *Evaluation Review, 15*(4), 471–481.

Greenberg, David, & West, Valerie. (2001). State prison populations and their growth, 1971–1991. *Criminology, 39*(3), 615–654.

Greenberg, David. (1977). The dynamics of oscillatory punishment processes. *The Journal of Criminal Law and Criminology, 68*(4), 643–651.

Greene, Judith, & Pranis, Kevin. (2005). *Alabama prison crisis: A Justice Strategies Policy report.* Brooklyn, NY: Justice Strategies. Retrieved November 29, 2007, from http://www.justicestrategies.net/Alabama_Prison_Crisis_Oct_2005.pdf.

Grey, Stephen. (2007). *Ghost plane: The true story of the CIA torture program.* New York: St. Martin's Press.

Grobsmith, Elizabeth. (1994). *Indians in prison: Incarcerated Native Americans in Nebraska.* Lincoln, NE: University of Nebraska Press.

Guerette, Rob. (2007). Immigration policy, border security, and migrant deaths: An impact evaluation of life-saving efforts under the border safey initiative. *Criminology & Public Policy, 6*(2), 245–266.

Guibord, Alberta S. B. (1917). Physical states of criminal women. *Journal of the American Institute of Criminal Law and Criminology, 8*(1), 82–95.

Gurley Flynn, Elizabeth. (1963). *The Alderson story: My life as a political prisoner.* New York: International Publishers.

Guy, Jasmine. (2004). *Evolution of a revolutionary: Conversations with Afeni Shakur.* New York: Simon & Schuster.

Haas, Kenneth C., & Alpert, Geoffrey P. (1989). American prisoners and the right of access to the courts: A vanishing concept of protection. In Lynne Goodstein & Doris Layton MacKenzie (Eds.), *American prison: Issues in research and policy* (pp. 65–87). New York: Plenum Press.

Hagelin, Rebecca. (2005b). *Home invasion: Protecting your family in a culture that's gone stark raving mad.* Nashville, TN: Thomas Nelson.

Hallett, Michael A. (2006). *Private prisons in America: A critical race perspective.* Chicago: University of Illinois Press.

Hamm, Mark. (1995). *The abandoned ones: The imprisonment and uprising of the Mariel boat people.* Boston: Northeastern University Press.

Haney, Craig, Banks, C., & Zimbardo, Philip. (1973). Interpersonal dynamics in a simulated prison. *International Journal of Criminology and Penology, 1,* 69–97.

Haney, Craig, & Zimbardo, Philip. (1998). The past and future of U.S. prison policy: Twenty-five years after the Stanford Prison Experiment. *American Psychologist, 53*(7), 709–727.

Hannah-Moffat, Kelly. (2005). Criminogenic needs and the transformative risk subject: Hybridizations of risk/need in penality. *Punishment & Society, 7*(1), 29–51.

Hannah-Moffat, Kelly. (2001). *Punishment in disguise: Penal governance and Canadian women's imprisonment.* Toronto: University of Toronto Press.

Harper, Ida. (1952). The role of the "fringer" in a state prison. *Social Forces, 31*(1), 53–60.

Harris, Jean. (1988). *They always call us ladies: Stories from prison.* New York: Charles Scribner's Sons.

Harris, Jean. (1986). *Stranger in two worlds.* New York: Macmillan Publishing Company.

Harris, M. Kay. (1987). Living in the new millenium: Toward a feminist vision of justice. *The Prison Journal, 67,* 27–38.

Harris, Mary Belle. (1942). *I knew them in prison.* New York: Vintage Press.

Harris, William. (1862). *Prison life in the tobacco warehouse at Richmond by a Ball's Bluff Prisoner, Lieut. Wm. C. Harris, of Col. Baker's California regiment.* Philadelphia: George W. Childs.

Harrison, Paige M., & Beck, Allen J. (2005). *Prisoners in 2004: Bureau of Justice Statistics bulletin.* Washington DC: U.S. Department of Justice. NCJ 210677.

Harrison, Paige M., & Beck, Allen J. (2004). *Prisoners in 2003: Bureau of Justice Statistics bulletin.* Washington, DC: U.S. Department of Justice. NCJ 205335

Hawkins, Gordon. (1976). *The prison: Policy and practice.* Chicago: The University of Chicago Press.

Haynes, F. E. (1948). The sociological study of the prison community. *Journal of Criminal Law and Criminology, 39*(4), 432–440.

Haynes, Peter, & Larsen, Clark R. (1984). Financial consequences of incarceration and alternatives: Burglary. *Crime & Delinquency, 30*(4), 529–555.

Healy, Charles. (1914). The outlook for the science of criminalistics. *Journal of the American Institute of Criminal Law and Criminology, 5*(4), 543–547.

Heffernan, Esther. (1974). *Making it in prison: The square, the cool, and the life.* New York: John Wiley.

Herrnstein, R., & Murray, C. (1994). *The bell curve: Intelligence and class structure in American life.* New York: Free Press.

Hogshire, Jim. (1994). *You are going to prison.* Port Townsend, WA: Loompanics, Unlimited.

Hooks, bell. (1981). *Ain't I a woman?* Boston: South End Press.

Hopper, Columbus B. (1969). *Sex in prison: The Mississippi experiment with conjugal visiting.* Baton Rouge, LA: Louisiana State University Press.

Hornblum, Allen M. (1998). *Acres of skin: Human experiments at Holmesburg Prison.* London, UK: Routledge.

House of Commons Foreign Affairs Committee. (2007). *Visit to Guantánamo Bay, Second report of session 2006–07 report, together with formal minutes and written evidence.* HC 44. London, UK: The Stationery Office, Limited. Retrieved March 20, 2009, from http://www.publications.parliament.uk/pa/cm200607/cmselect/cmfaff/44/44.pdf.

Hudson, Barbara. (2002). Punishment and control. In M. Maguire (Ed.), *The Oxford handbook of criminology* (2nd Ed.) (pp. 233–263). Oxford, UK: Oxford University Press.

Huff, C. Ronald. (1974). Unionization behind the walls. *Criminology, 12*(2), 175–194.

Human Rights Watch. (2008). *Locked up alone: Detention conditions and mental health at Guantánamo.* New York: Human Rights Watch.

Human Rights Watch. (2007). *Ghost prisoner: Two years in secret CIA detention.* New York: Human Rights Watch. Retrieved July 4, 2008, from http://hrw.org/reports/2007/us0207/us0207webwcover.pdf.

Human Rights Watch. (2006). *World Report, 2006.* New York: Human Rights Watch. Retrieved March 8, 2009, from http://www.hrw.org/legacy/wr2k6/wr2006.pdf.

Human Rights Watch. (2004a). *No second chance: People with criminal records denied access to public housing.* New York: Human Rights Watch.

Human Rights Watch. (2004b). *Guantánamo: Detainee accounts.* New York: Human Rights Watch. Retrieved July 3, 2008, from http://www.hrw.org/back grounder/usa/gitm01004/gitm01004.pdf.

Human Rights Watch. (2000). *Out of sight: Supermaximum security confinement in the United States.* New York: Human Rights Watch.

Human Rights Watch. (1998). *Locked away: Immigration detainees in jails in the United States.* New York: Human Rights Watch. Retrieved July 18, 2008, from http://www.hrw.org/reports98/usimmig/Index.htm#TopOfPage.

Human Rights Watch. (1997). *Cold storage: Super-maximum security confinement in Indiana.* New York: Author.

Human Rights Watch. (1996). *All too familiar: Sexual abuse of women in U.S. prisons.* New York: Author.

ICRC. (2008). *U.S. detention related to the events of 11 September 2001 and its aftermath — the role of the ICRC.* Retrieved March 17, 2009, from http://www .icrc.org/Web/eng/siteeng0.nsf/html/usa-detention-update-121205.

ICRC. (2007). *ICRC visits to detainees in Afghanistan.* Retrieved March 17, 2009, from http://www.icrc.org/Web/eng/siteeng0.nsf/html/afghanistan-interview-131207.

Ignatieff, Michael. (2004). *The lesser evil: Political ethics in an age of terror.* Princeton, NJ: Princeton University Press.

Ignatieff, Michael. (1983). State, civil society and total institutions: A critique of recent social histories of punishment. In Stanley Cohen and Andrew Scull (Eds.), *Social control and the state: Historical and comparative essays* (pp. 75–105). Oxford, UK: Robertson.

Ignatieff, Michael. (1978). *A just measure of pain: The penitentiary in the Industrial Revolution, 1750–1850.* New York: Pantheon.

Imai, Kent. (2007). *Analysis of CDCR death reviews 2006: Public version.* San José, CA: California Prison Health Care Receivership Corp. Retrieved November 14, 2007, from http://www.cprinc.org/docs/resources/AnalysisOfCDCRDeathReviews2006.pdf.

Immarigeon, Russ. (1985). Private prisons, private programs, their implications for reducing reliance on imprisonment in the United States. *The Prison Journal, 65,* 60–74.

Irwin, John. (1970). *The felon.* Englewood Cliffs, NJ: Prentice Hall.

Irwin, John, & Cressey, Donald. (1962). Thieves, convicts, and the inmate culture. *Social Problems, 10,* 142–155.

Irwin, Lee. (2006). Walking the line: Pipe and sweat ceremonies in prison. *Nova Religio: The Journal of Alternative and Emergent Religions, 9*(3), 39–60.

Jackson, George. (1970). *Soledad brother: The prison letters of George Jackson.* New York: Bantam Books.

Jacobs, James. (1982). The limits of racial integration in prison. *Criminal Law Bulletin, 18,* 117–153.

Jacobs, James B. (1980). The prisoners' rights movement and its impacts, 1960–1980. In Michael Tonry & Norval Morris (Eds.), *Crime and Justice* (Vol. 2) (pp. 429–470). Chicago: The University of Chicago Press.

Jacobs, James. (1979). Race relations and the prisoner subculture. *Crime and Justice, 1,* 1–27.

Jacobs, James. (1977). *Stateville: The penitentiary in mass society.* Chicago: The University of Chicago Press.

Jacobs, James. (1975). Stratification and conflict among prison inmates. *The Journal of Criminal Law & Criminology, 66*(4), 476–482.

Jacobson, Michael. (2007). Testimony to a hearing of the Joint Economic Committee. Retrieved October 12, 2007, from http://www.jec.senate.gov.

Jacobson, Michael. (2005). *Downsizing prisons: How to reduce crime and end mass incarceration.* New York: New York University Press.

James, Joy (Ed.). (2003). *Imprisoned intellectuals: America's political prisoners write on life, liberation, and rebellion.* Lanham, MD: Rowman & Littlefield.

Jarvis, Brian. (2004). *Cruel and unusual: Punishment and U.S. culture.* London, UK: Pluto Press.

Jesness, K. (1996). *The Jesness inventory manual.* North Tonawanda, NY: MultiHealth Systems.

Jimenez, M. A. (1990). Permanency planning and The Child Abuse Prevention and Treatment Act: The paradox of child welfare policy. *Journal of Sociology and Social Welfare, 17*(3), 55–72.

Johnson, Norman. (Ed.). (1994). *Eastern State Penitentiary: Crucibles of good intentions.* Philadelphia: Philadelphia Museum of Art.

Johnson, Norman. (1973). *The human cage: A brief history of prison architecture.* New York: Walker and Company.

Johnson, Paula. (2003). *Inner lives: Voices of African American women in prison.* New York: New York University Press.

Johnson, Roberta Ann. (1975). The prison birth of Black power. *Journal of Black Studies, 5*(4), 395–414.

Justice, William Wayne (1990). The origins of Ruiz v. Estelle: The Phleger lecture. *Stanford Law Review, 43*(1), 1–12.

Kann, Mark E. (2005). *Punishment, prisons, and patriarchy: Liberty and power in the early American republic.* New York: New York University Press.

Kaplan, Amy. (2005). Where is Guantánamo? *American Quarterly, 57*(3), 831–858.

Karmen, Andrew. (1990). *Crime victims: An introduction to victimology.* Pacific Grove, CA: Brook/Cole Publishing Co.

Karpman, Benjamin. (1948). Sex life in prison. *Journal of Criminal Law and Criminology, 38*(5), 475–486.

Katz, Michael. (Ed.). (1993). *The "underclass" debate: Views from history.* Princeton, NJ: Princeton University Press.

Kelling, George, & Coles, Catherine. (1996). *Fixing broken windows: Restoring order and reducing crime in our cities.* New York: Free Press.

Kennedy, Anthony. (2008). Written opinion in U.S. Supreme Court decision, Boumedienne v. Bush 533 U.S. ___ (2008).

Kilbride, Daniel. (2005). The cosmopolitan South: Privileged southerners, Philadelphia, and the fashionable tour in the Antebellum era. *Journal of Urban History, 26*(3), 565–590.

King, Roy. (1999). The rise and rise of supermax: An American solution in search of a problem? *Punishment & Society, 1*(2), 163–186.

King, R. (1991). Maximum-security custody in Britain and the U.S.A.: A study of Gartree and Oak Park Heights. *The British Journal of Criminology, 31*(2), 126–152.

Kinsey, Alfred. (1948). *Sexual behavior in the human male.* Philadelphia: W. Saunders.

Kirby, Georgiana Bruce. (1887). *Years of experience: An autobiographical narrative.* New York: Putnam.

Kleinig, John. (1983). *Paternalism.* Totowa, NJ: Rowman & Allanheld.

Kleinig, John. (1973). *Punishment and desert.* New York: Springer.

Korn, Richard. (1988a). The effects of confinement in the High Security Unit at Lexington. *Social Justice, 15*(1), 1–19.

Korn, Richard. (1988b). Follow-up report on the effects of confinement in the High Security Unit at Lexington. *Social Justice, 15*(1), 20–29.

Kraska, Peter. (Ed.). (2001). *Militarizing the American criminal justice system: The changing roles of the armed forces and the police.* Boston: Northeastern University Press.

Krasmann, Susanne. (2007). The enemy on the border: Critique of a programme in favour of a preventive state. *Punishment & Society, 9*(3), 301–318.

Krutschnitt, Candace. (1984). Sex and criminal court dispositions: The unresolved controversy. *Journal of Research in Crime and Delinquency, 21*, 213–232.

Krutschnitt, Candace. (1982) Respectable women and the law. *The Sociological Quarterly, 23*, 221–234.

Krutschnitt, Candace, & Gartner, Rosemary. (2005). *Marking time in the Golden State: Women's imprisonment in California.* New York: Cambridge University Press.

Krutschnitt, Candace, & Krmpotich, Sharon. (1990). Aggressive behavior among female inmates: An exploratory study. *Justice Quarterly, 7*(2), 371–389.

Kunioka, Todd, & McCurdy, Karen. (2006). Relocation and internment: Civil rights lessons from World War II. *PS: Political Science & Politics, 39*(3), 503–511.

Kupers, Terry. (1999). *Prison madness: The mental health crisis behind bars and what we must do about it.* San Francisco: Jossey-Bass.

Kurnaz, Murat. (2008). *Five years of my life: An innocent man in Guantánamo.* London, UK: Macmillan.

Lafree, Gary, & Hendrickson, James. (2007). Build a criminal justice policy for terrorism. *Criminology & Public Policy, 6*(4), 781–790.

Lanier, C. S. (1993). Affective states of fathers in prison. *Justice Quarterly, 10*(1), 49–66.

Lawes, Lewis F. (1932). *Twenty thousand years in Sing Sing*. London, UK: Constable & Co. Ltd.

Lawyers Committee for Human Rights. (2002). *Review of states' procedures and practices relating to detention of asylum seekers*. Retrieved August 21, 2008, from http://www.humanrightsfirst.com/refugees/reports/cntry_rev_02/Full_countryreview.pdf.

Lazarus, Liora. (2004). *Contrasting prisoners' rights: A comparative examination of England and Germany*. Oxford, UK: Oxford University Press.

Lerner, Barron H. (2007). Subjects or objects? Prisoners and human experimentation. *New England Journal of Medicine, 356*(18), 1806–1807.

Levinson, Robert. (1999). *Unit management in prisons and jails*. Lanham, MD: American Correctional Association.

Levinson, Robert B. (1974). Behavior modification programs in federal prisons: The "Clockwork Orange" issues. *New England Journal on Prison Law, 1*(2), 167–179.

Levitt, Steven D. (1996). The effect of prison population size on crime rates: Evidence from prison overcrowding litigation. *The Quarterly Journal of Economics, 111*(2), 319–351.

Lewis, Charlton T. (1903). Reform in penal law. *Journal of Social Science: Proceedings of the American Association, 41*, 110–115.

Lewis, W. David. (1965). *From Newgate to Dannemora: The rise of the penitentiary in New York, 1796–1848*. Ithaca, NY: Cornell University Press.

Lewisohn, Sam. (1942). How the prisons can help in national defense. *The Prison Journal, 22*, 176–182.

Liberman, Peter. (2006). An eye for an eye: Public support for war against evildoers. *International Organization, 60*(3), 687–722.

Lichtenstein, Alex. (1995). *Twice the work of free labor: The political economy of convict labor in the New South*. New York: Verso.

Lichtenstein, Alex. (1993). Good roads and chain gangs in the progressive South: "The negro convict is a slave." *The Journal of Southern History, LIX*(1), 85–111.

Loader, Ian. (2002). Policing, securitization and democratization in Europe. *Criminology and Criminal Justice, 2*(2), 125–153.

Loader, Ian. (1997). Policing and the social: Questions of symbolic power. *British Journal of Sociology, 48*(1), 1–18.

Loader, Ian, & Mulcahy, Aogán. (2003). *Policing and the condition of England: Memory, politics and culture*. Oxford, UK: Oxford University Press.

Loader, Ian, & Walker, Neil. (2007). *Civilizing security*. Cambridge, UK: Cambridge University Press.

Logan, E. (1999). The wrong race, committing crime, doing drugs and maladjusted for motherhood: The nation's fury over "crack babies." *Social Justice, 1*, 115–131.

Long, Harold S. (1990). *Surviving in prison*. Port Townsend, WA: Loompanics, Unlimited.

Loury, Glenn. (2007). Mass incarceration and American values. Testimony before the Joint Economic Committee of the United States Congress, Washington, DC, October 4, 2007. Retrieved October 12, 2007, from http://www.jec.senate.gov.

Lyon, Patrick. (1799). *The narrative of Patrick Lyon who suffered three months severe imprisonment in Philadelphia Gaol; on merely a vague suspicion of being concerned in the robbery of the Bank of Pennsylvania: With his remarks thereon*. Philadelphia: Francis and Robert Bailey.

MacDonald, Heather, Hanson, Victor Davis, & Malanga, Steven. (2007). *The immigration solution: A better plan than today's*. Chicago: Ivan R. Dee, Publisher.

MacDonald, Heather. (2004). Crime & the illegal alien: The fallout from crippled immigration enforcement. *Center for Immigration Studies, Backgrounder, June 2004*. Washington, DC: Center for Immigration Studies. Retrieved

March 16, 2009, from http://www.cis.org/articles/2004/back704.pdf.

MacKenzie, Doris L., & Souryal, Claire. (1994). *Multisite evaluation of shock incarceration.* Rockville, MD: NCJRS. Retrieved June 27, 2008, from http://www.ncjrs.gov/pdffiles/mse.pdf.

MacKinnon, Catherine A. (1982). Feminism, Marxism, method, and the state: An agenda for theory. *Signs: Journal of Women in Culture and Society, 7,* 515–544.

Mahan, Sue. (1984). Imposition of despair: An ethnography of women in prison. *Justice Quarterly, 1*(3), 357–383.

Maher, Lisa. (2000). *Sexed work: Gender, race and resistance in a Brooklyn drug market.* Oxford, UK: Clarendon Press.

Malkin, Michelle. (2004). *In defense of internment: The case for "racial profiling" in World War II and the War on Terror.* Washington, DC: Regnery Publishing, Inc.

Mancini, Michael. (1996). *One dies, get another: Convict leasing in the American South, 1866–1928.* Columbia, SC: University of South Carolina Press.

Mann, Coramae Richey. (1984). *Female crime and delinquency.* Tuscaloosa, AL: University of Alabama Press.

Manza, Jeff, & Christopher Uggen. (2008). *Locked out: Felon disenfranchisement and American democracy.* New York: Oxford University Press.

Marquart, James W., & Crouch, Ben. (1982). Co-opting the kept: Using inmates for social control in a Southern prison. *Justice Quarterly, 1*(4), 491–509.

Martin, Steve J., & Ekland-Olson, Sheldon. (1987). *Texas prisons: The walls came tumbling down.* Austin, TX: Texas Monthly Press.

Martinson, Robert. (1974). What works? Questions and answers about prison reform. *The Public Interest, 35,* 22–54.

Marvell, W. (1994). *Andersonville: The last depot.* Charlotte, NC: University of North Carolina Press.

Marwick, Arthur. (1978). *The development of the modern state.* London, UK: Hutchinson and Co.

Mathiesen, Thomas. (2006). *Prison on trial* (3rd Ed.). Sherfield-on-Loddon, UK: Waterside Press.

Mathur, Shubh. (2006). Surviving the dragnet: "Special interest" detainees in the U.S. after 9/11. *Race & Class, 47*(3), 31–46.

Mauer, Marc, & King, Ryan S. (2007). *Uneven justice: State rates of incarceration by race and ethnicity.* Washington, DC: The Sentencing Project.

Mauer, Marc. (2003). Comparative international rates of incarceration: An examination of causes and trends presented to the U.S. Commission on Civil Rights. Washington, DC: The Sentencing Project. Retrieved January 24, 2007, from http://www.soros.org/initiatives/justice/articles_publications/publications/intl_incarceration_20030620/intl_rates.pdf.

Mauer, Marc, (1999). *Race to incarcerate.* New York: The Free Press.

Mauer, Marc (1994). The fragility of criminal justice reform. *Social Justice, 3,* 14–30.

Mauer, Marc, & Chesney-Lind, Meda. (Eds.). (2002). *Invisible punishment: The collateral consequences of mass imprisonment.* New York: The New Press.

Mawby, Ron, & Walkate, Sandra (Eds.). (1994). *Critical victimology: International perspectives.* London, UK: Sage Publications.

McCorkel, Jill. (2003). Embodied surveillance and the gendering of punishment. *Journal of Contemporary Ethnography, 32*(1), 41–76.

McKelvey, Blake. (1936). *American prisons: A study in American social history prior to 1915.* Chicago: The University of Chicago Press.

McLeery, Richard H. (1957). *Policy changes in prison management.* East Lansing, MI: Michigan State University Press.

McLennan, Rebecca M. (2008). *The crisis of imprisonment: Protest, politics and the making of the American penal state, 1776–1941.* New York: Cambridge University Press.

Media Monitor. (1994). Crime down, media coverage up. *Overcrowded Times, 2*, 7.

Melossi, Dario. (2003). In a peaceful life: Migration and the crime of modernity in Europe/Italy. *Punishment & Society, 5*(4), 371–397.

Melossi, Dario, & Pavarini, Massimo. (1981). *The prison and the factory: Origins of the penitentiary system* (Trans. Glynis Cousin). London, UK: Macmillan.

Mendoza, Luis. (2003). The re-education of a Xicanindio: Raul Salinas and the poetics of Pinto transformation. *Melus, 28*, 1–25.

Meranze, Michael. (1996). *Laboratories of virtue: Punishment, revolution, and authority in Philadelphia, 1760–1835.* Chapel Hill, NC: University of North Carolina Press.

Merton, Robert. (1957). *Social theory and social structure* (revised and enlarged). London: The Free Press of Glencoe.

Messerschmidt, James. (2007). We must protect our Southern women: On whiteness, masculinities, and lynchin'. In Mary Bosworth and Jeanne Flavin (Eds.), *Race, gender, and punishment: From colonialism to the War on Terror* (pp. 77–94). New Brunswick, NJ: Rutgers University Press.

Miller, Lisa. (2008). *The perils of Federalism.* New York: Oxford University Press.

Miller, Lisa. (2004). Rethinking bureaucrats in the policy process: Criminal policy agents and the national crime agenda, *Policy Studies Journal, 32*(4), 569–588.

Mitford, Jessica. (1973). *Kind and usual punishment: The prison business.* New York: Alfred A. Knopf.

Moller, Lorraine. (2003). A day in the life of a prison theatre program. *The Drama Review, 47*(1), 49–73.

Morris, Norval. (Ed.). (1995). *The Oxford history of the prison: The practice of punishment in Western society.* New York: Oxford University Press.

Morris, Norval. (1974). *The future of imprisonment.* Chicago: The University of Chicago Press.

Morris, Roger. (1988). *The devil's butcher shop: The New Mexico prison uprising.* Albuquerque, NM: New Mexico University Press.

Morrison, Wayne. (2006). *Criminology, civilization, and the new world order.* London, UK: Routledge Cavendish.

Moskos, Charles. (1973). The American dilemma in uniform: Race in the armed forces. *Annals of the American Academy of Political and Social Science, 406*, 73–106.

Muhlhausen, David B. (2007). *Challenging crime rates: Ineffective law enforcement grants and the prison buildup.* WebMemo, No. 1355. Washington, DC: The Heritage Foundation.

Muller, Eric L. (2001). *Free to die for their country: The story of the Japanese American draft resisters in World War II.* Chicago: The University of Chicago Press.

Murray, Charles. (1984). *Losing ground: American social policy 1950–1980.* New York: Basic Books.

Myers, J. C. (1849). *Sketches on a tour through the Northern and Eastern states, the Canadas, and Nova Scotia.* Harrisonburg, PA: J. H. Wartmann.

Myers, Martha. (1998). *Race, labor and punishment in the New South.* Columbus, OH: Ohio State University Press.

Nagel, William. (1973). *The new red barn: A critical look at the modern American prison.* New York: Walker.

National Commission on Law Observance and Enforcement. (1931). *Report on law observance and enforcement (Wickersham Report).* Washington, DC: U.S. Government Printing Office.

National Institute of Corrections (1999). *Supermax prisons: Overview and general consideration.* Longmont, CO: U.S. Department of Justice, National Institute of Corrections.

National Institute of Corrections (1997). *Supermax housing: A survey of current practice, special issue in corrections.* Longmont, CO: U.S. Department of Justice, National Institute of Corrections.

National Prison Project of the American Civil Liberties Union. (2006a). *Abandoned & abused: Complete report.* Washington,

DC: ACLU National Prison Project. Retrieved March 10, 2009, from http://www.aclu.org/pdfs/prison/oppreport20060809.pdf

National Prison Project of the American Civil Liberties Union. (2006b). *Testimonials from inmates incarcerated at Orleans Parish Prison during Hurricane Katrina.* Washington, D.C.: ACLU National Prison Project. Retrieved March 10, 2009, from http://www.aclu.org/images/asset_upload_file182_23418.pdf.

Newburn, Tim. (2002). Atlantic crossings: "Policy transfer" and crime control in the USA and Britain. *Punishment & Society, 4,* 165–194.

Newburn, Tim, & Jones, Trevor. (2005). Symbolic politics and penal populism: The long shadow of Willie Horton. *Crime, Media, Culture, 1,* 72–87.

Newton, Huey. (1969). Prison, where is thy victory? In Joy James (Ed.), (2003), *Imprisoned intellectuals: America's political prisoners write on life, liberation, and rebellion* (pp. 81–83). New York: Rowman & Littlefield Publishers, Inc.

New York State Special Commission on Attica. (1972). *Attica: The official report of the New York State Special Commission on Attica.* New York: Bantam Books.

Ngai, Mae. (2004). *Impossible subjects: Illegal aliens and the making of modern America.* Princeton, NJ: Princeton University Press.

Nolan, James L., Jr. (2001). *Reinventing justice: The American drug court movement.* Princeton, NJ: Princeton University Press.

Novkov, Julie. (2008). Bringing the states back in: Understanding legal subordination and identity through political development. *Polity, 40*(1), 24–48.

Obama, Barack. (2009a). Executive order. Review and disposition of individuals detained at the Guantánamo Bay Naval Base and closure of detention facilities. Retrieved February 18, 2009, from http://www.whitehouse.gov/the_press_office/ClosureOfGuantanamoDetentionFacilities.

Obama, Barack. (2009b). Executive order. Ensuring lawful interrogations. Retrieved February 18, 2009, from http://www.whitehouse.gov/the_press_office/EnsuringLawfulInterrogations.

Obama, Barack. (2007). Statement on U.S. Senate floor, May 23, 2007. Retrieved March 1, 2009, from www.whitehouse.gov/agenda/immigration.

Ohlin, Lloyd. (1974). Correctional stages in conflict. *Proceedings of the American Philosophical Society, 118*(3), 248–253.

Okun, Peter. (2002). *Crime and the nation: Prison and popular fiction in Philadelphia, 1786–1800.* New York: Routledge.

O'Malley, Pat. (1999). Volatile and contradictory punishment. *Theoretical Criminology, 3*(2), 175–196.

Osborne, Thomas Mott. (1924). *Prisons and common sense.* Philadelphia: J. B. Lippincott Company.

Osborne, Thomas Mott. (1917/1918). Common sense in prison management. *Journal of the American Institute of Criminal Law and Criminology, 8,* 806–822.

Osborne, Thomas Mott. (1916). *Society and prisons.* New Haven, CT: Yale University Press.

Osborne, Thomas Mott. (1914). *Within prison walls: Being a narrative of personal experience during a week of voluntary confinement in the State Prison at Auburn, New York.* New York: D. Appleton.

Oshinsky, David. (1997). *"Worse than slavery": Parchman Farm and the ordeal of Jim Crow justice.* New York: Free Press.

Oswald, Russell G. (1972). *Attica: My story.* New York: Doubleday.

Otis, M. (1913). A perversion not commonly noted. *Journal of Abnormal Psychology, 8,* 113–116.

Owen, Barbara. (1998). *"In the mix": Struggle and survival in a women's prison.* Albany, NY: SUNY Press.

Paine, Lewis W. (1852). *Six years in a Georgia prison. Narrative of Lewis W. Paine, who suffered imprisonment six years in Georgia for the crime of aiding the escape of a fellow-man from that state, after he had fled from slavery. Written by himself.* Boston: Bela Marsh Publisher.

Palmer, J. V., & Sawhill, I. (Eds.). (1982). *The Reagan experiment: An examination of economic and social policies under the Reagan administration.* Washington, DC: The Urban Institute Press.

Parsons, Talcott. (1961). *Theories of society: Foundations of modern sociological theory.* New York: Free Press.

Parsons, Talcott. (1951) *The social system.* London, UK: Routledge.

Peck, James. (1962). *Freedom ride.* New York: Simon & Schuster.

Peck, James. (1958). *We who would not kill.* London, UK: L. Stuart.

Peltier, Leonard. (1999). *Prison writings: My life is my sun dance.* New York: St. Martin's Press.

Perkinson, Bob. (2008). *Texas tough: The rise of a prison empire.* New York: Henry Holt and Company.

Petersilia, Joan. (2003). *When prisoners come home: Parole and prisoner reentry.* New York: Oxford University Press.

Petersilia, Joan. (1999). Parole and prisoner reentry in the United States. In M. Tonry & J. Petersilia (Eds.), *Prisons* (Vol. 26) (pp. 479–530). Chicago: The University of Chicago Press.

Petersilia, Joan. (1981). *Report of the Task Force on Incarcerated Minorities.* Sacramento, CA: California Health and Welfare Agency.

Pew Charitable Trusts, The. (2009). *1 in 31: The long reach of American corrections.* Washington, DC: Pew Charitable Trusts. Retrieved March 9, 2009, from http://www.pewcenteronthestates.org/uploadedFiles/PSPP_1in31_report_FINAL_WEB_2-27-09.pdf.

Pew Charitable Trusts, The. (2008). *One in one hundred: Behind bars in America, 2008.* Washington, DC: Pew Charitable Trusts. Retrieved March 10, 2009, from http://www.pewtrusts.org/uploadedFiles/wwwpewtrustsorg/Reports/sentencing_and_corrections/one_in_100.pdf.

Pew Charitable Trusts, The. (2007a). *Public safety, public spending: Forecasting America's prison population 2007–2011.* Washington, DC: Author. Retrieved November 27, 2007, from http://www.pewpublicsafety.org/pdfs/PCT%20Public%20Safety%20Public%20Spending.pdf.

Pew Charitable Trusts, The. (2007b). *Alabama case study.* Retrieved November 28, 2007, from http://www.pewpublicsafety.org/pdfs/Alabama%20Case%20Study%202-22-07.pdf.

Philipose, Liz. (2007). The politics of pain and the end of empire. *International Feminist Journal of Politics, 9*(1), 60–81.

Pickering, Sharon, & Weber, Leanne (Eds.). (2006). *Borders, mobilities, and technologies of crime.* New York: Springer.

Platt, Anthony. (1977). *The child savers: The invention of delinquency* (2nd ed.). Chicago: The University of Chicago Press.

Platt, Anthony M. (1969). *The child savers: The invention of delinquency.* Chicago: The University of Chicago Press.

Pollock, Jocelyn. (1998). *Counseling women in prison.* Thousand Oaks, CA: Sage Publications.

Porporino, Frank. (1990). Difference in response to long-term imprisonment: Implications for the management of long-term offenders. *The Prison Journal, 70,* 35–45.

Potocky-Tripodi, Miriam. (2002). *Best practices for social work with refugees and immigrants.* New York: Columbia University Press.

Pratt, Anna. (2005). *Securing borders: Detention and deportation in Canada* (Law and Society Book Series). Vancouver, BC: University of British Columbia Press.

Pratt, Anna, & Valverde, Mariana (2002) From deserving victims to "masters of confusion": Redefining refugees in the 1990s. *Canadian Journal of Sociology, 27*(2), 135–161.

Pratt, John. (2007). *Penal populism.* London, UK: Routledge.

Prelinger, Catherine M. (1975). Benjamin Franklin and the American prisoners of war in England during the American Revolution. *The William and Mary Quarterly, 32*(2), 261–294.

President's Commission on Law Enforcement and Administration of Justice.

(1967). *The challenge of crime in a free society.* Washington, DC: U.S. Government Printing Office. Retrieved March 15, 2009, from www.ncjrs.gov/pdffiles1/nij/42.pdf.

Prison Journal, The. (1924). Surgery; A specific for the criminal impulse. *The Prison Journal, 4,* 8–9.

Quinney, Richard. (1979). The production of criminology. *Criminology, 16*(4), 445–458.

Quinney, Richard. (1978). The production of a Marxist criminology. *Contemporary Crises, 2,* 277–292.

Rafter, Nicole. (1997). *Creating born criminals.* Urbana, IL: University of Illinois Press.

Rafter, Nicole. (1985). *Partial justice: Women, prisons, and social control* (1st ed.). New Brunswick, NJ: Transaction.

Rafter, Nicole. (1992). Claims-making and socio-cultural context in the first U.S. eugenics campaign. *Social Problems, 39*(1), 17–34.

Rawls, John. (1971). *A theory of justice.* Oxford, UK: Oxford University Press.

Reagan, Ronald. (1984). Remarks at the Annual Conference of the National Sheriff's Association in Hartford, Connecticut, June 20, 1984. Retrieved December 5, 2005, from http://www.reagan.utexas.edu/search/speeches/speech_srch.html.

Reagan, Ronald. (1982). Radio address to the nation on federal drug policy, October 2, 1981. From the Presidential Papers. Available at www.presidency.ucsd.edu.

Reagan, Ronald. (1981). Proclamation 4831–Victim Rights Week, 1981. April 8, 1981. From the Presidential Papers. Retrieved August 8, 2008, from http://www.presidency.ucsd.edu.

Rediker, Marcus. (1996). A motley crew of rebels: Sailors, slaves, and the coming of the American Revolution. In Ronald Hoffman & Peter J. Albert (Eds.), *The transforming hand of revolution: Reconsidering the Revolution as a social movement* (pp. 155–198). Charlottesville, NC: University of North Carolina Press.

Reiman, Jeffrey. (1979). *The rich get richer and the poor get prison: Ideology, class, and criminal justice* (1st ed.). Somerset, NJ: Wiley.

Reprieve. (2008). *"Human cargo": Binyam Mohammed and the rendition frequent flyer program.* London: Reprieve. Retrieved March 12, 2009, from http://reprieve.org.uk/documents/2008_06_10Mohamed-HumanCargoFinalMedia.pdf.

Rhodes, Lorna A. (2004). *Total confinement: Madness and reason in the maximum secure prison.* Berkeley, CA: University of California Press.

Richards, Stephen C. (1998). Critical and radical perspectives on community punishment: Lessons from the darkness. In Jeffrey Ian Ross (Ed.), *Cutting the edge: Current perspectives in radical/critical criminology and criminal justice* (pp. 122–144). Westport, CT: Praeger.

Richards, Stephen, & Ross, Jeffrey. (2001). The new school of convict criminology. *Social Justice, 28*(1), 177–190.

Richie, Beth. (1996). *Compelled to crime: The gender entrapment of battered Black women.* New York: Routledge.

Rideau, Wilbert, & Wikberg, Ron. (1992). *Life sentences: Rage and survival behind bars.* New York: Time Books.

Rierden, Andi. (1997). *The farm: Life inside a women's prison.* Amherst, MA: University of Massachusetts Press.

Rinaldo, Suzanne Gelber, & Ian Kelly-Thomas. (2005). *Comparing California's Proposition 36 (SACPA) with similar legislation in other states and jurisdictions.* Berkeley, CA: The Avisa Group. Retrieved August, 5, 2008, from http://www.prop36.0rg/pdf/ComparisonProp360therStates.pdf.

Roberts, Dorothy. (2004). The social and moral costs of mass incarceration in African American communities. *Stanford Law Review, 56,* 1270–1305.

Roberts, Dorothy. (2002). *Shattered bonds: The color of child welfare.* New York: Basic Books.

Roberts, J. W. (Ed.). (1996). *Escaping prison myths: Selected topics in the history of federal corrections.* Washington, DC: American University Press.

Roberts, J. W. (1994). Work, education, and public safety: A brief history of Federal Prison Industries. In FPI, Inc. (Ed.), *Factories with fences: The history of Fedral Prison Industries.* Sandston, MN: Author.

Robins, Glenn M. (2007). Race, repatriation and galvanized rebels: Union prisoners and the exchange question in Deep South prison camps. *Civil War History, LIII*(2), 117–140.

Robinson, Greg. (2003). *By order of the president: FDR and the internment of Japanese Americans.* Cambridge, MA: Harvard University Press.

Robinson, Louis N. (1942). Should prisoners work? *The Prison Journal, 22,* 183–184.

Robinson, Louis N. (1931). *Should prisoners work?* Philadelphia: John C. Winston.

Rock, Paul. (2007). Cesare Lombroso as a signal criminologist. *Criminology & Criminal Justice, 7*(2), 117–134.

Rodríguez, Dylan. (2006). *Forced passages: Imprisoned radical intellecutals and the U.S. prison regime.* Minneapolis: University of Minnesota Press.

Rolland, Mike. (1997). *Descent into madness: An inmate's experience of the New Mexico State Prison riot.* Cincinnati: Anderson Publishing Company.

Roman, Caterina Gouvis, Irazola, Geri, & Osborne, Jenny W. L. (2007). *After Katrina—washed away? Justice in New Orleans.* Research Report. Washington, DC: Urban Institute. Retrieved December 6, 2007, from www.urban.org.

Romero, Anthony D. [ACLU] (2007). Foreword. In *Broken promises, 2 years after Katrina, August 2007.* Washington, DC: ACLU. Retrieved March 14, 2009, from http://www.aclu.org/pdfs/prison/brokenpromises_20070820.pdf.

Rose, David. (2004). *Guantánamo: America's war on human rights.* London: Faber and Faber.

Ross, Jeffrey Ian, & Richards, Stephen C. (Eds.). (2002). *Convict criminology.* Belmont, CA: Wadsworth.

Ross, Luana. (1998). *Inventing the savage: The social construction of Native American criminality.* Austin, TX: University of Texas Press.

Rostow, Eugene V. (1945). The Japanese American cases—A disaster. *The Yale Law Journal, 54*(3), 489–533.

Rothman, David. (1980). *Conscience and convenience: The asylum and its alternatives in progressive America.* Boston: Little, Brown.

Rothman, David. (1971). *The discovery of the asylum.* Boston: Little, Brown.

Rubenstein, Gwen, & Mukamal, Debbie. (2002). Welfare and housing—Denial of benefits to drug users. In Marc Mauer & Meda Chesney-Lind (Eds.), *Invisible punishment: The collateral consequences of mass imprisonment* (pp. 37–49). New York: Free Press.

Runyon, Tom. (1954). *In for life.* London, UK: Andre Deutsch Limited.

Rusche, Georg, & Otto Kirchheimer. (1939, 1968). *Punishment and social structure.* New York: Columbia University Press.

Ryan, Mick. (1983). *The politics of penal reform.* London, UK: Longman.

Ryder, Maj. Gen. Donald J. (2003). *Assessment of detention and correction operations in Iraq.* Washington, DC: U.S. Department of Defense.

Sabol, William J., & Couture, Heather. (2008). *Prison inmates at midyear 2007.* Bureau of Justice Statistics Bulletin. Washington, DC: U.S. Department of Justice. NCJ 221944.

Sabol, William J., Couture, Heather, & Harrison, Paige M. (2007). *Prisoners in 2006.* Bureau of Justice Statistics Bulletin. Washington, DC: U.S. Department of Justice. NCJ 219416.

Sabol, William J., Minton, Todd D., & Harrison, Paige M. (2007). *Prison and jail inmates at midyear 2006.* Bureau of Justice Statistics Bulletin. Washington, DC: U.S. Department of Justice. NCJ 217675.

Sabol, William, & McGready, John. (1999). *Bureau of Justice Statistics special report: Time served in prison by federal offenders, 1986–97.* Washington, DC: U.S. Department of Justice. NCJ 171682.

Salinas, Raul. (1980). *Un trip thru the mind jail y otras excursions.* Houston: Arte Público Press.

Sanborn, F. B. (1899). Past and present requirements of prison science. *Journal of Social Science, Containing the Proceedings of the American Association, 37,* 127–135.

Sanchez, Lisa E. (2007). The carceral contract: From domestic to global governance. In Mary Bosworth and Jeanne Flavin (Eds.), *Race, gender, and punishment: From colonialism to the War on Terror* (pp. 167–183). New Brunswick, NJ: Rutgers University Press.

Sanders, Charles W. (2005). *While in the hands of the enemy: Military prisons of the Civil War.* Baton Rouge, LA: Louisiana State University Press.

Santos, Michael. (2006). *Inside: Life behind bars in America.* New York: St. Martin's Press.

Sanville, Florence L. (1934a). A study of women in the county jails of Pennsylvania: Part I—the prisons. *The Prison Journal, 14,* 84–107.

Sanville, Florence L. (1934b). A study of women in the county jails of Pennsylvania: Part II—the women. *The Prison Journal, 14,* 108–131.

Scalia, John. (2001) *Federal drug offenders, 1999 with trends 1984–99.* NCJ 187285. Washington, DC: U.S. Department of Justice.

Scalia, John, & Litras, Marika F. X. (2002). *Immigration offenders in the federal criminal justice system, 2000.* Washington, DC: U.S. Department of Justice, Bureau of Justice Statistics. NCJ 191745. Retrieved March 16, 2009, from http://www.ojp.usdoj.gov/bjs/pub/pdf/iofcjs00.pdf.

Schaich, Warren, & Hope, Diane. (1977). The prison letters of Martin Sostre: Documents of resistance. *Journal of Black Studies, 7*(3), 281–300.

Schlanger, Margo. (2003). Inmate litigation. *The Harvard Law Review, 116*(6), 1555–1706.

Schmid, Muriel. (2003). "The eye of God": Religious beliefs and punishment in early nineteenth-century prison reform. *Theology Today, 59*(4), 546–558.

Schultheiss, Dirk, & Engel, Rainer M. (2003). G. Frank Lydston (1858–1923) revisited: androgen therapy by testicular implantation in the early twentieth century. *World Journal of Urology, 21,* 356–363.

Scranton, Phil, Sim, Joe, & Skidmore, Paula. (1991). *Prisons under protest.* Milton Keynes, UK: Open University Press.

Scull, Andrew T. (1977). *Decarceration: Community treatment and the deviant—a radical view.* Englewood Cliffs, NJ: Prentice Hall.

Sellin, Thorsten. (1976). *Slavery and the penal system.* New York: Elsevier.

Selling, L. (1931). The pseudo-family. *American Journal of Sociology, 37,* 247–253.

Sentencing Project, The. (1998). *Crack cocaine sentencing policy: Unjustified and unreasonable.* Washington, DC: Author. Retrieved June 9, 2008, from http://www.sentencingproject.org/Admin/Documents/publications/dp_cc_sentencingpolicy.pdf.

Shakur, Assata. (1987). *Assata: An autobiography.* London, UK: Zed Books, Ltd.

Shakur, Assata. (1978). Women in prison: How it is with us. *The Black Scholar, April,* 8–15.

Shaylor, C. (1998). "It's like living in a black hole": Women of color and solitary confinement in the prison industrial complex. *New England Journal of Criminal and Civil Confinement, 24,* 385–416.

Sim, Joe. (1990). *Medical power in prisons: The prison medical service in England, 1774–1989.* Milton Keynes, UK: Open University Press.

Simon, Jonathan. (2007a). *Governing through crime.* New York: New York University Press.

Simon, Jonathan. (2007b). Wake of the flood: Crime, disaster, and the American risk imaginary after Katrina. *Issues in Legal Scholarship, Catastrophic Risks: Prevention, Compensation, and Recovery. Article 4.* Retrieved August 8, 2008, from http://www.bepress.com/ils/iss10/art4.

Simon, Jonathan. (2000a). Megans's Law: Crime and democracy in late modern America. *Law & Social Inquiry, 25*(4), 1111–1150.

Simon, Jonathan. (2000b). From the big house to the warehouse: Rethinking prisons and state government in the 20th century. *Punishment & Society, 2*, 213–234.

Simon, Jonathan. (1998). Refugees in a carceral age: The rebirth of immigration prisons in the United States. *Public Culture, 10*(3), 577–607.

Simon, Jonathan. (1997). Governing through crime. In Lawrence Friendman & George Fischer (Eds.), *The crime conundrum* (pp. 171–190). Boulder, CO: Westview Press.

Simon, Jonathan. (1993). *Poor discipline: Parole and the social control of the underclass, 1890–1990.* Chicago: The University of Chicago Press.

Simon, Rita. (1975). *Women and crime.* Lexington, MA: Lexington Books.

Skidmore, Rex A. (1948). Penological pioneering in the Walnut Street Jail, 1789–1799. *Journal of Criminal Law and Criminology, 39*(2), 167–180.

Smith, Anthony D. (1986). *The ethnic origins of nations.* Oxford, UK: Blackwell.

Smith, Anthony D. (1981). War and ethnicity: The role of warfare in the formation, self-images and cohesion of ethnic communities. *Ethnic and Racial Studies, 4*(4), 375–397.

Sommerville, Diane Miller. (1995). The rape myth in the Old South reconsidered. *The Journal of Southern History, 61*(3), 481–518.

Spalding, Warren F. (1914). Proceedings of the American Prison Association Congress. *Journal of the American Institute of Criminal Law and Criminology, 4*(5), 724–732.

Sparks, Richard, Bottoms, Tony, & Hay, Will. (1996). *Prisons and the problem of order.* Oxford, UK: Clarendon.

Spaulding, Edith. (1915). The results of mental and physical examinations of 400 women offenders: With particular reference to their treatment during commitment. *Journal of Criminal Law and Criminology, 5*, 704–718.

Spidle, Jake. (1975). Axis prisoners of war in the United States, 1942–1946: A bibliographic essay. *Military Affairs, 39*(2), 61–66.

Stanford, Ann Folwell. (2004). More than just words: Women's poetry and resistance at Cook County Jail. *Feminist Studies, 30*(2), 277–301.

Stanley, Leo. (1940). *Men at their worst.* New York: D. Appleton Century Company, Inc.

Stanley, Leo. (1922). An analysis of one thousand testicular substance implantations. *Endocrinology, 6*, 787–794.

Stanley, Leo, & Kelker, George. (1920). Testicular transplantation. *Journal of the American Medical Association, 74*, 1501–1503.

Steffensmeier, Darrell J., & Steffensmeier, Renee Hoffman. (1980). Trends in female delinquency. *Criminology, 18*(1), 62–85.

Steffensmeier, Darrell J., Rosenthal, Alvin S., & Shehan, Constance. (1980). World War II and its effect on the sex differential in arrests: An empirical test of the sex-role equality and crime proposition. *The Sociological Quarterly, 21*(3), 403–416.

Stemen, Don. (2007). *Reconsidering incarceration: New directions for reducing crime.* New York: The Vera Institute of Justice.

Stephan, James J. (1997). *Census of state and federal correctional facilities, 1995.* Washington, DC: U.S. Department of Justice, Bureau of Justice Statistics. NCJ-166582. Retrieved March 5, 2009, from http://www.ojp.usdoj.gov/bjs/pub/pdf/csfc95ex.pdf.

Stephan, James J., & Karberg, Jennifer C. (2003). *Census of state and federal correctional facilities, 2000.* Washington, DC: U.S. Department of Justice, Bureau of Justice Statistics. NCJ 198272. Retrieved March 5, 2009, from http://www.ojp.usdoj.gov/bjs/pub/pdf/csfcf00.pdf.

Stimpson, Sally. (1989). Feminist theory, crime and justice. *Criminology, 27*(4), 605–632.

Stone, Diane. (2000). Non-governmental policy transfer: The strategies of independent policy institutes. *Governance:*

An International Journal of Policy and Administration, 13(1), 45–62.

Stone, Douglas, Major General, Deputy Commanding General, Detainee Operations, Multi-National Force—Iraq. (2008). Detainee operations, March 23, 2008. Retrieved March 12, 2009, from http://www.mnf-iraq.com/index.php?option=com_content&task=view&id=17793&Itemid=128.

Strom, K. J., Smith, K. S., & Snyder, H. N. (1998). *Juvenile felony defendants in criminal courts.* Washington, DC: U.S. Department of Justice, Bureau of Justice Statistics.

Sudbury, Julia. (Ed.). (2005). *Global lockdown: Race, gender, and the prison-industrial complex.* New York: Routledge.

Suleman, Arsalan. (2006). Detainee Treatment Act of 2005. *Harvard Human Rights Journal, 198,* 257–265.

Sykes, Gresham. (1958). *The society of captives: A study of a maximum-security prison.* Princeton, NJ: Princeton University Press.

Sykes, Gresham, & Messinger, Sheldon. (1960). The inmate social system. In R. A. Cloward, D. R. Cressey, G. H. Grosser, R. McCleery, L. E. Ohlin, G. M. Sykes, & S. L. Messinger (Eds.), *Theoretical studies in the social organization of the prison* (pp. 5–19). New York: Social Science Research Council.

Taguba, General Antonio S. (2004). *Article 15–6 investigation of the 800th Military Police Brigade.* Department of Defense. Retrieved February 19, 2009, from http://www.npr.org/iraq/2004/prison_abuse_report.pdf.

Tannenbaum, Judith. (2000). *Disguised as a poem: My years teaching poetry at San Quentin.* Boston: Northeastern University Press.

Teeters, Negley K. (1955). *The cradle of the penitentiary: The Walnut Street Jail at Philadelphia, 1773–1835.* Philadelphia: Pennsylvania Prison Society.

Teeters, Negley K. (1939). Prison idleness in America is one of our national curses. *The Prison Journal, 19,* 562–563.

Tewksbury, Richard, Ericson, D., & Taylor, J. (2000). Opportunities lost: The consequences of eliminating Pell Grant eligibility for correctional education students. *Journal of Offender Rehabilitation, 31,* 43–56.

Thomas, Jim. (1989). The "reality" of prisoner litigation: Repackaging the data. *New England Journal of Civil and Criminal Confinement, 15*(1), 27–53.

Thomas, Jim, Keeler, Devin, & Harris, Kathy. (1986). Issues and misconceptions in prisoner litigation: A critical view. *Criminology, 24*(4), 775–797.

Thomas, Piri. (1967). *Down these mean streets.* London, UK: Barrie and Jenkins.

Thompson, George. (1855). *Prison life and reflections, or a narrative of the arrest, trial, conviction, imprisonment, treatment, observations, reflections and deliverance of Work, Burr, and Thompson, who suffered an unjust and cruel imprisonment in Missouri penitentiary for attempting to aid some slaves to liberty. Three parts in one volume.* Hartford, CT: A. Work.

Tichenor, Daniel. (2002). *Dividing lines: The politics of immigration control in America.* Princeton, NJ: Princeton University Press.

Toby, Jackson. (1979). The new criminology is the old sentimentality. *Critical Criminology, 16*(4), 516–526.

Toch, Hans. (1997). *Corrections: A humanistic approach.* Monsey, NY: Criminal Justice Press.

Toch, Hans. (Ed.). (1980). *Therapeutic communities in corrections.* New York: Praeger.

Tonry, Michael. (Ed.). (2007). *Crime and justice.* Chicago: The University of Chicago Press.

Tonry, Michael. (2004). *Thinking about crime: Sense and sensibility in American penal culture.* New York: Oxford University Press.

Travis, Jeremy. (2005). *But they all came back: Facing the challenges of prisoner reentry.* New York: Urban Institute Press.

Travis, Jeremy. (2002). Invisible punishment: An instrument of social exclusion. In Marc Mauer & Meda Chesney-Lind (Eds.), *Invisible punishment: The collateral consequences of mass imprisonment* (pp. 15–36). New York: The New Press.

Travis, Jeremy, & Michelle Waul (Eds.). (2004). *Prisoners once removed: The impact of incarceration and reentry on children, families and communities.* New York: Urban Institute Press.

Trounstine, Jean. (2001). *Shakespeare behind bars: The power of drama in a women's prison.* New York: St. Martin's Press.

Trulson, Chad, & Marquart, James W. (2002). The caged melting pot: Towards an understanding of the consequences of desegregation in prisons. *Law & Society Review, 36*(4), 743–782.

Trulson, Chad, Marquart, James W., Hemmsn, Craig, & Carroll, Leo. (2008). Racial desegregation in prisons. *The Prison Journal, 88*(2), 270–299.

Useem, Bert, & Kimball, Peter. (1989). *States of siege: U.S. prison riots, 1971–1986.* New York: Oxford University Press.

U.S. Department of Justice. (2001). *Delinquency cases waived to criminal court, 1989–1998.* Washington, D.C.: U.S. Department of Justice, Office of Juvenile Justice and Delinquency Prevention.

U.S. Department of Justice, Bureau of Justice Statistics. (1982). *Prisoners 1925–1981.* Bulletin. NCJ-85861. Washington, DC: U.S. Department of Justice.

U.S. Immigration and Customs Enforcement. (2008). *Operations manual, ICE performance-based national detention standards.* Washington, DC: U.S. Department of Homeland Security. Retrieved March 11, 2009, from http://www.ice.gov/partners/dro/PBNDS/index.htm.

U.S. Immigration and Customs Enforcement. (2007). *Semiannual report on compliance with ICE National Detention Standards, January-June 2007.* Retrieved August 19, 2008, from http://www.ice.gov/doclib/pi/news/newreleases/articles/semi_annual_dmd.pdf.

U.S. Immigration and Customs Enforcement. (2000). *Detention operations manual.* Washington, DC: U.S. Department of Homeland Security. Retrieved March 11, 2009, from http://www.ice.gov/pi/dro/opsmanual/index.htm.

U.S. Immigration and Customs Enforcement, Office of Detention and Removal Operations. (2008). *Protecting the homeland: Semiannual report on compliance with ICE National Detention Standards, January–June 2007.* Washington DC: US Immigration and Customs Enforcement. Retrieved March 11, 2009, from http://www.ice.gov/doclib/pi/news/newsreleases/articles/semi_annual_dmd.pdf.

U.S. Sentencing Commission. (1997). *Special report to Congress: Cocaine and federal sentencing policy.* Washington, DC: U.S. Sentencing Commision.

U.S. Sentencing Commision. (1995). *Special report to Congress: Cocaine and federal sentencing policy.* Washington, DC: U.S. Sentencing Commision.

VanVoorhis, Patricia. (1994). *Psychological classification of the adult, male prison inmate.* Albany, NY: SUNY Press.

VanVoorhis, Patricia, & Brown, K. (1996). *Risk classifications in the 1990s.* Washington, DC: National Institute of Corrections.

VanVoorhis, Patricia, & Presser, L. (2001). *Classification of women offenders: A National assessment of current practices.* Washington, DC: National Institute of Corrections.

von Hirsch, Andrew. (1976). *Doing justice: The choice of punishments: A report of the Committee for the Study of Incarceration.* New York: Hill & Wang.

Wacquant, Loïc. (2005). The great penal leap backward: Incarceration in American from Nixon to Clinton. In J. Pratt (Ed.), *The new punitivism: Current trends, theories, perspectives* (pp. 3–26). Collumpton, UK: Willan.

Wacquant, Loïc. (2002). From slavery to mass incarceration: Rethinking the "race" question in the United States. *New Left Review, 13*, 41–60.

Wacquant, Loïc. (2001a). Deadly symbiosis: When ghetto and prison meet and mesh. *Punishment & Society, 3*(1), 95–134.

Wacquant, Loïc. (2001b). The penalisation of poverty and the rise of neo-liberalism. *European Journal on Criminal Policy and Research, 9*, 401–412.

Wacquant, Loïc. (2000). The new "peculiar institution"? On the prison as a surrogate ghetto. *Theoretical Criminology, 4*(3), 377–389.

Wacquant, Loïc. (1999). Suitable enemies: Foreigners and immigrants in the prisons of Europe. *Punishment & Society, 1,* 215–222.

Wallman, Joel, & Blumstein, Alfred. Epilogue, 2005: After the crime drop. In Alfred Blumstein & Joel Wallman (Eds.), *The crime drop in America* (Rev. Ed.) (pp. 319–347). New York: Cambridge University Press.

Ward, David A., & Kassebaum, Gene. (1965). *Women's prison: Sex and social structure.* Chicago: Aldine.

Ward, Robert Davis, & Rogers, William Warren. (2003). *Alabama's response to the penitentiary movement, 1829–1865.* Gainesville, FL: University Press of Florida.

Warner, James H. (1992). *Guns, crime, and the culture war.* Washington, D.C.: The Heritage Foundation. Retrieved March 16, 2009, from https://www.policyarchive.org/bitstream/handle/10207/12758/92266_1.pdf?sequence=1.

Watterson, Kathryn. (1996). *Women in prison: Inside the concrete womb.* (Rev. Ed.). Boston: Northeastern University Press.

Waugh, Joan. (1997). *Unsentimental reformer: The life of Josephine Shaw Lowell.* Cambridge, MA: Harvard University Press.

Webb, Jim. (2007). Opening statement at Joint Economic Committee Hearing on Mass Imprisonment: At What Cost? October 4, 2007. Retrieved December 4, 2007, from http://webb.senate.gov/newsroom/record.cfm?id=284989.

Weber, Max. (1978). *Economy and society* (Vols. 1 & 2). Berkeley, CA: University of California Press.

Weinstein, C., & Cummins, E. (1996). The crime of punishment: Pelican Bay maximum security prison. In E. Rosenblatt (Ed.), *Criminal injustice: Confronting the prison crisis* (pp. 308–321). Boston: South End.

Welch, Michael. (2003). *Detained: Immigration laws and the expanding I.N.S. complex.* Philadelphia: Temple University Press.

Welch, Michael. (1996). The immigration crisis: Detention as an emerging mechanism of social control. *Social Justice, 23*(3), 169–185.

Welch, Michael, & Schuster, Liza. (2005). Detention of asylum seekers in the UK and US: Deciphering noisy and quiet constructions. *Punishment & Society: An International Journal of Penology, 7*(4), 397–417.

Welsh, Robert Z. (2008). *Tough on crime and the budget: The difficult balancing act of public safety and skyrocketing prison costs, special report.* Atlanta: Georgia Budget and Policy Institute. Retrieved July 24, 2008, from www.gbpi.org/pubs/gabudget/20080111.pdf.

Wenner, Jann. (2000). Bill Clinton: The Rolling Stone interview, December 28, 2000. In Jann Wenner & Joe Levy (Eds.), (2007). *The Rolling Stone interviews* (pp. 399–408). New York: Back Bay Books.

West, Heather C., & Sabol, William J. (2008). *Prisoners in 2007.* Bureau of Justice Statistics Bulletin. Washington, DC: U.S. Department of Justice. NCJ 224280.

Western, Bruce. (2007a). Testimony before the Joint Economic Committee. Retrieved October 12, 2007, from http://www.jec.senate.gov.

Western, Bruce. (2007b). *Punishment and inequality in America.* New York: Russell Sage Foundation Publications.

Westly, Steve. (2006). *California Department of Corrections and Rehabilitation Review Report. Healthcare delivery system.* Sacramento, CA: California State Controller. Retrieved November 14, 2007, from http://www.sco.ca.gov/aud/specreport/prison_healthcare_rpt.pdf.

Wicker, Tom. (1975). *A time to die: The Attica Prison revolt.* New York: Quadrangle.

Williams, George. (1883). *History of the negro race in America from 1619 to 1880. Negroes as slaves, as soldiers, and as citizens; together with a preliminary consideration of the unity of the human family, an historical sketch of Africa, and an account of the negro governments of*

Sierra Leone and Liberia. New York: G. P. Putnam's Sons.

Williford, M. (Ed.). (1994). *Higher education in prison: A contradiction in terms?* Pheonix, AZ: Oryx.

Wilson, James Q. (1983a). *Thinking about crime* (Rev. Ed.). New York: Basic Books.

Wilson, James Q. (1983b). *Crime and public policy*. Richmond, CA: ICS Press.

Wilson, James Q. (1975). *Thinking about crime*. New York: Basic Books.

Wilson, James Q., & Boland, Barbara. (1981). The effects of the police on crime: A response to Jacob and Rich. *Law & Society Review, 16*(1), 163 – 170.

Wilson, William Julius. (1987). *The truly disadvantaged*. Chicago: The University of Chicago Press.

Wines, Enoch C. (1871). *Transactions of the National Congress on Penitentiary and Reformatory Discipline. Held at Cincinnati, Ohio, October 12–18, 1870*. New York: Argus Co.

Wormley, Margaret J. (1945). Adult education in federal prisons. *The Journal of Negro Education, 14*(3), 425–430.

W. N. (1899). Review of proceedings of the Congress of the National Prison Association of the United States, Held at Boston, 1888 by Frederick Howard Wines. *The American Journal of Psychology, 2*(2), 338–339.

X, Malcolm, & Haley, Alex. (1965). *The autobiography of Malcolm X*. New York: Grove Press.

Yackle, Robert. (1989). *Reform and regret: The story of federal judicial involvement in the Alabama prison system*. New York: Oxford University Press.

Yale Law Journal. (1973). The sexual segregation of American prisoners. *Yale Law Journal, 82*(6), 1229–1273.

Yates, Jeff, & Fording, Richard. (2005). Politics and state punitiveness in Black and White. *The Journal of Politics, 67*(4), 1099–1121.

Young, G., & Perkins, W. B. (2005). Presidential rhetoric, the public agenda, and the end of presidential television's "golden age." *The Journal of Politics, 67*, 1190–1205.

Young, Jock. (1999). *The exclusive society*. Thousand Oaks, CA: Sage Publications.

Young, Jock. (2003). To these wet and windy shores: Recent immigration policy in the UK. *Punishment & Society, 5*(4), 449–462.

Young, Vernetta D., & Spencer, Zoe. (2007). Multiple jeopardy: The impact of race, gender, and slavery on the punishment of women in antebellum America. In Mary Bosworth & Jeanne Flavin (Eds.), *Race, gender, and punishment: From colonialism to the War on Terror* (pp. 65–76). New Brunswick, NJ: Rutgers University Press.

Zedner, Lucia. (2005). Securing liberty in the face of terror: Reflections from criminal justice. *Journal of Law and Society, 32*, 507–533.

Zedner, Lucia. (2003). Too much security? *International Journal of the Sociology of Law, 31*, 155–184.

Zedner, Lucia. (2002). The dangers of dystopias in penal theory. *Oxford Journal of Legal Studies, 2*(2), 341–366.

Zimmerman, Jane. (1951). The penal reform movement in the South during the Progressive Era, 1890–1917. *The Journal of Southern History, 17*(4), 462–492.

Zimring, Franklin. (2007). *The great American crime decline*. New York: Oxford University Press.

Zimring, Franklin, & Hawkins, Gordon. (1995). *Incapacitation: Penal confinement and the restraint of crime*. New York: Oxford University Press.

Zimring, Franklin, & Hawkins, Gordon. (1973). *Deterrence: The legal threat in crime control*. Chicago: The University of Chicago Press.

Zimring, Franklin, Hawkins, Gordon, & Kamin, Sam. (2001). *Punishment and democracy: Three strikes and you're out in California*. New York: Oxford University Press.

Zwerman, Gilda. (1988). Special incapacitation: The emergence of a new correctional facility for women political prisoners. *Social Justice, 15*(1), 31–47.

Index

About the Author

Mary Bosworth is Reader in Criminology and Fellow of St Cross College at the University of Oxford in Oxford, England. Her major research interests are in punishment, incarceration, and immigration detention, with a particular focus on how matters of race, gender, and citizenship shape the experience and nature of confinement. She has published widely on these issues, as well as on qualitative research methods. Her books include *Engendering Resistance: Agency and Power in Women's Prisons* (Ashgate Press, 1999) and *The U.S. Federal Prison System* (Sage Publications, 2002). She has also edited the two-volume *Encyclopedia of Prisons and Correctional Institutions* (Sage Publications, 2002) and, with Jeanne Flavin, *Race, Gender, and Punishment: From Colonialism to the War on Terror* (Rutgers University Press, 2007). Currently, she is coediting *What Is Criminology?* with Carolyn Hoyle (Oxford University Press, 2010). She is a member of the editorial board of the *British Journal of Criminology* and coeditor with Simon Cole of *Theoretical Criminology*.

SAGE
PINE FORGE
CORWIN
CQ PRESS